HOW AND WHY WE AGE

HOW AND WHY WE AGE

Leonard Hayflick, Ph.D.

With a Foreword by
Robert N. Butler, M.D.

BALLANTINE BOOKS · NEW YORK

Copyright © 1994 by Cell Associates, Inc.
Foreword copyright © 1994 by Robert N. Butler, M.D.

All rights reserved under International and Pan-American Copyright
Conventions. Published in the United States by Ballantine Books, a
division of Random House, Inc., New York, and simultaneously in
Canada by Random House of Canada Limited, Toronto.

Library of Congress Cataloging-in-Publication Data
Hayflick, Leonard.
How and why we age / Leonard Hayflick.
p.   cm.
Includes bibliographical references and index.
ISBN 0-345-33918-5
1. Aging—Popular works. 2. Aging—Physiological aspects.   I. Title.
QP86.H39   1994
612.6'7—dc20   94-211
                                                              CIP

TEXT DESIGN BY DEBBY JAY

Manufactured in the United States of America

First Edition: August 1994

10   9   8   7   6   5   4   3   2   1

THIS book is dedicated to my mother, Edna Hayflick, on the occasion of her eighty-eighth birthday, for encouraging my interest in science; to the memory of my father, Nathan Hayflick; and to the memory of my teachers in the biology of aging, Sir McFarlane Burnet, Joseph T. Freeman, Robert Kohn, Sir Peter Medawar, George Sacher, and Nathan Shock.

Contents

PART FOUR: **Why Do We Age?**

PART FIVE: Slowing Aging and Increasing Life Span

PART SIX: **The Future of Human Aging and Longevity**

Foreword

WHEN I was a child of seven or eight, I invented my own theory of aging. I was a slender youngster, so when I laid down to sleep at night, the sound of my beating heart was particularly noticeable. I could not escape hearing the thump, yet it was a reassuring sound. I realized that having to listen to my heart was a worthy trade-off for the only possible alternative. I decided then that individual human beings, and the human race as a whole, had a finite number of heartbeats allotted to them. When the beats were used up, I concluded, death would occur. About the same time, I also developed my "psychological defense theory of senility," as deterioration of memory and dementia were then called. Senility must occur, I reasoned, in order to help free older individuals from the pain of aging and the prospect of death by dulling their awareness of what is going on.

Theories such as these from my youth undoubtedly are formulated in the minds of many children (and even adults!) when they become conscious of the realities of aging, dying, and death. The need to understand how and why we age, and why we die, is deeply rooted and ubiquitous. It is therefore amazing that, as far as I am aware, there has never been a sensible, nonsensational, nonideological book written in the English language for the general public explaining how and why we age, unless one counts the technically difficult but excellent book by Alex Comfort, *Aging: The Biology of Senescence*, published nearly thirty years ago. That is, there hasn't been such a book until now. *How and Why We Age*, by Leonard Hayflick, one of the most respected pioneers in the biology of aging, fills a great void. It has a clear point of view, yet provides an unbiased, comprehensive, and thoughtful account of what is presently known about the biology of aging, a subject that has fascinated humanity since its very beginnings and one which is becoming even more interesting and critical in our own times. The biological theories of aging are beautifully described in this book, and the psychological and sociological implications of both longevity and the increasing numbers of older people are discussed as well. Not everyone will agree with all of Dr. Hayflick's observations and conclusions, but I doubt if anyone can dispute his efforts to be objective and balanced in his arguments.

How do we age? Why do we age? The answers to these questions are important, not only to satisfy our existential curiosity, but also to solve the problem of causation of disease. What causes diseases? As far as we know, there are only three categories of such causes: the "environment" (including the quality of our air and water, what we eat, what we do in our lives, and so on); genes, especially defective ones; and, finally, changes related to aging. Comparatively speaking, the first two of these categories (environmental and genetic causes) have received more research attention than aging has. This is unfortunate since, for example, 50 percent of all cancers occur after age sixty-five and 80 percent after age 50, and the rates incidence of other age-associated diseases, such as coronary heart disease, osteoporosis, and Alzheimer's disease, also rise with increasing age.

In the twentieth century, we have witnessed the extraordinary growth of aging populations throughout the world, and chances are that this trend will continue into the twenty-first century. Consequently, we must recruit brilliant minds into the fields of gerontology and geriatrics, or we may have a calamity on our hands. The widely expanded last chapter of life has created many needs, but few people to meet them. I hope that *How and Why We Age* will be on the shelves of public libraries, and that it will be read and studied by educators and writers of grammar school, high school, and college textbooks, all of whom should cover the fields of gerontology and geriatrics more comprehensively in the materials they prepare and present to students.

In my own childhood, and that of many physicians I know, the books *The Microbe Hunters* by Paul de Kruif, *The Horse and Buggy Doctor* by Arthur Hertzler, Victor Heiser's *The American Doctor's*

Odyssey, and Sinclair Lewis's novel, *Arrowsmith*, were inspirational and contributed to our decisions to become doctors. I believe that *How and Why We Age* has the potential to make the same kind of impact on young minds. The fact is that we no longer have the luxury of ignorance. Our changing demography necessitates that we have an informed public and attract more scientists to the field to help us confront the profound worldwide revolution in longevity.

—ROBERT N. BUTLER, M.D.

Preface

THIS book is written for the intelligent reader of any age who is curious about biogerontology, the biology of aging. It is intended not only for those who are aging or aged, but also for young people who want to know what to expect as they too grow old. Knowing what changes to expect after maturity is just as important as knowing what to expect as one changes from an infant to a sexually mature adult.

In the past decade there has been an enormous surge of interest in human aging. The popular media have produced an increasing number of articles and stories about the subject, and biogerontologists have been besieged with lecture requests. Most of what has been written for a general audience about the biology of aging has not, however, been written by professional biogerontologists, and regrettably, much of the information that has appeared in the popular media is either erroneous or badly distorted by efforts to be brief or to meet unreasonable deadlines, or both. Consequently, what the public believes about the aging process is largely a mélange of folklore, surmise, unsubstantiated convictions, and downright false information. One of the purposes of scientific inquiry is to explode myths with verifiable data. Throughout this book I will separate fact from fiction wherever possible and will evaluate whether certain assumptions and beliefs are fads or will stand the test of time.

I have conducted research in the biology of human aging for more than thirty years. By dint of good fortune it is during this period that we have made our greatest advances toward understanding the aging phenomenon. The following chapters have been shaped by the university and public lectures I have given on aging in these three decades and by the many questions that my students and general audiences have posed to me.

I believe that scientists have an obligation to make known to the public the results of their work and to distill the essence of complex fields into easily readable texts. The story of scientific advances is best told by those who are active participants in the research, for they can grasp the nuances and communicate the thrill of discovery and the scientific way of thinking. In research, facts are collected, hypotheses formed, and preconceptions challenged. The mind of a scientist must be open to new ideas, no matter how heretical. Every principle must be questioned continuously, no matter how fundamental it may be to an established body of knowledge. Because biogerontology is such a new field, facts are scarce and conclusions often more speculative than those in better-established scientific disciplines. Within the field it is common for respected scientists interpreting the same set of facts to reach different, or even opposing, conclusions. Few biogerontologists—none in recent years—have been willing to interrupt their work long enough to summarize the status of this huge field for the public.

In this book, I present the prevailing views, then emphasize the one that the majority of scientists hold or that best fits my own biases. Of course, it is vital to recognize that my biases are just that—biases. I make no pretense of being omniscient about this field, nor do I believe that my interpretations of facts are invariably correct. Surely, as this field of research matures, I will be found to be wrong on some counts. My two major objectives have been accuracy and the fair presentation of contrary views. I have attempted to explain why so many cherished beliefs about aging are false and to demystify the subject in light of modern scientific research.

I have made only one assumption about my readers—that most will have only a passing familiarity with biology. Consequently, I have avoided the use of scientific jargon, but readers should be aware that doing so creates another danger: When the apparently arcane language of science is translated into ordinary language, accuracy suffers. Scientific communication, often incomprehensible to the layman, aspires to convey exact meaning with maximum precision. Everyday words for many scientific concepts, objects, or living processes simply do not exist. The transition from scientific language to ordinary language inevitably introduces imprecise words and generalities that compromise accuracy. Where this occurs I have attempted to indicate that the generalization may have exceptions or that the concept may be more complex. I hope that my colleagues, who may be critical of some of my oversimplifications, will appreciate why this has been done. I will take refuge in the words of Oliver Wendell Holmes, Jr., who said, "No generalization is wholly true, not even this one."

This book is not intended as an encyclopedia of the biology of aging. There are aspects of the field that I have not discussed because the available results are not definitive or are hopelessly controversial. I have covered only those areas in which there is agreement on general principles and where controversy is based on easily understood differences in reasoning or opinion. Also, I have made little attempt to discuss nonbiological aspects of aging. The biological aspects of aging are distinguishable from the medical aspects of old age in that the former represents the normal state of affairs and the latter the abnormalities. As the reader will learn, the illnesses of old age occur as the normal aging process increases vulnerability to disease and illness. I have covered the medical aspects of old age—called geriatric medicine—only to the extent that they are necessary considerations in discussing the biology of aging. I have made little effort to cover issues in gerontology that are strictly sociological, psychological, or nonbiological.

This book will tell you what is presently known (or thought to be known) about aging, why age changes occur, and where the frontiers of the science of gerontology are today. It provides statistical information on a wide variety of issues associated with aging and includes discussions of the ethical dilemmas posed by the possibility of manipulating aging and delaying death. If we succeed in slowing aging, we will be confronted with many extremely difficult decisions, and I believe strongly that we all need to start considering the consequences *now*.

Because biogerontology is a young science, researchers have not reached universal agreement on the meaning of some terms. One such term is "senescence," and, as a result, I have avoided its use. Other terms used in the study of the biology of aging that are also in general use have been defined early in the text. I do not mean to imply that the definitions given here are universally accepted. I have also adopted the convention of not identifying people as Doctor, or Dr. It should be understood that most of the scientists mentioned are entitled to be addressed by that title.

As a university teacher, I confess to a hope that young readers who have aspirations to be scientists will be sufficiently stimulated by the fascinating developments in biogerontology to choose it as a career. The biology of aging has come a long way from being the domain of quacks and merchandisers bent on exploiting people's vanity to sell cosmetic repairs. Today it is a respected science. It is also one of the last major biological frontiers. The secrets of aging and longevity are certain to yield to those courageous enough to become biogerontologists and clever enough to do the right experiments.

Acknowledgments

I HAVE drawn on several hundred sources for the information covered in this book. The sources have ranged from technical books, including the past and current scientific literature, to discussions and private communications with colleagues. For those who wish to learn more about a specific subject, I have listed some of my major reference materials under the heading "Further Reading" at the end of this book.

I wish to thank the many colleagues whose comments on drafts of sections of this book have helped to improve its accuracy and clarity. I confess to having some anxiety that there exists somewhere in the vast scientific literature a report that would negate statements I present as fact. Professional scientists will sympathize with my anxiety. I encourage readers who discover errors of omission or commission to bring them to my attention so that corrections may be made in future editions.

I am indebted to the following colleagues whose criticisms of various parts of this book have added to its accuracy, balance, and fairness: Patricia P. Barry, Graham Bell, Herman T. Blumenthal, Harold Boxenbaum, Harold Brody, Jacob Brody, William Ted Brown, Paul D. Coleman, William Dement, J. Fred Dice, Charles J. Epstein, John A. Faulkner, James F. Fries, Barbara A. Gilchrest, Gerald J. Gruman, Denham Harman, S. Mitchell Harman, Ronald W. Hart, William R. Hazzard, Robin Holliday, John O. Holloszy, Steven Horvath, Marvin L.

Jones, William B. Kannel, Robert Katzman, Albert M. Kligman, Edward G. Lakatta, Takashi Makinodan, George R. Martin, Edward Masoro, Zhores Medvedev, Joseph Meites, Kenneth L. Minaker, Jaime Miquel, Robert H. Mohlenbrock, Harold Morowitz, George C. Myers, Daphne J. Osborne, Leslie Robert, Michael R. Rose, Ira Rosenwaike, Isadore Rossman, George S. Roth, Jacob S. Seigel, Steven Shak, David W. E. Smith, Raj S. Sohal, John Stecker, Cynthia M. Taeuber, George B. Talbert, Andrus Viidik, Roy Walford, and Marc E. Weksler.

I am especially indebted to Bernard L. Strehler, who reviewed the entire manuscript.

Finally, I wish to thank my wife, Ruth, who suffered through the long gestation period of this project.

Introduction

IN this era of relative scientific enlightenment we have triumphed over many causes of death. Knowledge of biological phenomena often extends to the molecular level, but our understanding of the basic causes of aging is nearly as primitive as it was a century ago. There are several reasons for this.

First, there is a long-standing belief in most religions and schools of philosophy, and in science, that prolonging life beyond its natural bounds is neither possible nor desirable. Second, many scientists consider aging research to be uninteresting and unlikely to yield useful results. Many scientists are afflicted, as are many nonscientists, with "ageism," a bias against aging and the elderly. Robert Butler, the first director of the National Institute on Aging, coined the term in 1968 to describe discrimination directed toward the elderly: a "conflict of the generations," promoted by ageist bigots, which favors economic, social and political confrontation between the young and the old. These extremists are concerned about people who "live too long" and their consumption of resources that would allegedly be better utilized by the young. This form of bigotry, based as it is on biological factors, is no different than racism or sexism. For many scientists, ageism is coupled with the belief that growing old is intractable, an absolute certainty that is best ignored. As recently as fifteen years ago, the few researchers working in the field of aging were sometimes derided or ridiculed by fellow scientists. Happily, that negative attitude is changing.

1

A third reason why aging research has been a backwater is that the field has been a magnet for unscrupulous persons who trade on the vanity, fears, or ignorance of the elderly, making promises that cannot be kept and bilking them of their resources. Science does not flourish encircled by charlatans and scoundrels.

A BRIEF HISTORY OF MODERN BIOGERONTOLOGY

Before you read the rest of this book, it may be helpful to have an overview of the recent history of biogerontology.

Early in the twentieth century, two terms associated with aging came into use—"gerontology" and "geriatrics." The word "gerontology," introduced by Élie Metchnikoff in 1903, means the scientific study of the aging process. The Greek *gérōn*, from which the word "gerontology" derives, means "old man"; the suffix "-ology" means "the study of." Gerontology is not, however, limited to studying men as they age, or even to studying humans. Rather, it is the study of aging in all living things. It has come to include not only the biology of aging but its sociological, psychological, and other aspects. To distinguish themselves from other gerontologists, most biologists in the field of aging research refer to themselves as biogerontologists.

"Geriatrics" can be more precisely defined. This field is concerned strictly with the medical problems of the elderly, just as pediatrics is concerned with the medical problems of young patients. The word was coined in 1909 by Ignaz L. Nascher, an American physician. He wrote the first American medical textbook on aging in 1914, entitled *Geriatrics: The Diseases of Old Age and Their Treatment.*

Several pivotal experiments have propelled the field of biogerontology into the present. I will cover them in detail later in this text but will describe a few briefly now. In 1912, Alexis Carrel, a charismatic French surgeon and Nobel laureate, and Albert Ebeling, working at the Rockefeller Institute in New York, claimed to have continuously grown cells from a chick heart in laboratory glassware for what eventually became thirty-four years, after which time they were purposely destroyed. The experiment's impact on thinking about the causes of aging was profound: If normal cells removed from animals are "immortal" when grown in laboratory cultures, the reasoning went, then aging cannot be the result of events that occur *inside* individual cells. Aging, therefore, must be the result of events that occur *outside* of cells. Although this revolutionary concept was overturned in the early 1960s, it provided a stimulus for many scientists to enter the field of gerontology. (For full discussion of Carrel's experiment and why it was flawed, see chapter 8.)

In the early 1930s a fundamental discovery was made that, unlike Carrel's, has been confirmed many times and to this day defies understanding. Working at Cornell University, Clive McKay found that feeding rats a diet containing all the necessary vitamins and minerals but low in calories extended their life span significantly. This discovery, called "undernutrition without malnutrition," has played an important role in modern research on aging. No one can say with certainty what the effect of undernutrition on humans might be. (Undernutrition is discussed extensively in chapter 17.)

In 1938, the Russians organized the first large international conference on aging in Kiev, and in 1939 a landmark book was published in the United States. *Problems of Ageing* resulted from a conference held at Woods Hole, Massachusetts, and was edited by E. V. Cowdry, an eminent anatomist at Washington University in St. Louis. The contributing authors were leaders in their respective fields, and the introduction was written by philosopher John Dewey. This landmark book, and the second, enlarged edition of 1942, collected virtually all that was then known about aging. (The Cowdry books, although published in the United States, used the British spelling of "ageing" rather than the American "aging," perhaps because of Cowdry's Canadian heritage. The English now sometimes mock the American spelling by pronouncing it to rhyme with "nagging.")

Publication of the Cowdry books was supported by the Josiah Macy, Jr., Foundation, founded in 1930 by Kate Macy Ladd. The Macy Foundation was unique in selecting aging as one of the areas of research that it would sponsor, and it played a central role in establishing the science of gerontology in this country. In 1940, it provided ten thousand dollars in start-up funds to establish a "unit on gerontology" at the Baltimore City Hospitals, directed by Edward Stieglitz and administered by the National Institutes of Health. In 1941, the late Nathan W. Shock, a physiologist and psychologist, was appointed to replace Stieglitz, who was returning to private medical practice. From 1941 to 1951, the Macy Foundation also supported annual meetings of scientists interested in the biology of aging.

The Russian gerontologist V. Korenchevsky, then living in England, and a disciple of the famous biologist, Élie Metchnikoff, encouraged the establishment of a scientific society on aging in the United States. The Club of Gerontology was founded, mainly composed of the contributing authors to Cowdry's book. Korenchevsky traveled with a test-tube culture of the bacillus that he used to prepare his daily ration of yogurt, because he fervently believed that Metchnikoff's ideas about the antiaging properties of yogurt were correct. The culture thrived in the warmth of its portable incubator, Korenchevsky's vest pocket. Before coming to the United States, Korenchevsky had fled the Communist regime for England, where he met Lord Nuffield, who had just established the Nuffield Foundation. Korenchevsky persuaded Lord Nuffield to provide funds to establish gerontology research units in several British universities, medical schools, and hospitals.

In 1945, the Club of Gerontology gave birth to what is now known as the Gerontological Society of America, the largest society of professional gerontologists in the world. Their motto is, "To add life to years, not just years to life"—an increase in life span is not a central goal. The American Geriatrics Society was founded three years earlier, and today it comprises the largest group of geriatricians in the world. Similar societies have sprung up in many other countries, and almost all of these national societies are members of an umbrella organization called the International Association of Gerontology.

On the European continent, gerontology was centered around the Hungarian emigrant Fritz Verzar, who championed a theory of aging called cross-linking. (This theory is discussed in chapter 15.) Verzar founded the Institute for Experimental Gerontology in Basel, Switzerland, in 1956 and attracted a large cadre of European and American scientists interested in the biology of aging. One of his major accomplishments was the establishment of a colony of two thousand aging rats that, for the first time, made it possible to study the aging process systematically in animals under well-controlled conditions.

At about this time, Dmitri Chebotarev was appointed Director of the Soviet Institute of Gerontology in Kiev. It was part of a four hundred-bed hospital and was a major research and training facility for gerontologists in the Soviet Union and eastern Europe.

In the last fifteen or twenty years, the international scientific community has come to recognize the importance of understanding the aging process. The result has been an explosion of interest in the phenomenon of aging. Several recent developments have further advanced research on aging. For example, the Baltimore Longitudinal Study of Aging (BLSA), which attempts to distinguish between the effects of normal aging and disease, was begun by Nathan Shock in 1958 and now has had about twenty-two hundred participants. The participants undergo a series of biological and psychological tests about every two years and continue to do so for the remainder of their lives. After thirty-five years the BLSA is now revealing enormous amounts of new information about the aging process. The results, discussed in chapter 9, have upset many of our most cherished beliefs about aging.

In addition to founding this longitudinal study, Nathan Shock published, periodically, a bibliography of virtually all publications on aging. These compilations did much to attract interest in the field.

In 1950, a National Conference on Aging was held in the United States, followed by the first White House conferences on aging in 1961. Subsequent White House conferences on aging were held in 1971 and 1981, and there is now discussion about organizing another. Each of these conferences attracted hundreds of gerontologists and geriatricians. They addressed the major health and welfare problems of the elderly, as well as research in the field. Recommendations made by participants have resulted in significant legislation benefiting the elderly and research on aging. The Older Americans Act, for example, passed in 1965, established Medicare. The American Association of Retired Persons (AARP) was established in 1955 by Ethel Percy Andrus. It now probably has more members—close to thirty million—than any other membership organization in the world.

It soon became evident that the study of the diseases associated with aging, and even their resolution, would not tell us much about the aging process itself. This realization, still not generally appreciated by many scientists or the general public, will be treated extensively in chapter 4. The distinction is crucial. Just as curing childhood diseases such as polio or measles does not tell us much about how a child becomes an adolescent, curing Alzheimer's disease or arthritis will tell us little about how a person ages. If we wish to understand the aging process, we must learn more about the normal age changes that underlie and increase our vulnerability to these and other diseases of old age. In 1974, the National Institute on Aging was established as a new institute within the National Institutes of Health in Bethesda, Maryland. The establishment of this institute, with its separate budget, expanding staff, and focus on aging, has done much to legitimize aging research in the United States. Today, for the first time, money has become available to fund studies of the aging phenomenon by many competent scientists.

Other important developments include the establishment in 1979 of EURAGE, a consortium of European government agencies organized in an effort to coordinate the research on aging done in their countries. In 1982, the World Assembly on Aging, organized by the United Nations General Assembly, was held in Vienna, Austria, providing an opportunity for high-level representatives of countries to discuss the medical, social, and economic implications of the increasing numbers of elderly. In 1973, an Expert Committee on Planning and Organization of Geriatric Services was formed by the World Health Organization.

Today, there is a growing belief that efforts should be made to extend life as much as possible, provided that the quality of life is maintained. The issue of what constitutes acceptable quality and who should make that decision is the basis for vigorous debate. Some argue for "prolongevity," believing that aging and death, like diseases, must be curable and that extending life is both possible and desirable. Others, including myself, believe that extending the human life span is probably not possible, nor is it desirable. Obviously, people living wretched, miserable lives—a condition that most people found themselves in until relatively recent times—will have no desire to extend their life span. But even a joyous life should not, in my view, last forever. The consequences of an ageless population would be bizarre, even terrifying, and will be discussed in chapter 21.

Currently, more than 12 percent of our population—about thirty million people—are over the age of sixty-five. Practitioners of ageism who consider the elderly a drain on society will, if they live long enough, become the victims of their own intolerance. The irony is all the greater when ageists become advocates of prolongevity, as many of them, becoming older, undoubtedly will.

Today, interest in the scientific study of the biology of aging is greater than it has ever been, both in the United States and in other developed countries. National research institutes are being established, and governments are making more funds available for researchers in universities and other institutions. Private fund-raising organizations have been established to support the work of young researchers or those who are new to the field, who often find it difficult to compete with more established scientists. The best-known, most successful organization of this type in the United States is the American Federation for Aging Research, with headquarters in New York City. Each year it raises over one million dollars for research in aging and thus attracts several dozen new researchers to the field. Perhaps the most significant sign of the coming of age of aging research has been the founding of biotechnology companies like Geron in Menlo Park, California, to explore the fundamental aging processes and to determine why old cells are more susceptible to disease than young ones.

Today, granting agencies struggle with the dilemma of how best to allocate their funds between research on the normal aging process and on the diseases of old age. Funds spent on the diseases of old age have more popular appeal but will tell us little about aging. Funds spent on the study of the normal aging process have little public appeal but it is this process that underlies the increased vulnerability of older people to disease.

Because aging changes virtually every cell in our body, its study has attracted scientists working in virtually every field of biology and medicine. As a consequence, biogerontology has become a vast subject in recent years. The highlights of our current knowledge about the biology of aging will be described in the following chapters.

PART ONE

What Is Aging?

CHAPTER 1

Defining Aging

How old would you be if you didn't know how
old you was?

—Satchel Paige

ONE of our earliest realizations as children is that most of the
things that we see or know, including humans, animals, and inanimate
objects, change or deteriorate with the passage of time. Some take aging
for granted, accepting it as the fate of most things with which they
are familiar and a normal consequence of the passage of time. Others
spend a substantial part of their time in activities designed to arrest or
thwart the unwelcome effects of aging on themselves and their surroundings. Many of the things in our homes or workplaces need to be
protected, repaired, and renewed with time. Other things, as they age,
come to be considered more beautiful and desirable.

With material objects, most of the ravages of time are the result of
oxidation—the combination of the molecules that compose the objects
with atmospheric oxygen. In iron-containing objects we call the phenomenon rust, but the avidity of oxygen for other material things also
produces changes that we associate with their aging. Other age
changes can be attributed to temperature changes, water, radiation,
trauma, microorganisms, or insects. If we own pets, we see changes in
them. We are literally surrounded with living and inanimate things

11

that are continuously changing with time. Aging is an omnipresent part of our material and living world, and eventually, we realize that the phenomenon is occurring even within ourselves.

Aging is the only fatal affliction that all of us share. Scientists long scorned conducting research in the field of biological aging because it was deemed uninteresting or fundamentally intractable. Happily, this attitude has changed in recent years, and a major effort has been mounted in many countries to understand the aging process. But in order to understand the process, we first need to define the changes that we call aging. After all, as the French aphorist put it, "Most troubles of mankind are a matter of grammar."

CHRONOLOGICAL VERSUS BIOLOGICAL AGE

Aging defies easy definition, at least in biological terms. Aging is not merely the passage of time. It is the manifestation of biological events that occur over a span of time. There is no perfect definition of aging but, as with love and beauty, most of us know it when we experience it or see it. We all recognize an old person when we see one, and some of us are quite good at estimating chronological ages. However, subjective determinations based on appearances are frequently wrong, and, more importantly, age in years does not directly correlate with biological age. What is needed is a measurement of something biological that changes as a function of increasing age—a measurement that distinguishes biological age from chronological age. The distinction is crucial.

Scientific knowledge advances only when we can measure or count things in some way. We can determine the age of woody trees by counting the annual rings and the age of some fish by counting the layers on their scales, but we have no reliable measurement to determine the biological age of humans and most other animals. Of course, with humans we can use birth certificates, but, even if they are reliable, they specify only a single point in time. Chronological age measures how much time, how many years, have elapsed since that point. It tells us when to celebrate birthdays and what number to put on forms when asked our age, but for gerontologists aging is chronological only in the legal or social sense. Time itself produces no biological effects. Events occur *in* time but not *because of* its passage. The biological events that follow birth happen at different times and occur at different rates in each of us.

When we remark with surprise that someone "looks young" (or old) for his or her chronological age, we are observing that we all age biologically at *different rates*. Gerontologists have much good scientific evidence that this apparent difference is real. It is likely that age changes begin in different parts of the body at different times and that the rate of annual change varies among various cells, tissues, and organs, as well as from person to person. Unlike the passage of time, biological aging, sometimes called functional aging, defies easy measurement. What we would like to have is one or a few measurable biological changes that mirror all other biological age changes without reference to the passage of time, so that we could say, for example, that someone who is chronologically eighty years old is biologically, or functionally, sixty years old. This kind of measurement would help explain why one eighty-year-old has so many more youthful qualities than does another eighty-year-old, who may be biologically eighty or even ninety years old.

In terms of aging, we resemble a clock shop. Each of our many tissues and organs behaves like an independent clock ticking at a rate different from that of the others. Because of this, a person of a given chronological age could be considerably younger or older *biologically*, depending on the average of how quickly or slowly all his or her clocks are ticking. Knowing our biological age would be much more informative than knowing our chronological age, but, alas, we have no way of measuring it.

That is not for lack of trying. Gerontologists have tracked various biological measurements for humans over time with the hope that the changes found could predict the rate of aging. They have measured hair color, ear length, grip strength, heart function, exercise capacity, and dozens of other variables. None of these studies has established an infallible measurement of biological age, for at least one important reason: There is too much individual variability in the potential markers of aging. Even at birth humans have an enormous range of difference in most variables that can be measured. The differences are frequently unrelated to age. It is as if each of us begins the aging race with our feet on a different starting line. For example, women are generally smaller than men and therefore have a reduced vital capacity. (Vital capacity is measured as the volume of air one can forcibly exhale after taking a deep breath.) Yet, women generally live longer than men, so measurement of vital capacity is obviously useless as a marker for the rate of biological or functional aging.

A better approach to determining biological or functional age might lie in measuring the nearness of death as a function of some earlier biological change. Of course, the population studied must consist entirely of people who died from a known cause, and the biological change must be a function of aging, not illness or lifestyle. Retrospective analyses on human populations have successfully determined some variables that have value in predicting impending death. This kind of study is called *risk factor analysis*. Smokers, for example, have been shown by this method to have a shorter life expectation than nonsmokers and those who quit smoking. This is valuable information, but it does not tell us anything meaningful about the rate of aging. Smokers do not age faster than nonsmokers; they simply die sooner on average.

Even if there were an accurate way to determine biological age, knowing a person's biological age might be a mixed blessing. It could give rise to some bizarre birthday celebrations. Think what a deliriously happy occasion it would be if you celebrated your fiftieth chronological birthday knowing that you were only forty years old biologically. However, it would be an unhappy party if you were chronologically fifty and biologically sixty! Husbands and wives might discover that, although one is chronologically older than the other, their biological ages are reversed. We might even find adult children who are biologically older than their parents! Should retirement age and life insurance premiums be based on biological, not chronological, age? If so, some people might be forced to retire or to increase their life insurance premiums at age fifty, others at age eighty, or later. These seemingly odd situations will become more likely if a reliable biological marker is ever discovered that can demonstrate someone to be much older or younger biologically than he or she is chronologically.

We do have fairly reliable biological markers for age in some other animals and in plants. Still, these markers tell us not about the rate of aging, but only the passage of time. The two are related, of course, but the passage of time does not measure the rate of aging. The most familiar example of a biological marker in the plant kingdom is the growth rings that are laid down annually by woody trees. Time-dependent rings or markings have also been found in some animals. In mammals, markings on teeth of seals and the horns of sheep, goats, and caribou have been used to determine chronological age. The earwax of whales also has time-dependent growth zones. No time-dependent markers have been found in birds, which is one reason bird-banding techniques are used. Growth zones are found in the bones of snakes and other reptiles and in the annual layers that form the scales of many fish species. The number of fin rays has been used to measure the age of catfish and sturgeon. Other signs that occur in some animals regularly over time include markings on shells and on otoliths, which are tiny stones found in the balancing organ of the inner ear.

Humans have none of these age markers, which is why we must rely on birth certificates, other written documents, hearsay, or memory to establish chronological age.

LONGEVITY, AGING, AND DEATH

Any serious consideration of biological aging must define all three of the phenomena that characterize the finitude of life. These are longevity, aging, and death.

Longevity is the period of time that an animal can be expected to live, given the best of circumstances. For newborn humans, average longevity (life expectation) in developed countries is about seventy-five years and maximum longevity (life span) is about one hundred fifteen years. The essential question about longevity is, Why do we live as long as we do?

Aging represents losses in normal function that occur after sexual maturation and continue up to the time of maximum longevity for members of a species. The essential question about aging is, Why do we grow old?

Death is the final event that ends life. It is not, as one wag said, nature's way of telling you to slow down. The essential question about death is, of course, Why do we die?

Death need not be related to aging at all. For example, the death of a child by accident or infectious disease is unrelated to aging. Death is linked to aging in the sense that, with age, the probability of death for all members of a species increases. The qualification "all members of a species" is important because certain subgroups may die before they have an opportunity to age. For example, the steep rise in the death rate for young men has nothing to do with the aging process; it has everything to do with automobile accidents and, in some communities, homicide.

HOW OLD ARE YOU—REALLY?

This question might seem silly. Most of us know our date of birth as well as we know our own name. However, in many less-developed countries dates of birth are often unknown. In China, on the other hand, even illiterate people can provide their precise date of birth. The Chinese, however, consider themselves to be one year old on the day of their birth and determine age according to a lunar calendar, which makes it very easy to miscalculate the ages of the Chinese according to the Western solar calendar or of Westerners according to the Chinese calendar. (There are 29.5 days in a lunar month. Thus, a twelve-month lunar year rapidly falls out of synchronization with the 365.25-day solar year. To compensate, the Chinese insert an extra lunar month at irregular intervals, which makes the year in which a month is added a leap year.)

Similar uncertainties about age occur when we ponder what it is in each of us that is one year older at each birthday. Ordinarily we think not about the aging of our cells, but rather about how we relate to our family and friends or to what we perceive that society expects of someone our age. But if you say figuratively that you are not the same person you were five or ten years ago, you are quite literally right. All of us are composed of billions of individual cells and the products that cells make. Most of the cells present in our body today were not present five or ten years ago. In fact, some were not present yesterday.

There are at least three kinds of tissue in which cells are in a constant state of division: the skin, the cells lining the digestive tract, and the cells that make red and white blood cells. Many of the cells in these tissues divide every day, and the older cells are simply discarded. Old skin cells at the outermost edge of our skin are ultimately sloughed into the environment. Old gut cells are sloughed into the digestive tract, (yes, we cannibalize ourselves!) and old blood cells are literally eaten by other cells called phagocytes. Cells in other tissues are replaced by new cells (a process called turnover) on a longer time scale.

Two important kinds of tissue are composed of cells that do not divide or turn over. These are nerve cells (found throughout the body, and including the brain) and skeletal and heart muscle cells. Most of the brain and muscle cells that you will possess for life are present at birth or soon thereafter and do not divide further. Muscles, hearts and brains become larger after birth partly because the cells that form them increase in size (not in number) and partly because *other* cells surrounding the neurons and muscle cells divide and contribute to size increase.

If many of your cells turn over in less than ten years, then how old are you, *really*? After all, the cells that turned over during the last ten years are gone and new ones may have replaced them several times, so your present cells may be younger than the cells that were present a decade ago. Most of your cells do not accompany you from the cradle to the grave, so you really are not the same person that you were even a few years ago, either figuratively or literally. The best answer to the question "How old am I?" is that you are as old as your oldest cells—those neurons and skeletal muscle cells you were born with and still have. When you celebrate your next birthday, accuracy demands that you celebrate the birthday only of your nerve and muscle cells and the cell products that haven't been replaced!

But before you plan the bizarre celebration of the birthday of your neurons and muscle cells, I will add another complication. Although we are all composed of individual cells and their products, the cells themselves consist of smaller units called molecules, which in turn are composed of atoms. The complication is that molecules may turn over, or be replaced, as a result of normal metabolic processes, without the individual cells in which they are packaged being replaced. What happens in an old cell is analogous to what might happen in an old car. If the car has had *every* part replaced it is not the same old car. If the cell has had *every* part replaced it is not the same old cell. The neurons you were born with might appear today to be the same cells, but in reality many of the molecules that composed them when you were born (except DNA) may have been replaced with new molecules. So nondividing cells may not be the same cells you were born with after all!

It is probable that turnover in nondividing cells does occur to some extent, although except for DNA we have no proof that it is complete. If most of the molecules in your nerve and muscle cells turn over, then your birthday celebration is going to be tricky for two reasons. First, if all but a few of the molecules in all of your cells have turned over, then you are literally a different person today. Second, all of your molecules, whether they have turned over or not, are composed of more fundamental units called atoms, most of which have been the same since our planet formed. You and I simply represent unique rearrangements of ancient atoms that are themselves billions of years old. We are really composed of billion-year-old atoms; we might actually claim to be immortal! In that sense we are all billion-year-olds no matter when we were born, and celebrating birthdays is absurd.

In partial compensation for the loss of birthday celebrations consider this benefit: The atoms in our bodies may have been part of the body of someone else long since dead. This is the only scientific basis for believing that we, the living, represent a form of reincarnation. When we die our atoms will dissipate into the environment, and some, perhaps, will become part of another human in a continuing pattern of recycling atoms. You could argue that this is scientific evidence for life after death; our atoms are immortal but we, as individuals, are not. Upon death our concept of self is gone forever, regardless of where our atoms came from or where they will go.

Attempting to precisely define the age of a living organism can obviously boggle the mind. About the best you can do, if you insist on painstaking accuracy, is to celebrate the birth of all of your dead cells because, although they no longer exist, those cells generated the cell lineages whose progeny you are today.

CHAPTER 2

Some Animals Age,
Some Do Not

The animal knows, of course. But certainly it
does not know that it knows.
—Teilhard de Chardin

IT is not unusual to see an old human, but aged animals exist only
in captivity. Usually, animals show extreme age changes only when humans have intervened in their lives. We allow zoo and domestic animals and our pets to age by providing protection from predation and
disease, which, in the wild, would kill them before they had the
chance to experience important age changes. In many cases we have
bred captive animals (and plants) in ways that would not permit them
to survive at all in the wild. Unlike the animals we choose to protect, wild animals do not age, at least not to the extent that humans do.
Wild animals do not usually reach extreme old age or even what in humans we call middle age. In this way wild animals are like ancient or
prehistoric humans who rarely, if ever, saw an old person. Of the three
hundred Neanderthals found, only one may have been a postmenopausal woman.

Nature begins to eliminate wild animals just as they begin to show
signs of aging and its associated functional losses or weaknesses. With

age, animals in the wild don't leap as high, run as fast, see as well, or react as quickly. Death may result from starvation as an aging animal becomes less successful in finding food, from disease as its immune system loses efficiency, or from predation as its ability to elude capture decreases. Wild animals die well before they reach what would be comparable to middle or old age in humans. Many functions begin to weaken after animals, including humans, reach sexual maturity. Such weaknesses begin to appear in humans at about the age of twenty-five or thirty. Strength and neuromuscular coordination peak in humans around nineteen or twenty and decline after that; this is why world-class sprinters are almost always in their late teens or early twenties. Stamina, on the other hand, peaks in the late twenties or early thirties, which explains why marathon records are held by athletes in that age range and seldom by older—or younger—athletes.

Researchers have estimated that after age thirty there is a loss in running speed of a few percent per year (figure 2–1). However, individual variability is great. It may take a healthy forty-year-old from two and one-half hours to more than two days to run a twenty-six-mile marathon.

FIGURE 2-1. World record marathon times for men, ages 10 to 79

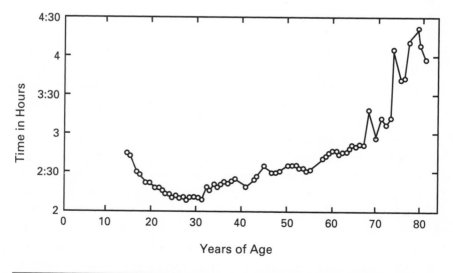

Years of Age

A vast amount of evidence supports the fact that not only physical vigor but also less obvious powers, such as the ability to resist disease and the physiological capacity of many major organs, peak and then decrease in humans and other animals soon after sexual maturation.

If you have a pet and protect it from predators, disease, and starvation, it will experience old age—something it couldn't do on its own. By tampering with the natural order of uncivilized life, we have similarly eliminated our own predators and most of the diseases of youth, so we live longer. This success compels us to experience the biological changes of aging. Odd as it may seem, aging, at least in its extreme manifestations, is an artifact of civilization! Nature planned things so that we would die well before we became old. If you believe that nature does things with a purpose, then aging is a phenomenon that nature never intended us to experience. In this sense efforts to extend life really are attempts to fool Mother Nature.

ANIMALS THAT DO NOT AGE

Animals that reach a fixed size as adults—including humans, all other mammals, and birds—*do* age. But some animals do not seem to age at all, even when protected by humans. If they do age, it occurs at such a slow rate that their aging has not been demonstrated convincingly. These animals increase in size indefinitely; their growth may slow as the years go by but, apparently, it does not stop.

Nonaging animals tend to be more primitive species. Typical examples are lobsters and many, but not all, fish (sturgeons, sharks), amphibians (alligators), and reptiles (the Galapagos tortoise). Nonaging animals do experience a peak in their physiological functions at some point after sexual maturation, but as they continue to grow, those functions do not seem to decline. The classic example of indeterminate growth associated with lack of aging is the fish called flounder in the United States and plaice in England. The female grows indefinitely and does not show age changes, but the male reaches a fixed size and ages. The reason for this difference is a mystery.

When protected by humans, who may put them in zoos or aquariums, nonaging animals simply grow bigger without seeming to grow older. Similar growth occurs in the wild. New catches frequently break previous records for the size and weight of several sport fish and amphibian species. The longer we keep records, the larger these

;ing animals seem to grow, so we can expect records to continue
broken.

...e Galapagos tortoise may live for one hundred seventy-five years,
the sturgeon for eighty-two years, and the carp for fifty years. Lobsters
have reached forty-four pounds, at which time they were probably between fifty and one hundred years old. Whereas animals that age experience an increase in reaction time, "old" lobsters close their claws
at the same speed regardless of their chronological age. If members of
these species become larger and larger without aging, why do they not
live forever and grow to gigantic size? They neither live forever nor
become gigantic because, like animals that do age, they still have a
constant annual chance of dying from accidents, disease, and predation. Although aging does not occur and the passage of time does not
increase their vulnerability, to disease, accidents, and predation, they
are not invulnerable. Their vital systems may not measurably decline
in function after sexual maturation, but this just makes them less likely
to die from these causes than are animals whose vulnerability increases with aging. Animals of indeterminate size live long, but they
are not immortal.

Some have claimed that the sea anemone is immortal, but this is not
true. The claim is based on a celebrated group of sea anemones that
were kept in an aquarium at the Edinburgh University zoology department from about 1862 until their mysterious death in 1942. Sea anemones are colonies of individual animals and behave like any other
colony of cells. Other colonial animals, like coral, were once thought
to be long-lived or even immortal, but now we can distinguish between the mortality of individuals within a population and the immortality of the entire population. *Individual* anemone cells are mortal,
but the *population* as a whole may be immortal. The same is true of
humans.

For animals that do age, the likelihood of death *increases* for each
year after progeny are raised to independence. For us this begins
around age thirty. Unlike us, animals that do not age have the *same*
chance of dying every year after sexual maturation. For an animal that
does not age, life is something like a game in which a coin tossed each
New Year's Day decides the animal's fate for that year. If heads means
life and tails death, then, although the animal has a fifty-fifty chance
of seeing heads each New Year's Day, it is very unlikely that it will do
so annually and forever. Each year that it escapes death the animal

will grow bigger and age little if at all. However, the animal is not immortal; it is a certainty that, given enough years and enough coin tosses, tails will eventually appear.

It seems peculiar that mammals, one of the latest and most sophisticated animal lines to evolve, have a limited life span (the maximum number of years they can live) and show the effects of aging, while more primitive species like sharks and tortoises do not seem to either have a fixed life span or to show age changes. One might have expected that more highly evolved animals would have learned how not to age, while more primitive species would age and have limited life spans. Some gerontologists speculate that aging and a limited life span are the "price" mammals and other highly evolved animals pay for maintaining fixed size in adulthood and the benefits of being more highly evolved.

AGING BY WEAR AND TEAR

There is an unusual functional loss in some animals that occurs with age yet may or may not be regarded as a biological marker for aging. It is analogous to the "wearing out" of some vital component in a machine that ultimately leads to its failure. Some animals—the African elephant, the mongoose, the shrew, some large carnivores, and domestic cattle—wear down their teeth to the extent that eating becomes impossible and they starve. (My guess is that animals in the wild die of other causes before they wear out their teeth.) It is debatable whether this phenomenon should be considered a form of aging: other than eroded teeth, the animal may show no life-threatening losses in physiological functions. It is possible to extend the life of prize cattle, which may command handsome prices as stud animals or producers of sperm for artificial insemination, by fitting them with dentures. In contrast, an old animal cannot be saved from the aging process, which affects most cells, by replacing or correcting only one worn-out organ or tissue.

Analogous kinds of wear and tear have been imagined to occur in animal and human organs, both in the cells that compose them and in the constituents of the cells themselves. This is one of the ideas that gave rise to the "wear and tear" theory of aging, which will be considered in chapter 15.

ANIMALS THAT REGENERATE

Some lower animals are capable of regenerating large parts of their body. This greatly complicates the process of assigning an age to the animal. Regeneration of the same organ may occur many times, with the result that some parts of the animal are older than other parts. Should the younger "spare parts" be considered in determining the age of the animal?

"BIG BANG" REPRODUCTION AND AGING

In several life-forms, aging occurs rapidly and immediately follows a single burst of reproductive activity. In the plant kingdom we see this most dramatically in annual plants. At the end of the growing season, the plant flowers, produces and disseminates seeds, then quickly ages and dies. A similar phenomenon occurs in the animal kingdom but in only a few species—lampreys, squid, and some fish, including eels. One of the most spectacular examples of "big bang" reproduction followed by aging and death is seen in the Pacific salmon, which after spawning, becomes an ugly, distorted version of its former self. Obvious outward signs of aging are a humped back, a hooked jaw, and skin that becomes mottled and covered with patches of fungi that begin to eat into the flesh. The catalog of internal changes is likewise enormous—quick deterioration occurs in almost all organs, including the stomach, liver, spleen, thymus, thyroid, pituitary, kidney, and cardiovascular system. This occurs in five species of the Pacific salmon, as well as in the Atlantic salmon. All of these events are thought to be accelerated age changes. Nevertheless, the interpretation of these findings has not been without controversy.

After the salmon has lived two or three years in the ocean, an unknown mechanism triggers its return to the river in which it was born. The location and operation of its navigational system is a mystery. The salmon neither rests nor eats once it enters the fresh water of the river. It has one ultimate goal: to find the specific region at the head of the river where conditions are suitable for spawning. After spawning, the salmon ages rapidly and dies. The question of what triggers the rapid aging process has been the subject of much research, and, although the answer is not known with certainty, we do have some interesting clues.

One possible trigger of the aging process in migratory salmon could be the change from the saline ocean to the sweet river waters. Once it enters the river, the fish does not eat but expends an enormous amount of energy climbing rapids and navigating upstream toward the spawning beds. This combination of marginal starvation and extreme exertion may also be a trigger. Evidence against both of these theories is provided by the kokanee salmon, which lives entirely in land-locked freshwater lakes but undergoes the same rapid aging after spawning as does the Pacific salmon. The most likely trigger for the rapid aging of salmon is certain hormonal changes in the adrenal glands, which lie on the surface of the kidneys. When the fish swims upstream, the adrenal gland grows to an enormous size, as does the pituitary gland in the fish's brain. The enlarged adrenal glands overproduce hormones called corticosteroids. (In humans there is a condition, called Cushing's syndrome, in which a similar overproduction of steroid occurs, but its clinical manifestations are not typical of aging.) The increased level of steroid hormones seems to shut down many metabolic activities in the fish and affects its immune system, making it more vulnerable to infection.

The whole process—migration from the sea, entry into the river, and the cascade of events that follows—seems to be programmed. That is, the sequence must be governed by a set of instructions somewhere in the cells of the animal. Although we haven't succeeded in locating this program, we do know how to perturb it; the salmon's life span is extended significantly if the fish are castrated before their gonads develop.

But, as is common in biology, what at first seems straightforward and understandable soon falls to some contradictory finding. In this case, that finding was made in the steelhead trout, which like the Pacific salmon migrates from the ocean to the rivers to spawn. The trout, however, does not always die after spawning and frequently returns to the ocean, where the degenerative changes that it experienced in the river are reversed. The animal becomes rejuvenated. What is more, the cycle of degeneration and rejuvenation can occur several times.

"Big bang" reproduction, followed by aging and death, is not limited to fish. It is also known to occur in the octopus, apparently after the release of a substance from the optic gland. And recently, the phenomenon has been observed in mammals. In Australia there are small insectivorous marsupials (pouched mammals) of the genus *Antechinus* that are commonly called marsupial mice. Six species in this genus display the "big bang" phenomenon, and the details are truly extraordinary. The young males in one carefully studied species leave their mothers' nest in May at the age of eight months, establish territories, and become sexually active. In August, which is late winter in Australia, the females become sexually receptive, and mating takes place in a brief period marked by much fighting among the males. Within the next two weeks all the males begin to rapidly lose weight, become sick, and show regression of their sex organs. Like the salmon, their adrenal glands enlarge, corticosteroids are overproduced, and the effectiveness of the immune system declines, making the animals vulnerable to infections. All of the males, except those developing in the uteruses of pregnant females, are dead by the end of August. All births occur in a two-week period in September, and weaning occurs in December. Since no male lives longer than a year and the population is synchronized, no male ever meets its father. A few females survive to breed a second time. If the males are prevented from mating, but not castrated, they may double their life span and live for another year. Mating costs them at least half of their lives!

Animals that reproduce only once are called *semelparous* animals. Animals that reproduce more than once during their lifetime are called *iteroparous* animals. Humans are iteroparous. Semelparous animals seem to age rapidly, almost to self-destruct, after the birth of offspring. Some semelparous species exhibit this phenomenon in astonishing ways. In the mite called *Adactylidium*, the offspring actually hatch inside the mother's body and eat their way out, killing their mother. The mother never ages but is killed before age changes can occur. A less dramatic example of single-burst reproduction and quick death may be found in the silkworm *Bombyx mori*. After the larval stage, the moth that develops is useful only for reproductive purposes. It starves to death in a few days because it has no mouth. Some butterflies experience this same phenomenon. In these instances one would be hard pressed to defend the idea that these animals age. They seem to be programmed to die without any opportunity to experience aging.

The key question about the salmon is this: Are aging and death triggered by some external condition, or are they part of a genetically determined program of self-destruction? Even if the answer were known, it is unlikely that it would tell us much about human aging because the changes that occur in "big bang" animals after the reproductive burst are very different from those that occur in aging humans or most other animals. It is debatable whether aging in "big bang" animals is really the same as aging in other animals. Nevertheless, advocates of programmed theories of aging and those who believe in "death hormones" have taken these "big bang" examples as evidence for their beliefs. These, and other theories of the cause of aging, will be discussed in chapters 14 and 15.

Wild animals that experience "big bang" reproduction seem to be exceptions to the generalization that wild animals do not age, although if the process truly is aging it occurs in an unusually brief span of time. There may, however, be another general exception to my belief that wild animals do not live long enough to age significantly. Human encroachments on previously wild environments have altered the normal patterns of life for many species. In some cases, animals considered economically valuable as sources of food or fur, or considered to be pests, have been destroyed in vast numbers. Humans also have interfered on a massive scale with the natural environment itself. All of these human activities have upset natural conditions and have resulted, for example, in the elimination of the predators of some animals, thereby permitting them to undergo greater age changes than they otherwise would. Caution must be exercised when evaluating the allegedly normal aging of wild animal populations.

HOW LONG DO ANIMALS LIVE?

Reliable information about the maximum life span of animal species is not easy to obtain. Many maximum age claims rely on anecdotal information, usually provided by someone who claims to remember a birth date or wishes to gain notoriety or bragging rights with some outrageous claim of longevity. Obtaining accurate information on the maximum life span of an animal species requires considerable work in evaluating a large number of animals. Consequently, the life spans are known reliably for only a few domestic animals and pets. Domestic animals other than pets are usually killed for economic reasons—for their meat or fur—well before they reach old age. The cost of keeping farm animals to old age would be prohibitive for those who raise animals for profit.

Furthermore, few animals are kept in sufficient numbers to allow reasonable certainty about their maximum longevity. The more members of an animal species that are observed, the greater the opportunity to find longer-lived individuals. For example, if you follow just five or ten humans from birth to death, the likelihood that one of them will live to be one hundred, or even ninety, is close to zero. With a larger group there is a greater likelihood of finding a centenarian. Many animals or humans must be tracked to obtain statistically reliable information for the preparation of what gerontologists call life tables. These important tables will be discussed in chapter 6.

In spite of these limitations, there are several sources of reliable information on the maximum age attained by a variety of animals, thanks to a few dedicated biologists who use recognized methods for the acquisition of their data. The small Pekingese may live as long as sixteen years and the spaniel fourteen, but the large mastiffs survive for only ten years. Unlike dogs, whose longevity is usually inversely proportional to the size of the breed, the life span of birds shows no relation to size. Cats are the longest-lived small domestic animal. The maximum reliable life span ever recorded for a cat appears to be thirty-one years.

Recently, data on the longevity of some insects has become available. The queens in social insect colonies are of particular interest because they live much longer than other members of their community, even though all members have the same genes. Larvae that are destined to become queens are simply fed differently. A larva in a bee colony will become a queen after being fed royal jelly. Her life span will then be measured in years while that of other community members will be measured in months. (Consider what it would mean if some humans had a special food that would give them a life span dozens or hundreds of times greater than that of their neighbors.) Ant and termite queens are among the longest-lived adult insects. A recent report from Finland shows that the life span of the queen ant, *Formica insecta*, may be as long as twenty-seven years, with some queens that old still living.

The earliest reliable longevity information for animals came from Chalmers Mitchell in 1911 and Major S. S. Flower, curator of the Cairo Zoo from 1925 to 1938. In addition to making painstaking efforts to locate credible information, they excluded information that was anecdotal or had been passed down for generations as legend. Regrettably, much legendary information still persists. One notable example is the common belief that elephants live for a hundred or more years. They do not. The maximum authenticated life span for an elephant is sixty-nine years. Humans are the longest-lived mammals.

   In more recent years, reliable longevity records have come to us from zoos. One of the most extensive and reliable lists of the maximum life spans of animals has been assembled by Marvin L. Jones, registrar of the Zoological Society of San Diego, California, to whom I am indebted for many of the figures included in Table 2–1. He began collecting this data in 1941, almost exclusively from the world's zoos. His is the first compilation of longevity data for every mammalian family in which a species has lived for more than one year in captivity. Most of Marvin Jones's records are for animals born in the wild and then brought to a zoo. In most cases, the animals arrived at the zoos around one year of age. Table 2–1 is not a complete list but is selected on the basis of what might be of interest to the nonspecialist.

TABLE 2-1. Longevity records for selected species
(in years, except as noted)

Mammals

Species	Years	Species	Years
Aardvark	23	Deer, red	26
Anteater, giant	25	Dog, mastiff	10[a]
Antelope, pronghorn	12	Dog, Pekingese	16[a]
Armadillo, nine-banded	10	Dog, spaniel	14[a]
Ass, Syrian wild	36	Dog, wolfhound	14[a]
Baboon, hamadryas	37	Dolphin, Amazon freshwater	9
Badger, American	26	Dolphin, Atlantic bottle-nosed	25
Bat, Indian fruit	31	Dormouse	8
Bat, Mexican fruit	6	Echidna, Australian	49
Bat, Mexican vampire	13	Elephant, African	48
Bear, Alaskan brown	36	Elephant, Asian	69
Bear, European brown	33	Fox, grey	13
Bear, grizzly	35	Fox, kit	20
Bear, polar	34	Gerbil, Indian	7
Beaver, American	15	Gibbon, pileated	34
Bison, American and European	33	Giraffe, Cape	36
Bobcat	32	Goat, domestic	21[a]
Buffalo, domestic water	28	Goat, North American mountain	14
Camel, domestic bactrian	35	Goat, Rocky Mountain	13
Cat	31[a]	Gopher, plains pocket	7
Cheetah	15	Gorilla, Western lowland	47
Chimpanzee	39[a]	Guinea pig	8[a]
Chimpanzee, troglodytes	56	Hare, European	7
Chinchilla, mountain	19	Hedgehog, European	6
Chipmunk, Eastern	7	Hippopotamus, river	54
Coyote	21	Hog, wild European	21
Deer, Eastern white-tailed	17	Horse	46[a]
Deer, fallow	15	Horse, Arabian	33[a]

TABLE 2-1. Longevity for selected species
(continued)

Horse, wild Mongolian	32	Squirrel, flying	12
Hyena, spotted	36	Squirrel, grey	23
Jackal, common	17	Tamarin, cotton-top	13
Jaguar	20	Tapir, South American	35
Kangaroo, Matschie's tree	16	Tiger, Bengal	26
Koala, New South Wales	17	Vicuna	25
Lemur, brown	35	Wallaby, Bennett's	10
Leopard	23	Wallero	19
Leopard, snow	15	Walrus	17
Lion	25	Whale, beluga or white	17
Lynx, Canadian	24	Whale, blue	12[a]
Manatee, Florida	30	Whale, humpback	47[a]
Mandrill	31	Whale, killer	12
Marmoset, silvery	11	Whale, pilot	11
Marmot, common	12	Wolf, maned	13
Mole, American	2	Wolf, timber	19
Monkey, capuchin	33	Wolverine, American	17
Monkey, Rhesus	23	Zebra, Chapman's	40[a]
Moose, American	17		
Mouse, common field	3	**Birds**	
Mouse, house	3[a]	Albatross, Laysan	37[b]
Mouse, white-footed deer	6[a]	Anhinga, American	18[b]
Musk-ox, Greenland	17	Blackbird, Brewer's	11[c]
Opossum, gray brush-tailed	14	Blackbird, red-winged	16[c]
Opossum, Northern	4	Bluebird, Eastern	8[d]
Opossum, ring-tailed	6	Bluebird, Western	4[d]
Orangutan, Sumatran	59	Bobolink	8[e]
Otter, Canadian	21	Booby, blue-faced	25[b]
Panda, giant	26	Booby, brown	28[d]
Platypus	17	Canvasback	22[e]
Polecat, marbled	8	Cardinal, Northern	16[c]
Porcupine, crested	24	Catbird, gray	11[d]
Puma	19	Chickadee, mountain	10[f]
Rabbit	15[a]	Chicken	12[g]
Rabbit, Old World	2	Cockatoo, greater sulfur-crested	56[a]
Racoon	20	Condor	52[a]
Rat, Nile	6	Condor, Californian	37[a]
Rat, slender-tailed cloud	13	Coot, American	22[e]
Reindeer	20	Cormorant, great	20[b]
Rhinoceros, African black	45	Cowbird, brown-headed	16[c]
Rhinoceros, great Indian	40	Crane, American	38
Seal, harp	5	Crane, Australian	47
Seal, leopard	7	Crow, American	15[f]
Seal, Pacific harbor	32	Cuckoo, yellow-billed	5[f]
Seal, Southern elephant	15	Dove, common ground	6[f]
Sea Lion, California	28	Dove, domestic	30
Sheep, Rocky Mountain	15	Dove, mourning	19[f]
Shrew, common tree	12	Duck, ring-necked	20[e]
Skunk, common	13	Duck, wood	22[e]
Sloth, Hoffman's	32	Eagle, bald	22[e]

TABLE 2-1. Longevity for selected species
(continued)

Eagle, Bateleur	55	Owl, burrowing	9[f]
Eagle, golden	46	Owl, common barn	15[f]
Egret, cattle	14[b]	Owl, eagle	68[a]
Egret, great	17[b]	Owl, great horned	21[e]
Emu	28[a]	Parrot, golden-napped	49[a]
Falcon, peregrine	12[b]	Parrot, Vasa	54[a]
Finch, house	12[e]	Pelican, brown	20[b]
Flicker, Northern yellow	9[f]	Pelican, rough-billed	41
Flycatcher, great crested	14[f]	Penguin, Adelie	14[g]
Flycatcher, Western	6[f]	Petrel, Leach's storm	31[e]
Flycatcher, yellow-bellied	4[f]	Phoebe, Eastern	9[f]
Frigatebird, great	30[b]	Pigeon, domestic	30[a]
Frigatebird, lesser	23[e]	Pigeon, white-crowned	12[f]
Goldfinch	16	Pintail, common	21[b]
Goose, Canadian	24[e]	Puffin, Atlantic	23[g]
Goose, domestic	35	Quail, California	7[b]
Goose, snow	20[b]	Raven, common	13[f]
Grackle, common	21[c]	Redstart, American	10[d]
Grosbeak, evening	15[c]	Redwing	17
Grouse, ruffed	8[e]	Robin, American	14[d]
Gull, California	31[g]	Sapsucker, yellow-bellied	7[f]
Gull, herring	28[e]	Shrike, loggerhead	12[d]
Hawk, red-tailed	21[e]	Shrike, Northern	3[d]
Heron, great blue	17[b]	Sparrow, house	13[c]
Hummingbird, Allen's	4[e]	Starling, European	15[d]
Hummingbird, broad-tailed	12[e]	Swallow, barn	9[f]
Hummingbird, ruby-throated	6[f]	Swallow, cliff	10[e]
Ibis, white	14[b]	Swan, mute	27[e]
Jay, blue	16[e]	Swan, trumpeter	24[b]
Jay, scrub	16[f]	Swift, black	6[f]
Jay, Steller's	16[e]	Swift, chimney	14[f]
Junco, Oregon	10[c]	Tanager, scarlet	10[c]
Kingbird, Eastern	12[f]	Tern, Arctic	34[b]
Kingbird, Western	7[f]	Tern, common	21[g]
Lark, horned	7[f]	Thrasher, brown	13[d]
Least tern	24	Thrasher, California	7[d]
Loon, common	8[b]	Thrush, Swainson's	10[f]
Macaw, blue and yellow	43	Titmouse, tufted Eastern	13[f]
Macaw, red and blue	38	Towhee, rufous-sided	12[c]
Magpie, yellow-billed	12[f]	Turkey	12[b]
Mallard	23[b]	Vireo, Philadelphia	9[d]
Mockingbird, Northern	9[d]	Vireo, warbling	13[d]
Nutcracker, Clark's	17[f]	Vireo, yellow-throated	6[d]
Nuthatch, brown-headed	6[d]	Vulture, king	40[a]
Nuthatch, white-breasted	10[d]	Vulture, turkey	17[b]
Oriole, Baltimore	12[c]	Warbler, black-and-white	11[f]
Osprey	23[e]	Warbler, hooded	8[d]
Ostrich	27	Warbler, prairie	10[d]
Oystercatcher, common	24[g]	Warbler, yellow	9[d]
Owl, barred	18[e]	Waxwing, cedar	7[d]

TABLE 2-1. Longevity for selected species
(continued)

Whippoorwill	4[f]	Bivalve, marine (*Arctica*	
Woodpecker, downy	11[f]	*islandica*)	220[i]
Woodpecker, hairy	16[f]	Bivalve, marine (*Pismo clam*)	53[a]
Woodpecker, pileated	9[f]	Cephalopod (*Nautilus*	
Woodpecker, red-bellied	12[f]	*pompilus*)	20[i]
Woodpecker, red-headed	10[f]	Earthworm	6[a]
Wren, cactus	6[d]	Lobster	50[a]
Wren, house	7[d]	Roundworm (*Wuchereria*	
Yellowthroat, common	10[d]	*bancrofti*)	17[a]
		Sea slug (*Dolabella*	
Reptiles and Amphibians		*auricularia*)	2[g]
Alligator	52[a]	Sea urchin	7[a]
Crocodile	56[a]	Snail, freshwater (*Viviparus*	
Frog, Bull	36[a]	*viviparus*)	11[i]
Lizard (*Anguis fragilis*)	33[a]	Snail, land (*Arianta*	
Snake (*Eunectes murines*)	29[a]	*arbustorum*)	17[i]
Terrapin, diamond-backed	40[a]	Snail, marine (*Haliotis*	
Terrapin, speckled	42[a]	*cracherodii*)	51[i]
Tortoise, Carolina box	129[a]	Sponge	90[a]
Tortoise, European pond	120[a]	Starfish	8[a]
Tortoise, Galapagos	100[a]	Tapeworm (*Taeniorrhynchus*	
Tortoise, giant	180[a]	*saginatus*)	35[a]
Tortoise, Marion's	152[a]	Tapeworm, dog	29[a]
Tortoise, snapping	58[a]	Threadworm, white	17[a]
Turtle, loggerhead	33[a]		
		Insects	
Fish		Ant (*Formica exsecta*)	27[j]
Beluga	75[a]	Ant (*Solenopsis invicta*)	6[j]
Betta	2[a]	Beetle (*Blaps gigas*)	10[a]
Carp	50[h]	Bee, queen	5[a]
Catfish	60[a]	Butterfly, adult stage	12 weeks[a]
Guppy	2[a]		
Halibut	60[a]	**Spiders**	
Molly	4[a]	Black widow (*Latrodectus mactans*)	
Pike	14[a]	28 months (female)	
Sturgeon	82[a]	4 months (male)[g]	
		Tarantula	20[a]
Invertebrates		Trap-door spider (*Ummidia* spp.)	
Bivalve, freshwater (*Margaritifera*		13 years (female)	
margaritafera)	116[i]	5 months (male)[g]	

SOURCES: Figures without symbols are from the records of Marvin L. Jones, registrar of The Zoological Society of San Diego, California. These figures were accurate as of 1979, when the last complete records were made; many animals have lived longer since then.

[a]Comfort, Alex, *The Biology of Senescence*, 3rd ed., New York: Elsevier North Holland, 1979.
[b]Clapp, R. B., M. K. Klimkiewicz, and A. G. Futcher, *Journal of Field Ornithology* 53 (1982):81, rounded to nearest year.
[c]Klimkiewicz, M. K., and A. G. Futcher, *Journal of Field Ornithology* 58 (1987):318, rounded to nearest year.

ᵈKlimkiewicz, M. K., Clapp, R. B., and A. G. Futcher, *Journal of Field Ornithology* 54 (1983):287, rounded to nearest year.

ᵉKlimkiewicz, M. K., and A. G. Futcher, *Journal of Field Ornithology* 60 (1989):469, rounded to nearest year.

ᶠClapp, R. B., M. K. Klimkiewicz, and A. G. Futcher, *Journal of Field Ornithology* 54 (1983):123, rounded to nearest year.

ᵍHazzard, D. G., H. R. Warner, and C. E. Finch, eds. "Alternative Animal Models for Research on Aging," *Experimental Gerontology* 26, no. 5 (1991).

ʰComfort, Alex, *The Process of Aging*, New York: Signet Science Library, 1964.

ⁱHeller, J., *Malacologia* 31 (1990):259.

ʲPamilo, P., Insect Society, 38 (1991):111.

CHAPTER 3

Redwood Trees
Are Not Old

If fifty million people say a foolish thing, it is still a foolish thing.

—Bertrand Russell

I
N chapter 1 we saw how difficult it is to define aging in animals. It can be even more difficult for some plants. Consider the redwood tree. Most of us have been taught to believe that it can live for millennia. The difficulty in devising a universal definition for aging is best illustrated by challenging this cherished conviction.

Whether the coast redwood trees (*Sequoia sempervirens*) growing in California and Oregon are among the oldest living things depends on what you mean by the word "living." A relative of the coast redwood, the giant sequoia (*Sequoiadendron giganteum*), is said to live more than twenty-five hundred years. Bristlecone pine trees, found in several states but most extensively studied in the White Mountains on the California-Nevada border, are thought to be even older. In the Snake Range of east central Nevada there is a bristlecone pine said to be more than forty-nine hundred years old. Regardless of the ages alleged for these trees, I am convinced that any reader over thirty years old is older than any of them! Here's why.

Annual growth rings are counted in woody trees to determine a tree's chronological age, but the cells in nearly all of those rings are dead. Just beneath the outermost ring of dead bark in a woody tree lies the living cambium layer. Further inside, one finds more dead cells. Thus, the band of living cells is sandwiched between the dead bark and the dead internal annual rings. By weight or by volume most of the substance of the trunk of an old tree is composed of dead cells. Of course, the age of those *dead* cells could very well be thousands of years, but is it correct to say that a tree is as old as its oldest dead cells? Logically, the fact that a tree has a live cambium layer should not make the tree as old as almost all of its cells which are *dead*.

Many redwood trees have survived fires that have all but destroyed the dead wood deep inside the trunk. In these chimneylike trees, not only are the cells that form most of the wood dead, but most of the dead cells no longer even exist! Most of the oldest bristlecone pines cling to life by a narrow ribbon of living tissue that snakes up the wall of the dead trunk. The oldest *living* cells in a redwood tree, giant sequoia, or bristlecone pine can be found in the needles and the cones, and they are no more than twenty or thirty years of age. That is why, if you are past your thirtieth birthday, I insist that you are older than what some mistakenly call the world's "oldest" trees!

AGING AND CELL LINEAGES

What is genuinely old in redwood trees or bristlecone pines is the cell *lineage* that has given rise to the present living cells in the cambium layer and the needles. Old cell lineages exist for all plants and animals, including humans. Like redwood trees, we can trace our cell lineages back thousands or millions of years, depending on where we draw an arbitrary line. Life is a continuum and does not begin or end at some arbitrary point. Despite the belief of some people that life begins at conception, all life, including human life, actually never ends. As the German biologist August Weissman postulated in the last century, our germ plasm (the source of sperm and eggs) is immortal. If it weren't immortal, we would not be here to discuss the matter. There is a good basis for believing that a mortal animal is simply a germ cell's way of making more germ cells, thereby optimizing the likelihood that they will fuse with germ cells of the opposite sex.

One difference between us and woody trees is that trees have devised a method for saving and piling up the skeletons of their dead cells and we have not. We cast off millions of dead cells every day. If we retained the tons of dead cells that we slough in a lifetime we would probably accumulate a mass as great as that of a good-sized redwood tree. A woody tree retains its dead trunk and limb cells in order to raise its living cells above other plants competing for sunlight. The fact that these trees do not dispose of their dead cells should not be a reason for believing that they become thousands of years old while you and I live at most to about one hundred years.

GRAFTS AND AGING

Age is even more difficult to determine in plants that can be propagated by cuttings. If you remove a cutting from a favorite plant and root it in soil or water, when was it "born"? When does it "die," if you can take a cutting again from the newly rooted plant and reroot it? If the cutting was left in its original place on the tree or plant it would eventually die, but rerooted it may live longer than the plant from which it came. If you reroot cuttings indefinitely, does the plant ever die?

Banana trees and some grapevines are propagated by cuttings in this way, so their age is not really known. The Reine Claude plum tree has been propagated by serial cuttings for about four hundred years, and the cabernet sauvignon grapevine for more than a thousand years. You might argue persuasively that these plants are, indeed, immortal.

ROOTS, SHOOTS, AND AGING

Many trees and shrubs propagate by sending up new plants from their roots as the roots spread underground. This process may be repeated for centuries or even millennia. If the original tree dies, how old are the remaining trees? Although most of the parental plant's tissue may be gone, the daughters represent its direct physical continuation. Trees such as the aspen, the coast redwood, and some elms and bushes like the creosote propagate in this fashion. Several kinds of prairie grasses reproduce in this way as well. Some of the trees and bushes that propagate by sending up new offspring from their underground roots are known to have perpetuated themselves in this way for periods far longer than the reputed age of the oldest bristlecone pine. A few aspen and creosote "clones" have been replicating in North American woods since the Wisconsin glacial period—over eleven thousand years ago!

Some mushrooms also propagate by sending up new plants from their roots. During the first year the mushroom sends out underground rootlike structures in all directions, like spokes emerging from the hub of a wheel. After a time the central or hub mushroom dies, but the rootlike structures live, sending up more mushrooms annually. The mushroom clone thus increases in size by forming concentric rings of increasing diameter. Some of these so-called fairy rings exist for years despite that fact that the original mushroom and its immediate daughters have long since died. Is the original mushroom potentially immortal although it does not remain standing? Are aspens, creosote bushes, prairie grasses, or fairy rings immortal? Do the individuals age? When is each born and when does each die? There are no simple answers.

One could also make a powerful argument that even trees and plants that propagate only by seeds are immortal. The seeds, although they eventually separate from the plant, are a physical continuation of the parent and give birth to living progeny. This argument applies equally well to humans and other animals, whose "seed" also separates from its producer, fuses with another cell, and starts a new individual. Individuals may die, but the germ plasm is immortal. If the germ plasm were not immortal, then the species would not last beyond one generation. The continuity of life through seeds and germ cells extends beyond the life of the individuals that produce them, frequently making age determinations difficult.

If the longest life span of an individual living thing occurs in the plant kingdom, so too does the shortest. Bacteria and yeast are plants, and many species have life spans of about twenty minutes.

PROGRAMMED AGING

In some higher annual or biennial plants, death occurs on a rigid schedule. Some desert annuals last only a few weeks. In annual plants, aging (or senescence, as it is called by botanists) and death follow after flowering and fruiting. Indeed, in many plants, seed maturation may occur *only* when the plant ages and dies. Examples are soybeans, corn, and many garden annuals. Some wheat varieties age and die in July, so the phenomenon is not necessarily triggered by the approach of winter. Still other popular plants survive for two years. During the first year they store food in their roots and during the second year they produce flowers and seeds, then quickly age and die. Examples of these biennials are carrots, beets, and onions.

Other plants have very long growing periods before they flower and fruit. The century plant and some bamboos grow for many decades before they produce flowers and fruit. Then they too quickly age and die. Recently, the bamboo tree whose leaves form the diet of the giant panda in China, flowered, fruited, aged, and died en masse after decades of growth. The pandas faced a serious food shortage and it was only by having humans supply them with bamboo leaves from other species that they were able to survive. The bamboos represent an extraordinary example of synchronized aging and death occurring in plants after the lapse of an enormous period of time. In the years 919 and 1114 the Chinese bamboo went to seed throughout the country. It did so in Japan between 1716 and 1735 and again between 1844 and 1847. The Japanese stock was introduced into other countries and in the late 1960s it flowered simultaneously in England, Alabama, Russia, and Japan. The cycle for flowering and seed production in this species appears to be one hundred twenty years! Other bamboo species have different periodicities that range from three to one hundred fifty years.

The location of the clock that times these events in the bamboo remains a mystery. One clue comes from the fact that parts of the same tree, when planted separately, give rise to plants all of which flower and seed at the same time. Botanists conclude that synchronized clocks must exist in all or most of the plant's cells. A similar long periodicity in mass reproduction can occur in the animal kingdom and is best exemplified by the cicada or seventeen-year locust.

Senescence and death that quickly follows the development of flowers, fruit, and seeds in plants is often referred to as "programmed aging" because the sequence of events seems to be written into the plants' genes. Indeed, senescence frequently seems to be a *prerequisite* for seed maturation and dispersal. There are a few comparable examples of programmed aging in animals, including the Pacific salmon and other "big bang" reproducers, discussed in the previous chapter.

THE LONGEVITY OF SEEDS

Humans are acutely interested in the longevity of seeds, probably in the hope of finding a truly immortal life-form. Great public interest is aroused when seeds are found during archaeological excavations. Seeds found in ancient Egyptian tombs have provoked excitement because of the expectation that the seeds might be made to germinate. Regrettably, claims of superlongevous seeds are as nonsensical as claims of superlongevous people (whose special case will be considered in chapter 12).

Gardeners and farmers know that the longer a batch of seeds is kept, the fewer seeds will germinate. Moreover, those that do will grow to maturity more slowly. Simple examination of seeds with the naked eye does not usually reveal whether they are dead or alive (unlike animals or plants, which usually exhibit distinct signs of death). The popular stories about finding viable wheat seeds in the excavated silos of ancient Egypt or the tomb of Tutankhamen at Thebes are not true; wheat seeds older than thirty or forty years do not germinate. Although physically intact wheat seeds four thousand to six thousand years old have been found, they are not viable. Usually these ancient seeds are found to have retained their form but to have decomposed to almost pure carbon, with traces of starch grains and cell wall remnants.

The oldest viable seeds are thought to be those of the canna lily (*Canna compacta*) that were discovered in part of a rattle necklace in the pre-Inca tombs of Santa Rosa de Tastil in Argentina. The necklace maker apparently put lily seeds into developing walnuts before the shells had formed and hardened. The mature, hardened walnuts then housed the lily seeds that made the rattle sound and apparently protected them for six centuries. A seed was germinated in 1968, and carbon dating found the walnut shell to be about six hundred years old. Although the seed germinated slowly and with some abnormal behavior, it produced a mature plant. The famous plant and its progeny can be found on the botany department grounds at the University of La Plata in Argentina. In 1923, a Japanese botanist discovered Indian lotus seeds in an ancient lake bed in China. He germinated thirty-five of the seeds, and other researchers repeated his success. There is some question about the accuracy of the carbon-dating method used with these seeds; they may be as young as four hundred years or as old as fifteen hundred. Another lotus seed was reportedly germinated successfully after about seven hundred years. Other authenticated examples of longevous seeds include those of two species of the cinnamon tree, germinated after 115 and 158 years, and a 221-year-old mimosa. Although they are not seeds, there is also a claim that pith cells in a nonwoody Australian grass tree appear to be alive after four hundred years.

In 1940, an air raid on London caused a fire in part of the British Museum's herbarium. The firefighters unwittingly wet part of the seed collection and some of the seeds germinated, producing mature plants. Some seeds in the herbarium were collected in China in 1793 and one, from a 1705 collection, germinated in 1942. In 1856, seeds from six hundred species were sent from Kew Gardens in England to start the botanical gardens in Melbourne, Australia. The seeds, however, were not planted until 1906; still, many were found to be viable. Two of the seed samples were then 105 years old. Seeds of barley, oats, and wheat were discovered in sealed glass tubes inside a foundation stone of the Nuremberg City Theatre in Germany. After 123 years, 12 percent of the barley seeds, 22 percent of the oat seeds, and none of the wheat seeds germinated. Hard-coated seeds, such as those of the canna lily, appear to remain viable longest.

A few years ago, during demolition at Farningham School in Kent, England, a bottle containing wheat seeds and a message was found in a wall. The message read, "Deposited in the Wall of this School Sept. 18th 1872 by Peter Ashenden. I leave this to some querist of a future day, as at this present time there is much curiosity in antiquity, and there is now growing the Mummy Wheat the seed of which is said to have been buried two thousand years. Some one of a future day may like to try this, and I wish you success. P.A." Botanists found the seeds to be dead. They were, however, awed by the inquiring mind and scientific forethought of Peter Ashenden.

In 1879, Dr. W. J. Beal put twenty samples of seeds from twenty-one different plant species in moist sand in unstopped bottles. He buried them with the open neck of the bottle down, eighteen inches below soil level on the grounds of Michigan State University. At intervals of five or ten years one bottle of seeds has been opened and planted. Some seeds were viable for seventy years; others germinated after ninety years. Three species germinated in 1979 after one hundred years.

In 1962, about two thousand old vegetable seed lots were transferred from the United States Department of Agriculture Horticultural

Field Station in Cheyenne, Wyoming, to the National Seed Storage Laboratory in Fort Collins, Colorado. Because of the limited number of seeds in each lot, only a few seeds have been tested for viability at regular intervals. The latest test was made in 1991. The oldest viable seeds were sixty years old and came from a strain of tomato; 82 percent were viable. Viable seeds were found after fifty years for certain strains of beets, corn, cucumbers, eggplants, muskmelons, okras, onions, peas, peppers, and watermelons; seed viability ranged from 2 to 98 percent. Bean, carrot, spinach, and Swiss chard seeds were viable after forty-five years, with viability ranging from 14 to 72 percent. These seed ages may not represent maximum numbers because the tests will continue in the future at regular intervals. Recent recognition of the necessity of preserving the germ plasm or seeds of important plants and trees, as more plants become extinct and wild lands are destroyed, has prompted forward-thinking scientists to establish the National Seed Storage Laboratory. Similar facilities have been organized in Europe and Japan, and all have as their goal the preservation for posterity of important seeds.

One promising method for seed preservation is suggested by the success of freezing living animal cells in liquid nitrogen for long-term storage. The "seeds" or sperm of humans and other animals have been preserved alive for many years in liquid nitrogen, as have cells and small pieces of tissue of many animals. I have stored living, normal human cells in liquid nitrogen for thirty-two years, which is currently the world's record. More recently, fertilized human eggs have also been stored in liquid nitrogen, recovered, and implanted into women, producing perfectly normal babies. Similar results have been obtained with the fertilized eggs of several lower animals. At the temperature of liquid nitrogen, which is three hundred and twenty degrees below zero Fahrenheit, virtually all biological activity stops. There is every reason to believe that living seeds, single cells, small bits of tissue, sperm, eggs, and fertilized eggs can remain in a viable state in liquid nitrogen indefinitely. Cells from my normal human lung cell strain, called WI-38, have remained alive for more than three decades. Thus, the question of the immortality of some kinds of *small* life-forms probably is settled. As long as they are properly frozen and kept at constant, very cold temperatures, their immortality seems to be assured.

I have suggested to the National Aeronautics and Space Administration that materials such as these could be placed into Earth's orbit with no refrigerant because the container could be oriented away from the sun and would thus remain sufficiently cold at the temperature of outer space. This orbiting "Noah's ark" of vital biological material might provide the most effective means for guaranteed long-term storage of vital germ plasm and the body cells of animals and humans. The ark would provide an opportunity to retrieve these materials if humans fail to stop the terrible destruction of plants and animals and their habitats that cause a species' extinction. The orbiting ark would also safeguard human, plant, and animal cells against species loss in the event of a nuclear war or other enormous disaster. My ark suggestion has fallen on deaf ears.

The world's champion oldest living life-form is a microorganism called *Bacillus circulans*. It was six hundred and fifty million years old when isolated from a salt deposit. Two other microorganisms are runners-up. *Enterobacter cloacae* and another member of this genus were found alive in the intestinal tract of a mastodon dead for eleven thousand years. Another living microorganism was found in a Roman archaeological site and dated at 1,890 years old, and a Porter yeast, grown from an 1825 shipwreck, has been used to commercialize a porter beer.

CHAPTER 4

Aging Is Not
a Disease

If I had known that I was going to live this long,
I would have taken better care of myself.
                                        —Eubie Blake

T O understand aging, it is necessary to distinguish between normal aging and the diseases that are associated with old age. Although the term "normal aging" is frequently used, it is not a good choice of words because it implies that there is such a thing as abnormal aging. That, of course, is absurd. No one experiences abnormal aging. Normal aging is simply aging.

When we speak of normal development, we mean the sequence of biological changes through which the fertilized egg becomes an adult. If a genetic mistake occurs during the embryonic phase of development we call it a birth defect or a congenital malformation. It is abnormal development. No similar "defects" occur during aging; we consider the aging process to be normal regardless of what changes occur. It would be absurd to say that someone who is more gray or more wrinkled than someone else is aging abnormally. Even if you don't become gray or wrinkled at all, you are not aging abnormally!

Both age changes and diseases produce impairments or deficits in

43

optimum functioning. Why, then, is it necessary to distinguish between changes that result from aging and changes that result from disease? And how can we make this distinction? If aging results in a physiological or functional loss leading to your inability to run as fast at age thirty as you did at age nineteen, is that a sign of disease? Is gray hair, wrinkled skin, farsightedness, or the loss of the ability to hear some high notes a disease? No one has been hospitalized or has died from gray hair, wrinkled skin, or the inability to hear a high C! These normal changes that occur with age are not diseases but are typical of hundreds of thousands of similar, though less apparent, nondisease changes that occur throughout our bodies as we age.

NORMAL AGE CHANGES

Some of the more obvious normal age changes include loss of strength and stamina, farsightedness, new hair growth in ears and nostrils, decline in short-term memory, balding, loss of bone mass, decrease in height, hearing loss, and the menopause. This brief, random list of normal age changes could be extended enormously. Most of the changes mentioned can be seen with the naked eye, but they have their origins at levels not readily apparent to our senses. As we age, thousands of changes occur in all of our organs and tissues, in the individual cells that compose them, and even in the cement that holds our cells together. Age changes occur even in the individual molecules of which our cells are composed and in the products that our cells produce. These less-apparent changes give rise to the more obvious manifestations of aging. The less-obvious normal age changes affect the cells in virtually all of our organs, including the immune, neuroendocrine, and cardiovascular systems. The important point is that these inapparent age changes are considered to be normal and not states of disease.

We are not sick because we experience normal age changes. But the likelihood that we will get sick increases with age because the normal age changes make us more vulnerable to diseases that in youth would be more easily repulsed. For example, as our immune system ages, it becomes less efficient in defending us and more likely to make errors in defense. It may mistake normal proteins in our bodies for foreign proteins, thus producing antibodies against our own cells. The result is an autoimmune disease.

The diseases associated with old age are *not* part of the norma
ing process. Cancer, heart disease, Alzheimer's disease, and stiokus
become more prevalent as we age because of our reduced capacity to
repel them. So, although the functional losses that occur in our vital
systems as we age are normal events, they do increase our vulnerability to diseases or accidents. And diseases, unlike aging, are not normal.

CAUSES OF DEATH

In truth, few people over the age of sixty-five die from what is written
on his or her death certificate. The normal age changes that occurred
before death simply increased vulnerability of the deceased to whatever was written on the death certificate. The real problem was not a
particular illness, but whatever changes within the body that made it
vulnerable to the illness. Even fatal accidents may not be the real
causes of death in old people if the accident was caused by the person's inability to see or hear well enough to detect danger or to react
quickly enough. It is also possible that a fall from which a young person would easily have recovered might be fatal for an older person
whose bones are more likely to break or whose normal physiological
age changes make recovery more difficult.

Furthermore, the older the person, the less likely it is that an autopsy will be performed to demonstrate the cause of death with scientific precision. Some gerontologists believe that we really do not know
what the cause of death is in people over, say, age eighty-five, sometimes called the oldest old. In the few studies that have been done,
most diseases of the elderly are found to have existed for a long time
without or with only minor, clinical signs. Some form of cancer is
found in more than half of autopsies on the oldest old people, but the
cancer didn't kill them. More than three-fourths of the oldest old have
from three to nine major pathological conditions. Obviously, designat-
ing a single cause for the death of a very old person is frequently inaccurate.

The cause of death in older people is a mysterious "black box."
Usually some standard cause of death is chosen from an approved list in
order to comply with legal requirements. A 1985 Connecticut study of
death certificates concluded that more than half of the causes of death
thus certified were wrong. Until we know the true causes of death in
the rapidly increasing population of older people, we can expect little

progress to be made in extending life. It is illogical to suppose that progress will be made in understanding the causes of death before those causes are known.

Until thirty or forty years ago, when the cause of death in an older person was not known, that fact was acknowledged on death certificates in the form of a statement attributing the death to "natural causes." At that time many people died of natural causes in the United States; today, few do. Who discovered the cause of "natural causes," and, more importantly, who discovered its cure? The scientific literature nowhere describes the cause and cure of the natural causes of death; the extraordinary modesty of the discoverers of the cause and cure of natural causes is unique in the annals of biomedical science. Furthermore, this monumental achievement apparently occurred without the expenditure of any research funds, and no health administrator has ever claimed credit for the feat when pleading for more funds before Congress! The Nobel committees as well have chosen to ignore these unsung heroes. It is one of the great enigmas of biomedical science that the resolution of a leading cause of death occurred almost without notice.

I believe, however, that if we succeed in preventing or curing the causes of death that now appear on death certificates, we will face an apparently renewed epidemic of "natural causes." Natural causes seem to have disappeared as a cause of death because physicians came to feel that writing "natural causes" on a death certificate, even when the cause of death was truly unknown, was too great an admission of ignorance in an age of increasing scientific enlightenment. Thus cardiac arrest, stroke, pulmonary infarction, cancer, or some other nameable cause became more acceptable, even when the real cause of death was unknown. One can only speculate as to the impact that this nonscientific, sociologically determined phenomenon has had on the statistics on the true causes of death in the elderly in the past fifty years.

Most biomedical research is directed toward resolving causes of death currently written on death certificates, but the primary cause of death, the *increase in vulnerability* to what was written on the death certificate, is largely ignored. That vulnerability results from the normal aging process. Even if cures are found for all the "certified" causes of death, we will still be fated to die of the physiological losses of old age because so little research is now being directed toward understanding the aging process. More basic research into the biology of aging would serve a double purpose: by increasing our knowledge of the fundamental aging process we would also gain insight into how to reduce our vulnerability to the causes of death now appearing on the death certificates of older people.

Only a few biomedical research scientists are now working on the underlying causes of aging that increase our vulnerability to chronic disease and accidents. Unless more attention is paid to the fundamental processes of aging, the fate of everyone fortunate enough to become old will be death on or around his or her hundredth birthday. And, despite what might be written on the death certificate, the true causes of those deaths will probably be unknown.

AGE-RELATED ILLNESSES

Although the distinction between normal age changes and diseases is important, it is not always easy to make, and on occasion may be impossible. For example, the menopause, a normal age-associated event, seems for many women to increase the risk of osteoporosis and atherosclerosis. Enlargement of the prostate gland occurs in almost all aging men, and the hormone changes that accompany it can result in several ailments, including cancer. One might argue that these are really examples of increased vulnerability, but it is a fine line. A better example of an age-related illness is the formation of cataracts, which result from normal changes in proteins that increase their opacity. These same protein changes occurring elsewhere in the body produce no discomfort, but in the lens of the eye the cloudy condition can lead to blindness. Here the distinction between age changes and disease is truly blurred (pun intended).

The difficulty in determining whether some aging processes are diseases is also influenced by two other concerns. If aging, like development to adulthood, is universal, then it should not be regarded as a disease because no disease is universal. Yet, as mentioned above, there are pathologies that are found in close to 100 percent of older people. Perhaps it is more appropriate to ask ourselves whether aging is like a disease because it is undesirable and therefore to be prevented or cured. If the prevention and cure of aging are desirable goals, then one might be justified in calling aging a disease. If not, then the processes of aging, like the processes that take us from infancy to adulthood, are desirable and therefore not diseases.

If we knew more about the changes that make a cell old and those that make a cell diseased at the molecular level, the differences might be difficult or impossible to distinguish. However, aging manifests itself differently from disease at higher levels of organization, through changes in cells, tissues, and organs. One general distinction is that physiological losses characteristic of aging eventually occur in the cells, tissues, and organs of *all* older members of a species, while changes due to disease occur only in *some* members.

POPULATION VERSUS INDIVIDUAL AGING

As we have noted, it is important to distinguish between the aging of a population and the aging of the individual members of that population. Even scientists can be misled by failing to make this distinction. For example, many microbiologists believe that one-celled animals, like paramecia, and one-celled plants, like bacteria or yeast, are immortal. After all, they argue, if these organisms are fed and cared for properly, they can be periodically transferred to new containers indefinitely. Because some microbial strains have been transferred for decades in this way, these scientists argue that the organisms do not age, that they are immortal. But this is not true. By that same faulty reasoning, humans would also be immortal. After all, we have been around for several million years and we are likely to survive indefinitely so long as we reproduce successfully and the necessities of life are provided.

The human *population*, like populations of one-celled animals or plants, is immortal, but *individual* humans are not. To an observer on another planet whose telescope lacks the resolving power to see bedrooms and what goes on in them, humans might appear to reproduce endlessly without the periodic mixing of genes. Mothers would appear to give birth with no apparent relationship to fathers. Sex, which might be defined as a mechanism for rearranging genes, results in the rejuvenation of the species. Although some might argue that sex rejuvenates individuals, I use the term here with a more narrow meaning. Most single-celled animal and plant populations have not been grown under circumstances where single individuals have been prevented from mixing their genes with those of others. In the few cases where this has been done, the organisms have been found to be mortal like humans. Like us, they must periodically reshuffle their genes with those of partners in order to ensure the continuation of their lineage.

An individual bacterium or paramecium divides by repeatedly splitting in two. Although the process, called fission, may seem to confer immortality on each individual, the protoplasm composing each one is diluted by half, or some other fraction, at each division. If the dilution is by one-half, then after about twenty-two generations, only about one molecule from the original bacterium will be found in each of the remaining bacteria. So, after twenty-two generations the physical identity of the original parent has essentially vanished. The substance within each of the cells is not immortal.

Because single-cell plants and animals replicate by dividing in half, they appear to produce no corpses. An old idea has it that if there is no corpse there cannot be death. (The idea appears in our legal system as the concept of habeas corpus.) However, if you carefully follow each cell lineage as division occurs, you will discover that many of the lineages do end in the death of the cell. So corpses do appear. If they did not, then after fifty consecutive fissions, several million tons of cells would be present! This, of course, never occurs. In the few lineages that do appear to be immortal, it is almost certain that exchange of genetic information (sex) occurs periodically. Like higher organisms, most bacteria have evolved means for periodically exchanging genetic information between pairs of organisms. As with humans, the mixing of genes from two individual bacteria will not make either one immortal, but it does have the potential of providing immortality to the entire population or species.

One species of yeast, used to make beer, does not divide in half to reproduce but multiplies by budding. The buds leave a scar on the surface of the mother yeast cell, and only about twenty-four daughter cells can bud from one mother even if more unscarred surface remains. There is a limit in the ability of the mother yeast cell to reproduce, just as there is a limit on the replicative capacity of normal cells taken from humans and animals, a discovery that will be discussed in detail later.

This discussion of population aging and how it differs from individual aging leads us now to consider the big population picture—how many old people there are (or will be), where they are located, how they live, and the effects that these factors have, or will have, on ourselves and our institutions.

PART TWO

Aging by the Numbers

CHAPTER 5

The Demographic
Facts of Life

It is now proved beyond doubt that [aging] is
one of the leading causes of statistics.
—with apologies to Fletcher Knebel

AMERICA has long thought of itself as a nation of young
people, but today, for the first time since the birth of the nation,
there are more middle-aged and older Americans than younger citizens.

In the past few decades an enormous amount of information has
been obtained on aging as it applies to the American population and
the populations of other developed countries. The demography of the
elderly is a particularly revealing subject, full of surprises and important information about both our present situation and the future. Most
of the data for the United States population have been generated from
the census, vital statistics reports from the Department of Health and
Human Services, and studies done by states, private foundations, universities, and insurance companies. Students of demography study the
statistics of the human population, especially its size, geographical distribution, and composition, as well as the determinants of these variables, such as fertility, mortality, and migration. Demographers have

taught us much about the dramatic changes that aging has made in our population.

THE GRAYING OF AMERICA

One of the most important demographic facts is the enormous increase in older people—both as a percentage of the population and in absolute numbers—that has occurred since our country's birth. The graying of America has been underway since the first census was taken in 1790. At that time half the population was under age sixteen. In 1990 less than 25 percent of Americans were under age sixteen and 50 percent were age thirty-three or older. Figure 5–1 shows the doubling of the median age (half of the population is older and half is younger than this figure) between 1790 and 1990.

Between 1980 and 1988 the number of older Americans increased by 18 percent, compared to an increase of 7 percent for those under age sixty-five. In 1990 there were 31 million people over the age of sixty-five in a total population of about 250 million. That is, people over age sixty-five made up about 12.5 percent of the population. Figure 5–2 shows the number of people age fifty-five or over, starting in 1900, with projections through the year 2050.

In the one hundred years from 1820 to 1920 in the United States, there was a general increase in the number of births, a reduction in the number of youthful deaths, and an increase in immigration. This has resulted in an increase in the *number* of people over sixty-five since 1900. The decline in the birth rate since the mid-1930s—with the exception of the post World War II "baby boom"—is the major reason for the increase now in the *proportion or percentage* of people over sixty-five.

While figure 5–2 shows the number of people in the four older age groups in the total population from 1900 to 2050, table 5–1 reveals that both the absolute numbers of older people and their percentage in the total population have increased dramatically. With the exception of the aging cohort of baby boomers, who are at this writing between the ages of twenty-seven and forty-seven, the population cohort whose numbers are increasing most rapidly today is people over the age of eighty-five. In the year 2010 the percentage of people over eighty-five will be twice what it is today; in forty years it will triple! The accuracy of these projections of future *percentages* will depend on how well we

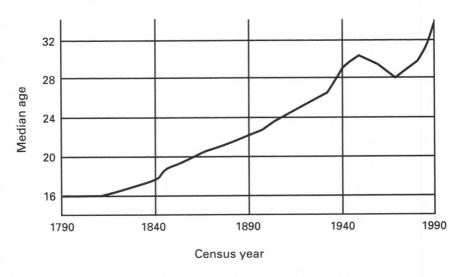

FIGURE 5-1. Median age of U.S. population, 1790–1990

SOURCE: Permission granted courtesy of *Statistical Bulletin*, Metropolitan Life Insurance Co., January–March 1990.

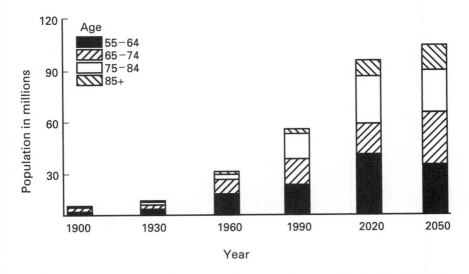

FIGURE 5-2. U.S. population age 55 and older, 1900–2050

SOURCE: U.S. Bureau of the Census. Decennial census,1900–1980; projections, 1990–2050, *Current Population Reports*, series P–25, no. 1018, January 1989.

TABLE 5-1. Growth of U.S. Population age 55 and older, 1900–2050
(numbers in thousands)

Year	Total population, all ages	55 to 64 Number	Percent	65 to 74 Number	Percent	75 to 84 Number	Percent	85 and older Number	Percent	65 and older Number	Percent
1900	76,303	4,009	5.3	2,189	2.9	772	1.0	123	0.2	3,084	4.0
1910	91,972	5,054	5.5	2,793	3.0	989	1.1	167	0.2	3,950	4.3
1920	105,711	6,532	6.2	3,464	3.3	1,259	1.2	210	0.2	4,933	4.7
1930	122,775	8,397	6.8	4,721	3.8	1,641	1.3	272	0.2	6,634	5.4
1940	131,669	10,572	8.0	6,375	4.8	2,278	1.7	365	0.3	9,019	6.8
1950	150,967	13,295	8.8	8,415	5.6	3,278	2.2	577	0.4	12,270	8.1
1960	179,323	15,572	8.7	10,997	6.1	4,633	2.6	929	0.5	16,560	9.2
1970	203,302	18,608	9.2	12,447	6.1	6,124	3.0	1,409	0.7	19,980	9.8
1980	226,546	21,703	9.6	15,580	6.9	7,729	3.4	2,240	1.0	25,549	11.3
1990	250,410	21,364	8.5	18,373	7.3	9,933	4.0	3,254	1.3	31,559	12.6
2000	268,266	24,158	9.0	18,243	6.8	12,017	4.5	4,622	1.7	34,882	13.0
2010	282,575	35,430	12.5	21,039	7.4	12,208	4.3	6,115	2.2	39,362	13.9
2020	294,364	41,087	14.0	30,973	10.5	14,443	4.9	6,651	2.3	52,067	17.7
2030	300,629	34,947	11.6	35,988	12.0	21,487	7.1	8,129	2.7	65,604	21.8
2040	301,807	35,537	11.8	30,808	10.2	25,050	8.3	12,251	4.1	68,109	22.6
2050	299,849	37,004	12.3	31,590	10.5	21,655	7.2	15,287	5.1	68,532	22.9

SOURCE: U.S. Bureau of the Census. Decennial census, 1900–1980; projections, 1990–2050, *Current Population Reports*, series P-25, no. 1018, January 1989.

have predicted future fertility, mortality, and immigration rates. On the other hand, we are sure of the *number* of present-day Americans who will be sixty-five years old or older through the middle of the next century because all of them are alive today, and we have excellent statistical evidence for their life expectations.

Despite the growing proportion of people sixty-five years of age and older in this country, the percentage here is lower than in many other countries. Most European countries and Japan have much greater proportions of older people in their populations than does the United States. African, Asian, and Latin American countries have smaller proportions of older people. These differences are mainly attributable to variations in patterns of migration, health status and birth rates. Where birth rates are high, the proportion of older people in the population is low. Where birth rates are low, the proportion of older people is high. For a complex blend of social, political, economic, and religious reasons, birth rates are highest in the least-developed countries. Thus a rule of thumb can be stated: The more developed the country, the greater its proportion of elderly; the less developed the country, the greater its proportion of youth.

THE STATISTICS TODAY

▪ Since 1900 the percentage of people in the United States over age sixty-five has tripled from 4 percent to 12.6 percent. The actual number has grown from 3 million in 1900 to 31.6 million in 1990, a tenfold increase.

▪ The oldest old (people over age eighty-five) are the fastest growing segment of our population (figure 5–3). Compared to the corresponding populations in 1900, in 1991 the 65–74 age group was eight times larger, the 75–84 group was thirteen times larger, and the 85 and older group was twenty-five times larger.

▪ A child born in 1991 can expect to live 75.5 years, or about twenty-eight years longer than a child born in 1900. Life expectation for a sixty-five-year-old increased by 2.4 years from 1900 to 1960, but, in half that time, from 1960 to 1990, it increased another 3 years.

▪ About six thousand people celebrated their sixty-fifth birthday each day in 1990, and each had an additional life expectation of 17.3 years. That's six years more than a sixty-five-year-old could expect to live in 1900, when reaching age sixty-five was unusual. In 1989 a

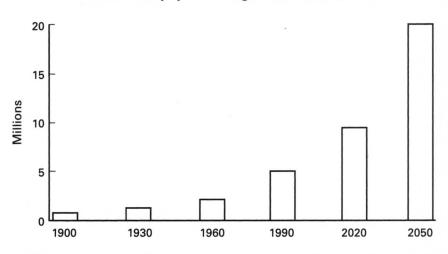

FIGURE 5-3. U.S. population age 85 and older, 1900–2050

SOURCE: U.S. Bureau of the Census. Decennial census, 1900–1980; projections, 1990–2050, Current Population Report, P–25, no. 922, October 1982.

twenty-year-old could expect to live fifty-six more years, or 13.4 years more than a twenty-year-old could expect in 1900.

▪ In 1990, the number of people turning sixty-five, minus the number of people sixty-five or older who died, yielded a net increase of 1,770 people aged sixty-five or older per day.

▪ In 1990 there were 123 women for each 100 men in the 65–69 age group (or 81 men for each 100 women). For persons 85 and older the ratio was 259 women for every 100 men (or 39 men for each 100 women). Why this difference occurs will be the subject of chapter 7.

▪ In 1991, almost half of all women over age sixty-five were widows. They outnumbered widowers five-to-one.

▪ Half of the female population over seventy-five, but only 20 percent of the male population over seventy-five, lives alone.

▪ Contrary to popular misconception, only 5 percent of people over sixty-five are institutionalized, almost all in nursing homes. More than twice as many of the institutionalized elderly are female.

▪ Ninety percent of persons sixty-five and over in 1989 are white; 8 percent are black. Eighty-four percent of the total population are white; 12 percent are black.

THE STATISTICS TOMORROW

▪ Although the number of people over sixty-five will continue to increase in the future, the rate will slow during this decade because so few births occurred during the Depression. (Fewer people born in 1930 means fewer people turning sixty-five in 1995.) The "baby boomers" will produce a rapid increase in the years 2010 to 2030 when they reach sixty-five (see last column in table 5–1). The baby boom will become the grandparent boom and then the great-grandparent boom. More accurately, it should be called the grandmother and great-grandmother booms, assuming women will continue to outlive men.

▪ There will be between thirty-two and thirty-eight million people over age sixty-five in the year 2000, depending on the accuracy of estimates about future death rates. Of these, more than six million will be over eighty-five.

▪ By 2030 there will be more than 66 million, or twice as many people over age sixty-five in the United States as there are today.

▪ The only age group that will experience a significant increase in numbers in the twenty-first century, given present birth rates and immigration patterns, will be people over age fifty-five.

SOME GEOGRAPHICAL FACTS

▪ In 1991, 52 percent of all people sixty-five and older lived in nine states: California (over three million); New York and Florida (over two million each); and Michigan, New Jersey, Illinois, Ohio, Texas, and Pennsylvania (over one million each). This is not too surprising because almost half of the United States population of all ages lives in these states.

▪ In 1991, 12.6 percent of the total United States population was over age sixty-five (table 5–2, figure 5–4). Florida had the highest proportion of people over age sixty-five with 18.3 percent, followed by Pennsylvania (15.5 percent), Iowa (15.4 percent), Rhode Island and West Virginia (15.1 percent each), Arkansas (14.9 percent), South Dakota (14.7 percent), and Missouri and Nebraska (14.1 percent each).

▪ Between 1980 and 1991, nine states showed a 40 percent or greater increase in the population sixty-five or older (figure 5–5). Nevada's older population swelled during this eleven-year period by 111

TABLE 5-2. U.S. population age 65 and older by state, 1991

State	Number (thousands)	Percent of total population	Percent increase (1980–1991)
U.S., total	31,754	12.6	24.3
Alabama	529	12.9	20.2
Alaska	24	4.2	105.1
Arizona	497	13.2	61.6
Arkansas	353	14.9	12.9
California	3,187	10.5	32.0
Colorado	340	10.1	37.5
Connecticut	451	13.7	23.7
Delaware	83	12.2	40.2
District of Columbia	77	12.8	3.5
Florida	2,432	18.3	44.1
Georgia	668	10.1	29.3
Hawaii	129	11.4	69.6
Idaho	124	12.0	32.8
Illinois	1,448	12.5	14.8
Indiana	708	12.6	21.0
Iowa	431	15.4	11.1
Kansas	346	13.9	13.1
Kentucky	472	12.7	15.1
Louisiana	474	11.2	17.3
Maine	166	13.4	17.7
Maryland	530	10.9	33.9
Massachusetts	824	13.7	13.5
Michigan	1,130	12.1	23.8
Minnesota	555	12.5	15.8
Mississippi	323	12.4	11.5
Missouri	726	14.1	12.0
Montana	108	13.4	28.1
Nebraska	225	14.1	9.4
Nevada	138	10.8	110.6
New Hampshire	128	11.6	24.2
New Jersey	1,041	13.4	21.1
New Mexico	168	10.9	45.1
New York	2,357	13.1	9.1
North Carolina	826	12.3	37.0
North Dakota	92	14.5	14.1
Ohio	1,432	13.1	22.5
Oklahoma	430	13.5	14.2
Oregon	401	13.7	32.3
Pennsylvania	1,858	15.5	21.4
Rhode Island	152	15.1	19.7
South Carolina	407	11.4	41.5
South Dakota	104	14.7	13.7
Tennessee	629	12.7	21.6
Texas	1,756	10.1	28.1
Utah	155	8.8	42.4
Vermont	67	11.9	15.5
Virginia	682	10.9	35.0
Washington	590	11.8	36.6
West Virginia	271	15.1	14.1
Wisconsin	661	13.3	17.1
Wyoming	49	10.6	30.7

SOURCE: A Profile of Older Americans, reprinted by permission from the American Association of Retired Persons, Washington, D.C., 1992.

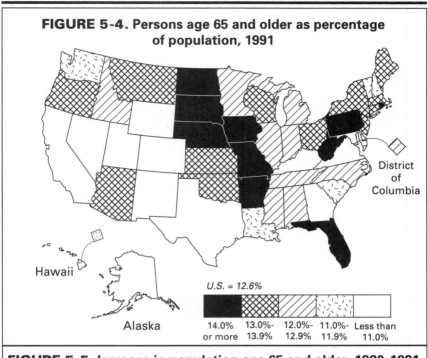

FIGURE 5-4. Persons age 65 and older as percentage of population, 1991

District of Columbia

Hawaii

Alaska

U.S. = 12.6%

| 14.0% or more | 13.0%-13.9% | 12.0%-12.9% | 11.0%-11.9% | Less than 11.0% |

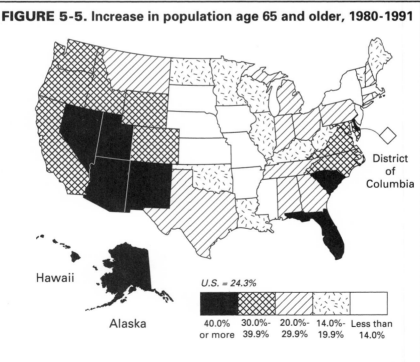

FIGURE 5-5. Increase in population age 65 and older, 1980-1991

District of Columbia

Hawaii

Alaska

U.S. = 24.3%

| 40.0% or more | 30.0%-39.9% | 20.0%-29.9% | 14.0%-19.9% | Less than 14.0% |

SOURCE: A Profile of Older Americans. Reprinted by permission of the American Association of Retired Persons, Washington D.C., 1992.

percent, Alaska's by 105 percent, Hawaii's by 70 percent, Arizona's by 62 percent, New Mexico's by 45 percent, Florida's by 44 percent, South Carolina's and Utah's by 42 percent each, and Delaware's by 40 percent. However, the numbers are deceptive; many of the changes are due more to the emigration of younger people from these states than to the immigration of older people.

■ Older people are less likely to move than younger people. In 1990 only 5 percent of older people had moved since 1989 while 20 percent of people younger than sixty-five had moved. Eighty percent of the older group that did move stayed in the same state. Of those that did move out of state, more than one-third moved from the northeast or midwest to the sunbelt, compared to 26 percent of the younger people who moved.

Growing old in America is a phenomenon that affects all of us, whatever our ages. The demographics of present and future age changes present convincing evidence that our concern about age changes must be broadened to include not only our personal concerns but also concerns about the growing number of people who will be our fellow travelers in time.

CHAPTER 6

Actuarial Aging

Life is 6 to 5 against.
                    —Damon Runyon

I N pursuit of the perfect definition of aging we should not overlook those made by actuaries. They would say that aging is the sum of the biological changes or functional losses that increase the likelihood of dying. Although this is statistically accurate, it doesn't help us to understand the biology of aging. Normal aging ultimately leads to death, but so can illness. For example, a life-threatening disease like leukemia may produce changes that increase even a young person's likelihood of dying, but the pathological changes attributable to leukemia are not the same as age changes. Another common definition describes aging as the reduced capacity to respond to environmental changes, but again, this condition is not unique to aging. Most leukemia victims, to continue our example, do not die of leukemia but of common yeast infections which overwhelm their compromised immune systems.

THE LIKELIHOOD OF DEATH

In 1825, a self-taught English actuary, Benjamin Gompertz, began to study the human demographic data that were then appearing for the first time in meaningful amounts. He made the startling discovery that, after the age of thirty, the likelihood that an individual will die doubles every seven years! He was the first person to demonstrate that the probability of death increased exponentially in human adults. The mathematical formula that he devised to express this fact helped to propel the growing nineteenth-century life insurance industry. The development of the Gompertz equation and more sophisticated actuarial tables gave the life insurance industry the same guarantee of financial success as that enjoyed by operators of gambling casinos, who also use statistical tables based on a large number of players and a knowledge of the laws of chance.

When you pay premiums to a life insurance company, you are betting that you might die soon. The insurance company happily takes your money in the more certain knowledge that it is unlikely you will die soon. The party that more often wins the bet is, of course, the insurance company. Just compare its resources with yours. But don't cancel your life insurance policy; you have purchased it to protect your dependents in the event that your demise *does* occur before the laws of chance say that, on the average, it should.

The specific factors that affect the probability of living a long life have fascinated gerontologists and actuaries for centuries. Even Alexander Graham Bell, best known for his invention of the telephone, made some interesting computations. Bell was a genealogist by vocation and, in that capacity, had access to the genealogical trees of many families. One of them was the family of William Hyde, who had over twenty-two hundred male and eighteen hundred female descendants. In 1918, Bell published an analysis of these descendants and found that Hydes whose parents both died at an age greater than eighty lived on average twenty years longer than those descendants whose two parents died before age sixty.

In a landmark book published in 1934, Raymond Pearl and Ruth DeWitt Pearl described an imaginative technique for determining the inheritance of longevity in humans. Using verifiable data for many people, they calculated a Total Immediate Ancestral Longevity index, or TIAL, by summing the ages at death of each person's six parents and grandparents. They argued that this number should be regarded as just as significant to an individual as his or her birthday, height, or weight. The maximum TIAL is 690, if all six parents and grandparents reach the maximum human longevity of 115 years. The minimum TIAL is about 78, based on the assumption that puberty is reached at the age of thirteen. Siblings will have the same TIAL.

The Pearls found that, for the longest-lived group of people, the TIAL ranged from the lowest found to the highest. However, the average TIAL for ninety- and one-hundred-year-olds was 16 percent greater than the average for all participants. Thirteen percent of these oldest participants had both parents die before age seventy, so extremely longevous people may be born of parents with low or average ages at death. But 87 percent of the nonagenarians and centenarians had at least one parent who lived beyond the age of seventy.

When both parents survive to age seventy or older, the likelihood that their children will reach ninety or one hundred is almost twice as great as that found for the general population. Among other findings, the Pearls reported that for every 3.7 years above the average in someone's TIAL score, one additional year of life over the average can be anticipated. Clearly, having long-lived parents and grandparents increases the likelihood of achieving great longevity, although it is no guarantee.

Similar studies have been made by life insurance companies, which have a strong interest in these matters and a great deal of pertinent information in their records. They have also found that longevous parents are more likely to have longevous offspring. What has not been revealed in these and other studies is whether one parent can influence the longevity of his or her offspring to a greater extent than the other parent. Put in a different way: Do certain people possess a genetic factor that can confer greater than average longevity on their children?

To help determine whether longevous parents and grandparents pass on to their children a genetic bonus or simply a lifestyle that favors above average longevity, it is interesting to study twins. There are two kinds of twins, those who develop from a single fertilized egg that separated into two distinct sets of cells early in development, (identical, or monozygotic, twins) and those who developed from two eggs fertilized by two separate sperm around the same time (fraternal, or dizygotic, twins). Identical twins, closer genetically because they developed from the same sperm and egg, are always of the same sex. Fraternal twins are as closely related genetically as two children born at different times to the same parents.

In one study, biogerontologists discovered that identical twins died within three years of each other, whereas fraternal twins of the same sex differed, on average, by more than six years in the times of their deaths. It is tempting to interpret this difference as an indication of a strong role for genetics in the determination of longevity. Although this may be true, it does not rule out the possibility that the difference in the time between deaths for the two kinds of twins may reflect a secondary role of genetics in the timing of the appearance of the disease that may have caused death.

Perhaps there is merit to the old saw that says, to increase your chances of living long, you should choose your parents, and grandparents, wisely.

ARE WE LIVING LONGER?

You have probably heard or read that we are living longer now than we ever have. This statement is true only if you include an important qualification based on the distinction between life span and life expectation. The belief that the triumphs of modern biomedical research have lengthened the human *life span* (maximum longevity) is not supported by either vital statistics or biological data. There is no evidence that the maximum human life span has changed from what it was about a hundred thousand years ago. It is still about 115 years. (Claims to the contrary will be considered later.)

Advances in biomedical research and the implementation of improved medical care in this century have certainly had an impact on human longevity, but only by allowing more people to approach the fixed upper limit of the human life span. The likelihood that you and I will live to be ninety or a hundred has certainly increased, but the maximum human life span has not changed. *Life expectation* has increased but *life span* has not; the distinction is critical.

Today, in the United States, life expectation at birth is about seventy-five years. That is, *on average*, an infant born today will live to celebrate its seventy-fifth birthday if it experiences the same chances of dying as existed for each future year of its life when it was born. Since the maximum human life span is about 115 years, we can conclude that the forty-year gap between life span and average life expectation at birth would vanish if we could prevent all causes of death now written on death certificates. Most people would then live to age 115, but no one would be immortal. Not even the monumental feat of conquering all currently recorded causes of death would allow us to exceed the 115-year maximum human life span, but even this limited miracle might not be an unmixed blessing, as we will soon see.

HOW MANY YEARS ARE LEFT?

We usually think of old age in terms of how close an individual is to age one hundred. Jacob S. Seigel, a leading demographer at the U.S. Bureau of the Census, points out that a different way of regarding age is becoming more popular because it seems to provoke greater interest in the social, legal, economic, and ethical aspects of aging. The new way of looking at the question of aging is to consider, for any particular age, the average number of years that remain until death becomes likely. Like life expectation at birth, this figure applies to groups of people and not to individuals; there is no method by which we can predict precisely when any given individual will die. According to this perspective, old age is the period of life that begins when a particular group of people has some average expected number of years left to live. For example, a group of white males aged seventy-three in 1988 had about ten years of life remaining on average; a group of white females of the same age had about thirteen years. The males, then, may be older than they think. This concept has been decisive in several recent court decisions: the fundamental question in this regard is whether economic and other privileges of later life should be conferred upon some people earlier because they have a shorter life expectation. Someone who is chronically ill and therefore expected to die sooner might have a basis for claiming old-age benefits earlier than a healthy person of comparable age.

This intriguing idea becomes even more complicated when we consider another trend in thinking about old age. Instead of knowing how many years of life you might have left, a more significant number might be what has been variously described as your "healthy," "active," or "functional" life expectation, that is, the number of years you can expect to live in good health. That information is known and we will consider this important idea soon.

THE TABLES OF LIFE

Some of the most valuable tools that the gerontologist has are life tables and the survival curves that can be drawn from the data they contain. The tables are easy to understand and yield an enormous amount of fascinating information. The data needed to compile one type of life table are obtained by identifying and tracking a large group of individuals all born during a specific time period. The group that is followed is called a cohort. After the cohort has been established, the deaths that occur within it are recorded until all members of the original group are dead. The end point in life tables is death, not aging. The tables are, nevertheless, valuable to gerontologists because we assume that deaths in the monitored cohort during the later years result from an increase in vulnerability—the hallmark of aging.

One of the first accurate life tables for humans was assembled by Edmund Halley, better known for his discovery of the comet that bears his name. Halley published his life table in 1693 under the title "An Estimate of the Degrees of the Mortality of Mankind Drawn from Curious Tables of the Births and Funerals at the City of Breslau." Halley found that life expectation for these citizens was about thirty-three years at birth, forty-two years at age five, thirty years at age twenty-five, twenty-two years at age forty, twelve years at age sixty, and six years at age eighty. The Northhampton Table, developed in England by Richard Price in 1783, was the first life table used to determine premium rates for selling life insurance because life expectation at several ages could be determined with reasonable accuracy. The table was skewed purposely to favor the insurance companies and to be unfavorable to the government, which was buying the annuity plans; two million pounds were lost by the government before the "error" was discovered. The first scientifically accurate life table was the Carlisle (England) Table, published in 1815 by Milne. It gave a life expectation at birth of 38.72 years for both sexes combined. Today, life expectation at birth in the United States is about seventy-five years for both sexes combined. It is not much different for other developed countries.

The most complete and longest-maintained series of life tables for humans are to be found in the Scandinavian countries. The tables for Sweden were begun in 1755, for Norway in 1821, and for Denmark in 1835. The Netherlands has records starting in 1816, France in 1817. Records for England and Wales begin in the mid-1800s. Life tables for the United States did not appear until early in this century. Even though the census was conducted in this country every ten years from 1790 on, essential facts about mortality did not become available until 1900. Death statistics were collected in 1900, but only in ten states and the District of Columbia. It was not until 1933, when Texas joined the Death Registration Survey, that life tables became available for the entire United States. From about 1850 to 1900, based on actuarial experiences in England, expectation of life at birth for males in the United States is estimated to have risen about four and a half years; for females, it rose about six years. With advancing age the gains became smaller until, for men about age thirty and older and women over forty, the gains were negligible.

The most important kind of life table is called a current, or cross-sectional, life table. The data in this type of table does not come from monitoring a cohort of people as described above. Instead, it applies the various causes of death known to occur today at each age to a hypothetical cohort of people, all born in some specific year. The data is projected into the future, applying current death rates each year into the future until the last member of the hypothetical cohort is dead. This kind of life table gives a "snapshot" of the current causes of death at each age and projects the long-range implications of current death rates into the future. Because current life tables permit us this look into the future, they have become the most popular kind of life table and have been prepared for many different populations, geographical areas, and time periods. Their major use is by insurance company actuaries, who consult current life tables to determine life insurance premiums. The older the applicant, the more he or she will have to pay because, with each passing year, the likelihood of death increases. Life tables are also used by government actuaries in planning, for example, social security and public health policies.

The most-used column in a current life table is the one that reveals average life expectation. It answers this question: Given my present age, on average, how many more years can I expect to live? The number, of course, diminishes with each birthday. A life table for 1989 from the National Center for Health Statistics is the latest to be published and is shown in table 6–1. It gives the number of years of life expectation for every age from birth to age eighty-five, assuming that the death rates for each age in 1989 are equally applicable for the next eighty-five years. Data for the oldest old, those over age eighty-five, are not available because the agency has chosen eighty-five as an ar-

TABLE 6-1. Expectation of Life at Single Years of Age, by Race and Sex: United States, 1989

Age	All races			White			All other					
							Total			Black		
	Both sexes	Male	Female	Both sexes	Male	Female	Both sexes	Male	Female	Both sexes	Male	Female
0	75.3	71.8	78.6	76.0	72.7	79.2	71.2	67.1	75.2	69.2	64.8	73.5
1	75.0	71.6	78.3	75.6	72.3	78.8	71.4	67.3	75.4	69.5	65.2	73.8
2	74.1	70.7	77.4	74.7	71.4	77.8	70.5	66.4	74.4	68.6	64.2	72.9
3	73.1	69.7	76.4	73.7	70.4	76.9	69.5	65.5	73.5	67.7	63.3	71.9
4	72.1	68.7	75.4	72.7	69.5	75.9	68.6	64.5	72.5	66.7	62.3	71.0
5	71.1	67.8	74.4	71.7	68.5	74.9	67.6	63.5	71.6	65.8	61.4	70.0
6	70.2	66.8	73.5	70.8	67.5	73.9	66.7	62.6	70.6	64.8	60.4	69.0
7	69.2	65.8	72.5	69.8	66.5	73.0	65.7	61.6	69.6	63.8	59.4	68.0
8	68.2	64.8	71.5	68.8	65.5	72.0	64.7	60.6	68.6	62.8	58.5	67.1
9	67.2	63.8	70.5	67.8	64.5	71.0	63.7	59.6	67.6	61.9	57.5	66.1
10	66.2	62.8	69.5	66.8	63.6	70.0	62.7	58.6	66.6	60.9	56.5	65.1
11	65.2	61.9	68.5	65.8	62.6	69.0	61.7	57.7	65.7	59.9	55.5	64.1
12	64.3	60.9	67.5	64.8	61.6	68.0	60.8	56.7	64.7	58.9	54.5	63.1
13	63.3	59.9	66.5	63.9	60.6	67.0	59.8	55.7	63.7	57.9	53.5	62.1
14	62.3	58.9	65.6	62.9	59.6	66.0	58.8	54.7	62.7	56.9	52.6	61.2
15	61.3	57.9	64.6	61.9	58.6	65.1	57.8	53.8	61.7	56.0	51.6	60.2
16	60.4	57.0	63.6	60.9	57.7	64.1	56.9	52.8	60.8	55.0	50.7	59.2
17	59.4	56.1	62.6	60.0	56.8	63.1	55.9	51.9	59.8	54.1	49.8	58.2
18	58.5	55.1	61.7	59.0	55.8	62.1	55.0	51.0	58.8	53.1	48.8	57.3
19	57.5	54.2	60.7	58.1	54.9	61.2	54.0	50.1	57.8	52.2	47.9	56.3
20	56.6	53.3	59.7	57.2	54.0	60.2	53.1	49.2	56.9	51.3	47.1	55.3
21	55.6	52.4	58.8	56.2	53.0	59.2	52.2	48.3	55.9	50.4	46.2	54.4
22	54.7	51.5	57.8	55.3	52.1	58.3	51.3	47.4	54.9	49.4	45.3	53.4
23	53.8	50.5	56.8	54.3	51.2	57.3	50.4	46.5	54.0	48.5	44.4	52.4
24	52.8	49.6	55.9	53.4	50.3	56.3	49.5	45.7	53.0	47.6	43.6	51.5
25	51.9	48.7	54.9	52.4	49.4	55.3	48.5	44.8	52.1	46.7	42.7	50.6
26	50.9	47.8	53.9	51.5	48.4	54.4	47.6	43.9	51.1	45.8	41.9	49.6
27	50.0	46.9	53.0	50.5	47.5	53.4	46.7	43.0	50.2	44.9	41.0	48.7
28	49.1	46.0	52.0	49.6	46.6	52.4	45.8	42.2	49.2	44.0	40.2	47.7
29	48.1	45.1	51.0	48.6	45.7	51.5	44.9	41.3	48.3	43.2	39.3	46.8
30	47.2	44.1	50.1	47.7	44.7	50.5	44.0	40.4	47.4	42.3	38.5	45.9
31	46.2	43.2	49.1	46.7	43.8	49.5	43.1	39.6	46.4	41.4	37.6	44.9
32	45.3	42.3	48.1	45.8	42.9	48.6	42.2	38.7	45.5	40.5	36.8	44.0
33	44.4	41.4	47.2	44.9	42.0	47.6	41.4	37.9	44.6	39.6	36.0	43.1
34	43.5	40.5	46.2	43.9	41.0	46.6	40.5	37.0	43.6	38.8	35.1	42.2
35	42.5	39.6	45.3	43.0	40.1	45.7	39.6	36.2	42.7	37.9	34.3	41.3
36	41.6	38.7	44.3	42.0	39.2	44.7	38.7	35.4	41.8	37.1	33.5	40.4
37	40.7	37.8	43.3	41.1	38.3	43.7	37.9	34.6	40.9	36.2	32.7	39.5
38	39.8	36.9	42.4	40.2	37.4	42.8	37.0	33.7	40.0	35.4	32.0	38.6
39	38.8	36.0	41.4	39.2	36.5	41.8	36.1	32.9	39.1	34.6	31.2	37.7

Age	1	2	3	4	5	6	7	8	9	10	11	12
40	36.8	30.4	33.7	38.2	32.1	35.3	40.9	35.6	38.3	40.5	35.1	37.9
41	35.9	29.7	32.9	37.3	31.3	34.4	39.9	34.7	37.4	39.6	34.2	37.0
42	35.0	28.9	32.1	36.4	30.5	33.6	39.0	33.8	36.5	38.6	33.3	36.1
43	34.1	28.1	31.3	35.5	29.7	32.7	38.0	32.9	35.5	37.7	32.5	35.2
44	33.3	27.4	30.4	34.6	28.9	31.9	37.1	32.0	34.6	36.7	31.6	34.3
45	32.4	26.6	29.6	33.7	28.2	31.1	36.1	31.1	33.7	35.8	30.7	33.4
46	31.5	25.9	28.8	32.8	27.4	30.2	35.2	30.2	32.8	34.9	29.8	32.5
47	30.7	25.1	28.0	32.0	26.6	29.4	34.3	29.3	31.9	34.0	28.9	31.6
48	29.8	24.4	27.3	31.1	25.8	28.6	33.4	28.4	31.0	33.1	28.1	30.7
49	29.0	23.7	26.5	30.2	25.1	27.8	32.4	27.5	30.1	32.2	27.2	29.8
50	28.2	23.0	25.7	29.4	24.3	27.0	31.5	26.7	29.2	31.3	26.4	28.9
51	27.3	22.3	24.9	28.5	23.6	26.2	30.6	25.8	28.4	30.4	25.6	28.1
52	26.5	21.6	24.2	27.7	22.9	25.4	29.7	25.0	27.5	29.5	24.7	27.2
53	25.7	20.9	23.5	26.9	22.1	24.7	28.8	24.2	26.6	28.6	23.9	26.4
54	24.9	20.3	22.7	26.1	21.4	23.9	28.0	23.3	25.8	27.7	23.1	25.6
55	24.1	19.6	22.0	25.3	20.8	23.2	27.1	22.5	25.0	26.9	22.3	24.7
56	23.4	18.9	21.3	24.5	20.1	22.4	26.2	21.7	24.1	26.0	21.5	23.9
57	22.6	18.3	20.6	23.7	19.4	21.7	25.4	21.0	23.3	25.2	20.8	23.1
58	21.8	17.7	19.9	22.9	18.7	21.0	24.6	20.2	22.5	24.4	20.0	22.3
59	21.1	17.1	19.2	22.1	18.1	20.3	23.7	19.4	21.7	23.5	19.3	21.6
60	20.4	16.4	18.6	21.4	17.5	19.6	22.9	18.7	21.0	22.7	18.6	20.8
61	19.7	15.9	17.9	20.7	16.8	18.9	22.1	18.0	20.2	21.9	17.9	20.1
62	19.0	15.3	17.3	20.0	16.2	18.3	21.3	17.3	19.5	21.1	17.2	19.3
63	18.3	14.7	16.7	19.3	15.6	17.6	20.5	16.6	18.7	20.4	16.5	18.6
64	17.7	14.1	16.1	18.6	15.1	17.0	19.7	15.9	18.0	19.6	15.8	17.9
65	17.0	13.6	15.5	17.9	14.5	16.4	19.0	15.2	17.3	18.8	15.2	17.2
66	16.4	13.1	14.9	17.2	13.9	15.8	18.2	14.6	16.6	18.1	14.5	16.5
67	15.7	12.5	14.3	16.5	13.4	15.2	17.4	13.9	15.9	17.4	13.9	15.8
68	15.1	12.0	13.8	15.9	12.8	14.6	16.7	13.3	15.2	16.6	13.3	15.2
69	14.5	11.5	13.2	15.2	12.3	14.0	16.0	12.7	14.5	15.9	12.7	14.5
70	13.9	11.0	12.7	14.6	11.8	13.4	15.3	12.1	13.9	15.2	12.1	13.9
71	13.3	10.6	12.1	14.0	11.3	12.8	14.6	11.5	13.3	14.5	11.5	13.2
72	12.7	10.1	11.6	13.4	10.8	12.3	13.9	11.0	12.7	13.8	10.9	12.6
73	12.1	9.7	11.1	12.8	10.3	11.8	13.2	10.4	12.1	13.2	10.4	12.0
74	11.6	9.2	10.6	12.2	9.9	11.2	12.6	9.9	11.5	12.5	9.9	11.5
75	11.0	8.8	10.1	11.6	9.4	10.7	11.9	9.4	10.9	11.9	9.4	10.9
76	10.5	8.4	9.6	11.0	9.0	10.2	11.3	8.9	10.3	11.3	8.9	10.3
77	10.0	8.0	9.2	10.5	8.5	9.7	10.7	8.4	9.8	10.7	8.4	9.8
78	9.5	7.6	8.7	10.0	8.1	9.3	10.1	7.9	9.3	10.1	8.0	9.3
79	9.0	7.2	8.3	9.5	7.7	8.8	9.5	7.5	8.8	9.5	7.5	8.8
80	8.5	6.9	7.9	9.0	7.3	8.3	8.9	7.1	8.3	9.0	7.1	8.3
81	8.1	6.5	7.5	8.5	6.9	7.9	8.4	6.7	7.8	8.4	6.7	7.8
82	7.7	6.2	7.1	8.0	6.6	7.5	7.9	6.3	7.3	7.9	6.3	7.4
83	7.3	6.0	6.8	7.6	6.3	7.2	7.4	5.9	6.9	7.4	6.0	6.9
84	7.0	5.7	6.5	7.2	6.0	6.8	6.9	5.6	6.5	7.0	5.6	6.5
85	6.7	5.6	6.3	6.9	5.8	6.6	6.5	5.3	6.1	6.6	5.3	6.2

SOURCES: National Center for Health Statistics. Vital Statistics of the United States, 1989; Life Tables Vol. II, Section 6. Washington D.C., 1992.

bitrary cutoff point. You may use this table to determine your own age group's *average* life expectation because the changes in life tables since 1989 will not be great.

Of course, it is not necessarily true that the death rates at each age today will remain the same in the future. The death rates for specific age groups may change because some of the present causes of death are reduced or eliminated or because other causes of death, like AIDS, increase. A war could change the life table. An environmental catastrophe that polluted the atmosphere might cause people to die from lung diseases at younger ages than they do today. An important disease could be completely cured, or an epidemic could cause enormous numbers of deaths. Current life tables are based on assumptions about the future that may not prove entirely accurate. Nevertheless, the predictions of past life tables have been reasonably accurate, so we can assume that today's life tables also will be good prognosticators of future human life expectation.

Table 6–2 lists the number of people in a cohort of 100,000 expected to still be alive at various age intervals, assuming that the death rate for each age stays the same as it was in 1989. Also listed is the number of people expected to die during each interval. Find your age in the table and determine the applicable numbers for yourself. The average life expectation at birth for the total United States population was 75.3 years in 1989 (table 6–1). The median age of death, when exactly half of this cohort born in 1989, is still alive and half is dead, was between seventy-five and eighty years of age (table 6–2). Provisional data from the National Center for Health Statistics reveals that life expectation at birth in 1991 equaled the 1989 record high of 75.3 years.

In 1989, white females had the highest life expectation at birth (79.2 years; (see table 6–1), followed by black females (73.5 years), white males (72.7 years), and black males (64.8 years). Life expectancy differences between whites and nonwhites have diminished considerably since 1900, when life expectation at birth was 15.7 years less for black males than for white males (reduced to 7.9 years by 1989) and 16 years less for black females than for white females (reduced to 5.7 years by 1989).

TABLE 6-2. Abridged life tables by race and sex, United States, 1989

Age interval	All races, both sexes			Male, all races			Female, all races		
	Number living at beginning of interval	Number dying during interval	Average years of life remaining at beginning of age interval	Number living at beginning of interval	Number dying during interval	Average years of life remaining at beginning of age interval	Number living at beginning of interval	Number dying during interval	Average years of life remaining at beginning of age interval
0–1	100,000	986	75.3	100,000	1,086	71.8	100,000	882	78.6
1–5	99,014	192	75.0	98,914	211	71.6	99,118	171	78.3
5–10	98,822	117	71.1	98,703	134	67.8	98,947	101	74.4
10–15	98,705	132	66.2	98,569	163	62.8	98,846	100	69.5
15–20	98,573	428	61.3	98,406	606	57.9	98,746	243	64.6
20–25	98,145	548	56.6	97,800	827	53.3	98,503	264	59.7
25–30	97,597	604	51.9	96,973	885	48.7	98,239	317	54.9
30–35	96,993	734	47.2	96,088	1,047	44.1	97,922	416	50.1
35–40	96,259	932	42.5	95,041	1,308	39.6	97,506	551	45.3
40–45	95,327	1,213	37.9	93,733	1,608	35.1	96,955	817	40.5
45–50	94,114	1,753	33.4	92,125	2,255	30.7	96,138	1,251	35.8
50–55	92,361	2,694	28.9	89,870	3,368	26.4	94,887	2,022	31.3
55–60	89,667	4,154	24.7	86,502	5,174	22.3	92,865	3,141	26.9
60–65	85,513	6,044	20.8	81,328	7,419	18.6	89,724	4,694	22.7
65–70	79,469	8,156	17.2	73,909	9,726	15.2	85,030	6,613	18.8
70–75	71,313	10,851	13.9	64,183	12,499	12.1	78,417	9,280	15.2
75–80	60,462	13,511	10.9	51,684	14,675	9.4	69,137	12,547	11.9
80–85	46,951	15,720	8.3	37,009	15,229	7.1	56,590	16,402	9.0
85 and over	31,231	31,231	6.2	21,780	21,780	5.3	40,188	40,188	6.6

TABLE 6-2. Abridged life tables by race and sex, United States, 1989 (continued)

Age interval	White, both sexes			White, male			White, female		
	Number living at beginning of interval	Number dying during interval	Average years of life remaining at beginning of age interval	Number living at beginning of interval	Number dying during interval	Average years of life remaining at beginning of age interval	Number living at beginning of interval	Number dying during interval	Average years of life remaining at beginning of age interval
0–1	100,000	814	76.0	100,000	908	72.7	100,000	715	79.2
1–5	99,186	170	75.6	99,092	187	72.3	99,285	151	78.8
5–10	99,016	108	71.7	98,905	123	68.5	99,134	93	74.9
10–15	98,908	124	66.8	98,782	154	63.6	99,041	93	70.0
15–20	98,784	409	61.9	98,628	565	58.6	98,948	245	65.1
20–25	98,375	487	57.2	98,063	731	54.0	98,703	237	60.2
25–30	97,888	526	52.4	97,332	775	49.4	98,466	267	55.3
30–35	97,362	625	47.7	96,557	898	44.7	98,199	341	50.5
35–40	96,737	784	43.0	95,659	1,104	40.1	97,858	454	45.7
40–45	95,953	1,055	38.3	94,555	1,394	35.6	97,404	710	40.9
45–50	94,898	1,569	33.7	93,161	2,013	31.1	96,694	1,119	36.1
50–55	93,329	2,474	29.2	91,148	3,080	26.7	95,575	1,862	31.5
55–60	90,855	3,942	25.0	88,068	4,933	22.5	93,713	2,957	27.1
60–65	86,913	5,863	21.0	83,135	7,275	18.7	90,756	4,478	22.9
65–70	81,050	8,048	17.3	75,860	9,694	15.2	86,278	6,439	19.0
70–75	73,002	10,906	13.9	66,166	12,696	12.1	79,839	9,220	15.3
75–80	62,096	13,747	10.9	53,470	15,115	9.4	70,619	12,628	11.9
80–85	48,349	16,105	8.3	38,355	15,756	7.1	57,991	16,685	8.9
85 and over	32,244	32,244	6.1	22,599	22,599	5.3	41,306	41,306	6.5

TABLE 6-2. Abridged life tables by race and sex, United States, 1989 (continued)

Age interval	Nonwhite, both sexes			Nonwhite, male			Nonwhite, female		
	Number living at beginning of interval	Number dying during interval	Average years of life remaining at beginning of age interval	Number living at beginning of interval	Number dying during interval	Average years of life remaining at beginning of age interval	Number living at beginning of interval	Number dying during interval	Average years of life remaining at beginning of age interval
0–1	100,000	1,630	71.2	100,000	1,757	67.1	100,000	1,499	75.2
1–5	98,370	279	71.4	98,243	305	67.3	98,501	253	75.4
5–10	98,091	155	67.6	97,938	175	63.5	98,248	134	71.6
10–15	97,936	163	62.7	97,763	198	58.6	98,114	126	66.6
15–20	97,773	509	57.8	97,565	776	53.8	97,988	232	61.7
20–25	97,264	827	53.1	96,789	1,282	49.2	97,756	386	56.9
25–30	96,437	992	48.5	95,507	1,460	44.8	97,370	552	52.1
30–35	95,445	1,298	44.0	94,047	1,857	40.4	96,818	775	47.4
35–40	94,147	1,722	39.6	92,190	2,477	36.2	96,043	1,040	42.7
40–45	92,425	2,167	35.3	89,713	3,002	32.1	95,003	1,421	38.2
45–50	90,258	2,863	31.1	86,711	3,810	28.2	93,582	2,002	33.7
50–55	87,395	3,975	27.0	82,901	5,114	24.3	91,580	2,912	29.4
55–60	83,420	5,450	23.2	77,787	6,688	20.8	88,668	4,247	25.3
60–65	77,970	7,340	19.6	71,099	8,490	17.5	84,421	6,169	21.4
65–70	70,630	9,085	16.4	62,609	10,141	14.5	78,252	7,945	17.9
70–75	61,545	10,832	13.4	52,468	11,555	11.8	70,307	10,017	14.6
75–80	50,713	12,272	10.7	40,913	12,075	9.4	60,290	12,385	11.6
80–85	38,441	13,568	8.3	28,838	12,061	7.3	47,905	15,031	9.0
85 and over	24,873	24,873	6.6	16,777	16,777	5.8	32,874	32,874	6.9

TABLE 6-2. Abridged life tables by race and sex, United States, 1989 (continued)

Age interval	Black, both sexes			Black, male			Black, female		
	Number living at beginning of interval	Number dying during interval	Average years of life remaining at beginning of age interval	Number living at beginning of interval	Number dying during interval	Average years of life remaining at beginning of age interval	Number living at beginning of interval	Number dying during interval	Average years of life remaining at beginning of age interval
0–1	100,000	1,863	69.2	100,000	2,004	64.8	100,000	1,717	73.5
1–5	98,137	303	69.5	97,996	332	65.2	98,283	272	73.8
5–10	97,834	167	65.8	97,664	192	61.4	98,011	141	70.0
10–15	97,667	176	60.9	97,472	214	56.5	97,870	135	65.1
15–20	97,491	550	56.0	97,258	855	51.6	97,735	237	60.2
20–25	96,941	921	51.3	96,403	1,449	47.1	97,498	424	55.3
25–30	96,020	1,134	46.7	94,954	1,681	42.7	97,074	626	50.6
30–35	94,886	1,544	42.3	93,273	2,229	38.5	96,448	912	45.9
35–40	93,342	2,067	37.9	91,044	3,023	34.3	95,536	1,215	41.3
40–45	91,275	2,625	33.7	88,021	3,644	30.4	94,321	1,709	36.8
45–50	88,650	3,366	29.6	84,377	4,507	26.6	92,612	2,337	32.4
50–55	85,284	4,529	25.7	79,870	5,887	23.0	90,275	3,275	28.2
55–60	80,755	6,031	22.0	73,983	7,253	19.6	87,000	4,757	24.1
60–65	74,724	7,971	18.6	66,730	8,917	16.4	82,243	6,913	20.4
65–70	66,753	9,648	15.5	57,813	10,501	13.6	75,330	8,600	17.0
70–75	57,105	11,171	12.7	47,312	11,563	11.0	66,730	10,656	13.9
75–80	45,934	12,273	10.1	35,749	11,658	8.8	56,074	12,783	11.0
80–85	33,661	12,949	7.9	24,091	10,900	6.9	43,291	14,913	8.5
85 and over	20,712	20,712	6.3	13,191	13,191	5.6	28,378	28,378	6.7

SOURCE: Vital Statistics of the United States, 1989, Life Tables, Vol. II, Section 6, Washington, D.C., 1992.

LIFE TABLES FOR ANIMALS

Life tables require data on a large population to maximize accuracy, so life tables for animals are rare. Tables 6–1 and 6–2 were derived from cohorts of 100,000 persons to obtain a high level of accuracy. It is rare to have data on such large numbers of animals. For this reason no life tables exist for most fish, reptiles, and amphibians. There are a few for birds and several for insects whose small size facilitates raising large numbers. We have reliable life tables for laboratory rats and mice, for which cohorts far smaller than 100,000 have been tracked by gerontologists, but none for mammals whose size is between that of a rat and a human. Such data would be useful for what it might tell us about the evolution of aging and longevity in mammals, fundamental physiological differences in the aging process, and variations in the rate of aging.

The thoroughbred race horse occupies a special place among domestic animals because life table data—births, deaths, and lineage—have been carefully recorded in England since medieval times. This is the only large animal for which gerontologists have reliable life table information that extends over many generations. The horse life tables are even better than most human data because they extend over more generations and the stud-book keepers seem to be more diligent and accurate than census takers. Perhaps more importantly, old horses, unlike old humans, can't lie about their ages! Other domestic animals usually are not kept until natural death occurs. However, there are life tables for a few dog breeds that approach reliability.

THE CURVES OF LIFE

When life table data is plotted on a graph, the shapes produced are called survival curves. An example of a human survival curve is shown in figure 6–1. Survival curves can also be plotted for animals or even inanimate objects. When animal populations that apparently do not age (discussed earlier) are tracked to provide data for life tables, the resulting survival curves resemble that seen in figure 6–2. This curve differs markedly from the survival curve for humans (figure 6–1). The curve for a population that does not age is quite different from the curve of aging. The force of mortality is constant in a nonaging population. Populations that age have different odds of dying each year. For humans the odds of dying are highest at birth, lowest at age

FIGURE 6-1. Schematic human survival curve

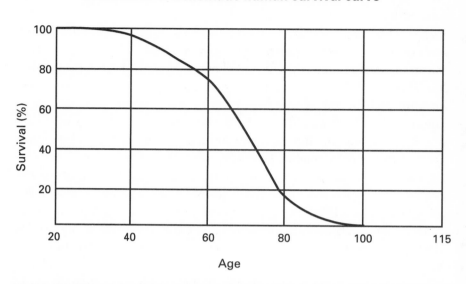

eleven or twelve and, as Gompertz found, double every seven years
from about age thirty. The Gompertz portion of a human survival
curve may be seen clearly in figure 6–1, where the curve begins to
drop around age thirty.

Notice, however, that the slope of the curve in figure 6–1 is less at
age eighty and above. Recently, the belief that the Gompertz equation
holds for all ages above age thirty has been challenged. It appears that
in extreme old age, say eighty and above, the likelihood of dying does
not double every seven years. It is only within the past few years that
we have had sufficient reliable data on very old humans to realize that,
in extreme old age, the probability of dying actually decreases! That is,
the likelihood of dying doubles at older ages in time intervals greater
than seven years.

Because it was thought that the Gompertz equation held for all animals that age, some recent studies on fruit flies and medflies are revealing. These animals are useful subjects for statistical studies in
biogerontology because millions of them can be studied accurately and
cheaply. Millions of individuals are needed to determine the Gompertz
curve accurately. It has been found that, like what has been seen recently in humans, the probability of dying in extreme old age also decreases in these flies.

One explanation for this new finding is that the frail members of a species die first and then the likelihood of dying decreases for the longest-lived because they have been selected for hardiness. A human who is fortunate enough to pass through the window of greatest vulnerability to disease, say between the ages of sixty-five and eighty, because of their greater hardiness, has a reduced likelihood of dying in subsequent years.

A nonaging curve like that in figure 6–2 is similar to the curve for a decaying radioisotope, where half of the radioactivity disappears during each successive time interval until there is very little left. We call each of these time intervals a half-life and the curve is called an exponential survival curve. This type of curve may indicate that the threat of predation, disease, or accidents (or all three) is so great that half of the population dies each year from birth onward. In many animal populations, including some insects, fish, birds, and amphibians, mortality from predation immediately after birth is even greater than 50 percent; in other species it is less than 50 percent. In any case, aging—diminishing physiological capacity over time—does not seem to occur in animal populations that exhibit this type of survival curve. An exam-

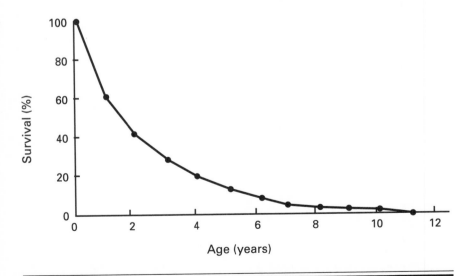

FIGURE 6-2. Survival curve for a nonaging population (460 lapwings banded as nestlings)

SOURCE: Lack, *British Birds* 36 (1943): 214 and Marion J. Lamb, Biology of Ageing, Blackie & Sons Ltd, Bishopbriggs, Glasgow, and John Wiley and Sons, New York, 1977, page 36. Reproduced with permission.

ple of a curve in which animals suffer an enormous death rate at every age was obtained from a bird study done in England on 460 lapwings banded as nestlings. In captivity the birds reach a fixed adult size and do age, but in the wild, rates of predation, accident, and disease are so high that a population with characteristic age changes does not have a chance to appear. As figure 6–2 shows, nearly half of the birds living at the beginning of a given year die during that year.

Nonaging survival curves can even be constructed for inanimate objects. One such population was studied years ago in a cafeteria. Several

---

FIGURE 6–3. Survival curve for annealed glass cafeteria tumblers

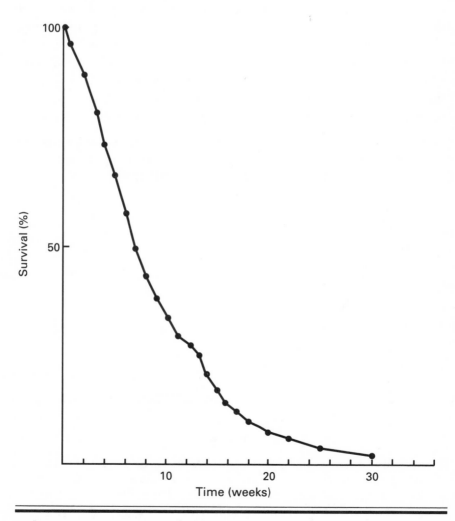

SOURCE: Alex Comfort, *The Biology of Senescence*, Third Edition, Elsevier North Holland, Inc., New York, drawn from the data of G.W. Brown and M.M. Flood (1947) Tumbler mortality, *Journal of the American Statistical Association*, Volume 42, page 562.

hundred new, annealed glass tumblers were distributed in the cafeteria and their fate tabulated roughly once a week (figure 6–3). After seven weeks, half had been broken. After thirty weeks, 90 percent were broken. A few lucky ones survived longer. The curve was almost identical to the curves for nonaging animal populations. However, the authors of the study concluded that a form of aging does occur in that the accumulation of abrasions on the lips of the tumblers predisposed them to later cracking. This is somewhat like the loss of efficiency in the immune system that may predispose older humans to death. But it is questionable whether lip abrasions in tumblers or immune system losses in humans have anything to do with the fundamental aging process.

Humans do not have the same risk of dying each year from birth to death. Because we exhibit the aging phenomenon, the force of mortality changes throughout our life. Consequently, our life tables generate

FIGURE 6-4. Human survival curves for various countries and times. As medical care and hygiene improve, fewer deaths occur in the earlier years. Elimination of all present causes of death would result in the hypothetical ultimate curve.

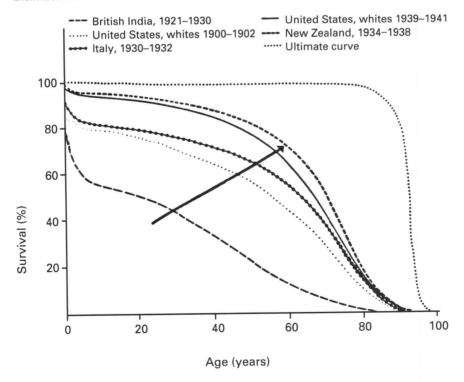

--- British India, 1921–1930   —— United States, whites 1939–1941

······ United States, whites 1900–1902   ---- New Zealand, 1934–1938

•••• Italy, 1930–1932   ······ Ultimate curve

SOURCE: Adapted from A. Comfort, *Aging: The Biology of Senescence*, (New York: Holt, Rinehart and Winston, 1964).

the typical curves of an aging population, like those in figure 6–4. These survival curves were obtained by plotting life table data for five groups of 100,000 people born in different countries and time periods. The curves, following the arrow from the data for British India, 1921–1930, to that for New Zealand, 1934–1938, show increasing rectangularization resulting from better hygienic conditions and medical care. In theory, the curves could become completely rectangular under ideal conditions or could decay to the non-aging type curve in circumstances where no medical care existed, where hygiene was unknown, or where, perhaps, predation by wild animals was a threat. These conditions probably existed in prehistoric times, which would account for life expectations at birth of eighteen years and the survival of so few people beyond the age of thirty that a truly old person was either rare or unknown. Figure 6–5 reveals this effect.

The family of human survival curves in figure 6–4 has another interesting attribute. Because the curves are all somewhat rectangular, or at least do not show the steep decline of the curves for lapwings (figure

FIGURE 6-5. Survival curves throughout human history

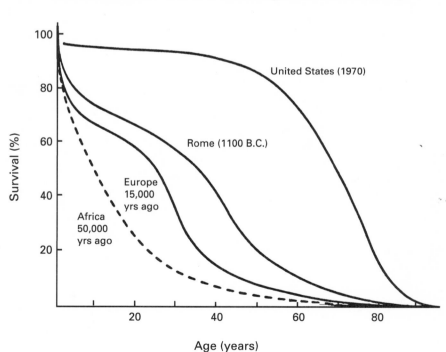

SOURCE: Richard Cutler in *Molecular Basis of Aging*, edited by A.K. Roy and B. Chatterjee, Academic Press, 1984, Orlando, Fl.

6–2) and tumblers (figure 6–3), we know that aging is taking place in all of these populations. In curves like these, where aging occurs, animals and humans are found to die from causes that may be different at different ages. One of the most remarkable achievements in developed countries in this century is that the survival curves of their citizens have improved so much that more than half of all babies born today will live to the age of seventy-five—almost two-thirds of the maximum, 115-year human life span.

RECTANGULARIZING THE SURVIVAL CURVE

Life tables and survival curves are major tools for our understanding of aging, longevity, and death in populations—or, more precisely, of the population's longevity and the pattern of deaths. More than fifty years ago, the pioneer gerontologist Raymond Pearl recognized that human survival curves constructed over intervals in developed countries were becoming more rectangular as the survival rates of youths improved. Rectangularization is continuing to occur: life expectation at birth has continued to increase in the United States and other developed countries, though the rate of increase has slowed in the past decade. The low degree of rectangularization in figure 6–4, compared to curves generated from more recent data, are understated because from 1930 to 1960 infant and child mortality declined rapidly in developed countries to current low levels, and declines in mortality at older ages started after 1960 as the result of reductions in cardiovascular disease mortality.

The bottom-most curve in figure 6–4 reflects the high rate of infant mortality in British India in the 1920s. Of every 100,000 babies born, 40,000 died before their fifth birthday! This is almost as bad as the experience of newborn lapwings or new tumblers put into a cafeteria. After the fifth birthday, deaths among the Indian children occurred less frequently, and a few lucky people reached about ninety-five years of age. The survival curve for the United States from 1939 to 1941 shows quite a different picture. Infant mortality was much lower; only about 3,000 children per 100,000 births died before the age of five. Once again, as in India, a few fortunate Americans lived to celebrate their ninety-fifth birthday.

In 1900, the leading causes of death in the United States were, in order of frequency, tuberculosis, pneumonia, and diarrhea (intestinal inflammation caused by a microorganism) and other infectious diseases. Cardiovascular diseases were in fourth place and cancer eighth. Today, cardiovascular diseases and cancer are in first and second place, re-spectively, and deaths attributable to tuberculosis, diphtheria, typhoid fever, syphilis, poliomyelitis, measles, whooping cough, and smallpox—common seventy-five years ago—are unknown, or almost unknown, in the United States and other developed countries. (Recently, however, the tubercle bacillus and other pathogenic microorganisms have shown a remarkable resistance to antibiotics, and the occurrence of many deaths caused by these once vanquished organisms is once again pos-sible.) As a result of the steep decline in infectious diseases as a cause of death in young people, survival curves for developed countries have become more rectangular with dramatic speed. Today, most of our youth live long enough to experience old age.

Analysis of survival curves reveals that there is always a concentra-tion of deaths at birth and immediately thereafter. Many of these deaths are due to poor prenatal care and birth defects. The fewest deaths occur just before puberty, around age eleven. Then, the death rate increases inexorably. In the Middle Ages, life expectation at birth was about thirty-three years in Europe, and it is not much different to-day in some undeveloped countries. In less-developed countries most deaths occur in childhood; in developed countries most deaths occur in old age. Today, in developed countries, most children can expect to grow old, which is a unique, twentieth-century phenomenon! At no other time in the history of human civilization could such a high pro-portion of infants expect to live long enough to experience old age.

What would happen to our survival curve if biomedical researchers were completely successful in reaching all of their goals? Or, put an-other way, suppose the research supported by the National Institutes of Health and private institutions in the United States and by similar organizations in other countries ended because all presently stated goals had been achieved. The world would then be one in which no one died from causes now written on death certificates. The ultimate survival curve would be achieved (figure 6–4): no one would die young; all would slip peacefully away during a narrow span of years, say between age 110 and age 115.

YES, WE ARE LIVING LONGER

Life expectation, as pointed out earlier, is the number of years, on av-erage, that someone at a particular age can expect to live. When no

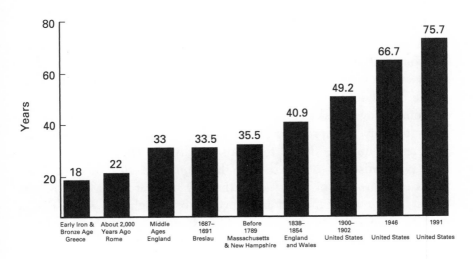

FIGURE 6-6. Human life expectation at birth, ancient to modern times

SOURCE: L. I. Dublin, A. J. Lotka and M. Spiegelman, *Length of Life*, The Ronald Press, New York, 1936 and U.S. National Center for Health Statistics, Washington, D.C.

age is specified in a discussion of life expectation, it is assumed that the stated life expectation is for newborns.

Unlike table 6–1, which shows life expectation at various ages for humans as of 1989, figure 6–6 depicts life expectations at birth for several places and times in history. Most are only approximations based on examination of the physical remains of relatively few people. In the early Iron and Bronze Age in Greece, a newborn infant could expect to live only about eighteen years because of the tremendous infant and childhood mortality. That same life expectation at birth was probably true for all humans from about 100,000 years ago to the Iron and Bronze Age, because if life expectation at birth were much less than eighteen years there would have been too little time for a significant number of humans to reach sexual maturity and raise infants to independence, which is the prerequisite for the survival of the species.

A life expectation at birth of eighteen years does not mean that no one lived beyond age eighteen. It just means that newborn babies had a fifty-fifty chance of reaching eighteen. Those who escaped death in infancy had a somewhat increased life expectation, but overall life expectation was still short compared to today. In one study of 173 paleolithic and mesolithic people, the three oldest were thought to have died when they were not much older than fifty. In paleolithic digs in China, most men were found to die from violence well before aging occurred. The rarity even of sixty-year-olds in ancient times is probably comparable to the rarity of today's centenarians. One reason why many cultures venerated their old members was that it was so unusual to see one. Old people were thought to have some special powers or wisdom to have lived so long. With several billion more humans living today than lived in prehistoric times, we are less impressed with the thousands who have defied the odds and lived to be ninety or more.

It is astonishing to realize that the human species survived hundreds of thousands of years, more than 99 percent of its time on this planet, with a life expectation at birth of only eighteen years. It was only in Roman times that human life expectation began to increase slowly, and only in this century has it reached seventy-five years. In coldly scientific terms, the physical survival of our species does not depend on the presence of old humans, but a longer life expectancy is no doubt crucial if we are to advance. It is probably true that most of the tyrants and evil-doers in recorded history were older than eighteen, but on balance adults have done more to improve the human condition than to worsen it. Still, asking whether the species is better off with so many people living well past age eighteen can spark enormously emotional debates.

Fertility, however, plays a larger role in determining the *proportion* of a population that is elderly than do changes in life expectancy due to medical progress. Consider an extreme situation: If no babies were to be born in or immigrate to this country for the next sixty-five years, then in the year 2058, the entire population would be sixty-five years of age or older regardless of what medical progress, or lack thereof, might have occurred. The proportion of elderly in a population will increase if either the birth rate or the mortality rate for older people drops. Decreases in *both* the birth rate and the mortality rate among older people have contributed to the "graying" of the United States and other developed countries.

An increase in the proportion of the elderly in a population is not evidence of medical progress, but an increase in life expectation might be. I say "might" because the increase may be a sign either of medical progress or simply of existing knowledge, such as good prenatal care, being put to greater use. Figure 6–6 shows how life expectation at birth has increased through the centuries. In 1900, it was not quite fifty years in the United States. Today's life expectation at birth, about seventy-five years, represents a gain of about twenty-five years in this century, roughly equivalent to that which took place from the Iron and Bronze Age to 1900! About twenty years of this gain occurred between 1900 and 1954.

The annual increase in life expectation has slowed in recent years. In 1991, life expectation for all infant boys was 71.9 years and for all infant girls, 78.7 years—record highs. Table 6–3 shows the gain in life expectation at birth and at age sixty-five for both sexes since 1850, with projections to 2050. Figure 6–7 is a graphic representation of increases in life expectation at several ages from 1900 to 1987. It is clear that, of all age groups, the young have benefited most from this century's advances in biomedical research. Over twenty-five years has been added to the life expectation of infants in the United States since 1900, largely due to our improving ability to combat infectious dis-

TABLE 6-3. Life expectation at birth and age 65, United States, 1850–2050

Year	Males		Females	
	At birth	Age 65	At birth	Age 65
1850	38.3	-	40.5	-
1890	42.5	-	44.5	-
1900	49.6	11.4	49.1	12.0
1910	50.2	11.4	53.7	12.1
1920	54.6	11.8	56.3	12.3
1930	58.0	11.4	61.4	12.9
1940	60.9	11.9	65.3	13.4
1950	65.3	12.8	70.9	15.1
1960	66.6	12.9	73.2	15.9
1970	67.1	13.1	74.8	17.1
1980	69.9	14.0	77.5	18.4
1990	71.8	15.2	78.6	18.8
2000	73.4	15.7	81.1	20.8
2010	73.9	16.1	81.6	21.3
2020	74.4	16.5	82.2	21.7
2030	74.9	16.8	82.7	22.2
2040	75.4	17.2	83.3	22.6
2050	75.8	17.6	83.8	23.1

SOURCES: 1850 and 1890 data (Massachusetts only), L. I. Dublin, A. J. Lotka, and M. Spiegelman, *Length of Life* (New York: Ronald Press, 1949); 1900–2050, Social Security Administration, Office of the Actuary, September 1982.

eases. Because we have been less successful in conquering chronic diseases, the gains made by all other age groups have been significantly smaller and slower. If you were a seventy-year-old male in 1900 your life expectation would have been about nine years; today it is about twelve years. Sixty-year-old males can expect, on average, eighteen more years, compared to about 14.5 years in 1900. Forty-year-old men can expect 34.5 years, up from about twenty-eight years. However, baby boys who could expect to live only about forty-eight years at the turn of the century can now expect to reach their seventy-first birthdays.

Although we have found ways to increase the average life expectation for most human age groups, a longer life may not always mean a happy outcome: many people have found that the added years are only an extended period of ill health. In recent years much debate has been provoked, centered around the extension of life and how to measure the quality of that life.

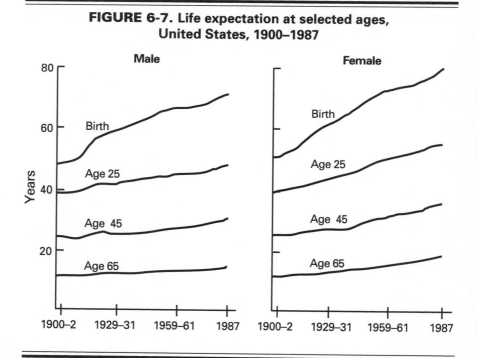

FIGURE 6-7. Life expectation at selected ages, United States, 1900–1987

SOURCES: National Center for Health Statistics, 1900–2 to 1979–81; *Statistical Bulletin*, Metropolitan Life Insurance Company, 1987. Permission granted courtesy of *Statistical Bulletin*.

CHAPTER 7

A Long and Healthy Life

I am tired of this thing called science. . . . We have spent millions on this sort of thing for the last few years and it is time it should be stopped.
　—Senator Simon Cameron, 1901

T HE notion of increased average life expectation is simple to understand, but it doesn't tell the whole story. We want to know whether all those added years will be healthy ones. The desire to measure this aspect of our final years has made a variant of the concept of life expectation, called active, healthy, or functional, life expectation, increasingly fashionable. Instead of considering death as the endpoint, active life expectation ends when someone's health declines to a point where he or she loses independence in matters of daily living and must depend on others for some form of care. For many of us, being able to anticipate the onset of dependency in later life is as important as anticipating the time of our eventual death. Active life expectation is equally important to long-term health planners and policy makers and is calculated much like life expectation itself—it might even be called health expectation.

WHAT IS YOUR ACTIVE LIFE EXPECTATION?

Because far fewer people have been studied to determine active life expectation than have been studied to determine life expectation, the resulting tables are not as reliable and are restricted to older people. In 1974, more than sixteen hundred noninstitutionalized people, sixty-five years old or over and living in the state of Massachusetts, were studied. As you would expect, older people had fewer years of independence left than the younger members of the study. Table 7–1 summarizes the results and reveals that active life expectation decreased with age from ten years for people in the sixty-five to sixty-nine age category to 4.7 years for those in the eighty to eighty-four age category. For those eighty-five and older, active life expectation was about 2.9 years.

Active life expectation is calculated based on the percentage of the noninstitutionalized population at each age that requires assistance with everyday activities. Judgments about what constitutes assistance

TABLE 7-1. Active life expectation among noninstitutionalized elderly people, Massachusetts, 1974

Age (years)	Number of persons	Active life expectation (years)	Life expectation (years)
Total			
65–69	446	10.0	16.5
70–74	329	8.1	14.1
75–79	248	6.8	11.6
80–84	132	4.7	8.9
85 and older	70	2.9	7.3
Men			
65–69	187	9.3	13.1
70–74	127	8.2	11.9
75–79	108	6.5	9.6
80–84	47	4.8	7.4
85 and older	26	3.3	6.5
Women			
65–69	259	10.0	19.5
70–74	202	8.0	15.9
75–79	140	7.1	13.2
80–84	85	4.8	9.8
85 and older	43	2.8	7.7

SOURCE: Active Life Expectancy, S. Katz, L. G. Branch, M. H. Branson, J. A. Papsidero, J. C. Beck and D. S. Greer, adapted from information appearing in *The New England Journal of Medicine,* Volume 309, pages 1218–1224, 1983.

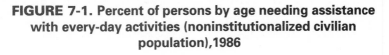

FIGURE 7-1. Percent of persons by age needing assistance with every-day activities (noninstitutionalized civilian population),1986

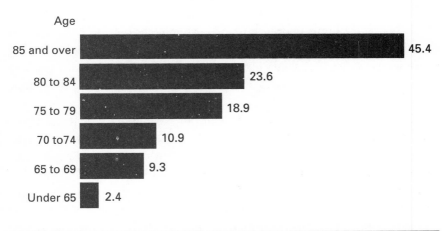

SOURCE: U.S. Bureau of the Census, *The Need for Personal Assistance With Everyday Activities: Recipients and Caregivers*, Current Population Reports, Series P–70, No. 19. U.S. Government Printing Office, Washington, D.C., 1990, Table B and Taeuber, C. M., *Sixty-five Plus in America,* U.S. Department of Commerce, Bureau of the Census, Current Population Reports, Special Studies, P23–178 RV, Washington, D.C.: U.S. Government Printing Office, 1993.

with daily living vary, but revealing studies can still be made. Not surprisingly the proportion of the population that requires assistance increases with age (figure 7–1). Most Americans over the age of sixty-five are healthy and live normal, productive lives but, with increasing age, health generally deteriorates and the need for care increases. In one study it was found that 45 percent of those over age eighty-five needed help with one or more basic activities such as shopping or meal preparation. About 22 percent of those over age eighty-five live in institutions or nursing homes and about half are disabled (defined by inability to use public transportation). Although data are not available for centenarians specifically, their characteristics probably do not differ significantly from all people over age eighty-five.

Unlike death, which is the endpoint for determining life expectation, disability, the endpoint for active life expectation, is sometimes reversible. Some of the people whose health makes them dependent will regain their health and become independent once again. Several such cycles may occur, but with increasing age the percentage of people who remain dependent once they reach a condition of dependency increases.

EXTENDING HEALTH AND COMPRESSING ILLNESS

When we grow old, some of us will die suddenly with few previous impairments to our health; others will die after some lingering chronic illness or illnesses. It would be useful to know the likelihood of one or the other fate. Some people, given the choice, would opt for a quick demise in old age. Alas, that choice is not ours to make. Nevertheless, what happens is of crucial importance to those who want to prepare for the worst and for medical planners who must budget for the public costs of medical care.

The continued rectangularization of our survival curves (figure 6–4) tells us something important about the state of our health as we age. Several social changes have occurred in recent years that, if continued, have the possibility of postponing death or eliminating illnesses. Examples include society's increasingly negative attitude toward smoking; improved personal health and lifestyle decisions, such as reducing the intake of fatty foods; and medical intervention, such as the development and use of drugs to reduce blood pressure and cholesterol levels. These changes in our health habits might have enormous effects on health budget planning, the social security system, and even the national debt.

If, because of these social changes and successes in biomedical research, the illnesses associated with older ages begin later and later in life, we will eventually spend fewer years suffering from the chronic diseases of old age. Within our 115-year fixed life span, the number of vigorous or healthy years would increase and the years spent in illness would decrease. This phenomenon is called *compression* because the illnesses of old age would be compressed into fewer years. Heart disease, for example, might begin to appear in seventy-year-olds instead of sixty-year-olds. Strokes might become more common in eighty-year-olds than in seventy-year-olds. Is compression occurring? We really don't know, mainly because we do not know if the human life span really is fixed.

Whether or not compression is occurring, the *total number* of people with a particular illness will increase. This is certain because the absolute number of old people in this and other developed countries will increase. All people who will be old during the next several decades are alive today. We know their numbers quite precisely. Recent data from the Bureau of the Census show that by the year 2050, persons eighty-five years of age and older will have increased from 2.3

million to about sixteen million. We know that about 20 percent of persons over eighty-five have severe mental impairment and require long-term care. Even if that proportion were halved by 2050, the number of individuals requiring long term care would increase from about a half million today to three times that number. By the same logic, the number of people with other age-associated ailments will also increase in absolute numbers, barring further significant breakthroughs in biomedical research.

IS LIFE SPAN FIXED OR CHANGING?

Although we believe that the human life span *has* remained fixed over the past 100,000 years, there is really no way of proving that it has not changed slightly since then. Our ability to obtain this important information is stymied by the difficulty in accurately determining the ages of very old people. If the human life span is really increasing, then, for example, we might find that the oldest humans were reaching the age of 100 years in 1850, 115 years in 1900, and 120 years in 1950. This would be good evidence that the maximum life span is increasing, especially if large numbers of people in each period reached these very old ages. The problem is that we really don't know whether today's alleged supercentenarians (over age 115) are as old as they claim to be. Furthermore, whether they existed at all before recorded history is entirely speculative. Even if some supercentenarians' claims today turn out to be true, there are too few of them to produce any reliable statistics.

Most gerontologists do not accept a maximum human life span that exceeds about 115 years of age. The reason for this skepticism is that there are no reliable, accurate markers like the tree rings and fish scales discussed earlier for determining the chronological age of humans. We have no way of physically verifying an individual's chronological age, so we are obliged to rely on written—or worse, oral records. Few, if any, birth records for people who claim to be older than 115 can be unambiguously authenticated. Acceptance of birth records for allegedly superlongevous people generally relies more on faith than on scientific standards of evidence. We will return, in chapter 12, to the fascinating question of whether superlongevous humans do indeed exist. In the 1980 United States census approximately twenty-five thousand people claimed to be centenarians. Most of their claims cannot be proven because birth registration was not legally required in most states until well into this century and most gerontologists believe the figure is greatly exaggerated. In any event, with so few authentic centenarians in proportion to the total population, a precise determination of the maximum human life span is not possible.

Our inability to verify birth dates for our oldest old not only keeps us from determining the maximum achievable human life span but also precludes our knowing whether our life span is changing. If the human life span in the United States increased or decreased, even by as much as five or ten years during this century, the change would go undetected because reliable baseline longevity data for the nineteenth century is virtually unobtainable and the accuracy of current supercentenarian age claims is unverifiable. Consequently, as good an argument can be made for a fixed human life span as for one that has increased or even decreased. Much more accurate age-at-death data exists for several Scandinavian countries, where records extend well into the last century, but no trend in the human life span can be observed in these records.

One reason that detecting changes in life span is difficult is that because so few people reach age 100 or older, attention is focused on individuals rather than populations. When each oldest person dies, attention shifts to a "new" oldest person. If the oldest person dies at 112 and the subsequent oldest person at 110, does that indicate a trend in life span? Gerontologists hope that accurate records will be kept of the ages of greater numbers of centenarians throughout the world so that future generations might be able to answer these kinds of questions.

DO SOME OCCUPATIONS FAVOR LONGEVITY?

Actuaries have made some informative, even amusing, studies in an effort to determine whether members of certain occupations live longer than the general population. Many of these studies are flawed because the population chosen for study is already old and the weaker members of the group have already succumbed. For example, if we decide to determine whether popes live longer than the general population, we could obviously only consider data for men who have achieved that rank. Since one of the prerequisites for the position is long experience in the church, the entire pool of candidates is already selected to be old. Do popes live longer than the general population? Yes, but only because the data is biased. The group that popes were chosen from represents the most vigorous survivors of a younger and larger qualified group.

Two studies reported by the Metropolitan Life Insurance Company do not seem to suffer from this flaw. One is a study to determine whether conductors of major regional and community symphony orchestras enjoy greater longevity than does the general population. The study was motivated by the popular belief that orchestra conductors represent a group of particularly longevous people: one thinks of Arturo Toscanini, Leopold Stokowski, Arthur Fiedler, and André Kostalanetz. Does this belief suffer from the same criticism as the one made for the allegedly greater longevity of popes?

Only male orchestra conductors were studied because there were too few women conductors to obtain statistically significant results. Unlike popes, the men studied ranged in age from twenty-four to ninety-one years of age. The study of 437 active and former conductors began in 1956 and ended in 1975 when 118 had died and more than 20 percent were eighty or older. Five were nonagenarians. Two died at age ninety-five during the study. The rate of death in the entire group of conductors was 38 percent below that of the general population. For conductors in the fifty to fifty-nine age group, the death rate was a remarkable 56 percent less than the general population. This period is generally thought to be the time when stress and professional responsibilities are at their greatest.

Another study, made in 1974 by Metropolitan Life, showed that the longevity of corporate executives is as high as that of orchestra conductors. These top executives outlived others at all lower levels of accomplishment in business. Can it be that one component of longevity is work fulfillment and the development of a successful strategy for coping with stress? Or can the differences be explained by assuming that with higher economic status comes better health care, diet, and behavior?

An earlier study in the United States revealed that the death rate for male musicians and music teachers—as opposed to conductors— was 62 percent *higher* than that found in the general population of working men. In a study in Britain, musicians, stage managers, actors, and entertainers showed a mortality rate 25 percent higher than that found in the general working population. A study of prominent American women, also made by Metropolitan Life, found a 43 percent higher mortality rate for performers and entertainers than for their contemporaries in the general population. The greater mortality rates among entertainers might be attributable to the general observation that, as a group, they have bad health habits.

In 1980, actuaries from Metropolitan Life examined the longevity of American presidents, reasoning that this must be one of the more stressful occupations. Life insurance companies, as you might imagine, are interested in whether or not a high stress job can shorten life. They found that presidents do not live as long as members of the general population who were born in the same year, or even as long as vice presidents. The mortality rate for presidents is about 30 percent higher than that for the general population and 10 percent higher for vice presidents. Of the thirty-five presidents deceased at the time of the study, thirteen had outlived their expected longevity and twenty-two had died earlier than expected. These results are in contrast to those found for orchestra conductors and top corporate executives. However, the presidents studied include four who were assassinated. If John F. Kennedy is eliminated from the data, then the life expectation of recent presidents is not much different from men in the general population. So, the question of the role of stress in longevity still remains open.

WHAT WILL HAPPEN WHEN ALL DISEASES ARE CURED?

In 1900, 75 percent of the people in the United States died *before* they reached the age of sixty-five. Today, this statistic is almost reversed: about 70 percent of people die *after* the age of sixty-five. Life expectation at birth has increased by more than 50 percent, from a little less than fifty years in 1900 to about seventy-five years in 1991. The increase in life expectation that occurred in the early part of this century was largely due to reductions in the mortality of newborns, infants, and mothers at childbirth. Today, the death rates for those younger than age fifty are so low (12.4 percent of all deaths) that completely eliminating all deaths prior to age fifty would only increase life expectation at birth by 3.5 years! Truly impressive increases in life expectation will occur only as we learn how to eliminate the causes of death that affect the elderly.

An interesting perspective on causes of death throughout the entire life span may be seen in figure 7–2 for the year 1979. The data is not

FIGURE 7-2. Causes of death as percentages of total deaths, 1979

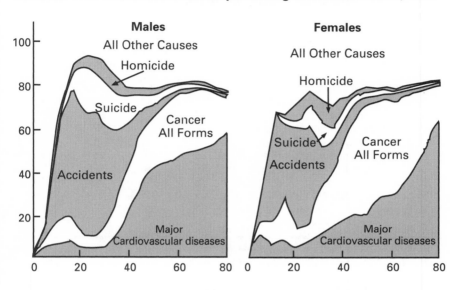

SOURCE: Permission granted courtesy of *Statistical Bulletin*, Metropolitan Life Insurance Co., Oct.–Dec., 1980, p.16.

too different from today. Contrary to popular belief, the incidence of cancer does not rise linearly with age. It peaks in the sixties and then diminishes. The distribution of accidents and homicides by age is also notable.

For people over age sixty-five, the causes of death, as written on death certificates, are shown in diminishing order of frequency in table 7–2. The top three, by far, are heart disease, cancer, and cerebrovascular disease (stroke). In fact, these three diseases represent the cause of death in about 75 percent of all people who die after the age of sixty-five. The successes of biomedical science and the implementation of better hygienic conditions since the turn of this century have eliminated so many major causes of death that a peculiar event has occurred. How we will die after reaching age sixty-five has been reduced to about three possibilities: cancer, heart disease, or stroke!

Let us consider the effect on our longevity if each of these major causes of death were eliminated (table 7–3); after all, that is the goal of much of our medical research. What if all that research is successful?

If cancer were cured tomorrow, about 3.1 years would be added to the life expectation of a newborn and about 1.9 years to the life expec-

TABLE 7-2. Rates of death by cause among people age 65 and older, 1988 (per 100,000 population)

Rank	Cause of death	Age (years)			
		65+	65 to 74	75 to 84	85+
	ALL CAUSES	5,105	2,730	6,321	15,594
1	Heart disease	2,066	984	2,543	7,098
2	Cancer	1,068	843	1,313	1,639
3	Stroke	431	155	554	1,707
4	Chronic obstructive lung disease	226	152	313	394
5	Pneumonia and influenza	225	60	257	1,125
6	Diabetes	97	62	125	222
7	Accidents	89	50	107	267
8	Atherosclerosis	69	15	70	396
9	Kidney Diseases	61	26	78	217
10	Blood infections	56	24	71	199

SOURCES: National Center for Health Statistics. "Advanced Report of Final Mortality Statistics, 1988." Monthly Vital Statistics Report Vol. 39, No. 7, Supplement (November 28, 1990); "Aging America" 1991 Edition, U.S. Department of Health and Human Services Publication No. (FCoA) 91-28001.

tation of a sixty-five-year-old. If you are between those two ages, then the gain would be between those two numbers. Most people who are asked to guess what they think the gain in life expectancy would be if cancer were cured will say ten to thirty years. Those estimates are far too high. The reason for such guesses is, in my view, the enormous individual and institutional attention that society has focused on cancer. The disease is associated with high costs for care, much emotional and physical pain, and a usually slow but inexorable course. Cancer is also resented as "unfair" because it frequently strikes young or middle-aged people in the prime of their lives. We have built a huge medical research and care enterprise directed toward the resolution and treatment of cancer, which employs thousands of scientists and caregivers and costs billions of dollars. The result is that many have come to mistakenly believe that our cancer research efforts, if successful, will add decades to our lives. I am not suggesting that these efforts should be diminished, but I do think that scientists and others who work in the field could be more publicly forthcoming to what effect a cure would have on our longevity.

By contrast, finding a cure for the leading cause of death in the United States—cardiovascular disease—would add 13.9 years to the life expectation of newborns and 14.3 years to the life expectation of

TABLE 7-3. Gains in life expectation due to elimination of various causes of death (years), 1978

Cause of death	Total		White male		White female		Nonwhite male[a]		Nonwhite female[a]	
	At birth	Age 65	At birth	Age 65	At birth	Age 65	At birth	Age 65	At birth	Age 65
Major cardiovascular diseases	13.9	14.3	10.6	10.1	16.4	17.4	10.6	11.2	20.3	22.1
Diseases of the heart	7.0	6.6	6.5	5.5	6.9	7.0	6.1	5.8	8.8	9.0
Cerebrovascular diseases	1.1	1.2	0.7	0.8	1.4	1.4	1.2	1.2	2.2	2.2
Arteriosclerosis	0.2	0.2	0.1	0.1	0.2	0.2	0.1	0.2	0.2	0.3
Malignant neoplasms[b]	3.1	1.9	2.8	1.9	3.1	1.7	3.4	2.6	3.3	2.0
Influenza and pneumonia	0.4	0.3	0.3	0.3	0.4	0.3	0.5	0.4	0.5	0.3
Diabetes mellitus	0.2	0.2	0.2	0.1	0.2	0.2	0.2	0.2	0.6	0.4
Motor vehicle accidents	0.6	–	0.9	0.1	0.4	–	0.7	0.1	0.3	–
All accidents excluding motor vehicle	0.6	0.1	0.7	0.1	0.3	0.1	1.0	0.2	0.5	0.2
Bronchitis, emphysema, and asthma	0.1	0.1	0.2	0.2	0.1	0.1	0.1	0.1	0.1	–
Cirrhosis of liver	0.3	0.1	0.3	0.1	0.2	0.1	0.5	0.1	0.3	–
Nephritis and nephrosis	0.1	–	0.1	–	0.1	–	0.1	0.1	0.2	0.1
Infective and parasitic diseases	0.2	0.1	0.1	0.1	0.1	0.1	0.3	0.1	0.4	0.2
Tuberculosis, all forms	–[c]	–	–	–	–	–	0.1	–	–	–

[a] Data for 1969–1971.
[b] Including lymphatic and hematopoietic tissues.
[c] Less than 0.05 years.

SOURCES: Prithwis Das Gupta, "Cause-of-Death Analysis of the 1978 U.S. Mortality Data by Age, Sex, and Race," U.S. Bureau of the Census, 1981 (unpublished manuscript); U.S. Public Health Service, National Center for Health Statistics, "U.S. Life Tables by Causes of Death: 1969–71," by T. N. E. Greville, *U.S. Decennial Life Tables for 1969–71,* 1, no. 5 (1975).

sixty-five-year-olds. That would be spectacularly rewarding. But even if we became able to prevent *all* causes of death now appearing on death certificates, the resulting increase in life expectation would not come close to the twenty-five-year increase that has occurred since the turn of the century! The period of rapid increase in human life expectation in developed countries has ended.

Table 7–3 indicates the gain in life expectation at birth and at age sixty-five, based on 1978 mortality experience, if each of the leading causes of death were eliminated. It suggests that if we succeeded in eliminating all causes of death written on death certificates, most people would live to be about one hundred years old. These centenarians would still not be immortal. But what would they die from? They would simply become weaker and weaker until death occurred. We could then either invent new terms to write on death certificates or return to using that old term, "natural causes," attributing death to the inexorable normal losses in physiological function that are the hallmark of aging.

When thinking about the effect of disease elimination on life expectation, some caveats must be appreciated. For example, if the causes of death attributable to cancer were eliminated, within a short time deaths would occur from other causes among those who were saved. The people who would have died of cancer would now live long enough to experience cardiovascular disease. Because both cancer and cardiovascular disease usually occur later in life, the additional time gained from curing either is not enormous. If most cancers occurred in humans between, say, the ages of thirty and forty and cardiovascular disease between ages sixty and seventy, then curing cancer would have a much greater effect on longevity than it does now when both diseases are separated by about ten years in their peak occurrence. Because two-thirds of all deaths now occur over age sixty-five, the time gained from eliminating one cause of death is somewhat less than simply adding that gain to the time gained from eliminating a second cause of death.

If the cause of most cancers and cardiovascular diseases is the greater susceptibility of aging cells to each, as I believe is the case, then eradicating any one of them will not have an enormous effect on longevity as table 7–3 suggests. An enormous effect might occur if we could reduce to the level of young cells, the susceptibility of old cells to these and other diseases.

WHY DO WOMEN LIVE LONGER THAN MEN?

William R. Hazzard of Wake Forest University has observed that a visit to almost any long-term care facility (except those run by the Department of Veteran's Affairs) will prompt the same question from even the most casual observer: "Where are the men?" *Why* do women live longer than men? The short, but correct, answer is that we do not know with certainty. Despite the profound effects that the longer lives of women have on our economic, political, and social institutions, the biological basis for the difference has attracted the interest of few researchers. With the emergence of biogerontology as a serious scientific discipline with growing financial support, the apathy of the past is waning, but we still know little about the reasons for the life expectation gender gap.

Not only do women, as a group, live longer than men, but women's rates of survival from major causes of death exceed those of men at almost every age. For example, as seen in table 7–4, men are from 1.12 to seven times more likely than women to succumb to such causes of death as heart attacks, strokes, cancer, respiratory diseases, accidents, liver cirrhosis, suicide, homicide and AIDS. The only exceptions are deaths caused by cancers that affect the female sex organs, complications of pregnancy or childbirth, and a few other relatively minor diseases. Many gerontologists believe that women live longer because men are more vulnerable to almost all causes of death and particularly to cardiovascular disease. Since cardiovascular disease kills almost as many people as all other causes combined and disproportionately more men than women, its cure would significantly reduce the difference in life expectation between women and men.

Although increased life expectation is generally deemed desirable, living longer does not necessarily mean more years spent living well. Women's greater longevity is accompanied by a higher incidence of many nonfatal diseases like rheumatoid arthritis, depression, and osteoporosis. Sadly, greater longevity often means more time to suffer from these ailments.

The only point in life at which males may have a biological advantage over females (based on absolute numbers but open to interpretation) is at conception: up to 170 males are conceived for each 100 females. However, about two-thirds of all conceptions end in spontaneous abortion, miscarriage, or stillbirth and of the fetuses lost, two-

TABLE 7-4. Sex differentials in causes of death: United States, 1991

Rank order[1]	Cause of death	Ratio of male to female deaths
. . .	All causes...	1.73
1	Diseases of heart...	1.89
2	Cancer including cancer of lymphatic and hematopoietic tissues...	1.47
3	Cerebrovascular diseases (strokes)	1.19
4	Chronic obstructive respiratory diseases and allied conditions....	1.74
5	Accidents and adverse effects	2.63
. . .	Motor vehicle accidents	2.39
. . .	All other accidents and adverse effects.....................................	2.94
6	Pneumonia and influenza	1.65
7	Diabetes mellitus	1.14
8	Suicide...	4.37
9	HIV infection...	7.44
10	Homicide and legal intervention..	3.84
11	Chronic liver disease and cirrhosis	2.25
12	Kidney diseases	1.54
13	Blood poisoning..	1.31
14	Atherosclerosis...	1.36
15	Certain conditions originating in the perinatal period[2]	1.27

[1]Rank based on number of deaths
[2]Inasmuch as deaths from this cause occur mainly among infants, ratios are based on infant mortality rates instead of age-adjusted death rates per 100,000 as for all other causes.

SOURCE: Monthly Vital Statistics Report, Vol. 42, No. 2, Supplement, August 31, 1993, National Center for Health Statistics.

thirds are male! The result is that only about 106 live males are born for every 100 females. From the moment of conception, female life expectation steadily gains on that of males. Most of the losses before birth are thought to occur because of imperfections in the genetic machinery of the sperm or egg or in the developing embryo. If you believe that nature does things for a purpose, then you may regard this huge loss of embryos and fetuses as a mechanism to ensure that most individuals born have a reasonable chance of surviving or to prevent serious genetic anomalies from being passed on to future generations (a phenomenon some have called "gene pollution"). Of course, the screening process is not perfect and some babies are born with serious congenital anomalies. Some die within a few hours, days or years, but others live long enough to reproduce. Why male embryos and fetuses are more likely to abort is unknown. Some people have speculated that males are not only the weaker sex after birth but in utero as well.

Whether we consider life expectation from conception, or from birth, we find that females have a much greater life expectation than males until adolescence, when, for the first and last time, males catch up. After that, the female advantage in life expectation becomes increasingly pronounced as we approach the maximum life span.

Between the ages of thirty and fifty-four the ratio of men to women is about even, and then it increasingly begins to favor the female. In time, the shift in favor of females becomes more and more striking. In 1990, for example, somewhat less than half of people in their thirties were female, but almost eighty percent of centenarians and older were women (table 7–5).

TABLE 7-5. Relative number of men and women by age group, United States, 1990

Age group	% Female	Number of males per 100 females
65–69	55.3	81
70–74	57.5	74
75–79	61.0	64
80–84	65.4	53
85–89	70.4	42
90–94	75.2	33
95–99	78.7	27
100 and older	78.7	27

SOURCE: Cynthia M. Taeuber, 65+ in America, U.S. Bureau of the Census, *Current Population Reports*, Special Studies, P23-178RV, Revised May, 1993.

Curiously, it was only during the early part of this century that it became clear that women's life expectation exceeds that of men; up to then so many women died in childbirth that their life expectation, as a group, was reduced almost to that of men. Indeed, in some south Asian and Middle East societies even today the life expectancy of males is equal to or greater than that of females. This may be attributable to female infanticide, a high maternal death rate in childbirth, or both. In 1915, when the numbers of deaths from childbirth were first recorded in the United States, six hundred mothers died for every 100,000 live births; in 1980 the figure was less than ten. In addition to the reduction in deaths during childbirth, the increase in female longevity can be traced to a variety of positive socioeconomic developments (health care, work opportunities, athletics) that, until recently, were not equally available to women.

The only nineteenth-century American data on this question is from Massachusetts, where from 1850 to 1900, the difference between life expectation at birth for males and for females was less than two years. By 1910 the difference widened to almost 3.5 years in analyses made in the eastern United States. It diminished to 2.2 years in 1920, returned to 3.5 years in 1930, then leaped to almost 5.5 years in 1940 and 5.8 years in 1950. The female advantage reached 6.2 years in 1954 and 1975, and peaked in 1979 at 7.8 years. Since then the gap in the United States has narrowed, but not dramatically. It recently stood at 5.8 years in the United Kingdom and 7.1 years in Canada. In Japan, since 1987 the most longevous country, it was 6.0 years in 1990, with a life expectation of 81.8 years for women and 75.8 years for men. It is no wonder, then, that so few old men can be found in most long-term care facilities in developed countries (table 7–5).

IS THERE A WEAKER SEX?

The consistently greater loss of males from conception to birth is often interpreted to mean that males are weaker than females even before birth. Further support for this idea is the fact that more boys than girls die before adolescence, mainly because boys are more susceptible to infectious diseases. By adolescence males have lost their numerical advantage over females. However, during and after adolescence males are more likely to die from suicide or homicide, which have little to do with physical weakness. The fact that accidents and violence are the major causes of death in young men accounts for the greater survival rate of young women (see figure 7–2); in some communities homicide is the leading cause of male death. It is after adolescence that the female advantage in *life expectation* becomes more and more apparent. Clearly, males are the weaker sex—more males are lost between conception and birth than are females, young boys are more susceptible to infectious diseases than are young girls, and women live longer than men.

Today, death during childbirth is relatively rare in developed countries, and the female longevity advantage is obvious. Males are more vulnerable than females to most diseases, especially the important ones. Is there some fundamental difference in the normal aging process that gives females an advantage, or are males more vulnerable to disease for reasons that have nothing to do with age changes? We could argue that if all the diseases to which males are prone were resolved, the gender gap would disappear. Like the resolution of childbirth as a major cause of deaths in females, the resolution of deaths caused by cardiovascular diseases would allow men to close the gender gap with women. It could be that there is really no fundamental biological cause for the difference in life expectation between the sexes, just a great vulnerability of one sex to some particular causes of death. It could be that as soon as those causes are resolved the gender gap will be reduced or eliminated.

Today, for each successive age group in developed countries, females outnumber males by larger and larger numbers. In the United States there are now about 84 men in the sixty-five to sixty-nine age group for every 100 women. In the eighty-five and older age group only 39 men can be found for every 100 women (table 7–5). These discrepancies occur in all developed countries.

Although it may appear contradictory, the difference in life expectation between the sexes declines with advancing age. Newborn girls have a life expectation 7.7 years greater than do newborn boys. At age sixty-five the difference narrows to 4.4 years, at seventy-five to 2.9 years, and at eighty-five to 1.4 years. These figures reveal that the more vulnerable males are eliminated more quickly than females from the aging population; at the older ages the remaining, healthier males have life expectancies closer to those of their female contemporaries. The greater number of deaths caused by heart attacks and strokes in middle-aged and older men give comparably aged females a survival advantage. But that advantage diminishes with age because only the males who are as robust as the females survive middle age. The maximum *life span* appears to be the same for both sexes—about 115 years. For humans over the age of one hundred, sex differences in life span are not significant. Thus the life span, or *potential* for maximum longevity, seems to be the same for both males and females, but *life expectation* favors the females.

Of the many economic and social effects that the sex differential in aging causes, none is more significant than the ratios of married and widowed older people. In 1990, 77 percent of men over sixty-five were married, compared to only 42 percent of women. Almost half of all older women were widowed (8.3 million), outnumbering widowers (1.7 million) almost five to one. It is clear who is more likely to live alone in old age and who, because they are alone, will become more dependent on others as health begins to fail. The situation is exacerbated because women are more likely to marry older men and thus widowhood for most American women lasts about ten years.

Although we cannot prove why sex differences exist in human life expectation, there is some basis for reasonable speculation. Greater female longevity seems to occur in most animal species, although it is by no means universal. A female advantage occurs in such diverse animals as spiders, rats, and humans. But male Syrian and Chinese hamsters and Guinea pigs live longer than the females. Several strains of laboratory mice and rats show no gender gap, but other strains do. Some geronologists have proposed that the female longevity advantage might be associated with the fact that females have two X chromosomes and males one X and one Y, but there are cases that contradict this conclusion. Birds have the same chromosome relationship, yet studies have shown that male pigeons, Japanese quail, and finches live longer than females; the stallion, with one X chromosome, lives longer than the mare; and male fruit flies also display greater longevity.

In one group of Amish men, part of the Y chromosome was found to be missing, and these men lived five years longer than the women in the group. One wit interpreted this to mean, "Too much Y and you die." In spite of these fascinating findings we must await the outcome of additional studies in order to place credence in chromosome differences as the basis for the longevity gap between the sexes. Even if these reports were correct, it would not be the chromosome difference per se that is important, but what the genes in those chromosomes do to cause the gender gap.

Some biogerontologists reason that men's higher metabolic rate, compared to that of women, reduces their average longevity. Others have proposed that the higher brain weight to body weight ratio of females gives them the longevity edge. There is also speculation that the amount and difference in sex hormones found in men and women makes women less susceptible to cardiovascular diseases. But alas, there is no solid evidence to support any of these imaginative ideas.

A study done in animals reveals that castrated male cats live longer than uncastrated males. A somewhat similar study was done on a group of castrated men at the turn of the century. Men committed to mental institutions at that time were frequently castrated, and these eunuchs did outlive other, uncastrated institutionalized men. However, neither group lived as long as noninstitutionalized men. In any case, even if the results were unambiguous, it is doubtful whether many men would opt for castration as a means of extending their lives. If castration were to be shown to significantly increase male longevity we might invert that famous line from *My Fair Lady* to read, "Why can't a man be more like a woman?"

ACCELERATED AGING IN HUMANS

Several human disorders, all extremely rare, superficially appear to mimic an acceleration of the aging process. Gerontologists are interested in the extent to which these disorders resemble natural aging.

The most important of these conditions is called progeria, and its victims display many of the characteristics of biological aging early in life. Although the child may appear to be perfectly normal during infancy, strange signs soon appear. Growth is retarded and the face takes on a birdlike appearance, with the eyes protruding and the nose hooked. All victims seem to look like each other. Heart disease and atherosclerosis usually appear, cholesterol levels and blood pressure may increase, the skin becomes thin and wrinkled, hair becomes sparse and falls out, and the patient usually succumbs to a heart attack or stroke. Their mental development does not seem to be impaired, however. The average length of life is twelve or thirteen years. About twelve living cases are known in the United States. The condition afflicts males and females equally and without discrimination as to race or national origin. There is no proven cause of the disease, although it is believed that each case represents a new sporadic dominant mutation. The children are not capable of reproducing, but if they were, half of their offspring would be expected to inherit the disease. Preliminary trials with human growth hormone made by the new recombinant DNA techniques are showing some promise for therapy.

Although progeria mimics some of the changes that occur in old age, not all of the signs of natural aging are present. The manifestations of progeria may simply mimic aging by coincidence. If progeria is truly accelerated aging, and a genetic error could be proved to cause progeria, this would strongly suggest that there is a genetic component to normal aging. However, no underlying genetic mutation has yet been discovered in patients with progeria.

Werner syndrome, which has its onset in adolescent humans, occurs about twice as often as progeria. The clinical manifestations of Werner syndrome are cataracts, loss and whitening of the hair, and a wasting away of the skin. Werner syndrome is definitely known to be the result of a genetic anomaly and is recessively inherited from both parents. Two other human conditions that are thought to resemble some aspects of aging are Cockayne's syndrome and Down's syndrome.

The relevance of these conditions to normal aging is debated continuously by gerontologists. They are thought to represent accelerated aging because they cause degenerative changes similar to those found in aged individuals. However, there are many other human conditions in which degenerative changes occur that do not seem to be accelerated aging. Progeria and Werner syndrome would seem to support the argument that degenerative changes associated with aging are not caused by wear and tear. This would argue against the popular wear and tear theory of aging, which will be discussed extensively in chapter 15.

An intriguing aspect of these rare conditions is the observation that when cells from progeria and Werner syndrome patients are grown in laboratory cultures, they age faster than do similar cells taken from age-matched controls. This active area of research will be discussed in part 3.

WHY ARE WE OLD AT AGE SIXTY-FIVE?

There is a common belief that humans somehow become old on their sixty-fifth birthday. Much of what we think about human aging is centered around the concept that the number sixty-five is somehow significant. What is the evidence for this, and will it stand the test of critical scientific scrutiny? The answer comes from a story, no doubt partly apocryphal, that we owe to the German chancellor Bismarck. It is said that he engineered his rise to power by making the astute observation that his rivals, all federally employed, were over the age of sixty-five. Seizing upon this observation, he allegedly masterminded legislation to retire all public servants who reached the age of sixty-five, then ascended to power with ease. Other countries also adopted sixty-five as the age for retirement, and we have suffered that legacy until relatively recent times. Happily, forced retirement at age sixty-five is no longer mandated in most American institutions. Regrettably, there still is a widely-held belief that, at age sixty-five, some mysterious biological event occurs that makes humans old at the stroke of midnight. I hope this book will help to dispel this absurdity.

PART THREE

How Do We Age?

Aging under Glass

A process which led from amoeba to man appeared to the philosophers to be obviously
progress—though whether the amoeba would
agree with this opinion is not known.

—Bertrand Russell

ALMOST everything that we can measure in humans and animals changes as time passes. Changes, however, do not always imply a loss. Some properties that can be measured over time increase, others decrease. Some biological properties don't change at all. Most of us are concerned about the things that decrease or are lost over time because some of those changes cause anxiety or may herald failing health.

Decreases and losses are odd things because much depends on how we perceive them. With age our skin may lose its smoothness and *acquire* wrinkles. From the standpoint of the major function of skin, which is to enclose our organs and protect us from the environment, it matters little whether our skin is wrinkled or smooth. Wrinkled skin is not unhealthy skin, but we are taught to believe that smooth skin is preferable. A pessimist might say that with time the skin loses its

111

smoothness; an optimist might say it gains wrinkles. The pessimist sees the change as negative and calls it a loss; the optimist sees it as affirmative and calls it a gain. Same change, different viewpoints. The appearance of gray hair signals old age for some, yet for others it is a sign of maturity and distinction. Like wrinkled skin, gray hair is a normal age change that does not affect health. It depends on your point of view whether it is a loss or a gain. If we acquire wisdom with age, that is surely a gain.

Functional changes, on the other hand, also occur normally over time but they result in real physiological losses, even to an optimist. We cannot run at age eighty with the same speed with which we ran at age twenty. That indicates a real physiological loss, but it certainly does not represent a disease or illness to a healthy eighty-year-old. There are hundreds of losses like this that are not signs of disease but rather part of the normal aging process. An incurable optimist might argue that the inability to run as fast at eighty as one could at twenty is not a loss at all but the acquisition of wisdom: our bodies wisely persuading us to avoid stressful exertion!

Later in this part of the book we will examine the changes that take place in our bodies as we age. I will not give a complete catalog of the changes that take place but will discuss those of greatest importance or interest. First, however, let us consider some developments in the field of cell biology that have provided novel insights into the aging process and longevity.

AGING IN A BOTTLE

At the end of the nineteenth century a new technique was introduced that revolutionized biological research and has given us important new insights into the aging process. The technique is commonly called "tissue culture" but would more accurately be called "cell culture." It's done by removing a small piece of living tissue from an animal or human and placing the tissue scrap, or more commonly the cells chemically released from it, into laboratory glassware. When the cell culture is then fed a fluid nutrient mixture and incubated at body temperature, the cells will grow, divide, and increase in number.

In the early part of this century an important experiment with cell cultures was done that had a profound impact on how people thought about human and animal aging. The experimenter was Alexis Carrel, a charismatic Frenchman who did most of his work at the Rockefeller Institute (now Rockefeller University) in New York City. Carrel removed a piece of tissue about the size of a matchstick head from the heart of a chicken and placed it in cell culture. He tacked the scrap of tissue to the floor of the glass culture vessel with a kind of biological glue, a blood clot similar to the kind that forms after a cut. Carrel made the clot by putting one drop of chicken blood plasma (blood without the red and white cells) on top of the tissue scrap together with one drop of an aqueous extract of chicken embryonic tissue. The technique is analogous to the preparation of epoxy cements that require one drop to be mixed from each of two different tubes.

Conveniently, the embryo extract and plasma contain the nutrients that the living cells placed in the clot require for growth. When the culture is incubated at the normal body temperature of the species from which it was obtained, after several days the tissue scrap (called an explant) is found to have increased in size (figure 8-1). The increase in size is due to cell division that occurs at the rim of the tissue scrap. This outgrowth of new cells ultimately extends in a concentric ring about an eighth of an inch around the original explant. Soon the cells stop dividing because they have reached the edge of the clot and have exhausted the nutrients. If one wants the cells to continue to divide, one must cut the enlarged tissue scrap into halves or quarters and introduce each segment into a new culture vessel, tacked to the floor with a fresh clot. This process can be repeated serially as each culture grows in size to the limit of the edge of the clot. In fact, Carrel and his colleagues claimed to have done so repeatedly with one explant from chick heart tissue for thirty-four years!

Albert Ebeling, a colleague of Carrel's, actually cultured the cells for most of the thirty-four years and discarded them in 1946, two years after Carrel's death. If each culture was halved each week, allowed to double in size, and then halved again the next week, the number of cultures would increase to astronomical proportions in a relatively short time. For example, if you started with one culture which doubles each week, you would have in twenty weeks about one million cultures which would in turn double in number each subsequent week. For practical purposes, only a few cultures are kept each week. Ebeling remarked that, if they had been saved over thirty-four years, the mass of chicken cells that would have accumulated would have been greater than that of the sun! In 1921 a New York newspaper called the *World* wrote that they would have formed a "rooster . . . big enough today to cross the Atlantic in a

FIGURE 8-1. Migration time of fibroblasts growing out from a tiny scrap of living tissue placed in culture varies inversely with age of the source. This has been ascertained for fibroblasts from chickens, rats and human beings and from several tissues, including heart, lung, and skin.

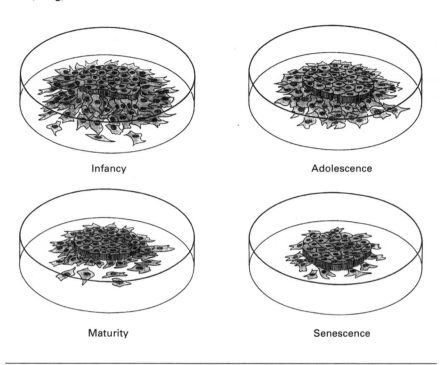

Infancy

Adolescence

Maturity

Senescence

stride; . . . so monstrous that when perched on this mundane sphere, the world, it would look like a weathercock." The *New York World Telegram* inquired after the health of the cells at the beginning of each new year; they mistakenly published a premature obituary for the cells in 1940.

The immortal chicken heart culture became a popular story and was a favorite with the Sunday newspaper supplements of the day. The imaginations of science fiction writers were stimulated and stories arose about a cell culture that had escaped from laboratory control, crept out of the room, spread into the hallways, oozed out of the building, and began to consume passersby. The imaginations of science fiction writers and cartoonists ran wild. Much attention was drawn to Carrel's laboratory and he reveled in the publicity.

Beyond selling newspapers to satiate the public's curiosity, this experiment had profound consequences for our understanding of the aging process. If it were true, as Carrel's experiment seemed to suggest, that normal cells taken from an animal could divide and function indefinitely in culture, then normal cells did not age and were inherently immortal! Furthermore, if normal cells are inherently immortal when grown outside an animal's body, as Carrel reported, then gerontologists could only conclude that the aging of similar cells in the body must be caused by events that occur outside of the cells, in the cement substance that binds cells to each other, perhaps, or to chemicals like hormones, released by specialized cells. Aging might even be caused by cosmic rays or other environmental factors. This conclusion affected thinking about the cause of human and animal aging for decades. The impact of Carrel's experiment on our understanding of aging was more profound than was its impact on any other area of biology.

Carrel's work with the chick heart cell culture led to a dogma that dominated the field of cell culture for fifty years: Once cells are put into culture and allowed to grow in the best conditions, they will divide and function indefinitely. The conclusion: Normal cells are immortal! A corollary of this axiom was that if cultured cells died, as often happened in laboratories at that time, their death must have been caused by some technical error. These failures were almost always attributed to errors in the preparation of the growth medium, inadequately washed glassware, or some other technical mistake. It was believed that Carrel and Ebeling were successful simply because they were so meticulous in their care of the supposedly immortal chick heart cell strain.

Carrel's idea that cultured cells were inherently immortal received additional support in the 1940s and 1950s when it was found that, *on rare occasions*, some normal cells cultured from rodents and humans seemed to acquire the property of immortality. The first immortal human cell culture was called HeLa. The name comes from the first two letters of the first and last names of Henrietta Lacks, a woman whose cervical tissue was cultivated at Johns Hopkins University in 1952. HeLa cell cultures have been in continuous culture since 1952 and have been distributed to research laboratories throughout the world since that time. The cells have been of enormous use in our understanding of cell biology. HeLa cells are to the cell culturist what the laboratory mouse is to the zoologist or the fruit fly to the geneticist.

However, the idea that *all* cultured cells are intrinsically immortal soon fell to a new observation that changed our view of the immortality of cultured cells. This new observation, made in my laboratory, illustrates not only how new scientific knowledge is often obtained but, perhaps just as important, how it is received.

AN OLD DOGMA DIES

> All truth passes through three stages. First, it is
> ridiculed. Second, it is violently opposed. Third,
> it is accepted as being self-evident.
>
> —Schopenhauer

About thirty years ago my colleague Paul Moorhead and I, working at the Wistar Institute in Philadelphia, discovered that Carrel was wrong. When we began our work in 1959, several dozen immortal cell populations, like the HeLa cells, were reported to have arisen spontaneously in cultures made from many different animal organs and grown in many laboratories. Although it was an uncommon event, the supposedly immortal cells arose in cultures grown from both normal and cancerous tissues taken from several different animal species and even from human organs. Paul and I agreed that the animal and human cell populations, like HeLa and the others described in the 1940s and 1950s, were immortal, but we felt that their biology must have differed significantly from mortal, normal cultured cells.

Our discovery occurred quite unexpectedly, as is often the case in scientific research, while we were looking for something else. We were growing cells from human embryonic tissue obtained from legal abortions sent to us from Sweden, trying to find viruses that might be implicated as the cause of human cancers. We reasoned that if cancer-causing viruses were present in human cancer cells, they might be able to infect normal cells, and we might be able to detect them by adding the growth fluids or extracts of cultured human cancer cells to cultures of normal human cells. We planned to determine whether the normal cells changed into cancer cells as a result of the exposure. We thought that embryonic cells would be the best normal human cells to use because adult cells might contain other viruses that would interfere with the interpretation.

The embryonic tissues that we received arrived from Sweden at random times, and we prepared ourselves to process the tissue whenever it arrived. In the 1950s, when we began our work, tissue was cultured quite differently than it was in the days of Carrel and those who followed him in the 1940s. The new method was simpler than clotting a scrap of tissue onto a glass surface and is still in general use today in laboratories throughout the world. Instead of being clotted to the floor of a culture vessel, the tissue scraps of interest are now exposed to a digestive enzyme called trypsin, which is found in the pancreas (trypsin from pigs is most commonly used). This enzyme dissolves the substances that cement the cells together into tissue but does not harm the cells themselves.

After the cement is dissolved, millions of individual cells are released, separated from the enzyme solution, and resuspended in a growth medium. The growth medium is a witch's brew of nutrients known to be required by cells, including amino acids, vitamins, and such essential minerals as sodium, potassium, and calcium. We know most of the nutrients that cultured normal cells require, but we do not know all of them. Therefore, it is necessary to add blood serum to the medium to supply any nutrients about which we are ignorant. The serum of many animals will do. Human cells grow well in bovine serum, the serum most commonly used today, and no better in human serum. It is a humbling realization.

After the cells are released from the original tissue, they are placed in a culture vessel containing the growth medium and incubated at body temperature. In a few hours the individual cells settle and attach themselves to the floor of the container. In about a day they begin to divide. The cells continue to divide until eventually the entire floor of the culture vessel—whatever its size—becomes carpeted with cells. Then they stop. Normal cells stop dividing in culture when they touch their neighbors. If additional cells are desired, it is necessary to remove the cells from the container and provide them with more room in which to divide. This process is known as subcultivating or splitting. It is possible to make three or eight or ten daughter cultures from the original culture, but the mathematics become complicated and the outcome is the same if you simply divide the contents of one vessel between two daughter vessels. This is called a one-to-two split ratio. The entire process is diagrammed in figure 8-2.

To subcultivate the cells one removes the used culture medium (the cells remain stuck to the vessel floor), then adds trypsin to release the cells from the vessel floor and to separate them from their neighbors. The cells are then removed from the enzyme preparation, divided into two equal portions, and placed into two daughter culture vessels.

FIGURE 8-2. Culture of normal human cells in the author's laboratory begins with the break-down of tissue into individual cells with the digestive enzyme trypsin. The cells are then transferred to a flat bottle, where they multiply until they cover the surface of the culture vessel. Then they stop multiplying. The cell population is now divided into equal halves, which are recultured. This process can be repeated only about 50 times with human fetal cells; it cannot be repeated as often with cells from older donors. Cells grown in this way are stored by being frozen in liquid nitrogen. Thawed and cultured years later, the cells "remember" the population-doubling level at which they were frozen and continue to divide until the total number of possible doublings is reached.

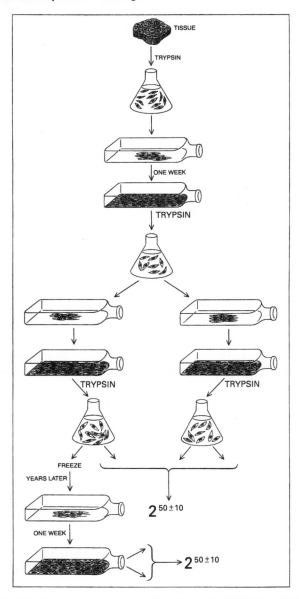

SOURCE: "The Cell Biology of Human Aging," by L. Hayflick, illustrated by Alan D. Iselin, *Scientific American*, January 1990, Vol. 242, No. 1. Reprinted with permission. Copyright © 1990 by Scientific American, Inc. All rights reserved.

When the cells in these cultures divide to the extent that they, too, cover the floors of their vessels, they again stop dividing and require another subcultivation. This process can usually be repeated every three or four days. The culture vessels, and hence the number of cells, increase in numbers exponentially. That is, they double in number at each subcultivation producing first one vessel, then two, then four, eight, sixteen, and so on. Like Carrel and Ebeling we saved only a few cultures each week, lest we be driven out of the laboratory and the research building by culture bottles.

This modern way of culturing cells is easy, and people in thousands of laboratories throughout the world do it every day. It is even possible to grow cells from one's own body in laboratory bottles by taking a small skin biopsy to start the first culture. (There are several ways in which the tissue can be taken virtually without pain.) I have grown my own cells in this way many times; there is something both thrilling and awesome in watching one's own living cells move, feed, and divide under the microscope. This same technology forms the basis for procedures now used in laboratories that do in vitro fertilization (in vitro means "in glass"). For in vitro fertilization the culture consists of a human egg to which sperm is added. The same kind of culture media, glassware, and incubators are used as previously described. After the fertilized egg divides several times it is implanted into the uterus of the biological or surrogate mother.

Returning to the story of our embryonic human cell cultures: Paul Moorhead, an expert on human chromosomes, determined that the cultures we were growing consisted of chromosomally normal cells, with no anomalies characteristic of abnormal or cancerous cells. We conducted many additional experiments to establish the essential fact that the cells were normal in every way. One critical experiment was designed to prove that the cells that we were growing were not cancer cells. Cancer cells, when inoculated into appropriate laboratory animals, will continue to grow; normal cells will not. When we inoculated the cells that we were growing into appropriate laboratory animals the cells did not grow. But when we inoculated immortal cells, like HeLa cells, into the same laboratory animals, tumors were formed from the growing HeLa cells. Many other tests confirmed that the cells we had grown were entirely normal. They also had only a limited ability to divide in culture, that is, they were mortal.

When I cultured the human embryo samples received from Sweden, I was not too surprised to find that each could only be subcultivated a certain number of times. The dogma that I was taught held that, although cells are inherently immortal, they will frequently die unless extraordinary precautions are taken to ensure that the growth conditions are perfect. Because I took no special precautions, I was not surprised to find that the cells eventually stopped dividing, remained alive for several months in the culture vessels, and then slowly died. However, my curiosity was piqued when I noticed that the cultures that were dying were those that had been subcultivated most often and kept in culture longest. Cultures that were only a few weeks or months old thrived while those many months old were dying. This was not consistent with the idea that cultured cells are immortal: if there was a mistake in our technique, then *all* the cultures should have been dying at the same time, not just the oldest ones. Since one person was using the same batch of growth medium and glassware to grow all of the cultures, it was hard to believe that some mysterious, fatal error in culturing would be made only with the oldest cultures.

I became even more curious when I realized that all the cultures that were dying had been subcultivated about fifty times over an eight-month period. At that point the cells stopped dividing and eventually died. Cultures that were subcultivated fewer than fifty times were luxuriating. Clearly, the dogma had to be challenged: Why were the cells dying if our technique was not at fault? Still, we were reluctant to publish our results. Our older and more knowledgeable colleagues insisted that we must be wrong and that we had simply made some technical error. Furthermore, Paul and I were at the beginning of our research careers, and we would be a laughingstock if someone discovered that we had made some dumb mistake; our future as credible scientists could be in jeopardy. Yet so much depended on whether our observation was valid. If our technique was not at fault then aging could originate within individual cells and not elsewhere, as was believed at that time. With so much at stake we had to either prove that our observation was correct or find our mistake.

In order to determine whether or not a mistake had been made, we devised the following experiment: Knowing that it is easy to distinguish between male and female cells based on the appearance of the sex chromosomes they contain, we mixed equal numbers of human female cells at the tenth subcultivation level (young cells) with human male cells at the fortieth subcultivation level (old cells). We also continued to subcultivate the unmixed cell cultures of each sex. (See figure 8-3.) Remember, our observation was that normal human cells of

FIGURE 8-3. Limit of replication of normal cells in culture was demonstrated by preparing a mixed culture of female and male fetal cells that were respectively "young" and "old." Unmixed cultures of each served as experimental controls. After 30 population doublings only the female control cells were still dividing. The male cells had exhausted their population-doubling potential and had stopped dividing several weeks before the mixture was examined. It is unlikely that technical errors or contaminating viruses could explain why only the male cells in the mixture had died off. Most likely explanation is that loss of ability to divide in normal cells is due to activity of an intracellular clock.

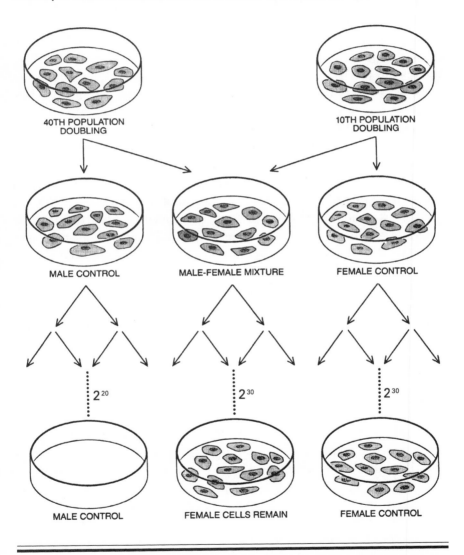

SOURCE: "The Cell Biology of Human Aging," by L. Hayflick, illustrated by Alan D. Iselin, *Scientific American*, January 1990, Vol. 242, No. 1. Reprinted with permission. Copyright © 1990 by Scientific American, Inc. All rights reserved.

either sex could undergo only about fifty subcultivations before they died. After about thirty more subcultivations we looked at all three cultures. In the mixed culture we found only female cells present. The male cells in the mixture had died several weeks before, when they had reached their maximum of fifty subcultivations; the female cells, at only the fortieth subcultivation level (10 + 30), were still dividing. The pure male cell culture had died several weeks before we decided to look at the mixture. The pure female cell culture, like the female cells in the mixture, was still luxuriating. It would be very unlikely that an error would have only affected the male cells! In fact, we then reversed the experiment, using young male and old female cells in the mixture. The result was as we expected. Only younger, still-dividing male cells were found in the mixed culture after the time that we had expected the older female cells to have died.

Although this evidence was quite conclusive, we thought of another way to alleviate our anxiety. We asked several of our doubting colleagues if each would agree to subcultivate one of our cell cultures in his own laboratory. Since they claimed that we must be making a mistake, we thought that if the same phenomenon occurred in *their* laboratories, then they would have to be guilty of making the same mistake! Would the cells be immortal in their hands, as the dogma claimed? Several colleagues accepted the challenge. We sent them cultures at the twentieth subcultivation level and told them that they should make two subcultivations each week. Based on our experience, we predicted that their luxuriating cultures would be dead in four months. They scoffed at the suggestion, but when they all telephoned us four months later to say that their cultures were dying our trepidation vanished and we decided to publish our findings. If we had made a mistake, so had our more senior colleagues, and any embarrassment would have to be shared. We would all go down in flames together!

In our paper we suggested that, contrary to what was formerly believed, normal cells have only a limited capacity to divide and function in cell cultures, just as they do in the animal from which they were obtained. We showed that the reason some cell populations are *immortal* is that they are *abnormal* in some way and they almost always become cancer cells. We suggested that normal cultured cells are mortal and cultured cancer cells are immortal. These principles were soon confirmed in many research laboratories and still hold to this day. We also proposed that the finite replicative capacity of normal cells represented aging at the cellular level and suggested that it be called the

Phase III phenomenon. We chose the name because we divided the life span of the mortal, normal cell cultures into three phases. Phase I occurred when the cells were introduced into the first culture vessel. Phase II began when the cells were subcultivated for the first time and continued while they multiplied vigorously for several months. Phase III was the time when the normal cells slowed down in their ability to divide until they finally died. We thought that Phase III must represent aging at the cellular level because we could think of no other reason why normal cells should slowly lose their capacity to function, stop dividing, and die. This was what happened to normal cells in an animal or human, so why shouldn't the same thing occur when the cells were cultured in bottles? Also the cultured cells approaching Phase III just looked as if they were becoming old!

Every cell culture we derived from human embryonic tissues demonstrated this phenomenon; all of them became old and died after forty to sixty successive doublings from the first culture. The average was fifty. The number fifty may be significant or it might be coincidental; it takes about forty doublings of a fertilized egg to produce a full-grown human adult, allowing for all of the cells that are shed from our bodies during a lifetime. (If we did not shed cells, we would assume the proportions of the giant rooster or redwood tree mentioned earlier). Could it be that a clock within all of our cells governs our longevity? Perhaps—but more about that later.

We decided, in 1961, to publish a description of our work and our interpretation that we had found aging at the cellular level. We submitted our article to the *Journal of Experimental Medicine*, one of the most prestigious scientific journals of the day. Several months later the paper was returned with a letter of rejection saying, among other things, "The largest fact to have come out from tissue culture in the last fifty years is that cells inherently capable of multiplying will do so indefinitely if supplied with the right [conditions]." As to our suggestion that the phenomenon that we had observed was aging at the cellular level, the reviewer commented, "The inference that the death of cells . . . is due to 'senescence at the cellular level' seems notably rash." Our paper was rejected because the editors were convinced of the validity of the very dogma that we claimed to have disproved! This letter rejecting our manuscript was signed by Peyton Rous, a world-famous virologist given credit for the first demonstration that viruses can cause cancer. He was later awarded a Nobel Prize for his discoveries.

We were deeply disappointed with this rejection but, convinced of the validity of our work and ideas, we sent the paper to another major scientific journal, *Experimental Cell Research*, where it was soon accepted. The paper has since risen to the status of what the Institute for Scientific Information calls a "classic"—one of the one hundred most cited scientific papers of the two million papers published in the world in the 1960s.

However, publication of a scientific paper does not in itself mean immediate acceptance of the work described. The scientific community is always skeptical of dramatically new principles or ideas that violate cherished beliefs, especially when the new idea does not seem to follow logically from what is already generally believed or expected to occur. To some extent this reluctance is beneficial, because it forces proponents of radical ideas to defend their position vigorously and to expose their work to the most critical examination. That is what we did for the next ten years. It took about a decade for the scientific community to accept our work and to seriously entertain the idea that aging could occur at the cellular level.

Reluctance to accept our conclusions also has an interesting psychological aspect. Everyone accepts the fact that animals and humans are mortal and that the individual cells that compose them die when the animal dies. Yet when cell mortality is seen to occur in a bottle, there is reluctance to believe that the same phenomenon is occurring. To this day there are a few skeptics who believe that we have merely not yet found that special growth medium that will allow cultured normal human and animal cells to live forever. This insistance echoes Ponce de Leon's belief that somewhere there is a fountain of youth.

TRANSPLANTING NORMAL CELLS

A novel experiment done several years ago should provide insight into the remote possibility that a "fountain of youth" medium might exist in which normal cells would be able to divide forever. The purpose of the experiment is to see whether normal animal cells will live forever when grown under the best possible conditions. The best possible conditions are, of course, in the animal itself. The question that this experiment is designed to answer is this: Will normal cells escape the aging process and live forever if they are serially transplanted to young animals? You can remove a small patch of skin, for example, from a laboratory animal and graft it to a younger host. When the young host ages, you can remove the skin patch and transplant it to another young host, repeating the process as many times as possible. Of course it is necessary to have a marker in the grafted cells so that they can be distinguished from the host cells. This can be done in several ways, including grafting male cells onto a female animal. Also, it is necessary to use inbred animals so that the grafts will always "take."

This experiment has been done with several kinds of tissues and the answer is clear. Normal cells transplanted in animals and living under these ideal conditions are, like the host animal themselves, mortal. That is, the serially transplanted normal cells will soon age and die just as they would if they were serially cultivated in laboratory bottles. The grafted cells, however, can function longer than the maximum life span of the animal from which they were taken. If you take a tissue sample from an old laboratory mouse, for example, and transplant it serially to young mice, the transplanted cells may outlive the old mouse but they do eventually age and die. The transplanted cells are mortal, which is the essential point; the fact that they may live longer than the animal that they came from suggests two possible explanations. First, the rate of aging varies for different kinds of cells. Perhaps the host animal aged and died sooner than its grafted cells because other kinds of cells in its body were weaker than the kind of cells that were grafted, and these more vulnerable cells led to the earlier death of the animal. A second explanation for why normal cells grafted in animals survive longer than those grown in culture is that, unlike cultured cells, only a small fraction of grafted cells divide at any point in time. Furthermore, the time necessary for each cell to divide is longer than for cultured cells. Proof for this reasoning is that, after several months, serial transplants do not reach a fraction of the mass that exponentially dividing cultured cells would reach in the same period of time.

The important point is that even though, under ideal circumstances, transplanted normal cells may function longer than cultured cells, they are not immortal. Like the clocks in a clock shop, cells in tissues age at different rates, stop functioning properly, and finally die. The fact that cells may perform longer when grafted than the life span of the species from which they came may simply provide evidence that cells must contain a greater capacity for division and function than is the minimum necessary for their owner to reach sexual maturation. We might conclude that, just as a chain is only as strong as its weakest link, the longevity of an animal is determined by the tissue or organ that ages fastest or has the shortest longevity.

The finite capacity to divide in culture is a characteristic of all *normal* cells. We do not know of any exceptions. Normal cells, whether cultured in bottles or grown as grafts in animals, are mortal; cancer cells are immortal in both circumstances.

AGING ADULT CELLS

Since the cells of normal embryos seem to have a built-in clock that limits them to about fifty doublings, it was important for us to know how many population doublings would occur if we started the cultures with cells obtained from older human donors. This was especially important in determining whether the phenomenon we had detected was really aging at the cellular level. Our first experiments using tissue from human adults did, indeed, show that cells taken from human adults doubled fewer times than did those from human embryos.

After we published our work, other scientists entered this new field of research, which we named cytogerontology (the study of cell aging). Other researchers found that normal cells from many different young donors and several kinds of tissue have a greater capacity to divide and function than do cells taken from the same kind of tissues from older people. The older the human donor, the fewer times the cultured normal cells divided. The tissues showing this phenomenon include skin, lung, white blood cells and cells from the aorta, liver, and the lens of the eye. The evidence seemed to be mounting that the Phase III phenomenon was really aging in cultured cells. If it was truly aging, then it would represent a real advance in our ability to design experiments that would help us to understand the aging process. It would be possible to do experiments in bottles of normal human cells that would be impossible to do in humans. Subsequent events proved that the phenomenon was truly aging at the cellular level.

ACCELERATED AGING IN A BOTTLE

In chapter 7 we discussed disorders that apparently cause accelerated aging in humans. These disorders, two of which are known as progeria and Werner syndrome, result in manifestations of age changes early in the chronological life of a victim. Progeria results in age changes before adolescence; Werner syndrome patients reveal age changes after adolescence. Soon after our announcement of the limited capacity of cultured normal human cells to divide, Samuel Goldstein, now at the University of Arkansas for Medical Sciences, and George M. Martin, of the University of Washington in Seattle, reported that cells taken by skin biopsies from these patients survived far fewer population doublings than did cells from normal subjects of the same chronological age.

These observations lent considerable support to the belief that the finite capacity of cultured normal human cells to divide might be a manifestation of aging at the cellular level. Nevertheless, many biogerontologists remain unconvinced that progeria and Werner syndrome are true examples of accelerated aging. They believe that the few similarities between the two disorders and true aging are simply coincidences and that true aging exhibits many changes that are not found to occur in progeria and Werner syndrome.

CARREL'S MISTAKE

Given that normal cells have a limited capacity to divide in cell culture and even in whole animals, how can we explain Carrel's apparently immortal heart cell culture? One obvious answer might be that his culture did not consist of normal cells. If they had changed to abnormal or cancer cells, then we would expect them to be immortal. But were Carrel's cells normal or abnormal?

There are several reasons why we believe that Carrel's cells were normal and thus mortal. First, the discovery that one could purposely "immortalize" a culture of normal mortal cells was made in the 1960s, well after Carrel had done his experiments and then only under circumstances where the normal cells were transformed to abnormal cells by purposeful exposure to such cancer-causing agents as radiation, chemical carcinogens, or cancer viruses. It is unlikely that agents such as these could have affected Carrel's culture or that it could have become immortal spontaneously. Second, we do not think that Carrel really had an immortal culture because hundreds of people have tried to repeat Carrel's experiment since his thirty-four-year-old culture was terminated in 1946. On only four occasions has someone succeeded in making normal chick cells multiply for more than two years and then only by exposing the cells to a chemical carcinogen.

Carrel's apparent success seems to have been the result of a mistake. The culprit was the chick embryo extract used to glue the heart tissue explant to the floor of the culture vessel. At least this was my guess until I had this idea confirmed in a most unexpected way. After a lecture I gave on the subject at the University of Puerto Rico School of Medicine in the mid-1960s, a woman in the audience came to see me saying that she had been one of Carrel's former laboratory technicians and that my surmise was correct. I was flabbergasted and asked how it had happened. She told me that during the first few years that she had contact with the "immortal" culture and was learning the culturing techniques, she grew increasingly puzzled by something that seemed anomalous. The clot in which the immortal culture sat frequently showed cell growth separated from the original explant by a region of empty clot. When her technical knowledge improved and her confidence increased she began to question the chief technician about this peculiarity. At first, it was passed off as unimportant. But as our heroine became more bold in her questioning, she was finally told to forget what she had seen or she would be dismissed. It was by now the early 1930s, and the Depression was at its height. She had no intention of losing her job so she remained silent. She told me that this was the first time that she had talked about the affair. What she had seen can be explained as follows:

The chicken embryo extract portion of the clot was prepared daily in Carrel's laboratory by extracting fluid from a chick embryo, placing the material in a tube, and then spinning the tube in a primitive centrifuge. Centrifugation is supposed to move all of the heavy materials in the mixture—broken pieces of cells and any whole cells that might have escaped the extraction procedure—to the bottom of the tube. The top portion of the tube should then contain only the clear, cell-free fluid used to form the clot. But the slow, primitive equipment Carrel used did not do an efficient job. Cell fragments and even whole living cells occasionally were retained in the surface fluid that supplied the drops of embryo extract used for feeding the culture and preparing new clots. In this way, fresh live chick cells were apparently introduced into the allegedly immortal culture almost every time that it was fed! A reexamination of the experimental details from Carrel's published studies makes this explanation highly likely. What the technician had seen were islands of new cell growth distant from the original immortal culture. The fresh cells supplied by the embryo extract appeared randomly distributed in the clot and formed isolated islands.

No wonder Carrel's chick cell line appeared to be immortal. He was adding new freshly prepared chick cells almost every time he fed the culture or subcultivated it! Was this a case of intentional scientific fraud? We will probably never know for sure. It could have been an honest mistake that was not appreciated until the publicity about the immortal chick cell strain became so great that it would have been extremely embarrassing to let the secret out. Also, there is no good evidence that Carrel himself knew about the error. The technicians may simply have wanted to protect the boss from enormous embarrassment.

Another clue lends support to the technician's explanation. I learned, some years later, that in the early 1930s the well-known Canadian cell culturist Raymond Parker was a guest researcher in Carrel's laboratory. In Canada he, too, was successfully using the clot technique. However, to avoid the tedium of preparing fresh chick embryo extract daily, he prepared the material weekly and froze the preparation for daily use. It was a great time-saver. He asked Carrel for permission to use the technique in carrying the immortal chick cell line. Carrel argued that it wouldn't work because freezing would destroy the extract's nutrient value, but Parker persuaded him to put the idea to the test. To the Canadian's astonishment, after a few weeks the immortal culture began to show signs of distress. Carrel argued that the experiment proved that he was correct and that freezing destroyed the nutrient value of the chick embryo extract. Parker was nonplussed. Carrel then showed that he could rescue the immortal culture by returning to the old method of using freshly prepared chick embryo extract. We now know that Parker was correct and Carrel was wrong. Freezing does not reduce the nutrient value of the chick embryo extract. What it does do is kill the fresh living cells that Carrel's technicians were inadvertently adding to the immortal culture when it was fed or subcultured. When the cells nurtured with frozen extract showed signs of distress, what they were showing was the Phase III phenomenon.

Because Carrel is dead we cannot question him about these matters. He may have been an innocent victim of a laboratory error kept secret from him or he may have been a coconspirator along with his technicians. We may never have an unequivocal answer. Nevertheless, the scientific method always demands confirmation of experiments by independent researchers, but numerous attempts to confirm Carrel's studies have consistently failed to do so.

LIFE IN THE COLD

Because normal human cells have a limited capacity to divide in culture, the subcultivation method described earlier allows us to work with any one strain of cells only for about eight months before it reaches the limit of fifty population doublings and dies. New strains could then be started, but this would be tedious. Furthermore, it is best to work with a single strain whose properties then become better known and whose behavior is therefore more reliable. A new development in a distant field of biology permitted us to solve this problem.

Several years before we began our work in 1959, a technique was developed for the cold storage of live animal cells. If cells are simply placed into a freezer they will die. The technique that worked was at that time used primarily in the cattle industry for the long-term storage of bull semen for use in artificial insemination. The semen was stored in small glass ampules that were then placed in a container of liquid nitrogen, not unlike a large thermos bottle. The key to successful storage of living cells in the cold was to add a chemical that would prevent destructive ice crystals from forming inside the cells and then to freeze the cells slowly. When thawed, the cells had to be thawed quickly. It was discovered that the live semen could be kept for months in the ultracold of liquid nitrogen, which is "minus" 196 degrees Celsius, or 320 degrees below zero Fahrenheit! We decided to adapt this technology for the preservation of our normal human cell strains. We took one of our normal human strains derived from embryonic lung, called WI-38, and placed several hundred glass ampules of the cells in liquid nitrogen. The experiment worked! We found that the living human cells could be frozen and kept alive for long periods of time and then thawed whenever they were needed. This allowed us to work with one strain of cells for a sustained period of time.

CELLULAR MEMORY

Once a single cell strain could be kept available for research for a long time, an intriguing question arose. If the cells were frozen at different population levels, say, from ten to fifty, how would the cells from each doubling level behave when they were resurrected? Because WI-38 came from a human embryo and therefore had a potential to double fifty times, would cells frozen at, say, the tenth doubling level, remember that number and go through only forty more doublings after they were thawed? Or would their internal clock be reset? We were anxious to find out.

We found that the cells do have at least a primitive form of memory! We thawed WI-38 cells frozen at many different population doubling levels. Each sample "remembered" at what population doubling level it was frozen and, when thawed, continued to divide until the total number of doublings before and after freezing equaled about fifty. How long can the cells remember? Ampules of WI-38 have now been frozen in liquid nitrogen for more than thirty years and their memory today is as good as it was in 1962 when the cells were first frozen! (This is a world record: the longest period of time that living normal human cells have ever been frozen.) In later experiments we found that normal older cells derived from adult human donors display the same kind of memory as those from human embryos. The only difference, of course, is that the total number of population doublings possible is less than fifty.

I still get a thrill when I look through my microscope at a culture of WI-38 cells resurrected after a frozen sleep of more than a quarter century. Within two hours of thawing, the cells stretch out on the floor of the culture vessel and look as healthy as I remember them to have been in 1962. In less than one day they begin to divide. Could it be that some day an extension of this technology could be used to delay the aging process or to preserve whole living humans? Would it be a blessing or a curse? We will consider this possibility later.

A PRACTICAL USE

Not only was WI-38 useful for research on human aging, but we also discovered that the cells were able to grow almost all of the then-known human viruses. Several previous unknown human viruses also were grown in WI-38. Today, WI-38 is used not only to isolate and identify human viruses in diagnostic laboratories throughout the world, but it and similar strains are also used to produce many of the world's human virus vaccines. These vaccines are made to combat such diseases as poliomyelitis, mumps, measles, rubella, respiratory virus infections, and rabies.

CELL AGING AND CELL LONGEVITY

Even though WI-38, like all normal human embryonic cell strains, can only divide about fifty times, the amount of cells that could be produced from one cell if they were all saved is staggering. In theory, more than twenty million tons of cells could be produced! This mass of cells is far more than anyone's body would need in a lifetime. Apparently nature has endowed us with cells that are mortal but that have sufficient division and functional capacity to satisfy our needs for far more than our maximum life span of 115 years. Perhaps this is yet another example of the overcapacity that our cells have acquired through natural selection—an important principle that will be discussed later.

Although our cells appear to have a counting mechanism that permits a maximum of fifty population doublings, I do not believe that we age or die because our cells run out of doublings. Even cultures made from the cells of very old human donors always have a few doublings left. More important are some of the findings made in the past twenty-five years about the behavior of aging human cells before they actually stop dividing and eventually die.

As cultured normal human cells double, age, and approach the end of their ability to divide, they undergo changes that affect almost every aspect of their biology, chemistry, and behavior. Literally hundreds of changes occur, including changes in enzyme activity; protein, fat, and carbohydrate synthesis; DNA; cell size; and hundreds of other aspects of biochemistry and cell behavior. Vincent J. Cristofalo, Paul Phillips, and their associates at the Medical College of Pennsylvania in Philadelphia have been especially successful in identifying much of the deterioration that takes place in cultured normal human cells as they age. Biogerontologists have now assembled a long catalog of functional changes that occur in normal human cells as they age in culture. Many of the changes are identical to those that we know occur in whole humans as we age; it is as if cells at the later doubling levels behave much like humans do in their later years!

Another striking finding is that when normal cells are taken from animals of different longevities, the cells from the most longevous species multiply more times before they die than do cells from less longevous species. For example, cells from newborn mice, which have a three-year life span, divide about fifteen times; cells from newborn chickens, which can live twelve years, divide about twenty-five times;

human cells divide about fifty times; the cells of a Galapagos tortoise, which has a maximum life span of about 175 years, divide about 110 times. There seems to be a direct relationship between species life span and the number of population doublings that its cultured cells will undergo. But the evidence for this observation is scanty and requires further study.

Now that the phenomenon of aging and the expression of different life spans have been demonstrated in cultured normal cells, we can construct experiments that might answer fundamental questions about these two processes. Neither aging nor life span determination at the cellular level can be studied easily using humans themselves.

As I've mentioned, I do not believe that people age or die because their cells stop dividing. I think that the range of changes that occur in cells before they lose their capacity to divide or function affects the whole body in such a way as to make it more vulnerable to the diseases of old age. Thus, people and animals eventually die, well before the maximum division capacity of their cells is reached, as the age changes within their individual cells increase their bodies' vulnerability to disease. I think that the doubling, or functional, limit coded into the genetic apparatus of the normal cell has evolved to give to each species its characteristic life span. In chapter 13 we will see how evolution might have selected the various life spans that are typical for each animal species.

The kind of cell that divides most in cell culture is called a *fibroblast*, and this is the type of cell that composes WI-38 and the other mortal human cultures that we studied. Fibroblasts are found in almost every tissue. They provide structure to tissues and produce important cement materials that hold cells together to form tissues. Our body is composed of thousands of different types of cells ranging from fibroblasts which divide frequently, to nerve and muscle cells, which do not divide at all. Other classes of cells have intermediate division capacities. When placed in culture, non-dividing cells simply function in the glass or plastic vessel for several weeks or months; then, like their rapidly dividing fibroblast cousins, eventually die. Aging and longevity are determined by what occurs in *all* cells, not only those capable of dividing most, like fibroblasts. In fact, it is likely that the most important age changes occur in the neurons and muscle cells that do not divide at all. Regardless of their potential to divide, all normal cells are mortal both in culture and in the animal itself. No individual cell and no individual animal is immortal.

I believe that the same fundamental process causes both dividing and nondividing cells to age. Furthermore, I believe that an identical process determines the longevity of these diverse cells. Cell division is governed by the same genetic signals and events that govern other functions in specialized cells that never, or rarely, divide. For this reason I think that the study of the loss of division capacity in dividing cells is fundamental to our understanding of the cessation of function in nondividing cells. Cell division and cell function are usually thought of as separate phenomena, but I believe that they are manifestations of the same genetic process.

The evidence that aging and the determination of longevity occurs within individual cultured human cells is now overwhelming. In recent years cytogerontologists have found evidence for the existence of a clocklike counting system in cultured normal cells. The clock that determines how long a normal cell will function in culture may also establish the life spans of its particular species. The events that lead up to the loss of cell function and the ultimate death of cultured cells may be the aging process itself occurring at the cellular level. Many biogerontologists are convinced that efforts to understand the nature of aging and the longevity clock at the fundamental level of the cell are certain to reveal more about the origins of both processes. Where is the clock located in the cell? How does it work? Can it be perturbed? Some important new knowledge has already been obtained.

Two of my former students, Woodring Wright, now at the University of Texas Southwestern Medical Center in Dallas, and Audry Muggleton-Harris, who now lives in England, did some interesting experiments in my laboratory that suggested that the clock is located in the nucleus of the cell. The nucleus is a discrete body present in all of our cells, with the exception of red blood cells. The nucleus is surrounded by the cytoplasm, in which most of the cell's metabolic activities take place. The nucleus is the location of the cell's genetic apparatus: it houses the chemical called DNA, which contains the fundamental genetic code and forms the genes on all forty-six human chromosomes. Using a recently developed technique, we were able to remove the nuclei from cultured normal cells. This left enucleated cells called cytoplasts. Using another new technique we then inserted nuclei from young cells into old cytoplasts and nuclei from old cells into young cytoplasts. The number of times that both kinds of hybrid cells divided led us to conclude that the age of the nucleus, not the age of the cytoplast, was what governed how long the hybrid cell divided in culture. This is why we concluded that the clock must be located in the nucleus of each cell. Recently, there have been reports that the longevity clock might be located in genes on either the first or fourth chromosome of the twenty-three pairs of human chromosomes.

Another of my former students, James Smith, and his wife, Olivia M. Pereira-Smith, both working at Baylor College of Medicine in Houston, Texas, have discovered an inhibitor of cell division that seems to become expressed by cells as they become older in culture. Eugenia Wang and her collaborators at the Lady Davis Institute for Medical Research in Montréal, Canada, discovered two more inhibitors of cell division that are also manufactured in normal human cells as they age in culture. Thomas H. Norwood, of the University of Washington in Seattle, had earlier provided an important clue that chemical inhibitors of cell division might be present. In a more recent development, Samuel Goldstein, of the University of Arkansas for Medical Sciences in Little Rock, has found evidence that specific genes within cells become "switched on" over time and inhibit cell function, thus initiating the aging process and indirectly determining the range of longevities in the cells of different animals.

An intriguing idea as to how a cell clock might actually work was first proposed in 1973, and Calvin B. Harley and his colleagues at McMaster University in Hamilton, Ontario, Canada, have since provided good evidence in its support. Each of our long, slender chromosomes terminates in a region called a telomere. Telomeres are made of DNA, the same chemical that composes all of the genes that form the chromosome. Telomeres, however, do not seem to contain any genetic information. They consist of a number of repeating subunits. We might think of the chromosome as a string of colored beads, each having one of four possible colors; the sequence of colors in a segment of adjacent beads would then specify a single gene. Each chromosome contains tens of thousands of different genes. The telomeres, found at the tips of the chromosomes, consist of a pattern of colored beads, say, two white beads followed by one black bead and three green beads, which repeats thousands of times until the very end of the chromosome is reached. Harley and his colleagues found that, with each cell division that takes place in cultured normal human cells, the repeated sequence in the telomeres is reduced. Because this happens at a fixed rate, the length of the telomeres might behave like a clock. Immortal abnormal cells seem to have found a way to keep their telomeres from shortening at each division, thus conferring immortality upon themselves. The immortal cells produce an enzyme called telomerase, which makes more telomeres. Normal cells lack this enzyme. The interpretation of telomere shortening in normal cells as a clock for longevity and aging is only speculative now. Biogerontologists are waiting anxiously for new developments as this fascinating story unfolds.

THE LATENT PERIOD

Another aging phenomenon, described in cultured cells in the late 1920s, has yet to be fully exploited or satisfactorily explained. At that time, tissue was cultured in clots (like the heart tissue in Carrel's laboratory). With this technique cells grow out from the periphery of a tissue scrap; if the scrap is circular, this results in an outwardly expanding ring of cells extending beyond the edge of the original tissue. The discovery was made that the older the donor of the cultured tissue, the longer it took for the cells to grow out from it and divide (see figure 8-1). This delay, called the latent period, has been found to occur with tissue from such diverse species as rats, chickens, and humans. The experiment has been repeated many times with the same result, but no one has provided a convincing explanation. Clearly, we are being told something new about the aging process at the cellular level, but we do not know what the message is.

The field of cytogerontology is now an active research frontier and scientists expect important new discoveries to be made in the next decade, especially as this field begins to exploit the dramatic new techniques of molecular biology. But nagging questions remain. Suppose we learn so much about the clock that we can perturb our longevity or the aging process itself? Is this desirable? Are we prepared for the consequences? I will discuss these important issues in a later chapter.

Although studies of aging and longevity in individual cells are important in our efforts to understand how we age and what determines our life span, most of us are more interested in how our whole body ages. Each of us is a private laboratory in which we can observe our own aging processes. But the aging process is highly variable; we cannot draw many conclusions applicable to most people from observations made in only one person. We need to study many people in order to make more accurate generalizations about the aging process. Let's see how this is done and what the results have been.

CHAPTER 9

The Baltimore Longitudinal Study of Aging

Old age is that period of life when more and more things happen for the last time and fewer and fewer things happen for the first time.

—Anonymous

MANY studies of normal human biology can be done relatively quickly and cheaply by studying almost any group of cooperative individuals. However, if we want to measure a change as a function of age, then special care must be taken in the choice of subjects and how the study is conducted. First, to study normal age changes you must have participants who are not sick, because disease can interfere with the measurement of many normal age changes. Many studies made on older people have been seriously flawed because they included sick subjects, leading researchers to erroneously attribute differences caused by disease in the older group to aging. Second, even in a group of healthy older people, you will find that there is great variability from person to person in almost any age change that you can measure. If there is a single indisputable fact about normal aging, it is the magnitude of individual variability.

Take gray hair, for instance. We all know people who began to gray in their twenties and others who do not gray until they reach sixty or later. If we choose at random men in their twenties, forties, and sixties to study graying of hair we might conclude that gray hair begins in the twenties, disappears in the forties (because by chance we chose middle-aged men who were not gray), and reappears in the sixties. Or, that gray hair begins only after the age of sixty. Or, that gray hair never occurs (because we happened to choose only men who were not gray or who were completely bald). This is called a *cross-sectional study* and, as the examples indicate, it is often a flawed method for studying age changes. The changes seen in such a study can be associated with aging only by inference—a dangerous business.

The best way to study age changes is by doing a *longitudinal study*. To study the graying of men's hair longitudinally, one would choose the largest number of young men possible, then study each one *periodically* until he ages or dies. In this way you would find the truth— that as men grow older the likelihood that their hair will turn gray increases, although the graying may start at a different time in each participant. You can also determine the rate of graying (for example, the number of gray hairs per year), which cannot be done in a cross-sectional study.

A story, presently circulating in gerontological circles, illustrates the dangers of interpreting cross-sectional studies in aging. It seems that a group of naive gerontologists decided to do a cross-sectional study on aging in Miami. When the study was completed, they found that most people there are born Hispanic and die Jewish!

Although a longitudinal study is the gold standard for measuring age changes, it suffers from at least three critical disadvantages. First, it is costly to follow a group of people for many years. Second, the subjects must be sufficiently dedicated to the study that they will be available for measurements periodically for the rest of their lives; those who volunteer for longitudinal studies thus tend to be better educated, more affluent, and healthier than the general population, and are usually disproportionately white Caucasians. Although this kind of self-selected population is a biased one, it is the best that we have at this time. A third problem arises in longitudinal studies which track people of different ages, because each age group (cohort) has been exposed to different environmental factors in its past. For example, if the study consists of twenty-, thirty-, forty-, fifty-, and sixty-year-olds, the younger cohorts will have had the benefits of more recent advances in medicine, hygiene, and nutrition that their older compatriots did not have.

Taken together these three pitfalls in conducting longitudinal studies are worrisome but, again, it's the best that we can do, and it is certainly better than a cross-sectional study. Longitudinal studies on the biology of aging humans are rare because of the cost and the enormous length of time that must pass before useful data is produced. Ordinarily, research grants are given for three to five years, after which time significant progress must be shown to qualify for additional support. Our current grant system is incapable of considering research projects, like longitudinal studies on aging, where results might not be available for decades.

THE BLSA

Despite the obstacles to such studies, several advanced thinkers and dedicated gerontologists began the most comprehensive and ambitious longitudinal study on aging ever attempted in 1958, and we are now beginning to reap the harvest of valuable information. The Baltimore Longitudinal Study of Aging, commonly known as the BLSA, is conducted in Baltimore, Maryland, at the Nathan W. Shock Research Laboratories, at the Gerontology Research Center, part of the National Institute on Aging. About 150 gerontologists conduct research there, and many work full-time on the BLSA. The study is designed to examine the physical, mental, and emotional effects of aging in healthy people. Called the "myth buster" by some people, the BLSA has yielded some fascinating results and even some major surprises that have changed our understanding of how we age. But before discussing the results, it is important to know more about the study itself, because it has had, and is destined to have in the future, a profound impact on our knowledge of how we age.

Credit for the foresight and determination to initiate this study must be given to the late Nathan Shock, a pioneer in the field of human aging and generally regarded as the father of gerontology in the United States. He spent many years engaged in fights with myopic administrators at the National Institutes of Health who, unconvinced of the value of the BLSA, tried every available means to prevent the birth of the project and to kill it once it was born. We owe much to Shock, who endured the tribulations that were heaped upon him, vigorously defended the BLSA project, and ultimately prevailed. Now, as the benefactors of his foresight and determination, we are harvesting a bounty of knowledge from one of the best studies of its kind in the world. Ironically, several of the myopic NIH administrators have, after the lapse of forty years, reached an age where they too are benefiting from the study they tried so hard to thwart.

Two other important figures in this story are William W. Peter and Arthur H. Norris, each of whom played a key role in recruiting subjects and sustaining their interest. Peter organized a vigorous campaign to recruit "healthy community-living" volunteers as subjects, but he himself lived only one year after initiating the program. Since 1958, more than one thousand five hundred male participants have entered the study, ranging from ages seventeen to ninety-six. Starting only in 1978, seven hundred women were enrolled so, unfortunately, less information is available on the female volunteers. All participants return to the Nathan W. Shock Research Laboratories in Baltimore every two years for two and a half days of testing that involves over one hundred procedures. They are paid nothing, not even their travel expenses. Some of the tests are uncomfortable or tedious, some require great mental or physical effort, and the questions asked can invade privacy. Nevertheless, there is a long waiting list to join the group.

Although the study began more than thirty years ago, most of the twenty-two hundred volunteers have been followed for an average of thirteen years, because many of the participants, already old when the study began, died within a decade or so after joining. Also, since half of the volunteers joined before the age of fifty, most have not reached advanced old age yet. This underscores the difficulty of obtaining reliable information about the aging process, to say nothing of the enormous costs involved.

Nevertheless, the study has revealed much new information and has confirmed some ideas previously only imagined to be true. For example, age changes were found to occur at a much slower rate than the developmental changes that occur before sexual maturity. Most, but not all, of the changes that occur during aging are associated with loss of function, but there is tremendous diversity. Older humans show a greater range of individual variation in many physiological and psychological measurements than do younger adults. This gives the lie to the old notion that all old people are essentially the same. The BLSA scientists have found extraordinarily "young" eighty-year-olds and extraordinarily "old" forty-year-olds. Many older persons performed as well as younger persons on several tests. Aging did not result in an inevitable loss in all intellectual functions. In some cases, performance was found to improve over time as a result of lifestyle changes, such as starting an exercise program.

As I have emphasized, although the incidence of disease increases with age among the BLSA volunteers, disease and aging are not the same thing. Aging is a normal process that occurs in all of us with the passage of time. Each disease is an abnormal process and does not occur in everyone. The predominant characteristics of old age are reduced capacity to adapt, reduced speed of performance, and increased susceptibility to disease. A disease that is minor in youth can be a major, even fatal problem, when it occurs in older people.

Shock and others believed that a longitudinal study was the only way in which the following critical questions about aging could be answered:

▪ How many of the age differences observed in cross-sectional studies are inevitable consequences of aging in all individuals?

▪ At what rate do age changes occur in different individuals?

▪ Is there a central aging clock that coordinates all the age changes that take place throughout the body? Or, are the changes that take place in one organ independent of those in other organs?

▪ Do or can critical events in our lives affect the aging process?

▪ Can patterns or levels of performance at one age predict longevity or performance at an older age?

▪ Can aging be distinguished from disease?

▪ How does age influence the outcome of a disease?

The BLSA researchers believe that there is no single cause of age changes. This general belief, shared by most gerontologists, holds that age changes have many causes, some of which may interact with others in extraordinarily complex ways. If you think cancer is complicated, try to understand the aging process! Cross-sectional studies of age changes show that a significant decline in many normal physiological functions is associated with advanced age, but the BLSA reveals that there is enormous individual variation, that some eighty-year-old subjects, for example, can perform as well as the average forty-year-old. Age changes are highly specific, not only for each one of us, but also for each of our organs. The clock shop analogy still applies. Our organs, like clocks in a clock shop, "tick" at different rates than do the corresponding organs in someone else. Thus, the rate of decline or failure of any particular organ is different for each of us.

These findings underline the vital distinction made earlier between biological and chronological age. We, or more precisely our organs and the cells that compose them, age at different rates. As we age, our individual changes are not in lockstep with those of other people born in the same month or the same year.

SEPARATING FACTS FROM MYTHS

We all have certain beliefs about how a person of a particular age should look and behave. We learn these beliefs from infancy when we first realize that people change as a function of the passage of time. Our biases are broad generalizations based on individual experiences of how the people we observe seem to perform or look at a certain age. Frequently our biases do not fit the facts.

I stated earlier that birthdays are a poor way to measure age changes. How many times have we said, upon learning how old someone was, that he or she doesn't look that old or that he or she certainly looks much older. Clearly, chronological age is not a reliable predictor of how an older person should look or perform. The BLSA scientists studied the lung function, basal metabolic rate, visual and hearing acuity, and motor coordination of over one thousand men. The researchers then independently assessed whether the men looked younger or older than their chronological ages. The men who looked older usually performed more poorly than younger looking men on the tests, but not all of them did; even experts frequently were unable to match chronological with biological age.

Following is a summary of the major findings made so far in the BLSA. A few of the conclusions are based on cross-sectional studies of the BLSA group, but most are based on longitudinal studies. As described earlier, the participants who have been in the study long enough to reveal useful information are mostly healthy, well-educated men and women who are working in, or are now retired from, high-level positions.

CHANGES IN APPEARANCE

▪ There is a gradual reduction in height, in both sexes, of about one-sixteenth of an inch per year beginning at about age thirty.

▪ With age the extremities become thinner and the trunk thicker. In men the diameter of the forearm diminishes after age sixty and the diameter of the calf, after age forty.

DENTAL CHANGES

▪ Chewing habits change markedly with age in both men and women.

▪ The number of cavities increases with age, as does the likelihood and severity of periodontal disease.

▪ The flow of saliva and its constituents are stable during aging.

WEIGHT AND METABOLIC CHANGES

▪ Weight increases to about the age of fifty-five, when it begins to fall. Contrary to popular belief, life expectation is not greatest for the leanest but for those who range from the middle of the "desirable" weight range (on the 1959 "ideal" height-weight insurance tables) to 20 percent over the midpoint. "Desirable" weights have been adjusted upward in the 1979 tables based on the BLSA studies. This remarkable finding will be discussed in detail later.

▪ The body consumes about 12 calories less per day for each year of age over thirty. At age forty, for example, your body needs 120 fewer calories per day than at age thirty.

▪ Weight declines between age fifty-five and age seventy-five, due mostly to loss of lean tissue, muscle mass, water, and bone. Bone loss is greater in women.

▪ Total body fat remains relatively constant with age but its distribution changes. More accumulates in the thighs and less in the abdomen, so "middle age spread" is not really due to increased fatty tissue. It probably occurs because muscle tone is lost, producing the characteristic sagging of the abdomen.

CHANGES IN THE CARDIOVASCULAR SYSTEM

▪ Cross-sectional studies show that blood cholesterol rises from early adulthood to age sixty or sixty-five and then falls.

▪ The Framingham, Massachusetts, Longitudinal Study, although not specifically designed to study aging, has identified risk factors for the development of coronary artery disease, which may be additive (that is, each risk factor you have adds further to your likelihood of developing coronary artery disease). The risk factors are cigarette smoking, hypertension, elevated serum cholesterol and low density lipoproteins, low vital capacity, diabetes, and obesity.

▪ When disease-free, the heart of an older person pumps just about as well as does that of a healthy young adult. There is no evidence that heart function declines with age.

▪ Maximum heart rate, what we also call the pulse rate, diminishes with age. This is not a health problem.

▪ Men and women develop a thickening of the heart wall with age.

▪ The incidence of coronary artery disease increases with age.

The cardiovascular system will be discussed in more detail in chapter 10.

CHANGES IN REACTION TIME

▪ Persons over seventy show a decline in their ability to detect and report small changes, such as the movement of a clock hand.

▪ After age seventy the reaction time to a noise increases.

▪ With age, responses to stimuli become slower and are more likely to be inaccurate. These effects become greater in tasks that become more complex. There is about a 20 percent slowing of reaction time from age twenty to age sixty.

▪ Vigilance, defined as a person's readiness to respond to infrequent and unpredictable stimuli, declines in people about seventy and older. Young and middle-aged people perform equally well.

COGNITIVE CHANGES

▪ Short-term memory declines with age.

▪ After age seventy, performance on tests of logic decreased for most BLSA participants, but no change occurred for some participants.

■ Ability to learn oral (as opposed to written) material decreases only in those over seventy.

■ Those older than sixty make more errors in verbal learning tasks than do young adults.

■ Top performers and individuals whose performance on mental tasks does not decline with age are found in every age group, including the oldest.

■ No relationship has been found between blood pressure level and intellectual performance.

■ Visual memory, measured by the ability to reproduce geometric designs from memory, declines slightly between ages fifty and sixty and falls greatly after about age seventy.

■ Vocabulary scores do not change with age.

PERSONALITY CHANGES

■ In the absence of disease, personality traits remain essentially the same throughout life but preference for fast-paced activities decreases around age fifty. The common belief that an older person's personality changes over time, that he or she becomes crankier or more mellow, is a myth.

■ No evidence has been obtained to support the belief that old people become hypochondriacs.

CHANGES IN SEXUAL ACTIVITY

■ Sexual activity decreases with age despite maintenance of normal levels of sex hormones. A slightly higher level of testosterone is present in men who are more sexually active.

■ No significant difference has been found in testicular size with age. Sperm counts per unit volume or per ejaculate remain the same, but the proportion of immature sperm present increases with age.

■ Enlargement of the prostate gland is common in men over age sixty. This development is unrelated to amount of sexual activity, number of sexual partners, or length or stability of marriage.

▪ Contrary to popular belief, older persons do not spend much time daydreaming about the past. Sexual daydreams decline in frequency and in intensity with age until after age sixty-five, when they virtually disappear. Sexual activity is correlated with frequency of sexual daydreams in men.

▪ Relative frequency of sexual activity does not change with age. The men who are most sexually active in their seventies were also highly active sexually in their twenties.

CHANGES IN THE SENSES

▪ Visual acuity decreases with age. With glasses, however, it is possible to maintain 20/20 vision or better into the eighties.

▪ There is a progressive loss in the ability to hear sound at all frequencies. Hearing loss in males seventy years of age and older is greatest at the highest frequencies. The *rate* of change for these men is faster in the speech range frequencies (0.5 to 2 kHz) than in the higher frequencies because their hearing has already diminished at the higher frequencies.

▪ With increasing age, the ability to taste sweet or sour things does not change much. Salty or bitter things become a little harder to detect.

▪ The ability to correctly identify odors declines with age in both men and women.

PHYSIOLOGICAL CHANGES

▪ Kidney function, measured by the ability of the kidney to clear nitrogenous wastes from the blood, decreases with age.

▪ Lymphocytes, a type of white blood cell, have a diminished capacity to kill cancer cells beginning as young as age forty. Other white blood cells that fight infectious diseases, called neutrophils, also become less efficient with advancing age.

▪ Pulmonary function declines with increasing age. In healthy men the decline is a significant risk factor for coronary heart disease.

CHANGES IN STRENGTH

▪ After age sixty-five, lower arm and back muscle strength declines. Power output, measured by turning a crank over a period of time, falls after age fifty, but there is good reason to believe that this is due to reduced coordination rather than loss of strength.

▪ Physical activity declines with age.

▪ Maximum exercise performance declines with age.

▪ Physical performance can improve over time as a result of lifestyle changes, such as doing daily exercises. Although physical performance may increase and some diseases might be delayed, eliminated, or slowed, there is no evidence that the basic causes of aging are affected by increased exercise.

▪ Grip strength increases until the thirties, then declines at an accelerating rate after age forty. Nevertheless, a substantial number of people at all ages show no decrease in grip strength over a period of ten years. Grip strength declines as muscle mass declines.

GENDER DIFFERENCES IN AGING

▪ Premenopausal women show no loss of bone density with age, while postmenopausal women show a faster rate of bone loss than men of comparable age.

▪ Aging men and women have different proportions of the several kinds of white cells found in the bloodstream.

▪ Contrary to previous belief, the thickness of the heart wall is not different in men and women.

▪ Older men have twenty percent higher maximum oxygen consumption capacity than do women; this difference is primarily due to the smaller muscle mass in women compared to that of men.

▪ In men, the predominant increase in abdominal fat occurs in the early adult to middle-age years. In contrast, women's fat is distributed less in the abdomen compared to men at all ages, and the increase in abdominal fat does not occur until after menopause.

▪ Weight loss in men produces a favorable change in fat distribution to reduce abdominal fat, whereas weight loss in women does not change the pattern of fat distribution.

▪ At most ages and audio frequencies, the longitudinal decline in hearing sensitivity is more than twice as fast in men as in women.

■ The ability to identify odors declines earlier and more rapidly in men than in women.

There are many other changes that occur with age, but those listed above were, except as noted, derived from the BLSA. A fair generalization is that, after age thirty, functional loss in several organs occurs at a rate of about one percent per year.

GENERAL CONCLUSIONS FROM THE BLSA

■ There is no evidence that a single factor or a single clock regulates the rate of aging in all of our organs.

■ Because there is a large amount of individual variation, chronological age alone is a poor predictor of performance. Some eighty-year-olds may perform as well as the average fifty-year-old.

■ Some things—for example, resting heart rate and personality—do not change with age.

■ Some slow losses are not caused by aging but rather by diseases, such as arthritis and Alzheimer's disease.

■ Some losses are inevitable consequences of aging, unrelated to disease. These physiological changes occur over time as part of the normal aging process: for example, reduced reaction speed and losses in short-term memory.

■ Sudden losses are the result of diseases—especially heart attack and stroke—rather than aging.

■ Primary changes can lead to secondary changes. Some normal changes that occur as we age may result from the body's attempts to compensate for some other normal loss. For example, with increasing age greater cardiac output is required after exercise.

■ Lifestyle decisions, notably adoption of a low-cholesterol diet or ending cigarette smoking, can influence the occurrence or progression of some age-associated diseases. There is no evidence for a direct effect on the fundamental aging process.

■ Longitudinal changes in functions help to distinguish age associated processes from disease.

The BLSA tells us that there is no single aging process. A person's rate of aging may vary significantly from what might be predicted from the averages. There is no general pattern of aging applicable to all of our organs. Aging results from the interaction of genetic, environmental, and lifestyle factors. Age changes are highly individualized. The disabilities frequently associated with old age may be caused more by the effects of disease than by the aging processes. Chronological age is an unreliable measure of aging—but a proven measure of the passage of time called birthdays and receiving presents.

CHAPTER 10

How We Change
with Age

> There are three early signs of old age. The first
> is loss of short-term memory, and ... I don't re-
> member the other two!
>
> —Anonymous

SEVERAL longitudinal studies, in addition to the BLSA, have produced much important information in the field of aging. These include the Duke University Longitudinal Study, begun in 1955 by Ewald W. Busse and a Veterans Administration study in Boston. Another large longitudinal study has been underway in Gothenburg, Sweden, since 1971. Gothenburg, with a metropolitan population of almost 1.5 million people, is the second largest city in Sweden. It is representative of the population of a country that has had the highest proportion of people over age sixty-five for the longest time. The Gothenburg study has emphasized studies on participants over the age of seventy. I chose to emphasize the BLSA because it has provided more information on biological changes and has been going on longer than any other study.

Studies of age changes on smaller groups of individuals have been made by hundreds of scientists. Most have been cross-sectional

150

studies, with the hazards of interpretation described in chapter 9. Nevertheless, a large number of additional normal age changes in men and women have been confirmed. What follows is certainly an incomplete list because of the impossibility of assessing all of the vast, and sometimes contradictory, scientific literature on this subject. Several thousand age-associated changes have been reported; in this chapter I discuss those that seem likely to be of the most general interest. I have organized the chapter by major organ systems because the changes that occur in some of these systems are the basis for some of the popular theories of aging that will be discussed in chapters 14 and 15.

THE CARDIOVASCULAR SYSTEM

There is little doubt that the incidence of cardiovascular disease increases exponentially with age. As a result, it is the leading cause of death in older age groups in virtually all industrialized countries. Curiously, deaths from cardiovascular disease have dropped over the last thirty years. There has been much speculation as to the reason for this, but a conclusive explanation remains to be established. Some scientists believe that it is the result of a greater public awareness of what constitutes a healthy lifestyle—that is, a reduced intake of fat and cholesterol and an increased emphasis on exercise. Earlier detection of and better diagnostic tests for heart disease, better control of hypertension, and a reduction in smoking might also have contributed. Nevertheless, cardiovascular disease is still the leading cause of death in the United States and most other developed countries. 60 percent of men who reach age sixty have a major narrowing in at least one coronary artery. In women, the 60 percent figure is not reached until age eighty.

Cardiovascular changes have been thought to be so central to the aging process that some people have believed that such changes are its cause. Based on his dissections of humans, Leonardo da Vinci wrote that the cause of aging is "veins which by the thickening of their tunics in the old, restrict the passage of blood, and by this lack of nourishment destroy the life of the aged without any fever, the old coming to fail little by little in slow death." A modern expression of the same idea is the cliché that we are as old as our arteries. But diseases of the cardiovascular system, although the leading cause of death in most developed countries, are not the cause of aging. The proof? People without cardiovascular disease also age.

It is a cardinal principle in gerontological studies that normal age changes cannot be detected confidently in the presence of disease, but the prevalence of cardiovascular disease can make it difficult to find enough old people with healthy hearts to study the normal aging process! To get around this problem researchers determine the state of health of potential older subjects' hearts while stressing them with vigorous exercise. Using this method, the number of individuals found to have cardiovascular disease doubles when compared to the same population measured at rest. The small fraction of remaining subjects are demonstrably normal and form the basis of the only meaningful studies. This method of selecting subjects is analogous to choosing a car on the basis of how it performs on the highway and not how the idling motor sounds in the showroom.

Until recently, it was believed that with age came an inevitable decline in cardiovascular function that could be detected even when the patient was at rest. Edward G. Lakatta and his colleagues, who are all researchers in the Baltimore Longitudinal Study on Aging, have found that in *normal* subjects—those free of cardiovascular disease—age has no predictable effect on the cardiac index or cardiac output, even though the volunteers, aged twenty-five to eighty, showed the usual decrease in physical activity over time. Peak systolic blood pressure (the first or top of the two numbers used to denote blood pressure) does increase with age, but diastolic pressure (the second or bottom number) does not change. The volunteers were not undergoing any physical training and represented average healthy city dwellers. It seems well demonstrated that in healthy hearts cardiac function does not inevitably decline with age as was previously thought.

Atherosclerosis, a thickening and hardening of the walls of the arteries, is responsible for most deaths after age sixty-five in developed countries. It begins early in life and may in later life produce a heart attack (myocardial infarction), angina (angina pectoris), or a stroke (cerebrovascular accident). A large number of atherosclerotic changes were seen at ages as early as twenty or thirty in autopsies done on male casualties of the Vietnam and Korean wars, but 80 percent of atherosclerotic cardiovascular disease in the United States occurs in people over age sixty-five.

There is general agreement that atherosclerosis is caused by a combination of three circumstances: genetic factors, normal age changes, and environmental influences, such as diet. It seems to be a disease unique to humans. It rarely occurs naturally in old animals. Some fortunate human populations seem to be exempt as well. We can therefore conclude that normal age changes do not themselves produce atherosclerosis but, as with all other diseases of old age, increase one's vulnerability to the disease. The dramatic increase in reported cases of atherosclerosis in recent decades is partly due to (*a*) better diagnostic methods, (*b*) resolution of diseases of youth—more people live long enough to experience atherosclerosis—and (*c*) the substitution of atherosclerosis for "natural causes" as a cause of death on death certificates. It is not known whether the incidence of this disease has actually increased in absolute terms.

The major normal age change that occurs in arteries is the slow increase in the thickness of the innermost of the three concentric rings of tissue which comprise the arterial pipeline. This innermost ring, called the intima, is, like the inside of a triple-layered pipe, in closest contact with the passing fluid, in this case, blood. The result of this thickening is a narrowing of the diameter of the artery and increased rigidity. Both are normal conditions and not life-threatening of themselves, but they may predispose or increase vulnerability to atherosclerosis when other factors are present. Other factors may account for the fatty streaks or fibrous plaques on the arterial wall which may eventually close it, causing a heart attack or stroke.

THE IMMUNE SYSTEM

The job of the immune system is to detect, inactivate, and remove microorganisms and other foreign materials from the body. Proper performance is vital for survival. One of the ways in which the immune system detects and inactivates foreign objects is to produce a class of proteins called antibodies. One of many amazing things about antibodies is their extraordinary specificity. Like keys, they are uniquely tailored to fit in locks represented by a myriad of different foreign substances that find their way into our bloodstream or tissues. Antibodies are not made against an entire invading organism or substance but against particular small parts on their surfaces. The surfaces may be thought of as a mosaic tiled floor. Each different tile or group of tiles elicits a different antibody. The body produces many different kinds of antibodies against a single microorganism or foreign cell. Imagine the billions of different possibilities: there are hundreds of millions of different viruses, bacteria, animal cells, and other large foreign protein molecules, and each can elicit from the immune system a different combination of antibodies or "keys" specific to the set of different proteins or "locks" on its surface.

The immune system is exquisitely sensitive to foreign proteins, and for decades biologists wondered how the system distinguished "foreign" proteins—those originating in some other living thing—from the incalculable number of "self" proteins that make up the animal or person that houses the immune system. If an animal or human made antibodies to its own proteins, it could deactivate vital protein molecules involved in essential life processes. Fortunately, the immune system has a remarkable scheme to prevent it from making antibodies to "self" proteins. The human immune system develops starting at a few months after conception, but it does not become "armed" to detect foreign proteins until about the time of birth. All of the proteins present in the body before the immune system is "armed" are automatically recognized by the immune system as "self" from that moment onward. Only new proteins, encountered by your immune system after arming, are recognized as foreign.

With age some of our normal "self" proteins incur minor changes that, in themselves, are harmless. But, the vigilance of the immune system is so exquisite that it will manufacture antibodies to these changed proteins, although the act might be characterized as a form of self-destruction. Thus, the superb sensitivity of our immune system, which serves us so well in youth, may in old age do us harm by attacking as foreign what is really a slightly changed "self" protein. This unpleasant circumstance is thought to be the cause of ailments called *autoimmune diseases.* Some examples of these are certain kinds of arthritis and a condition called lupus erythematosus, which is a chronic degenerative condition found in older people. Some gerontologists believe that the likelihood of developing these autoimmune conditions increases as we grow older as the immune system responds to subtle changes in an increasing number of our aging proteins.

Although nearly all of the complex functions of the immune system change with age, these changes vary in each individual. The thymus gland, which is found beneath the sternum in the chest, plays a crucial role in immune system performance. Mysteriously, after sexual maturation, it degenerates—or technically, undergoes involution—during the first half of our lives. It is believed by some that this normal change in the thymus triggers aging of the immune system. Humans at fifty years of age retain only 5 to 10 percent of the original mass of the thymus. The thymus produces hormones whose levels begin to decline around age twenty-five and are undetectable after age sixty. A class of white blood cells, called lymphocytes, some of which are found in the thymus, also changes in the proportion of its various subpopulation components with age. These cells are vital in maintaining the integrity of the entire immune system.

The immune system is exceedingly complex and consists of hundreds of vital components, many of which are known to change with age. The result is that older people are less efficient in mounting an immune response when it is required; a decline in the ability of the immune system to produce antibodies to foreign substances is coupled with a greater chance of its producing antibodies to "self" proteins. Some gerontologists believe that the increased incidence of cancer with age is the result of an immune system less capable of detecting and destroying cancer cells than it was in youth.

THE ENDOCRINE SYSTEM

The endocrine system, which is composed of the cells and tissues that produce hormones, has long been thought to play an essential role in producing normal age changes. The profound effects that hormones have on virtually all cells of the body, and the fact that the level of several hormones falls with age, explain why hormone replacement therapy has often been touted as a means of "rejuvenating" the old. Hormone manipulations do reverse age changes in several physiological processes. For example, stimulation of the hormone-producing hypothalamus in the brain can reinitiate the cycle of egg maturation and release (estrus cycle) in old female rats who have stopped breeding, elevate protein synthesis, and induce tumor regression. The levels of growth hormone and thyroid hormone are reduced in old age. When the levels are artificially raised by administering hormones to old rats, the efficiency of the immune system increases and the thyroid, whose size has decreased with age, is stimulated to increase in size. Recently, it was reported that growth hormone, administered to older men, increased muscle mass and reduced fat tissue—a reversal of the normal aging process.

In spite of these impressive results, intervention with hormones has not yet been demonstrated to arrest or reverse the entire aging process or to convincingly increase longevity. One of the reasons for skepticism is that hormone studies done with laboratory rodents may interfere more with feeding patterns than with the aging process. Captive rodents that have food constantly available differ from wild rodents, which have a feast-or-famine lifestyle. Wild rodents may have a longer life span because of their reduced caloric intake (a phenomenon that will be described in a later chapter). Perhaps the hormone manipulations that have apparently extended the longevity of laboratory rodents have been effective only because the injected hormones made the animals eat less.

Like the immune system, the endocrine system affects virtually all the cells in our body. Thus, it is also a prime candidate for the origin of all age changes. Hormonal changes with age could very well reduce the physiological reserve in our tissues and organs that, in youth, allowed us to respond efficiently to a variety of stresses. In old age, hormonal changes may erode this vital reserve, increasing our risk of maladies common in the elderly. The decreased ability of older people to recover from burns, wounds, or the trauma of surgery, or to respond to the stresses of heat and cold, may be due to impairments in hormone expression or balance. Even menopause—an obviously normal age-related phenomenon—is triggered by changes in the endocrine system. Enlargement of the prostate gland, almost universal in older men, is also thought to result from hormone changes.

The secretion of many hormones—including testosterone, insulin, androgens, aldosterone, and thyroid and growth hormones—has been found to decrease with normal aging. To complicate the picture, hormones act by first attaching to a receptor on their target cells; experimentation has shown that these receptors also frequently decline in numbers or efficiency with age. It is therefore possible that changes that have been attributed to decreases in hormone production are really due to decreases in the ability of target cells to respond to hormones.

The ability of the blood to maintain a normal level of glucose (sugar) declines with age, and the amount of blood sugar increases slightly when studied in subjects who have fasted overnight. This phenomenon has been the subject of research by endocrinologists since it was discovered about seventy years ago. The body's ability to utilize glucose—a fundamental source of energy—is controlled by such hormones as insulin and glucagon, which are secreted by the pancreas. A "glucose tolerance test" is used widely to study the behavior of insulin;

when fasting subjects are fed sugar, the level of insulin in the blood increases sharply. Other hormones, like growth and thyroid hormones, also play a role in blood sugar levels.

THE FEMALE REPRODUCTIVE SYSTEM

In most animal species, including humans, there is a large difference between males and females in length of reproductive life. Women lose the ability to reproduce about forty years after sexual maturation, or when they are about fifty years old. Healthy men appear to be capable of sexual reproduction until extreme old age. In all other primates that have been studied, such as monkeys and chimpanzees, female reproduction is possible for a much greater proportion of the average life span than it is in human females. Unlike human females, female members of other primate species do not show a gradual decline in the maturation of their eggs with age. In the few species that do have a menopause, egg maturation ends more or less abruptly. (Reliable information on reproductive decline in most domestic animals is generally unavailable. However, the chicken, because of the economic importance of its eggs, has been studied, with at least one remarkable finding: A hen in the first year of egg laying may produce as many as 175 eggs. The number of eggs laid in subsequent years is a fixed percentage of the number laid in the first year. Generally, one finds that egg laying declines in the second year to about 75 percent of the number of eggs laid the first, peak year, and in the third year, egg production falls to about half that of the first year.)

As women approach fifty years of age, the number of immature eggs in each ovary approaches zero. Surprisingly, about half of the immature eggs that a woman is born with are lost even before puberty. Very few of the eggs remaining at puberty go on to mature, escape from the ovary, and become expelled during menstruation. Fewer still become fertilized. In women approaching menopause, the number of living normal eggs produced decreases. Chromosomal defects are more common in the eggs of older women and account for a large proportion of the abnormal eggs produced by women approaching menopause. The reason for this is unknown, but it may account for the decreased fertility of older women, as well as the greater likelihood of having a baby born with a birth defect. The fact that chromosomal defects occur is well documented; their connection to birth defects is best exemplified by Down's syndrome, which is known to be more common in babies born to older mothers.

Postmenopausal women show rapid reductions in the levels of several circulating hormones, such as estradiol, but testosterone concentration declines more gradually. Although profound changes occur in the ovaries of menopausal women, it would be wrong to assume that changes in these organs are the basic cause of reproductive failure. Most of the functional capabilities of the ovary are in turn governed by hormones secreted by the pituitary gland at the base of the brain, and this is controlled by more basic changes in hormones secreted by the hypothalamus, located in a cavity between the cerebral hemispheres. It is likely that the hypothalamic changes result from even more fundamental changes in the part of the nervous system that controls it. No one knows what the ultimate trigger is. Not surprisingly, the whole system is called the "hypothalamic-pituitary-gonadal axis."

Changes also occur in other organs of the female reproductive system with age. The weight and size of the uterus decreases after menopause until about age sixty-five, when it is half the weight of what it was at age thirty. In postmenopausal women who are not receiving estrogen, the vagina becomes smaller both in length and diameter. The vaginal wall frequently becomes thinner and local glandular secretions diminish. These changes frequently result in discomfort during intercourse and necessitate a physician's advice. The breast also changes as a result of the complex hormone modifications that occur after menopause. Breast glandular tissue after menopause, much like the thymus after puberty, undergoes degeneration or involution. The pattern of change varies according to the individual. Generally the breasts decrease in size and become more flaccid with age, but for unknown reasons the breasts of about 10 percent of women show an enlargement after menopause.

Two-thirds of all breast cancers occur in women over the age of fifty, which, although not normal, might be related to normal age changes. Normal age changes are also thought to predispose postmenopausal women to osteoporosis (loss of bone calcium) and, perhaps, to atherosclerosis. Premenopausal women have only one-fifth the incidence of heart disease found in similarly aged men, but postmenopausal women have almost two and a half times the risk of heart disease of menstruating women of the same age. This is the basis for the belief that estrogens may have some protective effect on the cardiovascular system.

However, estrogen therapy is not without its own risks; its use has been reported to increase the incidence of cancer of the uterus.

THE MALE REPRODUCTIVE SYSTEM

Compared to the conspicuous reproductive aging that occurs in women, the senescence of the male reproductive system is a more gradual affair. In fact, there is controversy as to whether a male menopause (or climacteric) occurs at all. Clearly, some men retain full reproductive capacity into extreme old age—there is at least one reliable report of a ninety-four-year-old man becoming a father. Nevertheless, reduced reproductive capacity has been clearly demonstrated in many older men and in older male animals. Animal breeders are particularly concerned about this question, but there is less concern with reduced reproductive capacity in older men since it is rarely important for them to father children.

Since sexual activity for both men and women at any age fulfills deeply felt personal needs, reinforces pair-bonding, is helpful in maintaining the stability of the family and therefore of our social structure, any loss of sexual drive and functionality is of significant concern. The same hormonal changes that regulate reproductive function also control sexual capacity and drive, so changes in sexual activity can be expected with old age.

As in women, the levels of several hormones in men increase or decrease with age. Sexual interest, activity, and capacity are also generally reduced, but these events have not been firmly linked to hormone changes. There is little agreement on whether changes in sperm motility, sperm counts, viability of sperm, or numbers of abnormalities in sperm occur as men age. The safest generalization is that there is great variability among individual men.

While most tissues and organs shrink with age, the heart, lungs, and prostate tend, for unknown reasons, to enlarge. The prostate gland, wrapped like a doughnut around the neck of the bladder, makes a variety of materials and fluid with which sperm mix during ejaculation. When it enlarges, it may constrict the emerging urinary canal, causing difficulty in urinating. Some enlargement occurs in 10 percent of all forty-year-olds and 80 percent of all eighty-year-olds. Most often the enlargement is due to benign cell growth, but sometimes the growth is cancerous, so the condition should be followed closely by a urologist to rule out the presence of cancerous tissue. Removal of the prostate may be advised to relieve the obstruction of the urinary canal.

There is some belief that intercourse maintains the prostate in good condition. This prompted one urologist to suggest that his patients remember the three stages of sexual activity: tri-weekly, try weekly, and try weakly—but do try.

THE SKELETAL SYSTEM

Normal aging produces loss of bone tissue in everybody but the *rate* of loss varies in each of us. Bone loss seems to begin in the fifties for both sexes, but then proceeds more rapidly in women than in men. In women the rate of loss is highest during the five- or ten-year period after menopause. Men lose about 17 percent of the bone mass that they had as young adults, women about 30 percent. The amount of bone in childhood is greater in males than in females and this relationship remains unchanged throughout life. Eighteen-year-old girls have 20 percent less bone mass in relation to body weight than do boys of the same age. One of the factors that determines the amount of bone an old person will have is the amount that he or she had at maturity.

When bone loss results in the collapse of a vertebra (one of the thirty-three bones composing the spinal column) or in great susceptibility to fractures, osteoporosis is the likely diagnosis. In this condition what bone remains is usually normal but there is simply too little of it. The condition is found predominantly in females. Its most recognizable manifestation is the bent, curved, or hunched back (kyphosis) that has become part of the caricature of old age.

The cause of osteoporosis is unclear but much evidence suggests that four variables play a significant role: (1) changes in concentrations of hormones such as estrogen, parathyroid hormones, calcitonin, corticosteroids, and possibly progesterone; (2) nutritional factors, especially deficiencies of calcium and vitamin D; (3) immobility caused by a sedentary lifestyle, illness, joint disease, or a fracture; and (4) status of bone mass at maturity. Other risk factors include being short, thin, and Caucasian.

Several studies have shown that exercise, estrogen therapy, and calcium supplementation of the diet can, separately or together, slow the rate of bone loss in postmenopausal women.

THE NERVOUS SYSTEM

The nervous system is the command center for all of our body's activities. Some gerontologists believe that the brain, which governs the central and peripheral nervous system, also governs age changes. The hypothalamus, located in the brain, is believed to initiate the menopause and the subsequent cascade of events associated with the aging of the female reproductive system. Evidence for this is based partly on experiments done in rats where stimulation of the hypothalamus in postmenopausal animals reactivated the ovarian cycles. The intimate relationship between the brain and the endocrine system is such that changes in one frequently produce changes in the other. A change in a chemical secretion in the brain may trigger a change in hormone secretion in, for example, the ovary or the adrenal glands. These latter changes may in turn affect the original triggering secretion in the brain. This kind of interdependency is called a *feedback loop*. These loops can be extremely complex, involve many chemicals, and even affect loops in other systems.

Many of the hormones and other chemicals secreted in the body are released with a remarkable degree of rhythmicity. Some chemicals are released about every hour, some every three hours, and some with other periods. It is known that the clock mechanisms become less precise with age and that many clocks seem to be governed by hormones released from the pituitary gland at the base of the brain. Some gerontologists have speculated that the effect of age on our internal clocks could account for the well-known changes in sleep patterns that occur as we grow older. These biological clocks and their effects on the aging process will be considered in detail later. Despite the profound importance of the nervous system, we have not been able to identify any changes within it that indisputably account for the entire aging phenomenon.

THE BRAIN

Although the brain is part of the nervous system I have chosen to discuss it separately because deterioration of the brain has enormous consequences for humans. Brain dysfunction strikes squarely at what makes us human beings—our ability to reason and to remember. Such dysfunctions already affect nearly two million Americans and the numbers are certain to increase. Even if one escapes senile dementia, there is still the possibility that a vigorous mind may occupy a body that will not respond properly to its commands. Parkinson's disease and other motor disorders are examples.

At birth the brain weighs about three-quarters of a pound; it increases in weight to a maximum of about three pounds around age twenty. Brain weight then decreases until, at approximately age ninety, it weighs about 10 percent less than it did at age twenty. The loss in weight can be seen on the surface of the aging brain, where shrinkage of the convolutions (gyri) is accompanied by a widening of the grooves (sulci) between the convolutions. This change can now be visualized in a living person by using a computerized axial tomography (CAT) scan or by magnetic resonance imaging (MRI).

The brain is an immensely complex organ composed of an estimated one hundred billion (10^{11}) nerve cells or neurons and billions more supporting cells, called glial cells. The neurons consist of a central cell body, one end of which consists of a tangle of branching fine strands called dendrites, which bring impulses to the neuron. From the other end of the cell body there extends a strand called the axon which directs information to other cells along the network or even out of the brain to distant muscle cells. The axon of one neuron may extend one thirty-second of an inch to an adjacent neuron or as much as a yard from the central part of the neuron. Each neuron receives an enormous amount of information transmitted to it from thousands of other cells, which may inhibit or stimulate the activity of the receiving neuron.

Neurons use chemical messengers called neurotransmitters to communicate with each other across the almost imperceptible spaces that separate them. One of these chemicals, called *acetylcholine*, is found in about 15 percent of brain neurons, where it is made at the neuron junctions by an enzyme called *acteyltransferase*. An excited neuron releases its acetylcholine at synapses, or junctions with other neurons, and the chemical then interacts with the other neurons via special receptor molecules on their surfaces. Eventually the acetylcholine is deactivated by another enzyme, *acetylcholinesterase*. These events occur in fractions of a second. Each neuron can interact with probably ten thousand others through the branched network of their terminals. In some parts of the aging brain the synapses, or contact points between neurons, are lost or altered in shape. The amount of the chemicals associated with neurotransmitter activity also decreases with age.

There is universal agreement that the weight of the brain decreases from young adulthood to old age. However, *what* is lost and *where* the loss occurs is in dispute. Cells and fluids are both definitely lost, and the brain also shows changes in the shape and form of its various parts. Not all animals show this effect. Dogs, cats, and monkeys do, but rats do not.

Many studies on human brains examined during autopsy have shown a loss of cells in some, but not all, parts of the brain with increasing age. As much as a 40 percent loss of cells has been observed in the aging frontal cortex, but other areas of the brain show no significant cell loss with age. Because these studies necessitate removal of the brain it is only possible to do a cross-sectional study and not a more accurate longitudinal study. It's difficult to know what was lost if you can't be certain of what existed before. You can only remove a brain once!

As long ago as 1894, the hypothesis was proposed that losses in mental function with age might be caused by loss of neurons. To this day a connection between decreased mental function and brain cell loss has not been proven, although loss of brain cells as we age does occur. One gerontologist calculated that in one part of the brain there is an average loss of about 100,000 neurons per day from the age of thirty. If we assume that this is true, you would lose about two billion cells in fifty years. The number seems large, but it accounts for less than one-seventh of an ounce of brain cells. The number of cells lost may not, in itself, be significant. However, if the loss occurs in cells whose vital functions cannot be assumed by other cells, then the loss could be significant.

If the brain, like other organs, has a surplus of cells beyond what is necessary for normal function, or if the regions in which the losses occur are not important, then the loss of two billion cells might not matter. Although new brain neurons do not replace lost ones, remaining neurons can sprout new connections and, within limits, repair or compensate for the short or broken circuits that occur when a neighboring neuron dies, restoring the aging brain to more or less its former condition. Neurobiologists refer to this capacity of the brain for adaptive or compensatory changes as its "plasticity."

In 1906 Alois Alzheimer, a German neurologist, first described a form of cognitive impairment in humans that has come to be called Alzheimer's disease. The prevalence of this disease increases from about 0.1 percent of all people ages sixty to sixty-five to as high as

47 percent in those over age eighty-five. Anatomically, the disease is characterized by a peculiar mass of fibers found in the brain cells of older people. In addition, many nerve cells in the brain are lost and, as already mentioned, there is a reduction in the number of crucial connections (synapses) between nerve cells. The synapses transmit electrical and chemical impulses from nerve cell to nerve cell and are vital for normal brain function.

The masses of fibers found in Alzheimer's disease are called neurofibrillary tangles. Under the microscope they resemble pairs of helices similar in shape to pairs of minute spiral staircases. They are found throughout the cortex of the brain in those suffering from Alzheimer's disease and other dementing disorders. Neurofilaments similar to these are also found in normal brains, but few look exactly like these. Other structures, called neuritic or senile plaques, which are composed of various materials like amyloid (a sugar-protein complex) and the dead parts of cells, are found in the brains of normal older people. Their density increases in the brains of victims of Alzheimer's disease. Some neurobiologists believe that the plaques occur almost in direct proportion to the decline in mental function. Although both tangles and plaques are found in the brains of older people, they are present in larger numbers in the brains of those with mental impairment. How tangles and plaques form is unknown, and whether or not they actually cause or contribute to the loss of mental function has not been established. Scientists do not believe in guilt by association, and simple coincidence is not acceptable evidence to prove a causal relationship.

From 1906, when Alzheimer described this disease, until less than ten years ago, public awareness of Alzheimer's disease was virtually nonexistent and the erroneous belief that "senility" was a normal consequence of aging was widespread. Today, interest in Alzheimer's disease is at an all-time high. This change has not come about because the incidence of the disease increased dramatically in the last decade. In fact, as best as can be determined, the incidence has not changed at all. What has changed is the public's awareness of the existence of Alzheimer's disease as a disease and not part of the usual aging process. This increased public awareness has been brought about by a constellation of forces including interest groups focusing on Alzheimer's disease, Congressional recognition of the social and financial costs of its devastating effects, and the appropriation of more than half of the recent budget of the National Institute on Aging to its cure. As desirable as this attention might be, resolution of this disease, or of cancer or cardiovascular disease, would not add to our understanding of the basic biological processes of aging. I do not advocate that efforts to resolve these diseases be diminished, but because diseases associated with old age are the proper concern of geriatricians and not biogerontologists, they will not be treated extensively in this text.

Recent advances in computer technology and the ability to trace the path of glucose in the brain has opened up a new field for the study of brain metabolism. Although it is known that there is a decline in the energy metabolism of the brain with age, these new techniques are expected to reveal much more about how the normal and diseased aging brain obtains and uses energy.

This decade's most profound discovery in our understanding of the aging human brain has come not from research laboratories but from our own attitudes. We have come to realize that loss of mental capacity with age is not inevitable. The old idea that senility is a normal accompaniment of aging is simply wrong. This realization has become more significant to our understanding of the normal aging process than any recent laboratory discovery about the aging human brain.

Short-term memory declines with age. When you begin to write reminder notes to yourself, the process is beginning. There is probably a direct relationship between the number of reminder notes that you write (or the frequency with which you forget things) and your age. It is firmly established that older people do not perform as well on memory tests as do younger people. Retrieving proper names seems to be particularly troublesome. It is the chief complaint of older people in respect to age-related changes in cognitive ability. Finding that a word is "on the tip of the tongue" was found by one researcher to be the most common complaint of subjects over the age of sixty-four from a list of twenty-eight kinds of memory failure.

The major organ systems discussed in this chapter all change with age. Because these systems are fundamental to life they are separately or collectively viewed by many biogerontologists as the major sources of age changes throughout the body. Theories of aging based on these organ systems will be discussed later. The age changes that occur in other parts of the body, discussed in the next chapter, are important to understand but are not thought to be the basic causes of all other age changes.

CHAPTER 11

Aging from Head to Foot

And so from hour to hour we ripe, and ripe,
And then from hour to hour we rot and rot,
And thereby hangs a tale.
—William Shakespeare,
As You Like It

UNLIKE age changes in major organ systems, the following changes are not thought to affect the entire body. Here, instead, we consider the consequences, in limited areas of the body, of the systemic aging events described in the previous chapter.

HEIGHT

The normal erect posture characteristic of young adulthood is only rarely found in late old age. There are many reasons for this, including changes in the skeleton and in the muscles. Virtually every study that has been done has shown that standing and sitting height decreases with age, beginning in males around age forty and in females around age forty-three. However, the loss is so small until about age sixty that

166

it is difficult to detect in any single individual. A cross-sectional study done in 1989 on 1,763 people revealed that, on average, the lifetime loss of standing height in women was almost two inches and in men about one and a quarter inches. Not unexpectedly, the rate at which height is lost increases with age, so the greatest losses occur at advanced age. The loss in height for men in this study is greater than that found in the Baltimore Longitudinal Study on Aging. Height diminution with age is thought to be attributable to a combination of factors such as water loss, weakening of muscle groups, postural changes, osteoporosis, spinal disk deterioration, and spinal deformities. In women, the predominant cause of decline in height with aging is osteoporosis.

It is important to study cohorts of humans born in the same year because, even though reduction of height with age is still universal, many populations have shown an increase in average height at almost every age in the past hundred years. The magnitude of this trend can be appreciated when one realizes that the average height of American army recruits increased by 0.7 inch between the two world wars and by a further half-inch by 1958—a total gain in forty-four years of 1.2 inches! At that rate the average height for men will exceed six feet before the end of the twenty-first century. The cause of this general increase in stature, which has been observed in both men and women, is unknown. Many specialists believe that it can be attributed to better nutrition, but that is only speculation. Whatever the cause, one cannot avoid the conclusion that the human species is becoming taller and that the rate of increase has risen dramatically in recent years.

WEIGHT

Virtually every study done has shown that weight increases in the middle years and decreases in old age. In a U.S. Health Examination Survey done in 1965, men achieved a maximum average weight of 172 pounds in the thirty-four to fifty-four age range. This declined to 166 pounds between fifty-five and sixty-four years of age, 160 pounds between sixty-five and seventy-four, and 140 pounds between ages seventy-five and seventy-nine. The women studied showed different results. The average weight in the twenty-five to thirty-four age range was 136 pounds. This rose to a maximum of 152 pounds between ages fifty-five and sixty-four. It then dropped to 146 pounds between ages sixty-five and seventy-four and 138 pounds between ages seventy-five and seventy-nine.

The fiftieth percentile (the value which an equal number of subjects fall above and below) of weight for women aged twenty-five to thirty-four was 130 pounds and for women seventy-five to seventy-nine, 137 pounds. For males, it was 168 pounds between twenty-five and thirty-four years of age and 146 pounds between seventy-five and seventy-nine.

CHEST SIZE

In general, chest diameter, circumference, and depth increases with age in both men and women.

ARM SPAN

The proportion of the outstretched arm span to height at maturity has been appreciated since Roman times and is represented in a famous drawing by Leonardo da Vinci. The length of the outstretched arm span diminishes less with age than does height.

FACE

Several studies have shown that both the nose and ears elongate with age. Other facial dimensions do not appear to change significantly after about age fifty.

SKULL

The several bones of the skull are separated from each other but are attached by fibrous joints called sutures. Many of these sutures start to fuse at ages seventy, eighty, or ninety. The bones of the skull also appear to thicken with age. Two longitudinal studies have shown that the circumference, breadth, and length of the head increase with age in both sexes.

SKELETON

Growth of some rib bones continues in some people until the seventh decade. In most people, the second of the five cylindrical bones that comprise the palm widens into the eighties.

BODY COMPOSITION

According to cross-sectional studies, internal organs become smaller with age, but until longitudinal studies are done this finding is suspect. For some organs—the prostate, heart, and lungs—enlargement is more common. There is general agreement, despite the lack of a longitudinal study, that the brain and kidneys diminish in size. Skin folds increase and muscle mass decreases. For obscure reasons, the amount of the element potassium present in our bodies declines with age; some researchers believe that it is related to the replacement of muscle tissue over time with fat and connective tissue. I am unaware of any studies designed to show whether diets supplemented with potassium would reverse this trend.

BODY WATER

One possible cause of the organ shrinkage, diminution of height, and lowered weight seen in most older people is the loss of body water. In young men, about 61 percent of body weight is water. Men aged fifty-seven to eighty-six were found to have 54 percent of their body weight as water. In young women, 51 percent of body weight is water. In women aged sixty to eighty-two, water represents about 46 percent of body weight. The loss of water with age may be due to the actual loss of cells with age or due to their reduced size. Because more than 50 percent of us is water, and about 30 percent of our protein is a cement substance called collagen that holds our cells together, it is surprising that there is enough mass left over to make us what we are!

The stuff of which all of our cells are composed is a complex gel called protoplasm. It was once thought that age changes occurred as water left this protoplasmic gel, causing all kinds of mischief that interfered with the cell's ability to function properly. As attractive as this hypothesis may be, there is no direct evidence that loss of water, per se, causes age changes.

SKIN

Although there are age-associated skin diseases, normal aged skin is not clinically significant. "It is not clear why one should bother to study cutaneous aging. After all, no one dies of old skin! The skin never really wears out or falls off. There is heart failure but not skin failure. We are well packaged to the very end," says Albert Kligman, a prominent dermatologist at the University of Pennsylvania, adding, "Everyone wants to live a long life, but no one wants to look old."

No one dies of old skin, but the skin does show dramatic changes with age. It is the organ the appearance of which frequently determines our stereotyped conclusions about a person's age. Its discoloration, wrinkled state, and deterioration are commonly regarded as a reflection of chronological age and even of general health. Other than clothing, the skin is most of what we see when we look at a fellow human being. It is for all these reasons that aging in humans is first recognized in the skin.

Two-thirds of all people over seventy years of age have skin conditions serious enough to make them seek out a physician. Many elderly have multiple skin conditions. Dryness and itching are exceedingly common complaints; the appearance of callouses, corns, athlete's foot, and changes in the nails also prompt older people to seek treatment.

Wrinkles

The first sign of wrinkles strikes terror into the hearts of many people. The true blame for this response, however, lies not with wrinkles but with our society's devaluation of older women and older men. Wounded vanity may have profound psychological effects leading to a loss of self-image and consequent changes in social interactions. In time, however, vanity usually gives way to acceptance and a more sensible response to the change.

Most skin lesions afflicting the elderly are preventable. With few exceptions, they are not the result of normal aging but represent an accumulation of environmental insults. The main cause of the skin changes that we see as a person ages is the ultraviolet component of sunlight, which produces an effect called photoaging or extrinsic aging. The effect is greatest on skin exposed to the sun and least common on unexposed areas like the buttocks. People who worship the sun in their youth will pay the price with deeper and earlier wrinkling in later life. That is why dermatologists recommend that everyone, regardless of how naturally dark their skin might be, use high-protection sunscreens every day, even in the winter. Sunscreens (or, even more effective, staying out of the sun) can also prevent the occurrence of skin cancer and its most dangerous manifestation, melanoma.

Although there is some dispute, the characteristic wrinkles of old age are believed to be caused by losses of a protein called collagen. Collagen is so abundant in the body that it forms the basis of a theory of aging that will be considered later. In addition to collagen loss, skin wrinkling is induced by the overgrowth of another protein, called elastin. Elastin increases in amount in sun-damaged skin and changes substantially with age, leading to both wrinkles and sagging skin. Photoaging—damage due to ultraviolet light—exacerbates the wrinkles. Even the way you sleep may affect the creases that run vertically on the face.

You can demonstrate the reduced suppleness and loss of elasticity in your skin as it ages. After pinching the skin on the back of your hand hard for several seconds, measure the number of seconds it takes to retract to its original smoothness. In a cross-sectional study it will take approximately two seconds until the age of about forty-five. At later ages the time increases rapidly, to about twenty seconds at age sixty-five and fifty seconds at age seventy. This time change is too inaccurate to be used as the much sought after biomarker of aging. Furthermore, the rate of skin retraction may be an indication of the rate of aging only in the skin and not in other parts of the body.

Some wrinkling is related to use. Habitual facial expressions like smiling and frowning accentuate the formation of wrinkles at right angles to the pull of the muscles used. This accounts for wrinkles of the forehead, "purse string" wrinkles around the mouth, and wrinkles that radiate from the corners of the eye. Other muscles in the face, chin, and neck are thought to cause wrinkles that parallel the direction of muscle pulls in those areas. Other wrinkles do not seem to be related to muscle use. A good example is the ear lobe, which frequently enlarges with age and develops wrinkles. Irregular or crisscross wrinkles elsewhere on the face, where facial muscles do not seem to play a role, may result from changes in underlying fat and connective tissue.

The skin is composed of two main layers. The outermost layer is called the epidermis and the layer beneath it is called the dermis. The epidermis is covered by a thin layer of dead cells that are sloughed constantly and replaced by new cells generated just below the surface. The dermis is a thicker layer and is where the hair, sweat glands, and sebaceous glands originate. Collagen is present in this layer.

The epidermis and the dermis appear to get thinner in old age. The dermis thins in old age because the number of dermal cells diminishes. Males have a thicker dermis than do females, which may be why female facial skin seems to deteriorate more quickly with age.

Sweat Glands

The aged sweat less because many sweat glands either disappear or become nonfunctional. The ability of each remaining gland to produce sweat as the temperature rises decreases with age. These are the main reasons why older people are at greater risk for heat stroke. The apocrine sweat glands, located in the armpits, are controlled by an androgen hormone, which begins to function during puberty. Apocrine sweat provides a substrate for bacteria, which is the source of the familiar acrid, pungent, human body odor. Androgen production slows in old age, especially in women after menopause. Thus, as pointed out by Albert Kligman and his colleagues, the elderly have less body odor and can stop using deodorants. This is one of the unsung benefits of growing old.

Temperature Control

Beneath the epidermis and dermis is a third skin layer called the subcutis. In addition to its role as a fat storage depot, it serves as a shock absorber and controls the loss of body heat. Much of the subcutis is lost with age, especially on the back of the hands, the face, and the soles of the feet. It is likely that the losses on the soles of the feet increase the trauma of walking and amplify foot problems in the elderly.

There is some reason to believe that the nerve cells in the skin become less efficient with age. This may explain why older people are less sensitive to skin pain than are younger adults. Burns tend to be more serious in the aged because reduced sensitivity to heat or pain increases the withdrawal reaction time. Touch sensitivity is also known to be reduced in older people.

The density of the skin's blood circulating system, consisting of small veins, capillaries, and arterioles, is reduced as we age. It is also the probable reason why older people feel cold sooner when the temperature falls. For older people a comfortable temperature is often ten or fifteen degrees higher than what would be comfortable for a younger person. Facial skin temperature has been found to drop with age. Measurements made of skin temperature from the groin area to the feet in older women revealed a temperature gradient much larger than that found in young adults. The average skin temperature drop from the groin to the feet was about sixteen degrees, and in some women it was as much as twenty-nine degrees. Every older person knows how fast his or her feet get cold when the temperature drops, but we do not know for certain why the temperature gradient occurs.

A more serious, potentially lethal, consequence of cold sensitivity in old age is hypothermia, which occurs when body temperature falls below a safe level. Even a short exposure to temperatures near freezing or to conditions in which body heat is wicked away—for example, wet clothes or a brisk wind—may produce this condition in some older people, who may not even realize they are at risk. Young people challenged by the cold survive because their tiny skin blood vessels constrict more, their muscles shiver more, and these reactions help generate more body heat.

Healing Capacity

A less efficient nerve response in older skin coupled with a decline in the immune system may also account for a reduced or slower inflammatory response to irritants. This reduced capacity of the early warning system may result in older persons exposing themselves longer to an irritant before a warning sign like redness appears. Then it may be too late to prevent some serious outcome.

Wound repair in the elderly is slower than in younger people, and the strength of the wound itself (resistance to tearing) is less until the healing process is completed, but the eventual repairs are equally good. An operation on an older person is rarely ruled out solely because of considerations about healing of the wound.

In general, the changes that occur in normal skin with age are restricted to areas of the body that are not usually covered with clothing. The main cause of the changes in exposed skin is not so much age as the ultraviolet radiation of the sun. Striking evidence for this has been found in experiments in which human skin cells were grown in laboratory bottles. Cells grown from skin obtained from areas protected from the sun (like the underarm) have a much greater growth capacity than do cells taken from the skin of the same person that was commonly exposed to the sun. Sun truly ages the skin in ways detectable even at the cellular level.

FINGERNAILS

Norman Orentreich, of the Orentreich Foundation for the Advancement of Science in New York City, and his colleagues have found that from the age of about thirty to the nineties fingernail growth slows by about 50 percent. Until age sixty, males have more rapid nail growth than females. After age eighty, nail growth in females exceeds that in males. Interestingly, in a study of people in the northeastern United States, nail growth slows at night and is greatest in November and least in July. W. B. Bean, who studied his left thumbnail from age thirty-two to sixty-eight, found seven-year cycles in which constant nail growth alternated with a declining growth rate. In youth, nails grow at a rate of roughly one millimeter per week. Many factors other than age may influence the rate of fingernail growth. Faster than average fingernail growth occurs in pianists and typists. Slower nail growth occurs in the first and fifth digits, in severe cold weather, and in the presence of several kinds of diseases. Height, weight, skin color, and use of nail polish and polish remover seem to have no effect.

Most changes that occur in the fingernails with age, such as dullness, color change (to yellowish or gray), longitudinal ridging, and splitting may be considered normal. Some dermatologists believe that they may be due to previous excessive exposure to the sun or to nutritional, temperature, or hormonal effects.

No changes in nail growth occur as a function of age in hamsters, guinea pigs, or rats. An increase in nail growth is found to occur in mice and rabbits as they age. The growth rate of the nail, or claw, of the beagle dog, however, diminishes with age.

Toenails grow at a rate one-quarter that of fingernails, or about one millimeter per month. In the few studies that have been done, toenail growth does not seem to change much with age.

HAIR

The changes that occur in hair growth with age are an unsolved riddle. The mystery deepens when we realize that hair growth decreases in some parts of the body but increases in others. The growth of hair on the scalp generally diminishes, but, hair nearby—in the ears, nostrils, and eyebrows—may undergo a burst of continuous growth. The suggestion that changes in the output of the sex hormones with age account for these changes is difficult to defend because of the contrasting changes that occur within such a small area. Perhaps the hormone receptors on the hair cells themselves change with age and account for this varied response; this, however, is only speculation.

In many women, hair growth above the upper lip occurs as the concentration of the female hormone estrogen falls after menopause. This is particularly demoralizing to many aging women, who try an assortment of techniques to rid themselves of facial hair that our society teaches them to consider unsightly. By age fifty-five about 40 percent of women develop a coarse facial hair which does not subsequently increase.

In general, however, body hairs become less numerous with age. Changes in color and growth patterns also occur. These changes are clearly different in men and women. Pattern baldness—that is, losing hair on the scalp—usually occurs in young men; it is genetically determined and appears to be related to changes in levels of androgen, the male hormone. Later in life, slower growth and loss of hair frequently occur in both sexes and do not seem to be genetically induced. Axillary hair, or hair in the armpits, tends to lessen as we age and, in older women, it often disappears. Racial differences play a large role in hair pattern growth and loss with age. For example, in postmenopausal Japanese women, axillary hair virtually disappears. Pubic hair is lost in a small percentage of women over age sixty, but is rarely absent in similarly aged men.

In youth, the human scalp has approximately a hundred thousand hairs; blonds have slightly more, redheads slightly fewer. The average period of growth for a scalp hair is one thousand days. However, scalp hairs are not always in an active stage of growth. The resting phase lasts about one hundred days, so at any time 10 percent, or ten thousand scalp hairs, are not growing. Hair is shed at a rate of about one hundred hairs per day. Studies of human scalp hair have revealed that with age, hair density, diameter, and breaking strength decrease. The percentage of coarse hairs decreases, that of fine hairs increases. Fewer hairs are found to be growing, more to be resting. Variations in the rates of these changes are well known. For example, the number of hairs lost per week may be twice as great in November as in June.

Graying of the hair is probably the most conspicuous sign of aging, but it is by no means universal nor does it occur at the same time in all people. It is caused by the loss of melanin-producing cells and the consequent loss of melanin. Melanin, produced by cells in the hair bulb (the tiny collection of cells in the skin from which the nonliving strand of hair grows), is a pigment that gives color to the hair and skin. Graying usually begins at the temples, then extends upwards to the top of the scalp. Axillary hair graying is common in men and rare in women.

In over fifty measurements of age changes one group of researchers found that graying of scalp hair was the most reliable indicator of the aging process. Yet, it only correlated about 65 percent with old age; 35 percent of older people are not gray, or do not become gray, until they are very old.

HEARING

The sense of hearing changes with age in most people. Just as the ability to see clearly the fine print in newspapers decreases as time passes (see the section on "Sight," later in this chapter), a decrease occurs in the ability to hear the higher frequencies (presbycusis). Neither of these changes is considered to be a disease. At the worst they might be considered annoyances. If you are not in the habit of looking at things close up, or you are not an audiophile who listens to the higher frequencies (3000 to 4000 hertz or higher), these changes might even go unnoticed, at least at first.

In most people, the ability to hear the higher sound frequencies begins to diminish in the thirties. However, there is considerable variation when the process begins and in the rate at which it occurs. In one large study, from two to five times more men, aged thirty to fifty-nine, showed a decline in ability to hear the higher notes than did women, and, whatever level of loss was found, it increased from one and a half to four times more in each subsequent decade. Age-related sensory changes can be traced to degeneration in some of the cells and cell products that compose the sense organ itself.

The diminution in ability to hear high notes is accompanied by a decreased ability to hear louder sounds. Loudness is measured in decibels (dB) and hearing loss is measured in the same way. A decrease in the ability to hear of more than 20 dB from a normal value is generally regarded as an early sign of impairment. A loss of 30 dB makes for some difficulty hearing, but a slightly louder voice will still be heard. At a loss of 40 dB normal conversation is not easily heard if there is other background noise. With a 50 dB loss there is considerable difficulty in hearing a normal voice, but loud speech can be understood with some lipreading. With more than a 50 dB loss it is not possible to hear either normal speech or very loud voices.

The vowel sounds of words are generally heard in the lower notes and consonant sounds mainly in the higher range. Because most of the information in speech is encoded in the consonant sounds, the loss of high-frequency hearing makes speech unintelligible. About one-third of people over age sixty-five have hearing impaired to the extent that some unfavorable social consequences occur. Interestingly, a substantial number of older people who believe they have a hearing loss actually suffer from blockage of the ear canal by the normal buildup of wax.

Many people can estimate the age of an older person from the sound of his or her voice, based on such signs as a lower pitch for females, a higher pitch for males, increased hoarseness, changes in the rate of speaking, and imprecise articulation.

TASTE

Contrary to previous beliefs, there does not seem to be a loss in the number of taste buds in older people compared to young adults. The belief that a loss occurs has been explained by the enormous variation in taste bud density on the tongues of humans regardless of age. The decreased ability to detect different tastes with age is not due to a decrease in the number of taste buds, but rather to degenerative changes within the individual cells that make up the taste bud. This illustrates once again the danger in drawing conclusions from cross-sectional data.

The ability to detect the four primary tastes (salt, sweet, bitter, and sour) decreases slightly with age but, again, there are large individual differences. In one study, older people were found to require from six to ten times the concentration of certain flavors to identify their source than did younger people. (The flavors used were cherry, grape, lemon, orange, tomato, bacon, cheddar cheese, chocolate, and mushroom.) Deficits in taste perception can frequently be traced to diseases or to the side effects of medications.

SMELL

A gradual decline with age in the ability to detect odors has been reported in most studies. The loss is not only in the ability to detect weak odors but a diminution in the ability to appreciate the magnitude of strong odors. The ability to identify different odors also diminishes with age. In one study, 45 percent of old people and only 4 percent of young people failed a test to identify the odors of cheese, chocolate, peppermint, and sardines. The loss of ability to detect odors appears to begin much earlier than other sensory losses. Diminished performance in odor detection has been found to begin in the early twenties. At any age women perform better than men.

All of these studies on the sense of smell are cross-sectional, and only longitudinal studies will provide a more conclusive understanding. Some perfumers and wine and other tasters claim that their odor detection facilities have not changed with age, but we lack an objective way to measure this. If they are right the explanation might be found in the principle "use it or lose it."

The failure in odor detection and identification might be attributable to degeneration of some cells in the organs that detect odor; another possibility might be the loss of brain cells associated with the sense of smell. The memory for faces is far less affected in the elderly than is the memory for odors. The difficulty of accurately determining losses in smell or taste with age is often complicated by illnesses present in the population studied.

Loss of the ability to detect odors is not only bothersome but also potentially life-threatening. Older people may be at risk if they fail to detect the odor of leaking gas or smoke.

There is some reason to believe that odors first detected in youth are better remembered in old age than odors first detected in later life. Similarly, the memory of youthful experiences is better retained than the memory of experiences in middle age.

SIGHT

Some gerontologists believe that it is not the graying of the hair but changes in the lens of the eye that come closest to being a universal normal age change in humans. The main finding is that the lens becomes thicker and heavier with age, reducing the ability to focus on close-up objects. The condition, called presbyopia, occurs in about 42 percent of people aged fifty-two to sixty-four, 73 percent of people aged sixty-five to seventy-four, and 92 percent of people aged seventy-five and over. Your first indication may be an inability to read the fine print in a newspaper held at the usual distance from your eyes—you find yourself holding the paper farther from your eyes to focus the image. The remedy is lenses that magnify things to be seen close up.

The formation of cataracts, caused by a change in the protein structure of the lens, is generally considered to be a disease, although some believe that if you live long enough its occurrence is inevitable. This is one of several examples that illustrate the difficulty in distinguishing between some normal age changes and disease. Other ocular changes that occur with age include an increase in pressure in the anterior chamber of the eye and decreased light transmission, both of which are arguably normal.

SLEEP

Sleep researchers have discovered that our eyes actually move under our closed lids as we sleep and that the rate of these movements discloses much about the depth of sleep. Rapid eye movement sleep is called REM, and nonrapid eye movement sleep is called NREM. The latter is divided into four stages. In normal young adults, about the first eighty minutes of sleep is in the NREM state. REM sleep then occurs and the two states alternate about every ninety to one hundred minutes. With age, changes occur in the amount of sleep and the distribution of the two sleep states. A normal older person usually experiences more frequent and longer periods of wakefulness and spends more time in the earliest stage of NREM sleep and much less in the last of the four stages of NREM sleep. The amount of time spent in the REM state seems to correlate well with general well-being. REM time seems to decrease with reduced intellectual function associated with organic brain syndrome (senile dementia) and some other physiological activities.

Older people usually spend more time in bed at night without attempting to sleep or unsuccessfully trying to sleep. Compared to young adults, older people also spend more time resting or napping during the day. After once falling asleep older people have greatly increased amounts of wakefulness, and the number of times that they wake up after first falling asleep increases. The number of midsleep awakenings is much greater for men than for women. One interesting experiment revealed that the threshold of arousal from sleep diminishes with age. A loud noise was used to determine how easily groups of young, middle-aged, and older volunteers could be awakened. The older group of both men and women awoke much more easily than did the two younger groups. Apparently, as we grow older we do not sleep as deeply. I am not aware of studies in which strong light or touch were used to provoke arousal.

Recently, it has been found that disturbances in breathing or respiration during sleep increase greatly with age. These disturbances are momentary stops (called apnea) in the normal breathing pattern. In a group of healthy men and women ranging in age from sixty-two to eighty-six, one-third experienced five to ten interruptions per hour in their sleep caused by disordered breathing. No difference was observed between men and women. These breathing disturbances might be the cause of the fragmented sleeping patterns that increase with age. The most important unanswered question remains, What is a normal sleeping and breathing pattern for a healthy older person?

Snoring almost always indicates an abnormality somewhere in the breathing airway. The condition can be serious because changes in blood chemistry caused by interference with the body's intake of oxygen can lead to other health problems. In one study, lifelong snoring was found to be a risk factor for developing cardiovascular disease and hypertension. The frequency of snoring increases with age; almost 60 percent of men in their sixties and 45 percent of similarly aged women are habitual snorers.

Another condition common in healthy old people, sometimes called restless leg syndrome, is marked by leg movements with a periodicity of twenty to forty seconds during sleep. Each movement may be accompanied by a brief arousal from sleep. Little is known about the cause of this condition which, in one random sample of people over sixty-five, occurred in one-third of the group.

Much of what we know about changes in our sleeping patterns with age is determined by observation or anecdote, and causes have not yet been established. Accurate description of biological events is a vital first step to understanding their cause, but studies on sleep in the elderly have not yet gone much beyond this descriptive stage.

NUTRITION

Only within recent years have the effects of aging on human nutrition commanded the attention of scientists. However, it has been known for some time that nutrition does influence such major diseases of old age as cardiovascular disease and some forms of cancer. One fact about the relationship of aging to nutrition in humans seems clear: food intake decreases with age. In the Baltimore Longitudinal Study on Aging it was found that the optimum energy intake of twenty-seven hundred calories per day at age thirty declined linearly to twenty-one hundred calories per day at age eighty. Caloric needs decrease with age in part because of a decline in physical activity. We know much less about the nutritional requirements of the elderly than about those of infants, children, and young adults. We don't even know whether the natural tendency of older people to eat less puts them at or below safe nutritional levels.

The amount of body fat increases up to about age sixty. Conversely protein, or lean body mass, decreases at a rate of about six pounds per decade from early adulthood. Most of the lean tissue loss represents lost muscle mass. Seventy-year-old men have about twenty pounds less muscle mass than they had when they were forty and about seven and a half pounds more fat and connective tissue. Bone mass commonly is also lost with age. Many other changes occur in the composition of the body with age, which, taken together, affect nutritional requirements. Malnutrition in older people is not unknown and may be caused by several factors: ignorance of the requirements for a balanced diet, poverty, loss of interest in food caused by social isolation, physical restrictions limiting the ability to obtain food, mental disorders, malabsorption of food due to intestinal conditions, substitution of alcohol as an energy source, losses in the senses of taste and smell, and use of therapeutic drugs that influence appetite, digestion, or absorption.

METABOLISM

Metabolism is the sum of all of the numerous and complex chemical events that occur in a living organism. The aspect of metabolism that is most important in aging is how the fuel that runs our bodies is stored and utilized. The rate at which fuel is utilized to provide energy for all of our physiological activities is called the metabolic rate. It is not unlike the rate of gasoline consumption by which we measure the efficiency of our cars. In cars we calculate fuel efficiency in miles-per-gallon; we express our basal metabolic rate as the number of kilocalories of energy expended per square meter of body surface per hour. Measurements of metabolic rate, like measurements of gasoline consumption, must be made under standard conditions so that the results can be meaningfully compared; we wouldn't learn much by measuring the gas consumption of one car as it climbed a mountain and another as it descended.

The basal metabolic rate, often abbreviated as BMR, decreases slightly with increasing age and has often been an important component of theories of aging. In 1928, Raymond Pearl proposed the "rate of living" hypothesis of aging. He argued that length of life is determined by the exhaustion of some vital substance that is consumed at a rate proportional to the metabolic rate. The theory has fallen into disfavor because there is now much evidence that contradicts it. However, in mammals there is a tendency for maximum life span to be greatest for species in which the BMR is lowest. Many believe that a slow-moving tortoise outlives a fast-moving hare because the former has a much slower metabolic rate. However, this is only partly true, because other important factors also play a role in life span. As we will learn later, brain weight in proportion to body weight and the BMR are two significant parts of a three-term equation—the third term is body temperature—that accurately describes the maximum longevity of virtually all vertebrates.

One interesting test of the relationship between BMR and longevity was done with hibernating hamsters. During hibernation the BMR drops considerably, so that one might expect that the animals that hibernate longest would live the longest. This is, in fact, exactly what happened. One group of hamsters was kept at room temperature and, as expected, did not hibernate. The second group was kept at a temperature close to freezing for six months of the year. Not all of the animals kept in the cold hibernated all of the time. When they were divided into three groups depending on the length of their hibernation, it was found that those that hibernated longest lived the longest. The shortest-lived hamsters were those kept at room temperature, which didn't hibernate at all. The same effect has been seen when fruit flies and domestic houseflies are kept at various temperatures. Although these insects do not hibernate, their BMR is lower at lower temperatures and, thus, they live longer.

When the domestic housefly and the fruit fly are made to undergo varying amounts of physical activity, which increases their BMR, it has been found that the greater the amount of physical activity, the shorter their life span. However, the opposite result has been found to occur in rats made to undergo various amounts of exercise. There was a small increase in the length of life of the animals that exercised most. One cannot extrapolate these results to humans, and we have no reliable evidence that there is either a positive or negative correlation between exercise and longevity. This important issue will be addressed in chapter 17.

Restricting the intake of calories increases the longevity of animals, but whether or not caloric restriction in humans is associated with changes in the BMR will also be discussed later.

Aging is frequently associated with a reduced ability to adapt to environmental changes. Conditions we easily adapt to in youth—say, the rigors of stress, pneumonia, or the flu—become more difficult to tolerate in old age. This difference is also apparent at the molecular level. Several years ago Richard Adelman, now at the University of Michigan, found that with age a vital class of proteins called enzymes are less able to adapt to changes they encounter in the proteins on which they act. Enzymes are catalysts of metabolic reactions. Without enzymes life would not be possible. Like the changes in individual cells described earlier, the reduced capacity of enzymes to adapt to change is an example of how the aging phenomenon manifests itself at the cellular and molecular levels.

Our bodies contain large stores of fuel in the form of fat tissue, which we metabolize during exercise and fasting. As we age, the mass of fat stored generally increases until age fifty or so. The results of several studies on stored fat after that age are inconclusive. As discussed previously, the Baltimore Longitudinal Study on Aging has found that in the middle years a modest increase in fat mass over that considered ideal in the old height-weight tables favors increased longevity. Gross obesity of course, reduces life expectation.

During times of starvation, when we run out of carbohydrate fuel our fat reserves will be consumed. If we then run out of fat, as a last resort, we will metabolize our proteins. Because we have no reserve stores of protein, the body will, in a sense, cannibalize itself, utilizing proteins that make up the structure of our cells or that are used in vital life processes.

CAPACITY FOR EXERCISE

Exercise tolerance and performance usually decrease with age. There is good reason for this. More than 150 years ago it was found that between the ages of thirty and eighty muscle strength decreases 30 to 40 percent in men and to a lesser degree in women. Grip strength is a good example. In men a force of about one hundred pounds is maintained from sixteen to forty-five years of age. This drops to about seventy-five pounds at age fifty-five and to fifty pounds at age seventy-five. In women the overall grip strength is also reduced with age. The loss in strength correlates well with loss of actual muscle mass as animals and humans age.

Maximum aerobic capacity generally decreases with age. However, older people who are physically active have aerobic capacities far greater than do similarly aged, or even younger, sedentary people, and their reaction and movement times are superior. In these respects physically active older people have exercise capacities similar to younger active people. This means that some physiological processes that decline with age can be modified with exercise and physical conditioning: we can improve cardiac efficiency, pulmonary function, and bone calcium levels. Nevertheless, despite the health benefits of exercise there is no good evidence that life expectation is increased in physically active older people. If it were, we would expect to find that all, or most, of our oldest people are, or were, physically active, and this is not true. Most, in fact, are sedentary. In chapter 17 we will consider, in detail, the effects of exercise on aging and longevity.

CHRONIC DISEASES

The chronic diseases most likely to afflict older people have been determined in extensive surveys conducted by the National Center for Health Statistics. The latest results (table 11–1), for 1985, are quite revealing.

One striking observation is that more than one-third of men and one-half of women over age sixty-five report some form of arthritis. About one-third of people over sixty-five report hearing impairment, hypertension, or heart disease. Many people in the study had more than one condition.

TABLE 11-1. Percentage of people over age 65 with various chronic conditions

Condition	% Men	% Women
Arthritis	36	55
Hearing impairment	36	25
Hypertension	35	46
Heart disease	33	29
Limb deformity	14	19
Cataracts	10	21
Visual impairment	10	9
Emphysema	8	2
Cerebrovascular disease	8	5
Ulcers	4	3
Glaucoma	3	4
Frequent constipation	3	7
Gastritis	1	3
Bone and cartilage disorders	0.7	3

AGING HAS ITS COMPENSATIONS

An essential feature of the aging process is the phenomenon of compensation. When a group of cells, a tissue, or part of an organ loses function, other groups frequently take over the job. This phenomenon is not restricted to age-related losses, and many other examples are known in which undamaged cells, tissues, or organs compensate for the loss or diminished use of an injured part of the body. Take, for example, the aftermath of a nonfatal heart attack. A heart attack is caused when the blood supply to part of the heart is blocked and the cells or tissue previously fed by that blood supply become injured or die. Compensation occurs when adjacent veins and arteries take over the job that the dead tissue is no longer capable of doing.

Many of the normal changes that occur as we age are the result of the body's attempts to compensate for some normal loss. For example, with increasing age, greater cardiac output is required after exercise because the blood vessels are not as supple as they were in youth. Both men and women develop a thickening of the left ventricular heart wall because the heart muscle must increase in strength in order to work harder. Compensation for normal age losses in physiological capacity occurs at virtually every level in our body. But, compensation, too, has its limits. Beyond those limits, further age changes are not compensated for and the inexorable forces of aging and mortality continue unchecked.

In part 4 we will examine why we age and the theories that have been proposed to explain the phenomenon.

PART FOUR

Why Do We Age?

CHAPTER 12

Centenarians and Supercentenarians

> With a little luck, there's no reason why you can't live to be one hundred. Once you've done that, you've got it made, because very few people die over one hundred.
>
> —George Burns

FTER performing the miracles that take us from conception to birth and then to sexual maturation and adulthood, nature chose not to devise what would seem to be a more elementary mechanism to simply maintain those miracles forever. This insight has puzzled biogerontologists for decades.

Virtually all biological events from conception to maturity seem to have a purpose, but aging does not. It is not obvious why aging should occur. Although we have learned much about the biology of aging and that it is possible, within limits, to increase our life expectation, we are still left with the inevitable outcome of purposeless aging followed by death. Our primitive ancestors probably began thinking about aging and death as soon as they realized that even those rare individuals fortunate enough to survive predators, starvation, accidents, diseases, and wars eventually changed and did not live forever.

SUPERLONGEVITY THROUGHOUT THE AGES

Most societies can trace their attitudes about aging and death to a primitive belief that they *were* once immortal, but that some folly committed by an ancestor caused an offended deity to punish the descendants with mortality. The story of Adam and Eve is illustrative of this pattern. One early means of confronting the fact of human mortality was to plead for supernatural intervention, attempting to placate the offended god and so regain immortality or obtain resurrection from the grave. This central concern may have been the origin of religion itself.

Legends and myths are at the heart of early human thought about aging and the prolongation of life. Literature and oral tradition have often expressed ideas about the existence of a time or place where some people live forever or for enormous lengths of time. This recurring theme is well exemplified by the life spans reported for the ten patriarchs in Genesis (5:3–32, 9:29), ranging from 365 years for Enoch to 969 years for Methuselah—well in excess of the baseline for superlongevity, 115 years. Noah is claimed to have lived 950 years; Abraham, 175; Isaac, 180; and Jacob, 140. Joseph lived to age 110, Aaron to 123, and Moses to 120. It is not known whether these claims are meant to be taken literally or simply as metaphors for longevity, or whether they are somehow attributable to the widespread use of the lunar calendar in biblical times.

Genesis 6:3 describes God's limitation of the human life span to 120 years; in Psalms 90:10 the life span is given as seventy or eighty years. Some interpreted this decrease to mean that the will of God is to shorten the human life span, not lengthen it.

Ancient people observed that snakes, lizards, beetles, and crabs periodically shed their skins or shells, and concluded that this was a process of rejuvenation. In both Greek (*gérōn*) and Latin (*senectus*) the words for old age refer to the shedding of an animal's skin. Legends about long-lived animals abound. The snake was believed to be capable of rejuvenating itself by periodically shedding its skin, and the eagle to do so by flying to India and bathing in the fountain of youth. Ancient Egyptians believed that a mythical bird, the phoenix, lived a thousand years. Today, several primitive peoples believe that their forefathers once knew how to rejuvenate themselves by shedding their skin like snakes.

Pliny, in the first century B.C., writes of people in the past who lived up to eight hundred years and then, sated with life and luxury, leaped into the sea. The idea of enormous longevity is also prevalent in the literature of ancient India. In those times, when travel was difficult, the exaggerated ages attributed to people living in distant lands or on isolated mountaintops were accepted because they could not easily be disproved. Belief in these exaggerated ages was a major stimulus for some of the ancient explorations to distant lands and unknown seas. On his third voyage, in 1498, Columbus claimed to have found the earthly paradise of immortality on the Venezuelan coast near the island of Trinidad.

The Garden of Eden is, perhaps, the best-known example in Western culture of a paradise in which immortality existed. The Greek legend of the Hyperboreans, which literally means "beyond the north wind," is a good example of belief in a distant land where the inhabitants are extremely longevous. The Hyperborean legend survives in contemporary literature in the 1933 novel *Lost Horizon*. This book by James Hilton, and the movie based on it, describes Shangri-La, a Himalayan paradise of superlongevous people (those who attain ages in excess of the known human life span of about 115 years). To this day there is the belief that in certain parts of Ecuador, the Ukraine, and Pakistan people can be found who have reached great ages (more about that later in this chapter).

Luigi Cornaro and the Spartan Life

The Venetian Luigi Cornaro produced a great contribution to thought about aging when, in the sixteenth century, he wrote a book on health and longevity. Cornaro found himself in poor health when he was about fifty years old and attributed his condition to a disorderly lifestyle, gluttony, and an overindulgence in sensual pleasures. He was warned by his physician that if he did not change his habits, he would die in a few months. In a remarkable about-face, he changed his lifestyle radically to one of temperance, abstinence, and order, and recovered his health completely. At the urging of friends, when he was eighty-three, he wrote a discourse describing his spartan ways. He added to his writings on this subject at the ages of eighty-six, ninety-one, and ninety-five. He died at age ninety-eight.

In his *Discourses on the Temperate Life*, Cornaro wrote that, contrary to the popular belief that life for the elderly was unattractive, "I never knew the world was beautiful until I reached old age." He described extensively the excellent status of his health and his physical and mental agility. His abstemious diet consisted only of bread, meat, broth with eggs, and new wine. The popularity of his book was dependent less on original ideas than on the fact that its author was unique in having attained such an old age and written clearly about how he did so.

As for dieting Cornaro said, "Whosoever wishes to eat much must eat little," meaning that eating little lengthens life, therefore providing more time to eat than would otherwise be possible. He also counseled, "The food from which a man abstains, after he has eaten heartily, is of more benefit to him than that which he has eaten."

Cornaro's writings were enormously popular. They were translated into several languages, and during the eighteenth and nineteenth centuries went through fifty editions in England alone. His work spawned a number of similar books advocating the virtues of an ascetic life as a means of achieving maximum longevity. Cornaro's book continues to be reprinted in the United States to the present day. Belief in his principles is accentuated by the popular conviction that many people have achieved great longevity by leading simple, spartan lives.

The physician, William Harvey, who discovered the circulation of the blood, autopsied Thomas Parr in 1635 and announced ex cathedra that Parr had died at the age of "one hundred and fifty-two years and nine months." Parr had been a poor farmer who had subsisted on a simple diet, been free of worry, and breathed the country air. Harvey believed that Parr's death at 152 years was actually premature and had been brought about by an unfortunate trip to London to be presented to the king, which exposed him to foul air and rich food, to which he was unaccustomed.

Descartes and Bacon

In the seventeenth century the philosopher René Descartes wrote about the possibility that science might find a cure for aging, a goal that he thought was desirable. Descartes seems to have emulated the lifestyle of Cornaro in an effort to increase his own longevity. His concept of the human body, working like a machine and following the laws of mechanics, led to important insights into biological phenomena.

A disciple of Descartes, the English philosopher Francis Bacon, regarded the extension of human longevity as the "most noble" goal of medicine. If it were achieved, physicians would no longer be reduced to administering "humble cures" but rather would be praised for bestowing the greatest of "earthly gifts" on humans. In order to defend himself against possible charges of sacrilege, he added that, although the maximum life span was determined by the Almighty, this did not preclude advocating measures that could help to reach it. (This is a bit like the man who prayed to God to permit him to win the lottery. After many prayers and lost lotteries he heard a booming voice that said, "At least meet me halfway—buy a ticket.")

Bacon published his ideas about a scientific basis for prolonging life in a book entitled *History of Life and Death*. He disdained many of the then-prevalent ideas about the causes of disease and aging. But though he denounced changes in "innate heat" and "innate moisture" as causes, he substituted similar notions. Bacon's book gave great prominence to the notion of increasing longevity because its author was a distinguished person who enjoyed enormous fame. Among his accomplishments, Bacon is given credit for stimulating the establishment of the Royal Society, which became the paradigm for subsequent scientific societies. He was also an early advocate of the replacement of defective organs and speculated on the replacement of old body "juices" as a means of increasing longevity. When Bacon's contemporary, William Harvey, announced his theory of the mechanics of blood circulation, the stage was set for blood transfusions. Of course, the need for asepsis and blood typing was unknown at that time.

Early Blood Transfusions

The historian of aging and longevity, Gerald Gruman, describes what happened next in his monumental work, *A History of Ideas about the Prolongation of Life*:

> The first successful blood transfusions in animals (dogs) were performed by the English physician and physiologist Richard Lower in 1650, and the new skill quickly was applied to trials of rejuvenation. Thus, we read in the *Philosophical Transactions* of the Royal Society of the experiment by Coxen in which "an old mongrel curr, all over-run with the mainge" was transfused with "14–16 oz." of blood from a young spaniel and was "perfectly cured." Similar investigations were reported as follows:
> "Mr. Gayant transfused the blood of a young dog into the veins of an old, which two hours after, did leap and frisk; whereas he was almost blind with age, and could hardly stir before."

From Italy in 1668 came the report that the blood of a lamb had a marvelous restorative effect on a decrepit, thirteen-year-old spaniel.

Meanwhile, the idea had been taken up by Jean Denis, a Paris physician, who attracted attention by a public demonstration of the revitalization of a mangy old canine by blood from a healthy young animal; a like test was carried out on an ancient horse. A supporter of Denis wrote to the *Journal des Savants* advocating the new method as a cure for all sorts of diseases and for rejuvenating the aged, and, during 1667, Denis performed the first human blood transfusion. We know of five cases in which the procedure was tried; curiously enough, none of these were senescent. Undoubtedly, the infusions would have been applied, sooner or later, to aged persons, but Denis' work was brought to an early end by the sudden death of one of his patients; this led to a lawsuit and finally to a moratorium by the powerful Faculty of Medicine on further experiments. Despite a few sporadic, ineffectual efforts by others, the further evolution of transfusion was delayed until the early nineteenth century.

Superlongevous Individuals

There were many reports of superlongevity during the seventeenth and eighteenth centuries. The Countess of Desmond was reputed to have lived beyond 140. And in the nineteenth century the important German physician, Christopher Hufeland, cited records of sixty people over the age of 111, twenty-nine over 120, fifteen over 130, six over 140, and Henry Jenkins, who, he said, died at 169. Most of these people, it was claimed, labored in the fresh country air, ate plain foods, and led simple lives, and this accounted for their extreme longevity. Hufeland maintained that the body is born with only a specific quantity of "vital power" which can be used up quickly or slowly depending on the lifestyle of the owner. One must live extensively, not intensively. This notion continued well into the nineteenth century, when ten "well authenticated" instances of persons reaching ages beyond 150 years were reported.

In the United States, Joice Heth, allegedly born in 1684 in Madagascar, was put on exhibit when 161 years old, by the circus man P. T. Barnum, who claimed that she was a slave of Augustine Washington and the nurse of his son George. In his promotional advertisement, Barnum wrote that she "was the first person to put clothes on the unconscious infant who in after days led our heroic fathers on to glory, to victory, and to freedom. To use her own language when speaking of the Father of his country, 'she raised him.' "

Modern Skepticism

In the late 1800s the tenets of Cornaro and his followers came under heavy fire. Discoveries made in bacteriology and pathology undermined the idea that the simple life was clean and healthy, and the emerging actuarial sciences provided sufficient ammunition to demolish unsubstantiated claims of superlongevity. The turning point in acceptance of such claims seems to have been the publication in 1873 of *Human Longevity: Its Facts and Its Fictions*, by William J. Thoms. Thoms was deputy librarian in the English House of Lords and noted for coining the word "folklore." He blamed physicians for the gullibility in uncritically accepting claims for superlongevity for which he argued there was "not a tittle of evidence."

Thoms was the first to apply critical scientific and historical methods to claims for superlongevity. His arguments rested on data from actuarial tables that were the bedrock of the life insurance industry, founded in England in 1706. He proposed rules for proving claims of great longevity and argued that the poor inhabitants of rural areas, who accounted for most of the claims, were the very people whose birth and death records were most suspect. Thoms insisted on documentary evidence of birth, death, or present age and identity. Since birth certificates were not made compulsory in England until 1837, authentic claims of ages over 115 could be evaluated only after 1952. To date, none have been made.

Thoms disproved the claims made for Thomas Parr, the Countess of Desmond, and Henry Jenkins. This caused a furor, because Henry Jenkins had been honored with a costly monument in a Yorkshire churchyard, and Thomas Parr had been interred in Westminster Abbey, near the grave of Charles Darwin. Neither Parr's remains nor the tablet inscribed with his name were removed. However the uproar provoked Thoms to call himself "one of the best-abused men in England." He insisted that the human life span was no more than one hundred years and that one could not hope to live beyond that age by the expedient of conserving one's "vital powers."

Thoms's unmasking of the superlongevity claims conformed with the revolutionary hypotheses put forth by Darwin less than fifteen years earlier. The notion of natural selection explained that humans and animals, by incurring physiological losses with age, became less fit and more vulnerable to disease and predation.

ARE THERE SUPERLONGEVOUS PEOPLE?

Gerontologists have often thought that one good way of finding out why we age might be to examine the lives of centenarians and those who reach the maximum human life span of about 115 years. Perhaps a common clue might be found that would tell us why the longevous live so long. If we could identify a factor or combination of factors that centenarians have in common, we might be able to infer what it is that delays the aging process or causes extraordinary longevity. That finding, in turn, might provide insights into why we age or, at least, why the rate of aging differs in different people. For example, if we found that all centenarians didn't smoke, didn't drink, exercised every day, ate well-balanced meals, and led a stress-free life, we would then have an important insight into how to achieve our maximum life span. However, no common factor or factors have been found. The oldest old do not have any attribute in common that accounts for their extreme longevity. What further complicates the problem is that many claims to be one hundred years old or older are simply not true. Before studying centenarians, you first must identify some—and this is trickier than you might think.

The popular media to this day often trumpet instances of individuals or groups of people alleged to have life spans far in excess of what gerontologists believe to be the 115-year limit for humans. Gullible or uncritical reporters assume their audience will want to hear these claims, so they repeat them without qualification. The result has been almost universal acceptance of exaggerated or outright false claims. In some cases jingoists in the claimant's homeland have promoted these preposterous stories through pictures on their nation's postage stamps. Several such philatelic advertisements were printed in the USSR, including a 1956 commemorative honoring Mukhamed Eivazov, an Azerbaijani farmer allegedly 147 years old. As recently as 1956 the *New York Times* reported that Xavier Pareira, a Colombian Indian allegedly 167 years old, would visit the city. A postage stamp issued by Colombia in his honor depicted Pareira, as well as his recipe for longevity: "Don't worry, drink lots of coffee, and smoke a good cigar." It seems that the chamber of commerce was more interested in promoting Colombia's chief exports than in telling the truth. Considering what Colombia's most publicized export is now, one wonders what might be printed on that stamp if it were issued today.

Musings about extraordinary longevity are not much different from the long-held belief in some civilizations that races of giant humans exist somewhere in the world. But the myth of giants has been torpedoed, while the idea of superlongevous humans persists. To this day many believe that in certain parts of the world people can be found who have reached great ages. Three specific geographical locations are usually mentioned: (1) the Abkhazia and Ossetia region in the Caucasus of the Georgian Republic in the Commonwealth of Independent States, (2) the Andean village of Vilcabamba in Ecuador, and (3) Hunza in the Karakoram Range in the Pakistani region of Kashmir. Isolated reports of supercentenarians also have surfaced in other countries. These claims of superlongevity are not true and, in view of widespread popular belief to the contrary, it is worth considering how we know they are not true.

In the Caucasus region of Georgia, claims have been made of three to fifteen centenarians *per ten thousand* inhabitants. To appreciate the magnitude of such claims one must realize that in the rest of the Commonwealth of Independent States (C.I.S.) and in Japan and the developed countries of the West, two or three centenarians are found *per hundred thousand* people. Even this rate is probably exaggerated. Also, in these countries, there are no authentic claims of individuals living beyond about 115. In the United States, one person *per million* reaches the age of 105, and only one in forty million will live to be 110. Yet, in the Caucasus, Vilcabamba, and Hunza, not only are higher proportions of centenarians claimed, but many individuals claim ages of 120 to 165 years old or older!

In 1959, the whole Caucasus area reported 4.5 centenarians per 10,000 population, and about five hundred people claimed to be between 120 and 165 years of age. In certain areas of Azerbaijan, claims of thirty to forty centenarians per 10,000 have been made. These claims pale by comparison with those made by the village of Vilcabamba in southern Ecuador. The 1971 census there recorded nine centenarians in this village of 819—or more than one in a hundred! This rate extrapolates to 110 centenarians per 10,000 persons— more than 100 times higher than the United States rate, which itself is almost certainly an exaggeration.

In Hunza, few statistical data are available, and the Hunzukuts, who have no written language, cannot even point to falsified birth certificates. The old Vilcabambans are isolated and their baptismal records were lost in a church fire. One gerontologist who made his second trip to the village, after a lapse of five years, was told by several alleged supercentenarians that during his absence their ages had increased by seven to ten years! Age exaggeration seems to correlate positively with extreme age, illiteracy, and absence of documentation. In Vilcabamba, matters are complicated further because relatively few family names exist—Toledo and Carpio are the most common. Many people have mistaken records of a parent for those of a child, and frequently a child will be given the name of a brother or sister who died earlier. Jose Toledo, who claimed to be 107 in 1970, was officially recorded as being 140 when he died a year later. Miguel Carpio Mendieta, who claimed to be 127 in 1976, was recorded as being 112 at his death.

In a study done in Vilcabamba in 1978, Richard B. Mazess of the University of Wisconsin and Sylvia H. Forman of the University of Massachusetts, found that none of the twenty-three alleged centenarians investigated had, in fact, reached one hundred years of age, and none of the fifteen alleged nonagenarians had reached ninety. Indeed, there was no evidence that anyone in the village had attained one hundred years and even the idea that the total population was unusually long-lived was discounted.

The Georgians' supercentenarian claims have been studied more extensively, and the findings are most revealing. The reasons for their claims are an odd mélange of social mores, pseudoscience, politics, and economics. First, the census data, like that obtained in many other countries, including the United States, relies entirely on verbal statements unsupported by written evidence. Zhores Medvedev, a Russian biogerontologist now retired from the National Institute for Medical Research in London, England, and the originator of the first error theory of aging, has made a detailed study of these claims and much of what follows is based on his findings. He points out that exaggerated age claims are almost always made by poorly educated individuals of lower socioeconomic status. Birth certificates simply did not exist at the time that today's superlongevous claimants were born; internal identity cards came in to use in the Soviet Union in 1932 for urban areas only, and dates of birth were recorded from oral information. Even if birth notations were made in church records or bibles, those names were frequently not used at home. In the Muslim area of the

Caucasus, where supercentenarian claims are most exaggerated, births are not registered at all. Furthermore, people do not use calendar ages in everyday life. It has been suggested that differences between the Gregorian and Muslim calendars caused some misunderstandings when the census takers arrived. In Christian areas of the former Soviet Union, birth records were kept before 1917 in special church registers, but because 90 percent of all churches were destroyed between 1922 and 1940, these records were almost completely lost. Not one of five hundred alleged supercentenarians questioned in the Caucasus could produce a valid document in support of his or her claim.

Westerners who have come to accept the superlongevity claims made in the Georgia censuses have had to rely on the interpretation of official documents by colleagues in the C.I.S. because few scientists in the West are able to read the Abkhasian, Georgian, or Azerbaijani languages. The problem is compounded by the fact that in the pre-glasnost U.S.S.R., challenging official statistical information was not looked upon kindly.

General census statistics in the former Soviet Union clearly show that for the ninety to ninety-nine year age group, the ratio of women to men is three to one, similar to that found in other developed countries. Yet, in the group of alleged Georgian centenarians, this sex ratio is reversed after age one hundred. Either this is a new biological phenomenon unique to these people or, more likely, older men exaggerate their ages more than do older women.

Cultural conditions in the Georgian Republic create strong motivations for age exaggeration, especially when no documentation exists and the few living witnesses are practicing the same deception. Extremely old persons in the region enjoy the highest levels of social authority, and are regarded almost as saints; the older a person is, the more respect and honor he or she receives. This stimulus has been compounded by the national and international attention given to people who make such claims and the villages in which they live. Before glasnost, supercentenarian tales were among the only "human interest" stories to emerge from the Soviet Union. The Novosti press agency sold stories and photographs about supercentenarian bands, choral groups, and dance ensembles for hard currency to its ingenuous Western counterparts. In 1970 it shamelessly reported that the oldest man in the Soviet Union was 165-year-old Shirali Mislimov (who died in 1973, allegedly 168 years old). Although it was by no means alone in its gullibility, *Life* magazine in 1966 published a long photographic essay centered around belief in Mislimov's claim. In 1981, the oldest male was allegedly an Azerbaijani, Yadigyar-Kaslhi, age 135. However, claims of superlongevity are not unique to males. According to *Pravda*, April 11, 1982, the oldest woman was Apruz, from the Azerbaijani village of Kirovsk. She was then allegedly 141 years old. The notoriety that accrued to the Georgian villages where allegedly superlongevous people live was also exploited by the former Soviet travel organization, Intourist, which organized tours and established spas in these regions to raise more hard currency from naive foreigners.

All of these rewards—fame, respect, and profit—have motivated townspeople to press their claims that their village has the oldest resident. The resulting circus atmosphere tends to propel the age claims upward, especially when political considerations are added to the account. Political propaganda unabashedly referred to the existence of centenarians as a special social achievement of the former Soviet Union. Articles appeared in central newspapers and magazines with such titles as "The U.S.S.R.—State of Longevity." Scholarly publications announced that "the Soviet Union is the country with the record longevity of human beings. The number of centenarians is increasing in parallel with our approach to the creation of a Communist Society." It is worth mentioning in this context that life expectation at birth in the former Soviet Union peaked in 1964 and has been declining ever since.

The fact that Joseph Stalin was Georgian is not inconsequential. He was greatly interested in the alleged supercentenarian phenomenon and local Georgian politicians were eager to provide him with information about as many cases as they could. It has been rumored that Stalin believed he shared the qualities of his Georgian comrades and would live well past the century mark. Official propagandists often referred to the alleged superlongevity of Georgians to convince people that a long life was possible for their Dear Wise Teacher.

There is yet another quite reasonable explanation for the origin of exaggerated age claims in the Georgian Republic. During World War I and the Russian Revolution there were hundreds of thousands of deserters and draft dodgers, many of them in the Caucasus. These people are not ethnic Russians and in fact have a tradition of despising them, feelings again made evident with the recent secession of the region from the former Soviet Union. The Caucasians did not want to serve in the Czar's army and chose the obvious course of exaggerating their ages in order to avoid conscription. Many used their fathers' birth records to support the fiction. When the wars ended many continued the masquerade for fear of reprisal, and eventually other benefits, already described, became apparent.

Although supercentenarian age claims have been substantially discredited, there still remains the possibility, remote though it may be, that clusters of legitimate centenarians exist in numbers disproportionately greater than would ordinarily be expected for a given population. If this is true of the three areas noted for exaggerating their ages, it is effectively masked by the exaggerations. In any case, there is no compelling proof that disproportionate numbers of centenarians exist in any part of the world.

The three parts of the world where superlongevity claims are most common are all rural. Some of these country folk may simply take delight in outwitting the city slickers. Many of those who believe the tales of inordinate concentrations of old people are unaware that the phenomenon is usually easy to explain. The younger people in the community may have moved away, probably for economic reasons; the older people may have quite practical reasons—social, political, or economical—to exaggerate their ages.

The United States is not immune from exaggerated age claims. Several examples could be given, but one case—fully documented by the late pioneer gerontologist Joseph T. Freeman, a private medical practitioner in Philadelphia—should suffice. Charlie Smith of Bartow, Florida, died on October 7, 1979, alleged to be 137 years old. Both of his legs had been amputated many years earlier, and he had a bullet in his hip, also of many years duration. In 1961, the Social Security Administration recorded an interview with Charlie Smith in which he claimed to have been born on July 4, 1842. The Social Security Administration was the only possible source of reliable, documented, birth information about Smith. Before Smith's death, Freeman had obtained his permission to receive a copy of the written records, but later the director of the Office of Information of the Social Security Administration replied, "I am very sorry but we goofed. I didn't know at the time of the original request that Charlie Smith's original file that contained those documents used to establish his date of birth had been lost." The Social Security Administration had previously concluded that "benefits based on Social Security credits began to be earned by picking oranges at age 113." However, Smith's marriage certificate, later located in Arcadia, Florida, gave his age on January 8, 1910, as 35. If correct, Smith would have been 104 years of age at his death in 1979. The 1980 edition of the *Guinness Book of World Records* duly eliminated Smith's claim to be the oldest American and in his place put a woman who died in 1928 at an alleged age of 113 years. The evidence used to substantiate this woman's claim is also suspect.

Those who believe that all or some of the supercentenarian age claims are valid have speculated at length on why the superlongevous live so long. Apparently, these diehards are unable to appreciate the absurdity of compounding conjecture with illusion. Scientific inquiry is better served by evaluating the claims of centenarians than chasing after alleged supercentenarians.

WHAT ABOUT CENTENARIANS?

Despite the fact that gerontologists do not believe the claims of supercentenarians, they do believe that a few people reach ages that approach 115 years. We are fascinated with people who live from 100 to 115 not only because they are rare but also because of what we might learn from them about why we age.

Centenarians certainly do exist, but it is often extremely difficult to authenticate their claims. This is less of a problem in many Scandinavian and other European countries, where meticulous birth and death records have been kept for several centuries. In the United States, however, accurate birth and death records are a relatively recent development, and death registration was not required for all states until 1933, when Texas became the last state to become a part of the Federal Death Register.

In Scandinavian countries, death records are directly linked to birth records. That is not done in the United States or most other countries. Linkage is important because it reduces the likelihood that a birth certificate could be said to apply to a person other than the one intended. This may occur under innocent circumstances or with an intention to deceive. Deception is not difficult in the United States because official birth records were not required by the states during the period when our present crop of alleged centenarians was born. Consequently, we must rely on weak evidence for the authenticity of their claims. This evidence might include notations in a family bible or church records, or simply memory; all are notably unreliable and present opportunities for error, exaggeration, or deception. Exaggerated age claims, as indicated earlier, are more often made by people who are illiterate and live in remote areas or regions without an adequate birth registration system.

In the United States, ages are overstated in censuses, on death certificates, and on the medicare and social security rolls. In underdeveloped countries the claims are exaggerated even more. It is not uncommon to find an unusual concentration of age claims around a number divisible by ten. Ansley Cole of Princeton University and Shaomin Li of AT&T cite the example of Iraq, where, in 1957, the census showed 14.4 times as many persons at the age seventy as the mean number of those at ages sixty-nine and seventy-one. A similar clustering of people at ages fifty, sixty, seventy and eighty was reported in the censuses taken in the former Soviet Union. So common is this aberration that it is known to demographers as the "index of accumulation of ages in round numbers." Iraq, with a total population of about 6.3 million in 1957, claimed 5,759 centenarians, while in 1961 West Germany, with a population of 54 million, reported only four hundred centenarians.

There is no absolutely reliable way to determine when a person was born. Birth certificates and even passports can be altered, forged, or fraudulently obtained. The nearest we may ever come to a positive identification that would satisfy the most hard-nosed scientist might be to place on the birth certificate some form of unalterable biological evidence of the identity of the named individual: the baby's footprint, handprint, or fingerprint, or better still, a DNA profile, now known to be unique for each individual. However, even these measures would probably not dissuade a determined cheater.

There are undoubtedly many centenarians, but skepticism should be exercised when considering people's claims to be members of this elite group.

THE INCREASED LIKELIHOOD OF
REACHING AGE ONE HUNDRED

Census Bureau and Social Security Administration data indicate that centenarians and the oldest old are among the fastest-growing groups of Americans. The population aged eighty-five and over is predicted to grow over sixfold from 1980 to 2080, while the number of centenarians will grow seventy-five-fold: In 1980 there were about 14,200 centenarians in the United States, in 1986 about 25,000. If present assumptions about the composition of future populations are correct, there will be over 100,000 by the year 2000 and, by 2080, over one million centenarians!

Some skepticism is appropriate here, however. Birth certificates have not been in use in this country long enough to unequivocally validate even Census Bureau and Social Security Administration data. Both depend on suspect evidence and verbal claims for the ages of the oldest members of their constituencies. With this important caveat, the "official" data for the United States look like this: Since 1950 the number of sixty-five-year-olds has more than doubled, the number of eighty-five-year-olds has quintupled, and the number of centenarians has increased tenfold. Despite this impressive growth rate, the total number of centenarians is still small in respect to our entire population. According to the Bureau of the Census, in 1990 there were twenty-two people aged one hundred or older per 100,000 inhabitants. However, as indicated earlier, this figure is almost certainly too high.

Today, the odds at birth of reaching age seventy-five in a developed country are about one-in-two, which is the definition of life expectation. In 1980, the odds at birth of reaching age one hundred were one-in-eighty-seven. In 1879, the odds at birth of reaching age one hundred in the United States were one-in-four hundred. The improvement has been enormous. For all babies born in 1980, the odds were 559-to-1 against their reaching age 105 and 4,762-to-1 against reaching 110. However, in 1980, while almost one baby girl in fifty could be expected to reach one hundred, less than one baby boy in two hundred could expect the same. Table 12–1 shows the ten states that have the highest and lowest rates of survival to age one hundred. Figure 12–1 shows how the chances of surviving to age one hundred have increased from 1900 to 1981.

Centenarian data for some European countries is worth considering because it is much more accurate than is the data for the United States. In Belgium there are five centenarians per 10,000 people; 70 percent are female. In Sweden there are seven people aged one hundred or more per 100,000 people; this proportion increased from 1900 until 1980, when it stabilized at the figure given. The proportion of centenarian females to males is three-to-one in Hungary, seven-to-one in France, and eight-to-one in the Netherlands. The rate of centenarians in the United States, as reported by the Census Bureau for 1990, is twenty-two per 100,000. Clearly, this rate is severalfold greater compared to what has been found when the highly reliable European rec-

TABLE 12-1. U.S. states with best and lowest chances of survival to age 100, 1969–71 and 1979–81

1969–71		1979–81	
State	Chances per 100,000	State	Chances per 100,000
Hawaii	794	Hawaii	1713
Florida	698	Minnesota	1444
Alaska	662	South Dakota	1392
Utah	660	Iowa	1379
Minnesota	659	Nebraska	1364
North Dakota	651	North Dakota	1362
Nebraska	649	Kansas	1339
Oregon	647	Florida	1336
Kansas	640	Idaho	1329
South Dakota	640	Arizona	1317
National average	542	**National average**	1150
Ohio	482	New Jersey	1044
New York	482	Ohio	1043
Illinois	481	Mississippi	1033
Kentucky	473	Kentucky	1018
Delaware	465	West Virginia	1012
Mississippi	462	Pennsylvania	1009
Dist. of Columbia	456	Nevada	1004
Pennsylvania	455	Louisiana	994
West Virginia	452	Dist. of Columbia	948
Nevada	444	Alaska	941

SOURCE: National Center for Health Statistics, U.S. Decennial State Life Tables for 1969–71 and 1979–81. Permission granted courtesy of *Statistical Bulletin*, Metropolitan Life Insurance Co., Vol. 68, No. 1, January-March, 1987, page 6.

ords are used. Several studies have been started, using this more reliable European data, in an effort to understand more about the centenarian population. In France, the Ipsen Foundation has funded a research effort called the "Chronos Project," in which a variety of biomedical, social, psychological, demographic, and economic studies have been undertaken on people one hundred years of age and older. Similar studies have been undertaken in Hungary and Sweden. Some results follow.

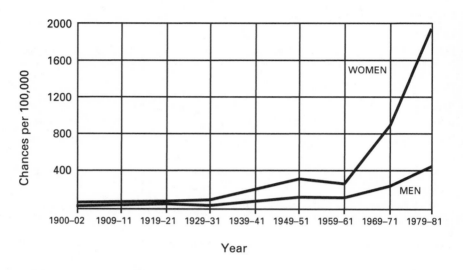

FIGURE 12 –1. Chances of survival to age 100, by sex, United States, 1900–1981

SOURCE: Permission granted courtesy of *Statistical Bulletin*, Metropolitan Life Insurance Co., Vol. 68, No.1, January–March, 1987.

SOME STATISTICAL CHARACTERISTICS OF CENTENARIANS

People in Sweden who live to be one hundred can expect to live, on average, only one more year; at the maximum, about fifteen years more.

In 1980, 90 percent of all people aged one hundred and over in the United States claimed to be less than 105 years of age; only 10 percent were 105 years old or older. The majority of American centenarians are female, white, widowed, and institutionalized; were born in the United States of Western European ancestry; and have less than a ninth-grade education. Ninety percent of American centenarians have an annual income of less than five thousand dollars, not counting food stamps, federal payments to nursing homes, or in-kind support from family and friends.

In a study of thirty Kentucky centenarians, ranging in age from 100 to 103, none currently smoke and only one did so in the past. There was no excessive use of alcohol.

There appear to be proportionally more centenarians in Okinawa than in the rest of Japan. One reason for this may be that Okinawans consume fewer calories than do those on the other Japanese islands. Gerontologists have long known that reduced caloric intake dramatically increases longevity in a variety of animals and even insects. This fascinating subject will be discussed extensively in chapter 17.

The older the group, the less we know about them. It follows, therefore, that we know the least about centenarians. It has only been in recent years, with the rapid rise of gerontology as a science, that interest developed in the biomedical characteristics of centenarians. Even the U.S. Bureau of the Census, until recently, lumped all people over the age of seventy-five or eighty-five into one group.

Why do centenarians live so long? Because of the lack of reliable, detailed information, we really do not know whether there is a common denominator responsible for this exceptional group's longevity. Perhaps the most convincing answer to date was offered by the centenarian who said, "I didn't die."

One other thing is certain about prospective centenarians. People born in 1899 or before, and who are still alive today, have a chance of living into the twenty-first century. Those who do will have lived in three different centuries and two millennia.

CHAPTER 13

Determining
Life Span

Poor man, he just stands and stares at a yellow
flower for minutes at a time. He would be far
better off with something to do.

—Charles Darwin's gardener

IN chapter 7 we saw that there is no reliable way to determine whether the human *life span* has changed in recent years. We are more certain, however, about life span changes that have occurred over the long term, that is, on an evolutionary scale. There is good evidence that the human life span increased rapidly until about 100,000 years ago, when the rate of change slowed considerably.

HOW LIFE SPAN RELATES TO BRAIN
WEIGHT AND BODY WEIGHT

The life span of many mammalian species is related to the average weight of the adult brain and the average weight of the adult body. This relationship is called the index of cephalization. The heavier the brain, as compared to the weight of the body, the more long-lived a species will be. This relationship, first reported in 1910, was independently rediscovered in 1955 and refined for mammals by the late, brilliant gerontological theorist George Sacher. Other organ weights, such as those of the adrenal glands and the liver, also seem to correlate well with species life span, but the brain has been studied most thoroughly.

The brain weight–body weight equation with weights expressed in grams, is

$$\text{Maximum life span in years} = 23 \, (\text{brain weight})^{0.6} \times (\text{body weight})^{-0.267}$$

Species with a greater brain weight to body weight proportionality are found to be the most longevous. Using this rule we can calculate the probable life span of extinct primates for which only skull fragments and a few other bones are available. By calculating the likely brain weight from the dimensions of a hominid skull and doing the same for the tissues in the rest of the body, a fairly good estimate can be made of the life span of a long-extinct hominid species.

We believe that early hominids had a life span far shorter than modern humans, because their considerably smaller brains weighed proportionately less than our brains, and their bodies were also smaller (table 13-1). Beginning with the evolution of *Australopithicus afarensis*, about three to four million years ago, early hominid life span was probably about fifty-seven years. We believe it increased to about sixty-eight years for *Homo habilis*, about two million years ago. The rate of increase in human brain weight compared to body weight was rapid after the hominid line became established four million years ago. But, about 100,000 years ago, at the time of Neanderthal man, the human brain weight to body weight ratio stopped changing and the human life span became arrested around the present 115-year maximum—double the life span of our hominid ancestors three to four million years ago. Relatively sudden stops and starts in evolutionary change have been recognized recently as the most likely way in which modifications in the characteristics of living things occur. The chief exponent of this concept is Stephen Jay Gould of Harvard University, who calls the phenomenon "punctuated equilibrium."

As evolutionary forces continue in the future, the human life span may increase, but changes will be difficult to detect for two reasons. First, as discussed in chapter 7, there is simply too much variability in the ages of those who live longest to reliably spot a trend over a short span of years. Second, brain weight–body weight measurements are not sufficiently sensitive to reveal small life span differences that may

TABLE 13-1. Maximum life span potential based on body and brain weight of pongids and hominids

Species	Cranial capacity (cm³)	Body weight (g)	Maximum life span potential (years) Observed	Maximum life span potential (years) Predicted	Time of appearance (millions of years ago)
Hominids					
A. afarensis	400	28,000		57.0	4.0–2.8
A. africanus	442	36,000		56.6	3.2–2.2
A. robustus	519	55,000		55.8	2.5–1.0
H. habilis	644	41,800		68.4	2.3–1.6
H. erectus	984	50,800		83.9	1.6–0.5
H. soloensis	1135	55,000		89.6	0.8–0.46
H. sapiens (pre-Neanderthal)	1314	59,800		95.7	0.3–0.1
H. sapiens sapiens	1460	63,800		100.3	0.04–0.01
H. sapiens recens (Australian aborigines)	1292	57,000	95	96.0	
Pongids					
Pygmy chimpanzee	343	35,250		48.8	
Chimpanzee	383	46,500	49	48.5	
Orang-utan	405	53,400	50	48.3	
Gorilla	503	105,000	42+	46.0	

SOURCE: Michel A. Hofman, "On the Presumed Coevolution of Brain Size and Longevity in Hominids," *Journal of Human Evolution*, 1984, Vol. 13, page 3.

have occurred over one hundred, one thousand, or even ten thousand years. Nevertheless, there is good evidence that the human life span did increase, at least until 100,000 years ago. If correct, this conclusion is important because it implies that the human life span, even if it has been fixed for the last hundred millennia, is plastic and may have the potential to increase in the future, if it is not already doing so. Recent evidence that animal life spans may increase has come from studies on Mediterranean fruit flies (medflies), insects that threaten destruction of fruit crops. Life span increases have also been observed to occur in the fruit fly (Drosophila), housefly, and a species of beetle. Studies have been limited to insects because definitive results can only be obtained by a statistical analysis of millions of animals.

An indirect argument that the human life span *is* increasing has been based on the belief that the death rates in very old humans may slow down, rather than increase at a constant rate, as they do from age thirty until, say, age eighty-five. The life spans of most mammals have increased over evolutionary time, and there is no evidence that the life span of any mammalian species has decreased. The inference is that humans should not be an exception to what appears to be, for most mammals at least, a law of increasing life span.

Life span can increase in several ways. The rate of aging might be slowed or the time of onset of age changes might be delayed. A more likely possibility is for natural selection to favor the survival to sexual maturity of individuals whose greater physiological capacity enables them to sustain good health longer and to continue to escape predators and capture prey efficiently. This might occur in circumstances where the force of natural selection favored a delay in reaching reproductive maturity. It is a remote possibility that the aging process might stop completely at some point, but this seems unlikely. We are left with the fact that life span has increased in humans and other animals over the millennia, but we can only speculate on how it may have happened.

Humans have the greatest brain weight compared to body weight and are therefore the longest-lived mammals. Contrary to popular mythology, the maximum life span of the elephant does not exceed that of humans but is only about seventy years (table 2–1), as predicted by the brain weight–body weight relationship.

When applied to humans, the equation gives a maximum life span of about one hundred years, which is close to the mark. This simple relationship shows a good fit for most other mammals with the exception of bats (which live four times longer than predicted by the equation) and mammalian insectivores (which have life spans two to four times shorter than would be expected from the equation). Bats may not fit well because their metabolic rate is slowed during hibernation, and the insectivores have a disproportionately high metabolic rate. There is one other exception to the brain weight–body weight relationship as it applies to the longevity of mammals. The deer mouse and the white-footed mouse have maximum life spans of about six years, twice as long as that of their cousin, the field mouse, yet the brain weight–body weight relationship of these three species is about the same. The reason for this discrepancy, like that of the bats and the insectivores, is a mystery. Otherwise, the life span figures calculated from the equation correlate with observed life span values with an accuracy of more than 98 percent.

BODY TEMPERATURE AND METABOLIC RATE

For the brain weight–body weight formula to hold for most vertebrate animal species, two other variables must be included: body temperature and metabolic rate (that is, the rate at which a body burns up food). A probable relationship between metabolic rate and aging was discovered in 1908 by Max Rubner. He found that many mammals metabolize about the same number of calories per pound of tissue over the course of their life span. In its two- to three-year life span, a mouse will burn from twenty-five thousand to forty thousand kilocalories per pound of tissue, or, say, about thirteen thousand kilocalories per pound per year. An elephant will burn about the same total number of calories per pound of tissue, but over a seventy-year life span, at a rate of maybe five hundred kilocalories per pound per year. The metabolic rate of a mouse, then, is much faster than that of an elephant. Humans are an exception to this rule. We burn about eighty thousand kilocalories per pound in our lifetime, more than any other animal. Figure 13–1 shows the relationship between calories burned per day and maximum longevity of some common mammalian species.

The value of expressing relationships between part of an organism and the whole organism (a subject called allometry) in an equation is that once we are certain the equations are accurate, they have both predictive and theoretical value. For example, if we know the brain weight–body weight proportionality for some mammal but do not know its life span, we can with some confidence determine its life span by finding where the brain weight–body weight relationship falls on the diagram based on animals for which all three variables are known. Conversely, if we know an animal's maximum life span, we can determine its brain weight–body weight relationship.

A second reason why quantifying relationships like these may be important is that it might reveal some fundamental information about the processes of aging and longevity. For example, because the weight of the brain in respect to the weight of the body correlates so well to longevity in mammals, some gerontologists believe that the brain may play the fundamental role in determining life span. As stated earlier, we know from measurements of fossil crania and other bones that human brain weight increased dramatically in proportion to the weight of the body about 100,000 years ago. Thus we believe that the human life span increased at that time to approximately what it is today, about 115 years. For animals that do not reach a fixed size in adulthood, such

FIGURE 13-1. Relationship between maximum lifespan potential (MLP) and specific metabolic rate (SMR) for some common mammals.

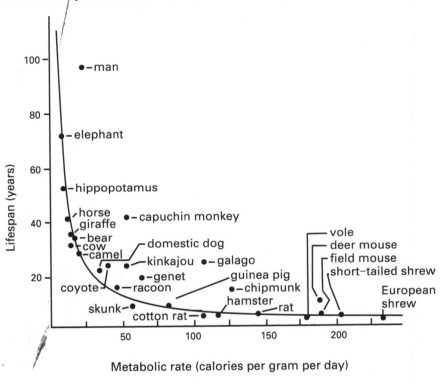

Metabolic rate (calories per gram per day)

SOURCE: Richard G. Cutler, "Evolutionary Biology of Senescence," in: *The Biology of Aging,* Editors: J. A. Behnke, C. E. Finch and G. B. Moment, Plenum Press, New York, 1978.

as sharks and alligators, both the nonneuronal brain cells and the body continue to grow indefinitely. Apparently, these animals experience no fixed life span or aging process.

LENGTHENING LIFE SPANS

There is good evidence that, at least for mammals, the life span of each species has increased as the species evolved. Richard Cutler of the National Institute on Aging compared the brain weight–body weight relationship of about 150 species whose fossilized remains have been studied, and found that the proportionality, and by inference the estimated life span, increased for every species that did not become extinct. He also found that the rate of gain in life span was greater for species closer to humans on the evolutionary tree and greatest for humans. Although our own life span appears to have reached its present maximum about 100,000 years ago, it may still be increasing because 100,000 years in evolutionary terms is not long. As the longest-lived mammals, it is believed that humans already age more slowly than any other mammal. If, however, our rate of aging were slowing further, the change would be imperceptible for many generations; we would need an evolutionary time frame of hundreds of thousands of years to recognize it.

If the longevity of a species is determined by its genetic constitution, then a fascinating question follows: How many genes are involved? In attempting to answer this question, Cutler has based his reasoning on his belief that the differences between chimpanzees and humans resides in about one percent of the genes, which are otherwise identical in the two species. Because one of the differences is the longer human life span, he speculates that longevity must be determined by less than one percent of the genes. He also reasons that for human longevity to have increased so rapidly up until about 100,000 years ago, only a few genes—he guesses a few hundred—must be involved. If life span is genetically encoded, it would take longer to alter a greater number of genes.

Two kinds of genes are known: structural genes—concerned with producing the materials of which bodies are composed—and regulatory genes, which act like switches to control chemical reactions. Cutler believes that longevity is governed by genes that act like switches, which he calls "longevity determinant genes." The late George Sacher, whose reasoning followed these same lines, preferred "longevity assurance processes."

Bernard Strehler of the University of Southern California argues against a genetically coded life span by pointing out that not only are the differences between humans and chimpanzees too great to be accounted for by only a few genes, but even if they were, the mutation rate in those genes would have to be unreasonably high for the differences between the two species to occur.

DID AGING EVOLVE?

> Descended from apes! My dear, let us hope that
> it is not true, but if it is, let us pray that it will
> not become generally known.
> —wife of the Bishop of Worcester

We know of no good reason why aging should happen.

In the last century, the German biologist August Weismann suggested that aging served to remove worn-out members of the species
who would otherwise clutter up the environment and deprive the
younger members of food and space. Many people still believe this
idea, but there is no evidence to support it. In the wild, you will recall, animals rarely live long enough to age. Furthermore, animals that
reach old age are not essential for the survival of a species, so there
should be no selective advantage favoring their survival. Weismann
pointed to an advantage in *limiting* their survival, but it is difficult to
see how evolution could select for a process like aging. Few, if any, animals ever lived long enough to participate in the selection process,
but members of wild species, who for million of years, have not experienced extreme aging, nonetheless reveal age changes when protected by humans as pets or in zoos.

There might be at least one case in which age changes do have a
selective advantage for the entire species, however. The late Sir Peter
Medawar, whose contributions to gerontological theory will be discussed later in this chapter, called to my attention the behavior of a
species of moths, which in the late stages of adulthood begins to
mimic the movements characteristic of the juvenile forms. By doing
this they lead predators away from the young moths and sacrifice their
own lives. It could be argued that the moths have evolved an age-
linked behavioral change that benefits the species by reducing the
force of predation on the young.

Some theoreticians believe that age changes evolved in the same
way as developmental changes. In development, the genetic program—a kind of blueprint—governs a sequence of carefully orchestrated events through which the fertilized egg becomes an adult
animal. Some gerontologists believe that the same genetic program
could also guide the adult animal from maturity to old age through the
sequence of changes that are characteristic of the aging process. Again,
it is difficult to imagine how a genetic program that governs age

changes could have evolved, given that few animals would have survived long enough to age and expose their age changes to evolutionary selection.

The fundamental question is this: Did aging evolve or did life span evolve? For the reasons just discussed, I conclude that age changes did *not* evolve. In the following section I present my reasons for believing that life span did evolve, but only indirectly.

THE IMPORTANCE OF REDUNDANCY

A bacterium lives for twenty minutes, a mayfly one day, a housefly one month, a mouse about three years, a dog twelve years, a horse twenty-five years, and a human up to 115 years. How have these extraordinary differences in the maximum life spans of various species evolved?

Some experts argue that evolution selects for a lengthening life span; however, short-lived animals that reproduce quickly may be just as successful in their environmental niche as animals that live longer and reproduce more slowly. Much depends, of course, on the frequency of deaths among the juvenile animals compared to the death rate of the adults. A female mouse that lives more than a year in the wild and produces four litters may be no more "fit" for the environment than another female mouse that lives for a few months and produces only one or two litters. Success depends on how many of their offspring survive and reproduce.

Despite the fact that a long life may not be necessary or "better" for a species, evolution does seem to favor increasing life spans. I believe this occurs indirectly. That is, evolution must favor some event that has nothing to do with life span determination directly, but that has a secondary effect that increases life span. How might this happen?

Most experts would agree with the premise that natural selection favors animals that are most likely to reach sexual maturity and give birth to vigorous offspring. The premise seems obvious; animals that fail to mature sexually will not reproduce and the species will soon vanish. But *how* does natural selection favor animals with the best chances of reaching sexual maturity? One good way is to select for animals whose vital systems are more robust and thus more capable of surviving predation, disease, and environmental extremes. As predators become more skilled in capturing prey, the prey that survives to reproduce does so by developing better avoidance techniques. In general, animals that have greater reserve capacity in their vital functions, faster sensory responses, or greater strength—that are in some way overengineered—will be better able to escape predators and survive disease and harsh environmental conditions. The issue, you recall, is survival to reproduce and nurture offspring to independence, not survival per se; but the favored animals will also tend to live longer, having developed what biologists call greater "redundant capacity" or "physiological reserve."

We humans have achieved redundant capacity in many of our organs. For example, we are overengineered in that we have two kidneys when one would do quite well. The same is true for our lungs. We can also survive with part of our liver, stomach, or intestines, or part of several vital systems. Some severely epileptic children have been substantially cured by removing the entire left hemisphere of the brain! They have half a brain and yet they survive quite well. Thousands of people get along after part of their heart muscle is destroyed by a heart attack. Reserve capacity has served all of these people well.

The price to be paid for redundant systems is the expenditure of more energy during development. Engineers know that to guarantee the performance of a complex machine in a harsh environment it is necessary to design backup systems for the most vital parts. The more backup systems the better. There are limits, of course. The machine may become too heavy or unwieldy if the redundancy built into it is too great. Space vehicles are good examples of the engineering principle of building in overcapacity or redundancy to ensure the success of a launch and the goal of the mission.

Similarly, natural selection favors animals that develop sufficient reserve capacity to increase their likelihood of surviving to sexual maturity. The favored qualities of increased vigor are then passed on to the triumphant animal's offspring. In this way greater reserve capacity in vital organs is favored, transmitted to the next generation, and slowly increases. After sexual maturation, the force of natural selection diminishes because, with increasing age after maximum reproductive capacity, the transmission of favored traits is not necessary for species survival. Thus, the condition of maximum physiological functioning reached at sexual maturity starts to decline. Maintenance of peak physiological functioning in postreproductive animals is unnecessary; a species betters its chances of survival by investing its resources and energy in reproductive success rather than individual postreproductive longevity. We might therefore conclude that animals age and are mortal because the resources that would be needed to maintain a perpetually youthful body are, in terms of survival of the species, better invested in strategies for better reproductive success.

How does all of this affect, or determine, the life span of an animal species? Natural selection determines life span *indirectly* because the greater reserve capacity favored to ensure an animal's survival to sexual maturity will also permit that animal to survive for some time *beyond* sexual maturity. How far beyond depends on how much surplus physiological reserve remains after the animal reaches reproductive maturity. So, although greater reserve capacity may have evolved only to guarantee that an animal reached sexual maturity, it indirectly determined the length of that animal's life span as well. Longevity, therefore, may have evolved as a by-product of the selection process. The differences in longevity of fruit flies, mice, and humans may reflect the evolution of differences in reserve capacity in the vital organs of each of these species at the time of sexual maturation.

Some biogerontologists contend that there is a trade-off between reproductive effort and life span. They maintain that high reproductive capacity correlates with a short life span and low reproductive capacity correlates with a long life span.

T.B.L. Kirkwood, of the National Institute for Medical Research in London, England, argues that animals make a trade-off between growing up fast and producing many offspring—a strategy that better favors the preservation of the organism's genes—and survival for a longer time, which may or may not benefit reproductive success. The energy costs of a perfect repair system would be so high as to put its possessor at an evolutionary disadvantage compared to an animal that puts less energy into maintenance and more into fecundity. For example, the lapwings discussed in chapter 6, with their high mortality rate in the wild, are, in terms of evolution, better served by producing many offspring quickly than by investing in strategies that might keep the animal alive somewhat longer. When adults have reasonably good chances of survival—that is, when adaptation or resistance to environmental hazards makes death by accident, disease, predation, or starvation less likely—animals tend to reproduce later. Elephants and humans, for example, have adopted this strategy of slow rates of growth and reproduction.

A rule of thumb is that the larger the proportion of resources allocated for reproduction, the smaller the chance that members of a species will survive. Stated in another way, poor odds for the survival of adult animals favor earlier sexual maturation and increased reproductive effort.

A recent experiment in Trinidad illustrates these principles. In one environment, a guppy predator fed on adults. Over time the fish matured at an earlier age and had more and smaller offspring per brood. In another environment, a different guppy predator fed on the juveniles; here the fish matured later and had larger offspring in smaller broods. This adaptability is heritable: the experimenters switched the two predators between the guppy populations and found that after eleven years and thirty to sixty generations, the guppies' reproductive patterns had reversed. Unfortunately, no data were given on changes in the life span of the two groups of guppies.

Kirkwood calls his hypothesis about the trade-off between reproductive success and life span the "disposable soma theory" because the demands of reproduction in an animal are greater than the demands for greater longevity, or maintenance of somatic cells. You can't have it all. Life span evolves indirectly from the priority given to traits that favor reproductive success over traits that might directly favor longevity. Somatic, or body cells, are disposable once reproductive success has been ensured. Stated another way, natural selection trades traits that favor greater longevity for traits that favor enhanced early fecundity. The force of natural selection then declines with age, an idea first emphasized by the late Sir Peter Medawar and championed in more recent years by Brian Charlesworth of the University of Chicago and Michael R. Rose of the University of California at Irvine.

As I mentioned earlier, space vehicles offer good examples of using redundancy to ensure that a goal is achieved. Alex Comfort of London, England, first suggested them as a good analogy to the relationships among redundancy, reproduction and longevity in animals. I have taken the liberty of greatly expanding Comfort's analogy in the light of newer developments in biogerontology. Suppose the goal of a space vehicle is to fly past Mars and, by radiotelemetry, send photographs back to Earth. That goal would be analogous to an animal's mission of reaching sexual maturity. Neither nature, which designed the animal, nor the engineers who designed the spacecraft, care what happens after the animal reaches sexual maturation or the spacecraft sends back its pictures. The engineers (or nature) simply do not need to make a spacecraft (or animal) that works perfectly forever. Neither nature nor the engineers believe that it is necessary to invest an enormous amount of resources in guaranteeing the immortality of the spacecraft or the animal because neither mission requires immortality. However, to best guarantee the success of both missions with the least expenditure of resources, it makes good sense for nature and the engineers to build some redundancy into the animal or the spacecraft—that is, to back up all vital systems. Two computers instead of one. Two kidneys instead of one. An auxiliary power supply in case the main supply fails. A pair of lungs instead of one.

Once the space vehicle has radioed its photographs back to Earth, or once the animal has reached reproductive success and raised its offspring to independence, neither the engineers nor nature cares what happens to it—mission accomplished. But, neither spacecraft nor parent vanishes immediately. The spacecraft survives beyond accomplishing its goal and continues on through the outer solar system. The animal accomplishes its goal and continues to participate in life's activities. However, after each goal is reached, glitches begin to occur in the space vehicle's vital systems, and losses of function begin to occur in the animal's vital organs. Both begin to age because neither was designed to function beyond the goal to be immortal. Nor was either specifically designed to be mortal. Mortality occurs because of the increasing likelihood for disorder to occur in both systems. It was unnecessary for nature and the engineers to design a specific self-destruct mechanism. It is completely unnecessary to have a program written in the computer's memory, or the cell's DNA, that instructs it how to age or how long to live.

After their goals are reached, deterioration and outright failures become more likely in both spacecraft and animal. Initially, the deterioration may not be critical: the paint on the spacecraft might become discolored, or some of the wiring frayed, from exposure to the sun's ultraviolet rays; the animal's ability to see, hear, or run may be slightly diminished, or its immune system a bit less efficient. Even slight deterioration, however, renders feral animals vulnerable to disease and predators. These animals will not live long enough to experience further changes in the aging process. Humans and the animals that we choose to protect, though, will live beyond this point and experience the more extreme manifestations of age changes. Similarly, the space vehicle, having no predators, will survive far beyond trivial age changes. With the passage of time, the minor fraying of the wires might increase the space vehicle's vulnerability to a serious short circuit, just as hardening arteries in a human might increase vulnerability to the formation of a life-threatening blood clot.

Even if the space vehicle's main power supply fails, all is not lost because the backup system will kick in. In the human or other animals, a lung clot or pneumonia that diminishes the capacity of one lung or reduces the blood supply to part of the heart may not be fatal because the other lung can easily handle the job and the heart can generate new small arteries and veins to maintain a somewhat less than perfect blood supply. In this way system failures are overcome by the reserve mechanisms that were engineered into the space vehicle and evolved in the animals' ancestors. However, no amount of redundancy will guarantee immortality. Even the repair processes known to exist in living cells are themselves incapable of performing error-free forever. All backup systems and reserve capacity will eventually be exhausted as the aging process continues inexorably. A fatal flaw will inevitably cause the space vehicle to fail and fly out of the solar system as a functionless mass of metal and electronic circuits. The animal will eventually loose peak physiological capacity, age, succumb to predation, accidents, or disease, and die.

Engineers have a term to describe the average period of time that they expect a mechanical device to survive. It is called the "average time to failure." Some people feel that cars are timed to self-destruct as soon as the auto loan is paid off. The average time to failure of a cheap car might be two years before some major repair is needed. A more expensive car might have an average time to failure of five years. "Average time to failure" refers to the period of time until half of a group of identical things will stop functioning. The average time to failure of today's babies is about seventy-five years; of every one hundred human babies born today, fifty will be alive in seventy-five years. Your average time to failure, or life expectation, based on your present age, may be determined by consulting table 6–1.

In both the spacecraft and the animal we find the three aspects of the finitude of life: aging, longevity, and death. If longevity is determined by our genes, albeit indirectly, and aging is not, then what causes the age changes that ultimately lead to our "system failure"— that is, death?

CHAPTER 14

Theories of Aging Based on Purposeful Events

We are all agreed that your theory is crazy. The
question which divides us is whether it is crazy
enough to have a chance of being correct. My
own feeling is that it is not crazy enough.

—Niels Bohr

MODERN biologists understand that in order to change
the course of a biological phenomenon—whether fetal development,
the progress of a disease, or the onset of age changes—for human benefit, one must first understand the phenomenon itself. Because our ancestors lacked an understanding of the aging process, their early ideas
about the control of aging were pure speculation. As the scientific
method evolved in the last few centuries, scientists learned that understanding a process first is a far better way to ensure the success of
any interventions. There are, however, some notable exceptions to this
approach: the use of aspirin to manage headaches and the use of cow-
pox to vaccinate against smallpox spring immediately to mind. In both

cases there was no complete understanding of the biological basis of the treatments at the time they were discovered.

Notwithstanding the exceptions, scientists generally believe that intervention in a biological process has a much greater likelihood of succeeding if we thoroughly understand the process itself (more accurately, if we *think* we understand the process). Efforts to understand natural phenomena are the reason that the scientific method has developed. The method is based on four principles:

1. observation of a phenomenon;
2. formulation of a hypothesis or theory, a plausible explanation for the observation;
3. testing the theory by experimentation; and
4. confirming the results.

Confirming the results of experimentation may lead to making more accurate observations or reformulating the hypothesis, in which case you loop back to step 1 or 2. Scientific investigators then repeat the cycle until they believe that the truth has been revealed.

Today, most biogerontologists would agree that we have sufficient observational data on aging to support experimental testing of several theories. Indeed, the recorded observations on how living things change with age are so numerous that they have spawned dozens of theories, and laboratory testing has become a growth industry in biogerontology. Current theories are in a continuous state of flux as new experimental results are reported. Some cynical biogerontologists claim that there are probably as many theories about the causes of age changes as there are biogerontologists.

Because of the profusion of theories, I will consider only those well supported by experimental evidence or receiving significant attention from the present scientific community.

EARLY IDEAS ABOUT AGING

Several modern theories on the causes of aging have their roots in old ideas. These early musings are useful to consider because they have influenced our current thinking.

The "Vital Substance" Theory

An early idea, still prevalent, is that animals begin their lives with a limited amount of some vital substance. As this hypothetical substance is consumed, age changes occur that eventually lead to a loss of vigor. When the vital substance is exhausted, the animal dies. In ancient times the vital substance was thought to be one or more vital "humors" that were believed to control all of human biology.

Francis Bacon challenged this view in the sixteenth century by arguing that aging might be overcome if the repair processes that occur in man and other animals were themselves made perfect and eternal. As examples of repair processes he cited the healing of wounds, tissue regeneration, and the capacity of the body to recover from disease. A modern variation of the vital substance argument posits that we are born with a limited capacity for, or a specific number of, heartbeats or breaths and, as we approach the limit, aging and death ensue. Variations in species longevity and individual life expectation are explained by differences in the amount of vital substance possessed by each animal or person at birth. As attractive as this idea might be, there is no evidence to support it.

Nevertheless, Bernard Strehler argues that the vital substance might be the DNA of essential genes present in multiple copies in nondividing cells. As copies of these vital genes are lost over time, (DNA repair is an imperfect process) protein synthesis, orchestrated by the vital genes and essential in maintaining peak physiological functions, is also compromised. Strehler believes the loss of the vital substance—copies of essential genes—is the fundamental cause of age changes.

The Genetic Mutation Theory

At the turn of this century, mutations were discovered to occur in cells, and in the 1950s genetics began to dominate thinking about the cause of aging and the determination of longevity. Mutations are changes that occur in genes and there are several kinds of changes that are known to occur. Some mutations are harmful, and if they occur in a developing human embryo, the embryo is likely to be spontaneously aborted. It is believed that this accounts for the high rate of spontaneous abortions in humans. Many spontaneous abortions occur without the mother's knowledge because, for all practical purposes, a miscarriage that occurs only a few weeks after conception is indistinguishable from a late menstruation. Nevertheless, a few beneficial mutations do occur. In fact, mutation is the engine that drives evolution and natural selection. Because of their essential role in the diversity of life and the adaptation of animals to their environment, mutations are a serious contender for the locus of the aging and longevity phenomena.

In the late 1940s several scientists began to explore the role of mutations in aging. The original proposal was made in 1947 by Paul Henshaw and tested later by Howard Curtis of the Brookhaven National Laboratory in Upton, New York. Other contributors were G. Failla, Bernard Strehler, Arnold Clark of the University of Delaware, John Maynard Smith of the University of Sussex, Brighton, England, and Leo Szilard, widely known for having persuaded Albert Einstein to write the famous letter to Franklin D. Roosevelt describing the potential of atomic power.

Because gene mutations are fundamental to life, changes in genes seemed to be a good candidate for the cause of aging. The early evidence in support of this idea came from observations suggesting that radiation, known to increase the mutation rate, also simultaneously accelerated the aging process in experimental animals. Later, it was observed that the radiation-induced changes in these animals only mimicked age changes. Such changes are reminiscent of progeria, discussed in chapter 7, also considered by many gerontologists to only mimic some age changes but is not true aging. Evidence was soon obtained showing that the amount of radiation necessary to produce a lifetime's worth of mutations in an experimental animal is insufficient to shorten the life expectation of rats. In fact, George Sacher found that moderate amounts of radiation actually increase life expectation! Another damaging blow to the hypothesis was found by Clark when he studied the wasp, Habrobracon. This insect has, like most other animals, two full sets of chromosomes or genes (diploidy). Unlike most other animals it can also be found normally with one set of chromosomes (haploidy). Clark reasoned that if both kinds of Habrobracon, which have identical life spans, are exposed to the same high dose of radiation, then the haploid insect should have a shorter life span than the diploid insect. He thought that this would be expected, because having two sets of essential genes should provide one backup or redundant system in case one gene fails or mutates. The results of the experiment showed this to be true; however, *unirradiated* insects had identical life spans. The conclusion was that normal background radiation does not accelerate aging. Because other kinds of mutations are now known to occur that are not accelerated by radiation, the possibility that these kinds of mutations might cause age changes cannot be excluded.

The late Sir MacFarlane Burnet suggested a unique twist on the mutation hypothesis in the early 1960s in Australia. He proposed that a class of cells called precursor cells might be the source of mutations. Precursor cells exist in many tissues and are the basic primitive cells that, by dividing many times, give rise to cells that ultimately become the mature functioning cells in a particular tissue. Burnet argued that a mutation in one of the precursor cells of the immune system, for example, would automatically give rise to millions of daughter cells carrying the same mutation. In this way it wasn't necessary for mutations to occur in many mature cells. Despite this novel proposal, no experimental evidence has been forthcoming to support it, so Burnet's version of the mutation theory of aging remains unproven.

The Reproductive Exhaustion Theory

One early idea that still has a few adherents is the belief that "reproductive exhaustion" is a precursor of aging. That is, after a burst of reproductive activity, an animal or plant is triggered to age and die rapidly. There is convincing evidence for this relationship in some fish like the Pacific salmon, some mollusks, the "big bang" animals discussed earlier, and some flowering and annual plants. Nevertheless, a burst of reproductive activity followed by aging and death is not a universal pattern in nature—many animals, humans included, give birth several times to one or more offspring—and universality is required in a tenable theory of aging.

WHY MODERN THEORIES OF AGING
ARE STILL SPECULATIVE

Because biogerontology is a young science, it lacks a firm foundation in experimentally confirmed facts. With little fundamental information, theories of aging are easy to construct. Many of them appeal more to the emotions than to reason, and some rest on the particular biases of their advocates. These circumstances have led to the present state of affairs, best described by this scientific axiom: In fields in which hypotheses cannot be tested, there is no such thing as being wrong. Alex Comfort aptly summarized the situation as follows:

> In almost any other important biological field than that of senescence, it is possible to present the main theories historically, and to show a steady progression from a large number of speculative, to one or two highly probable, main hypotheses. In the case of senescence this cannot profitably be done. . . . It is a striking feature of these theories (of senescence) that they show little or no historical development; they can much more readily be summarized as a catalogue than as a process of developing scientific awareness.

Virtually all theories of aging suffer from another important difficulty: any proposed cause of aging may, itself, be the result of some more fundamental cause. Therefore, for each theory of aging that is offered one must ask not only if it is testable but also whether it might be merely the manifestation of some more basic event.

Another fact makes theories of aging easy to propose. Virtually anything biological that can be measured changes over time, and most, but not all, of the changes that occur with age are losses in some measurable activity. Thus, any one change can be proposed as the cause of all other age changes. For example, our immune system loses its efficiency in protecting us from diseases as we age; therefore, one modern theory of aging claims deficiencies in this system as the basic cause of aging. But, similar losses occur in other vital systems, so how can we identify any single system as *the* site of the basic cause of aging? Other losses clearly have nothing to do with the cause of aging. For example, most people experience graying of their hair with age. But although this change occurs over time one would not get far in defending the theory that aging is caused by gray hair, because it is intuitively wrong. It may also be just as wrong to believe that any other time-dependent change causes the entire constellation of less obvious age changes. It is more probable that the causes of gray hair, losses in immune system efficiency, and other physiological losses are all dependent on some even more fundamental change. That common denominator is likely to be found in the molecules that form, or are produced by, the basic building blocks that compose our body: cells. Today, most biogerontologists believe that there is not a single cause of aging but many causes, and that several mechanisms may be operating simultaneously.

No one has provided absolute proof that a single mechanism can explain why we age or account for differences in species longevity, but there are several good theories. We simply do not have enough fundamental information to answer the questions with authority. But this circumstance is not unusual. For example, we know that the blueprint for development from conception to adulthood is dictated by genetic events, but we do not know exactly how it happens, even though studies on biological development have been going on for a century or more. Other than descriptive studies, the modern era of research in biogerontology is only about forty years old, so it should not be surprising that we know so little about it.

Unlike any other area of biology, gerontology has become involved in two debates that heretofore had been the province of theology and philosophy. One question is whether living organisms, especially humans, are potentially immortal or inescapably mortal. The other is more subjective: whether aging is good or evil. Virtually every author of a theory of aging states a position on one or the other of these issues, though it is rarely stated explicitly.

RULES OF THE GAME

In an effort to eliminate some of the weaker theories of aging, Bernard Strehler proposed a set of requirements to be satisfied before any theory of aging be considered tenable. He postulated that an acceptable theory of aging must explain why the phenomenon is (a) *deleterious*, that is, why losses in physiological function occur; (b) *progressive*, why the losses are gradual; (c) *intrinsic*, why the losses cannot be corrected; and (d) *universal*, why the losses occur in all members of a species, given the opportunity. Strehler's guidelines are useful because they define what is meant by biological aging with a good degree of precision and, most importantly, they exclude other biological phenomena with which aging is often confused. Diseases, for example, fall outside of the rules because no specific disease ordinarily occurs in all members of a species although the effects of many, though not all, are intrinsic.

Two factors are worth emphasizing when we consider the possible causes of age changes. First, we must distinguish between normal age changes and the diseases of old age. Many diseases are progressive, intrinsic, and deleterious but, unlike age changes, none is universal. Second, we must distinguish between longevity and aging. The life span of a species is generally believed to be genetically determined, although indirectly. The decrements that occur after sexual maturation and before maximum longevity is reached are called age changes. Age changes, and not the determination of life span, are the object of the theories of aging that follow.

IS AGING ACCIDENTAL OR PROGRAMMED?

Theories of aging can be divided into two broad groups: those that presume a preexisting master plan, and those based on random events. Chief among the former group is the idea of a biological clock based on a series of chemical events or physical changes in specific molecules. Examples include the theories that age changes are determined by switching on "death" genes or by hormones secreted at a certain time by the hypothalamus or pituitary gland in the brain. The latter group of theories postulates that aging results from random, accidental events that are not purposefully programmed. Such theories may attribute aging to the accumulation of errors in important molecules such as DNA, the results of wear and tear, or the accumulation of waste products.

First we will consider two theories that postulate the existence of a clocklike mechanism.

AGING BY DESIGN

In 1908, the American anatomist Charles Sedgwick Minot wrote, "the condition of old age is merely the culmination of changes which have been going on from the first stage of the germ up to the adult, the old man or woman. All through life these changes continue. The result is senility."

Minot expressed the popular idea that aging is simply a continuation of the biological development that occurs from conception to sexual maturation. Implicit is the idea that the genetic blueprint that governs those events also governs the changes that follow adulthood, which we call aging. According to this way of thinking a purposeful genetic program is at work. Minot's idea also means that aging begins at birth—which is about the most conservative position that one could take. (Although Minot's idea about programmed aging may be defendable, his conclusion that age changes always result in senility is not. If there is one important fact that biogerontologists have learned in the last decade or two, it is that the majority of us are *not* fated to suffer from senility. This important matter will be discussed later.)

Minot's view that age changes from conception to death are programmed into our cells and that we start to age at conception, has been defended by the following line of reasoning. Around the time of birth, the specific growth rate falls. That is, in the nine months from conception to birth, one cell grows to billions, from an almost insignificant weight to, say, seven or eight pounds. At no other time of life does human weight proportionately increase so much or so rapidly. There is a popular misconception that many human cancers are characterized by rapid growth, yet no human cancer grows as rapidly in nine months as does a developing human fetus! After birth, the growth rate slowly declines until it stops around the early twenties. If the growth rate did not slow down after birth, then even assuming that the fertilized egg weighed as much as one ounce (it weighs far less) and that at birth a baby weighed seven pounds, the baby would weigh over seven hundred pounds before its first birthday! Minot essentially believes that the decline in growth rate after birth represents the beginning of aging.

Some biogerontologists who disagree with the notion that aging begins at birth have taken a slightly less conservative position, suggesting that aging begins immediately after the "actuarial prime of life," that is, when the force of mortality is lowest. As can be seen in table 6-2, the time at which the fewest people die in the United States (and in most other developed countries) is between five to ten years of age. Actually, the actuarial prime of life is at about seven years of age. At that age the likelihood of living another day or month or year is higher than at any other time of life. Because aging is often defined as an increase in the force of mortality, some gerontologists argue that aging begins after that age.

Abstractly, programmed aging is an attractive hypothesis. It seems to correlate well with programmed cell death, a phenomenon universally recognized by biologists. An example is the process by which the fingers and toes are molded during embryonic development. The tissue composing those regions starts as a single mass of cells, but the cells in the areas that become the spaces between the digits are destined to die. In this way discrete fingers and toes are formed. Thus, perfectly healthy cells are programmed to die in order to give shape and form to structures during development. We know that the program to do this is determined genetically, but we don't know whether this mechanism underlies the aging process. I am certain we do not age because of massive cell death, but the complex molecular changes that precede cell death might cause age changes and death of the animal well before the cells themselves die.

The modern interpretation of Minot's idea holds that the DNA in each of our cells provides the blueprint for what happens not only from fertilization of the egg to sexual maturation, but also from young adulthood through the entire aging process. This hypothesis is beguilingly simply because it rests on the current dogma that grants DNA and the genetic apparatus a virtual monopoly on determining almost everything about us. Nevertheless, there is a major problem with this hypothesis. As we found in chapter 13, there were never enough old members of a species around, and none for a long enough time, to allow evolution to directly select for aging processes. For this and other reasons the programmed theory of aging is unpopular today. "Big bang" animals, like the Pacific salmon, might be exceptions, but they are programmed to die quickly. It is arguable whether the changes that precede their death are age changes.

THE NEUROENDOCRINE THEORY

The endocrine glands release chemical messengers called hormones into the blood, which then act on target cells in the body. Hormones regulate many kinds of activities involved in metabolism, reproduction, protein synthesis, immune function, growth, and behavior. Their importance in the maintenance of normal life processes would be difficult to exaggerate. Hormones, in large amounts, are known to be capable of accelerating some aging processes and slowing others. The suggestion that changes in the endocrine or hormone-secreting glands are causes of aging is certainly not a new idea. Hormones have been used experimentally in attempts to reverse age changes since 1889. However, modern gerontological endocrinologists are more interested in the role of hormones as possible causes of age changes than as means of rejuvenation.

One of the common changes that heralds the onset of aging is the decline in reproductive capacity. This decline is almost as accurate an indicator of aging as is the increased force of mortality. In animals

which produce young in litters, decreased litter size is an early warning of the approach of more dramatic age changes. As stated earlier, a
leghorn hen, during the first year of laying, will lay more eggs than
in any subsequent year. After the first year, egg laying diminishes
annually.

The decline in reproductive capacity is governed by the neuroendocrine system, which is also associated with several kinds of biological clocks. These are compelling reasons to examine the role of the
neuroendrocine system in aging and as a potential site for the origin
of other age changes. It was not until the 1960s and 1970s that serious
study of the role of the neuroendocrine system in aging was begun.
The earliest studies were designed to understand the relation of the
hypothalamus, one of several candidates for a biological clock, to reproductive decline in old female rats. It had been learned that neither
the ovaries nor the pituitary gland were responsible for the loss of the
estrous cycle in old female rats. Joseph R. Meites of Michigan State
University found the cause to be in the hypothalamus.

The hypothalamus has been studied for other reasons as well. When
some animals are raised on a diet that contains all of the essential nutrients but is low in calories their longevity may double. It has been
suggested that caloric restriction slows aging by somehow retarding
the hypothalamic chronometer in the brain. Caloric restriction is one
of the few ways known to perturb the aging process. It will be discussed extensively in chapter 17. By contrast, a rapid acceleration of
a putative biological clock may explain those rare cases described in
the medical literature of people who, after a severe trauma to the
head or an emotional shock, suddenly acquire several of the stigmata
of aging, such as gray hair and a general decline in physiological capacity.

A few years ago, a little understood hormone, secreted by the adrenal glands, was found to have some interesting associations with the
aging process. The hormone is called dehydroepiandrosterone
(DHEA). It is found in greater amounts in young adults, then diminishes with age. When administered to mice it seems to reduce the incidence of breast cancer, delay immune system dysfunction, increase
longevity, and make the animals "look younger." But DHEA-treated
mice eat less—perhaps they don't like the taste of the drug if it's fed,
or don't eat well if it is inoculated—and some biogerontologists believed that the increase in longevity attributed to DHEA may instead
be a manifestation of the longevity extending effect of caloric restric-

tion. Other researchers believe that the DHEA effect is real. The effects of DHEA on aging are under investigation by several research groups but too little is known at this time to make any substantive claims.

Like those who claim that the immune system is the seat of all age changes (see chapter 15), advocates of the neuroendocrine system theory marshal powerful arguments about the influence of the system on the entire body and argue that any changes in so vital a system must play a profound role in aging. The neuroendocrine system and the immune system even interact to regulate each other's functioning. Their influence on each other and on the body as a whole is not in dispute; as is common in science, the dispute is not over the facts but over their interpretation.

Few parts of the body act in isolation from nerve cells or hormones. Perturbations in hormone secretion or nerve cell activities will have profound effects on health, and possibly on aging. As expected, there is a veritable catalogue of age-related changes associated with alterations in hormones or neural factors. Menopause provides good examples of age-related hormonal events that affect the entire body. Some hormone levels also drop in men as they age, yet one must be careful not to overinterpret this phenomenon. After all, the menopause only occurs in women; men continue to be fertile while simultaneously aging. Despite the profound effects that the neuroendocrine system has on our bodies, there is no direct evidence that it is the origin of all age changes.

DOWN THE BRAIN-CELL DRAIN

A controversial question in biogerontology is whether or not we lose nerve cells as we age. (In fact, the question should be asked of all cells, not just neurons.) The brain, like many other parts of our bodies, shrinks in weight and size during normal aging. As mentioned in chapter 10, brain weight decreases about 10 percent, the convolutions narrow, and the spaces between them widen. The shrinkage may be due to loss of neurons, water, or both, but its cause and significance remain in dispute.

Recently the dogma that neurons cannot replicate in adult animals has been challenged. Research on the brains of adult songbirds has revealed several seasonal cycles of dying and replicating neurons. We don't know what the implications of this are for humans. Profound changes certainly do occur in the brain as we age and it is plausible that these changes might trigger age changes elsewhere.

A proposal made several years ago suggested that the brain was the origin of all age changes. Despite considerable attention in the popular media, the supporting evidence ranges from weak to nonexistent. The theory was that the brain produced a substance popularly referred to as a "death hormone." The hormone, allegedly made by the pituitary gland, was formally known as *decreasing oxygen consumption hormone*, or DECO. It was postulated to initiate and then orchestrate the aging phenomenon. The chief advocate of this notion was Donner W. Denckla, formerly of the Roche Institute in Nutley, New Jersey. He postulated that DECO circulates in the body and interferes with protein synthesis and cell division. In this way it is capable of causing widespread mischief. Despite some evidence for the existence of DECO offered by Denckla, the idea has fallen on hard times because no one else has been able to confirm the studies and Denckla himself no longer pursues this line of research.

Nevertheless the brain remains a serious candidate for the role of master orchestrator of normal age changes. Tantalizing evidence that supports this idea has come from experiments showing that removal of the pituitary gland, located at the base of the brain, may cause some rejuvenation in animals that survive the heroic surgery. The pituitary gland, often called the master endocrine gland of the body, secretes many hormones which regulate vital processes involved in growth, maturation, and reproduction.

The brain controls or influences virtually every other organ in the body, either through connections with other nerve cells or by way of hormone messengers. It consumes more energy for its weight than any other organ, representing about 2 percent of body weight but consuming 20 percent of the oxygen used by the entire body. In addition, the mysterious relationship of the brain's weight to that of the whole body and to life span, described in chapter 13, keeps the brain in consideration as a possible origin of all age changes.

Like the immune theory of aging, the neuroendocrine theory suffers from lack of universality, that is, not all animals that age have the complex neuroendocrine systems found in higher vertebrates. Moreover, the age-associated deficits that occur in the neuroendocrine system may be the result of more basic changes that occur in all, or most, of the cells in the body. Consequently, there would be no more compelling reason to select the neuroendocrine system over any other system as the primary orchestrator of age changes.

The modern theories of aging that will follow are not based on genetic design but rather on the occurrence of random events. The events may be the result of accidents at the molecular level and may affect important molecules. As a group they seem to be more attractive hypotheses.

CHAPTER 15

Theories of Aging Based on Random Events

A theory is a cluster of conclusions in search of a premise.

—N. R. Hanson

THE theories of aging discussed in this chapter are based on the concept that aging does not occur according to some master plan, but rather that it is the result of chance events.

THE WEAR AND TEAR THEORY

An early theory of aging, articulated in 1882 by the great German biologist August Weismann is called the "wear and tear" theory. "Death," he said, "occurs because a worn out tissue cannot forever renew itself." As the name suggests, the theory contends that animals age because their vital systems accumulate damage from the normal abuse of everyday life, which some biogerontologists think of as a form of stress. Wear and tear erodes the normal biochemical activities that occur in cells, tissues, and organs. Weismann was correct in his hypothesis that normal cells cannot divide or function forever, but that does not explain *why* age changes occur.

Wear and tear might be an important source of age changes, but interpreting its role could be a trap for the unwary. In chapter 2 we discussed the wear and tear that occurs in horses and other grazing animals whose teeth wear down at a fairly constant rate. As the erosion progresses, the animal's ability to gather and masticate its food diminishes. Its ability to obtain nourishment is reduced and it slowly starves. A knowledgeable person can determine, with reasonable accuracy, the age of a horse based on how far down the teeth are worn (hence the expression, "Don't look a gift horse in the mouth"). However, worn-down teeth are neither a cause nor an effect of aging. The wear is caused by trauma to the teeth. A young horse which loses its teeth in an accident might be as likely as an old horse to starve to death in the absence of any signs of old age. Worn teeth themselves do not affect the aging process (except, perhaps, briefly, by reducing caloric intake; the effects of such restriction on longevity are discussed in chapter 17), but they offer a good example of the danger that exists in interpreting the wear and tear of anything that changes as a result of age.

Possibly the best example of wear and tear associated with aging occurs in adult insects. The cells that comprise the bodies of most adult insects do not divide, with the exception of the sex cells and, perhaps, some cells in the gut. None of the cells in the adult fruit fly divides. Biogerontologists have been intrigued with the aging of the flight muscle cells of insects not only because they do not replace themselves, or turn over (the scientific term), but because flight muscle cells have an extremely high energy requirement and are therefore good indicators of age changes. We are impressed to learn that a hummingbird's wings beat about 70 times per second. However, the homely young fruit fly can beat its wings up to 300 times per second. A young, week-old fruit fly can beat its wings about two million times, sustaining flight for 110 minutes. An aged, month-old fly can sustain flight for only about nineteen minutes, beating its wings only 170,000 times. We do not understand *why* there is a loss of wingbeat frequency over time, whether it causes other age changes, or whether it is the result of a more fundamental cause. Old male houseflies have frayed wings and can't fly after two weeks of adulthood. This situation may be as close as we can get to a perfect example of wear and tear as an effect of the aging process and ultimate cause of death. But it is an effect, not a cause, of aging in the fly; when a young fly's wings are removed, it does not age faster.

The most serious problem with the wear and tear theory is that wear and tear is too difficult to measure in most animals. Although it might be accurately defined when applied to a fly's wings or to an automobile tire, wear and tear is difficult to describe or quantify in most biological systems. We simply do not know what normal wear and tear is when applied to most living cells, their individual parts, or the molecules of which they are composed. Because we cannot measure what cannot be defined, the wear and tear theory presently languishes in a scientific backwater and attracts few advocates.

Recently, the biogerontologist Jaime Miquel of the University of Alicante, Spain, suggested that wear and tear might occur in individual cells when free radicals, the subject of a theory discussed later in this chapter, are formed by normal metabolic processes. These highly active chemicals are known to inflict damage on other molecules, and Miquel proposes that an accumulation of this damage over time could produce age changes. If Miquel's idea is correct, then the basic cause of age changes is not wear and tear but the more fundamental process of free radical formation.

If wear and tear is a fundamental cause of age changes then the most likely arena for its effects is at the molecular level. Important molecules might incur damage over time and not be replaced as quickly as they are lost, or they may not be replaced at all. Although there are systems that can repair some kinds of molecular damage, these systems themselves are imperfect. Cells, tissues, organs, and repair systems may gradually lose physiological efficiency, decline, and ultimately fail.

Miquel has suggested that molecular wear and tear may directly affect the "mitochondria," the "power plants" that provide energy for all the cell's activities. Damage to the power plants of cells would be just as disastrous as damage to the power plants that supply a city with its energy. The mitochondria, which are located outside of the cell nucleus, contain their own small piece of DNA, which contains instructions for the manufacture of thirteen proteins required for energy generation. The DNA of mitochondria, which is close to the site for energy production, seems more susceptible to damage than the DNA in the nucleus of the cell. Furthermore, unlike the nucleus, the mitochondria do not seem to have a repair system for damaged DNA. In many animal species the mitochondria in old cells show a decrease in numbers, an increase in size and various structural abnormalities. Even cultured normal cells reveal these mitochondrial changes at the end of their lifetime. It is easy to imagine ways in which the mitochondrial power plants might suffer damage over time and the effect that this damage might have on the vital activities of cells. Miquel believes that it could be a fundamental cause of aging.

Because mitochondria contain DNA and have an exclusive maternal lineage, they become important players in the quest for knowledge about the origin of age changes. There is some evidence, both in humans and in animals, that longevity may be more strongly influenced by a mother's longevity than by a father's. At fertilization, only the nucleus in the sperm head, which does not contain mitochondria, enters the egg to fuse with the egg's nucleus. Therefore, all of the remaining cell material outside of the fertilized egg's nucleus comes from the mother. In all subsequent divisions of the fertilized egg that give rise to the adult, all the cells contain mitochondrial DNA inherited only from the mother.

The difficulty in interpreting wear and tear as a cause of age changes is the same at the molecular level as it is at the level of horses' teeth. That is, wear and tear at the molecular level might, like the wear and tear on horses' teeth, have nothing to do with the fundamental causes of aging or its effects. Until experiments are devised to test directly whether mitochondrial damage causes age changes we can only admire the ingenuity of the biogerontologists who have developed such an interesting theory.

THE RATE OF LIVING THEORY

The rate of living theory is based on the belief that animals are born with a limited amount of some substance, potential energy, or physiological capacity that can be expended at various rates. If it is used up rapidly, aging begins early. If it is consumed slowly, then aging will be slowed. The theory is often referred to as the "live fast, die young" theory.

The germ of the theory was first articulated in 1908 by the German physiologist Max Rubner, who, as I mentioned in chapter 13, discovered the relationship between metabolic rate, body size, and longevity. Rubner found that in several species of animals of different sizes and life spans, each animal spent about two hundred kilocalories per gram of tissue during its lifetime. Bigger, long-lived animals spent fewer calories per gram of tissue per year than did smaller, short-lived species. The idea was discussed extensively in a 1928 book by the pioneer American gerontologists Raymond Pearl and Ruth DeWitt Pearl. They wrote that "in general the duration of life varies inversely as the rate of energy expenditure." This idea became known as the "rate of living" theory. Like Rubner, the Pearls proposed that what was finite was metabolic capacity, and when it declined age changes occurred. That is, an animal species is born with the ability to expend a finite amount of energy. Animals can expend energy quickly, age faster, and have a short life span, or they can spend energy slowly, age more slowly and have a longer life span.

Other rate of living theories focus on different limiting factors that, when exhausted, produce age changes. Suggested factors have included the amount of oxygen consumed (or even the number of breaths taken) and the number of heartbeats spent. However, both of these may really be governed by the metabolic rate or temperature— further examples of the difficulty of distinguishing between cause and effect. The heart of a mouse, during its three-and-a-half-year life span, and that of an elephant, in a seventy-year life, have each been found to beat about one billion times. A human heart, however, beats about three billion times in a seventy-five-year period. There are few biogerontologists who would defend the theory that the number of heartbeats has anything to do with the aging process. If it did, then the transplantation of a young heart into an older recipient would thwart aging and delay death. There is no evidence for this, however. (If there were, "young at heart" operations would present awesome ethical problems).

Wear and tear and the rate of living might work together in humans. Comparing a person with an automobile may provide a useful illustration. Let us assume that depletion of the capacity for living does not begin until the car is built or the human is fully developed. Suppose the car has only five thousand gallons of gasoline available, permitting it to travel one hundred thousand miles at twenty miles per gallon on a level highway with a few stops. Assume that this is equivalent to a human's having the ability to burn a specific number of calories in one hundred years in a stress-free, unhurried lifestyle. If you run the car a thousand miles a week, even on level highways, gasoline will be consumed rapidly, wear and tear will be great, aging will be rapid, and without repairs functional failure will occur in about two years. If a human burns up all of his or her allotment of calories in forty-five years, he or she too will have aged rapidly and died soon. Worse, if the car is driven in heavy traffic and up a lot of hills, it will incur greater wear and tear, consume fuel more rapidly, and age faster or fail sooner, just as a human might if he or she consistently metabolized at the highest level. On the other hand, if the car runs a hundred miles a week on level highways it will age more slowly, require fewer repairs, and run for twenty years before exhausting its fuel. Similarly, a life spent at a low metabolic rate will reduce wear and tear and last longer.

In humans, life in the fast lane is also called "burning the candle at both ends." The slower lifestyle might be labeled "being laid back." The rate of living and the wear and tear theories would argue that if you live a laid-back life you will age more slowly and live longer. This is an appealing idea, but like many other appealing ideas in biogerontology, there is little evidence to support it.

Not only is the substance or entity that supposedly becomes depleted in animals unknown, but there is no solid evidence that it even exists. For example, a human centenarian's heart has beaten about four billion times—four times more than that of the oldest elephant or mouse—and humans metabolize about eight hundred kilocalories per gram of tissue in a lifetime, also four times greater than the value found in other animals. We have no evidence, even anecdotal, that the aging process is accelerated in people or animals whose rate of living or energy expenditure is high, no matter how the theory is defined. Birds as a group have long life spans and high metabolic rates. And among humans, there is no evidence that stevedores, lumberjacks, athletes, or harried business people age faster than sedentary folks. Also, some centenarians have led physically active lives, while others have been inactive. There is no pattern. The rate of living, however defined, does not seem to explain human or animal longevity.

THE WASTE PRODUCT ACCUMULATION THEORY

If cells accumulate more waste than they can dispose of efficiently, a kind of cellular constipation results. In time, so the theory goes, the accumulated toxins and refuse could hamper normal cell function and slowly kill the cell.

There is some evidence that waste accumulation does occur. A substance called lipofuscin, or age pigment, accumulates in many kinds of cells as an animal or human ages. The cells most commonly found to contain age pigments are nerve cells—frequently those in the brain— and heart muscle cells. These surely are vital cells, and interference with their activities could have significant consequences. The brownish pigment is formed by a complex reaction that binds fat in the cells to proteins. It accumulates in cells as small granules that increase in size as the animal ages and is isolated by the cell within tiny membranous packages. There is some speculation that the pigment forms as the result of the free radical reactions described later in this chapter. A writer of colorful prose called age pigments "the ashes of our dwindling metabolic fires."

The waste product hypothesis has several virtues. The lipofuscin hypothesis of aging, unlike some other theories, does meet the criterion of universality. There is no dispute about the presence of age pigment in non-dividing cells in almost all old animals that have been examined. However, as attractive as the waste product theory might be, there simply is no good evidence that the presence of age pigment actually interferes with normal cell function. The material can be seen, frequently in large amounts, within cells, but the cells do not seem to show signs of distress. Also, not all nerve cells or cardiac muscle cells contain age pigments and in some old animals these cells contain little or no age pigment. However, it is not possible to examine all of the billions of cells. Despite its indisputable presence in some old cells, few biogerontologists believe that age pigment plays a key role in the aging process.

Anxious to trade on the ignorance of the public, some unscrupulous merchants have promoted the use of a drug called centrophenoxine, which in laboratory animals, seems to reduce the lipofuscin content of cells. When studied in humans, the drug does reduce blood sugar levels and increase oxygen consumption. However, there simply has never been proof that this or any other drug perturbs the fundamental processes of aging.

THE CROSS-LINKING THEORY

Water aside, most of the stuff of which our cells are composed is protein or proteins combined with complex forms of carbohydrates or lipids. Similar chemicals form the cement that holds our cells together to form tissues. Next in this progression are organs, each of which is composed of several different tissues. One of the most important and common proteins, found in tendons, ligaments, bone, cartilage, and skin, is called collagen. Almost one-third of all of the protein in our body is collagen. Collagen is sometimes called the "skeleton" of soft tissues, and in bone it has been compared to the reinforcement bars in concrete. You probably know collagen best as gelatin or aspic, which is made by boiling animal tissue and bones containing collagen. It is probably even more familiar to you under the trade name Jell-O, which is made by simply flavoring animal collagen.

The collagen protein is complex but consists primarily of parallel molecules that, like the two legs of a ladder, are held together by rungs called cross-links. Imagine rows of ladders with the usual rungs or cross-links but with the legs of each ladder linked to its neighboring ladders by more rungs. In young animals cross-links are found to join only a few neighboring ladders. The ladders are relatively free to move up and down; the collagen is pliable. But as animals age cross-links form a scaffold that connects a larger number of neighboring ladders to each other. In time, the cross-links increase the scaffold size, and the tissue becomes less pliable and actually shrinks. The effects of cross-linking are apparent in the behavior of our largest organ, the skin. Young skin is soft and pliable because of the small number of cross-links in the collagen. Old skin is more heavily cross-linked and, consequently, less soft and pliable.

The cross-link theory of aging postulates that with age some proteins, including collagen, become increasingly cross-linked and may impede metabolic processes by obstructing the passage of nutrients and wastes into and out of cells. This recalls the waste product theory of aging, but in that theory constipation is intracellular and not, as in the cross-link theory, mostly extracellular. Cross-linking is also thought to occur in more important molecules than collagen. Cross-links may appear in nucleic acids, the molecules of which our genes are composed; the consequences are analogous to what might occur using a faulty blueprint or template. Molecules whose structure is determined by a faulty blueprint or gene possess mistakes that may have serious consequences. Advocates of the cross-linking theory believe that as errors accumulate in diverse molecules over time, age changes are produced.

There are many normal chemicals in our body that, at least in theory, can cause proteins and nucleic acids to cross-link. The chemicals are called, not surprisingly, cross-linkers. Probably the best known cross-linkers are chemicals used for the industrial tanning of leather. The cross-link theory of aging, then, maintains that as we age the proteins and nucleic acids in our body actually undergo a process not unlike the tanning of leather.

Fritz Verzar, the founder of the famous Institute of Experimental Gerontology in Basel, Switzerland, developed an ingenious way to measure the shrinkage of collagen. At the time he did his experiments the phenomenon of cross-linking was unknown. Verzar placed collagen fibers from the tails of rats of different ages in test tubes. Tails are rich in tendon fiber bundles that contain collagen. Verzar determined that the older the rat, the longer it took for the collagen to shrink. Verzar was able to measure the relative age of rats by this method.

Why is the cross-linking theory of aging not more popular? The idea that cross-linking of important molecules causes age changes is appealing, but it is based more on deductive reasoning than on direct experimental evidence. There is little doubt that cross-linking occurs in collagen and some other proteins, but the idea that it occurs in the DNA of live aging animals is only speculation. And even if it does occur, there is no good experimental evidence that it actually impedes metabolic processes or causes the formation of faulty molecules. Perhaps cross-linking is only one of the many biochemical changes that occur over time and that contribute to various aspects of aging—it does not seem to be the most important contributor.

THE FREE RADICAL THEORY

No, the free radical theory is not based on a political conspiracy. It is based on a complicated chemical reaction that occurs when certain susceptible molecules in cells encounter oxygen and break apart to form highly reactive pieces. These molecular fragments are called free radicals. They are unstable and try to reunite with any other molecule that happens to be in the vicinity. When a free radical unites with an important molecule, mischief may result. The affected molecule might be deactivated or made to perform incorrectly. Denham Harman of the University of Nebraska is the chief proponent of the free radical theory of aging, although the germ of the idea was first introduced by R. Gerschman in 1954.

The chemistry of free radical formation and their subsequent reactions with other molecules is complex. Like cross-linking and waste product accumulation, the fact that free radicals occur is not in question. What is in dispute is whether the phenomenon of free radical formation plays a central role in aging.

The free radical theory of aging is supported by the finding that free radicals not only form the age pigments, but also produce cross-links in some molecules and can damage DNA. Free radicals have also been implicated in the formation of the neuritic plaques that are characteristic of dementia of the Alzheimer type. Because free radicals can react with so many different substances, including DNA, a strong inferential foundation has been laid to support a major role for free radicals in the aging process.

The most convincing evidence that free radicals are involved in age changes are experiments that have been done with another group of chemicals that is known to inhibit the formation of free radicals. These chemical inhibitors are called antioxidants because they prevent oxygen from combining with susceptible molecules to form damaging free radicals. Many antioxidants have been identified, and some, like vitamin E, are natural products. Our body even makes several important antioxidants, which further persuades some biogerontologists that free radicals must be important. The most important antioxidants in our body are vitamin E and maybe vitamin C. Enzymes called superoxide dismutase (SOD), catalase, and glutathione peroxidase also destroy some free radicals. Animals with longer life spans appear to have higher levels of SOD to detoxify the free radical called superoxide. Humans have the highest levels of SOD of all species studied. SOD has been touted to the gullible as an antiaging drug, but the cognoscenti know that when it is ingested it decomposes into its basic amino acids, which do not recombine to form SOD.

Antioxidants are frequently added to processed food to prevent oxygen from combining with food components. Without them some foods would become rancid, stale, or otherwise inedible as oxygen combines with their molecules over time. Antioxidants, listed on the labels of many breakfast cereals and baked products as preservatives, are analogous to antirust compounds, which prevent oxygen from combining with iron and turning it to iron oxide—rust. In a similar fashion, antioxidants in the body prevent oxygen from producing free radicals that might, in turn, damage important molecules. I don't recommend that you eat more breakfast cereal, Hostess Twinkies, or the antioxidants themselves, because there is no evidence that they slow the aging process in humans and the evidence for an antiaging effect in animals is weak.

The principle experimental efforts to prove that free radicals play a role in aging have involved feeding laboratory animals food containing large quantities of antioxidants. The animals have then been monitored to determine whether they live longer than control animals that have received no antioxidants. Although the results of such experiments are uneven, they have tended to show that the animals fed antioxidants do live longer than the controls. This result has been obtained with mice, rats, fruit flies, nematodes (a primitive worm), rotifers (a small pond animal), and the mold called neurospora. In mice, increases in longevity up to 30 percent have been observed.

However, before jumping to the conclusion that free radicals play a role in aging, several important points must be considered. First, animals fed large amounts of antioxidants are believed to dislike the taste of food treated in that way. As a result, it has been argued that they eat less than the controls and live longer because of the resulting caloric restriction, not because the antioxidants prevent free radical reactions. To answer this criticism, subsequent experiments have ensured that the total food intake was identical for the untreated, normally fed control animals and those fed antioxidants. The experimental animals still lived longer than the controls. Nevertheless, it's possible that the presence of antioxidants in the diet might affect digestion or absorption of food such that even if the experimental animals eat as much as the controls, the antioxidants may impede their digestion. This could have the same effect on life expectation as putting them on a calorie-restricted diet.

However, there is a more important criticism of the role free radicals play in aging. When experimenters say that the antioxidant-fed animals "lived longer" they usually mean that the *life expectation* of the treated animals was greater than that of the controls. However, to prove that antioxidants, or any other factor for that matter, influence the aging process, it is necessary to show an increase in the *life span* and not in average length of life. Why is this so?

Let us consider an extreme example to illustrate this important point. Suppose we enact legislation that bans the use of motor vehicles. What effect would this legislative miracle have on our life expectation and life span? As shown in table 7-3, it would add about 0.6 years to the life expectation of a newborn: on average, each baby could expect to live about 0.6 more years if traffic accidents were eliminated as a cause of death. Since eliminating motor vehicles would surely increase life expectation, should we conclude that motor vehicles cause aging? I think not. Banning motor vehicles would have no effect on what appears to be the fixed maximum human life span of about 115 years. It might extend our longevity if all motor vehicles were banned or antioxidants were administered, but neither result can be interpreted as a change in the aging process. In order to show that a substance perturbs the aging process, the experimenter must prove that its administration increases *life span* and not life expectation. It has not been proven unequivocally that free radicals affect the molecules that produce age changes, nor has the feeding of antioxidants been shown unequivocally to increase life span.

Nonetheless, the free radical theory deservedly enjoys much popularity, and many biogerontologists continue to study the phenomenon. They hope to prove categorically whether or not free radicals are a major cause of age changes. They have been encouraged by the finding that the rate of production of these free radicals is greater in shorter-lived species. Perhaps longer-lived species have evolved a method for producing more antioxidants or free radical destroying enzymes, thus reducing the number of damaging free radicals. Also, there is some evidence that more free radicals are produced in older animals, so there may be a direct link with age. The free radical theory may also be linked to the rate of living theory, the mutation theory and the wear and tear theory because all four may be affected by the rate and the production of free radicals.

Regardless of what the mechanism might be, the administration of antioxidants does increase the average length of life. The increase may not be caused by the effect of antioxidants on the aging process but instead by a process that delays the expression of age-associated diseases. The most intriguing aspect of studies done with free radicals is, perhaps, not what they *might* be telling us about aging but what they *are* telling us about disease. The administration of antioxidants to animals clearly seems to postpone the appearance of cancer, cardiovascular disease, degenerative diseases of the central nervous system, and depression of the immune system. The real reason antioxidant-fed animals live longer may be that the diseases that would otherwise have killed the animals at an earlier age are postponed.

Because these same diseases are postponed when animals' caloric intake is restricted, skeptics still believe that feeding antioxidants in some mysterious way mimicks the calorie restriction experiments. Regardless of the role that antioxidants might play in the fundamental biology of normal aging, they, like caloric restriction, are certainly sending us an unambiguous message about their ability to delay the appearance of the *diseases* of old age, and that message should not be ignored.

THE IMMUNE SYSTEM THEORY

Because the functional capacity of most organ systems declines or changes with age, theories have been built around the idea that functional losses in an important organ system are the main causes of aging. The systems most commonly advocated as the orchestrators of all age changes are the neuroendocrine system, discussed above, and the immune system.

The immune system is the most important line of defense against any foreign substance that may enter our body. As with any good defense force, the weapons are varied. White cells in the blood can deactivate and digest such invaders as bacteria and viruses. Other specialized white cells produce ammunition in the form of antibodies, which circulate in the blood, deactivate foreign substances, and prepare them for digestion by other cells.

The immune theory of aging rests on two major findings. The first is that, with age, the immune system's ability to produce antibodies in adequate numbers and of the proper sort declines. The second is that the aging immune system may mistakenly produce antibodies against normal body proteins. Ordinarily, the immune system should make antibodies only to foreign proteins or other chemicals that are introduced from outside. As discussed in chapter 10, antibodies mistakenly directed against "self" proteins may damage or destroy the normal proteins of the body. This results in what are called autoimmune diseases, not all of which are limited to older people. Good examples of autoimmune diseases that may occur in older people are some forms of arthritis.

When first described in 1900, the autoimmune phenomenon evoked dread because it suggested the possibility that a person's immune system might be turned from a defensive organ to an offensive one. The immune system could kill you by making antibodies against your own cells. The phenomenon was aptly named "horror autotoxicus."

Advocates of the immune system as the cause of aging argue that, as a result of a less efficient immune system or the production of self-antibodies, we are more likely to acquire and manifest the diseases and other pathologies of old age. For example, an immune system that might, in youth, have kept cancer cells or microorganisms in check, might, in later life, be less able to do so. A potential trigger for the decline in immune function with age may be the thymus gland, found in the upper part of the chest. This gland produces an important component of the immune system, called T cells. These white blood cells are essential in the body's continuing efforts to combat disease. The thymus begins to wither after adolescence, and it has been suggested that this triggers the eventual dysfunction of the entire immune system. (See chapter 10).

Despite the innate appeal of an altered immune system as the central cause of age changes, the theory suffers from several flaws that apply to other organ-based theories of aging, as well. First, it is not universal; some animals that age do not have a well-developed immune system. Thus one of Strehler's requirements for a tenable aging theory is not met. Second, the most likely change that indicates the decline in immune function with age is the greater incidence of disease, but disease is pathological, not normal. Immune system decrements have not been shown to influence the normal aging process.

The immune system is also subject to control by some hormones and by the nervous system, so there could be a more basic source for the changes found in the immune system as we age. Likewise, it is possible that the development of autoimmune diseases, which the immune system theory attributes to the system's mistakes in making antibodies to "self" proteins, is caused by some of our proteins' changing shape or chemistry as we age. If so, the production of antibodies against "self" proteins would be a normal, appropriate response to proteins the immune system did not recognize, and not a dysfunctional one at all. These are yet more examples of the difficulty gerontologists may have in distinguishing causes from effects. Clearly the immune system, like other systems, shows some functional decline with age, but there does not seem to be anything unique about the immune system that would argue for its being *the* master chronometer. Functional losses in the immune system, like functional losses in most other systems over time, might simply add to the totality of the entire body's age changes. As I have noted before, the body's many systems are interrelated in complex ways and all are affected by aging; so far no one has demonstrated that any one system is the master producer of all age changes.

THEORIES OF ERRORS AND REPAIRS

Nothing works perfectly forever. Every automobile owner knows that, given enough time, all mechanical things ultimately fail. If repair processes exist, the repairers themselves may make mistakes, or the processes they use may be inadequate or inappropriate. The impossibility of having perfect repair processes may explain why formerly "perfect" systems age and fail.

The production of proteins and the reproduction of DNA are fundamental to the maintenance of life, but these molecules are not always produced with absolute fidelity. Proponents of various error theories argue that an animal's manufacturing machinery incurs errors and, furthermore, that natural repair processes are incapable of making perfect repairs every time and may be flawed to begin with. As a result, errors creep into the molecules that compose or are produced by our cells. Advocates of the error theory argue that faults in various molecules accumulate to a point where metabolic failures occur, resulting in age changes and, finally, death. This is an attractive theory. There is indisputable evidence that errors do occur and that, although repair processes exist, they are not perfect and do not function forever.

The idea that errors might produce age changes is, to some extent, derivative of the earlier idea that gene mutations produce age changes. Mutations are random events—errors, in a sense—that occur in the genetic apparatus of cells. When mutations occur in the genes of a sperm or egg, the offspring that result might differ somewhat from their parents. Natural selection may then either favor the change, and permit it to be passed on to that animal's progeny, or reject the change, in which case the animal will die or fail to achieve reproductive success. Deleterious or lethal mutations are usually not passed to subsequent progeny. Beneficial mutations are retained by the animal because they give the possessor a reproductive advantage over the competition. These mutations drive evolution forward, making a species better adapted to its environment. Mutations may also be neutral and not affect the animal at all.

The mutation theory of aging holds that if mutations occur in the cells of our body—in the somatic cells, as distinguished from germ cells, which give rise to sperm and eggs—they could result in aging. Evidence for the mutation and error theories is weak, however, and their popularity, though quite high a decade or two ago, has declined significantly in recent years.

In 1952 Sir Peter Medawar, an Englishman who was awarded a Nobel Prize in 1960 for his studies on acquired immunity to tissue transplantations, proposed an ingenious variation of the error hypothesis of aging. The theory was further developed by an American, George C. Williams, in 1957. These scientists suggested that as animals evolve they develop, along with entirely well-behaved genes, genes that behave well in early life but begin to misbehave in later life. Williams postulated that successful animals would be those that developed a method for suppressing or delaying the action of misbehaving genes until after sexual maturation, when their expression would do less harm to the species. These good-genes-gone-bad then would not interfere with successful reproduction but would express themselves later in life as the physiological losses that we call aging. The late-acting genes could thus be regarded as having become aging genes.

There is a good model for this idea in the disease called Huntington's chorea in humans. It is a dominant genetic disease revealed later in life and characterized by constant rapid, jerky, involuntary movements. Victims usually show no symptoms until after reaching reproductive maturity, and they produce normal children, although these children might also be carriers of the faulty gene. Similarly, we might imagine some genes to behave normally until after sexual maturation and then to express age changes in the postreproductive period of life. Late-manifesting genes of this kind are essentially unaffected by the forces of natural selection. Michael Rose of the University of California at Irvine suggests that as the force of natural selection diminishes, the hypothetical late-acting genes would express themselves. The benefit to the species of deferring expression of age changes until after reproductive success would be the better preservation of the most precious cells that an animal possesses—the germ or sex cells. Without their preservation in optimum condition and their fusion with germ cells of the opposite sex, the species would be doomed. Genes involved in favoring the survival of an animal to sexual maturation might be regarded as "selfish" genes, in that all else is sacrificed to guarantee their perpetuation, even the greater longevity, or potential immortality of their possessor.

A corollary of this idea about late-acting genes is the notion that aging is an artifact of civilization because it is expressed only in civilized animals—humans or the animals humans choose to protect. No non-human animal spends two-thirds of its life span undergoing a slow loss in physiological function. We have learned how to change our environment so that we can live well beyond sexual maturation and experience the phenomenon called aging that perhaps we were never intended to discover. The theories of Medawar and Williams are clever and appealing, but testing them has defied the ingenuity of biogerontologists because we do not know how to do the right experiments.

A more general error theory was first postulated in 1961 by Zhores Medvedev, who then lived in the Soviet Union. By a quirk of fate he now works at the National Institute of Medical Research in London, where the late Sir Peter Medawar was once director. Medvedev suggested that errors might occur in either the mechanism by which self-duplicating molecules reproduce or in the cell machinery that synthesizes new protein molecules. He postulated that the errors might have many different causes, including free radicals, cross-linkers, and other components of complex chemical reactions. Repair processes, he felt, were insufficient to correct all errors.

In 1963 Leslie Orgel of the Salk Institute proposed a special case of Medvedev's error hypothesis. He suggested that because the machinery for making proteins in cells is so essential to life, an error in that machinery could be catastrophic. Proteins are molecules that are designed by DNA and are essential for almost all of a cell's vital processes. It is well known that errors in proteins cause many diseases. Could other errors in proteins be the cause of normal aging? How might this occur? To attempt to answer these questions we must know something about the manufacture and structure of proteins themselves.

Proteins are manufactured in cells with the aid of enzymes, which are themselves proteins. Enzymes are catalysts, so one or a very few enzyme molecules can manufacture thousands of copies of some essential protein. If an error occurs in an enzyme, then all of the proteins made by that enzyme would themselves be defective. Orgel called this an "error catastrophe" and postulated that it could result in age changes. The idea is analogous to the mischief that would occur in an automobile (cell) if a small error occurred in one of the machine tools (enzymes) used to manufacture other machine tools, thus propagating the fault to produce an "error catastrophe." All of the auto parts (proteins) produced by the machine tools (enzymes) would be faulty, and all of the resulting cars (cells) would malfunction or not function at all. Malfunctioning machine tools in an automobile factory would create faulty parts for *all* of the cars produced, and that would surely be catastrophic.

When first presented, this theory enjoyed some popularity. Best of all, it was testable. Alas, most of the test results did not support the theory. A few did, but only weakly. Old cells were not found to contain enough inaccurate proteins to account for age changes and clever efforts to force cells to make faulty proteins did not accelerate the aging process. Nevertheless, the basic idea of error accumulation as a cause of age changes has not been disproved, and there is some intriguing evidence that the accumulation of errors in enzyme proteins may contribute to aging.

Proteins are composed of long strings of amino acids, of which there are more than twenty kinds. A protein is comparable to a long string of beads of different shapes and sizes. Each type of bead represents one of the twenty-plus amino acids. The protein string may consist of thousands of amino acids, with varying numbers of each type. But proteins are even more complex than that. Just like a dropped string of beads, proteins can fold in almost limitless ways, and every twist and turn is absolutely vital to its ability to function! It is the structural properties created by the twists and turns, not the sequence of the amino acids (beads), that can be distorted most easily. In fact, errors in the twists and turns of proteins have been found in some proteins in old cells. Perhaps these kinds of folding errors are at the root of some age changes.

Most proteins also turn over, that is, most do not last a long time and must be constantly replaced. Proteins produced by an old animal's cells may be fine structurally, but may be produced too slowly to replace older damaged proteins. One protein that doesn't turn over rapidly is the crystalline protein found in the lens of the eye. Over time, however, it incurs structural changes that lead to lens opacity and, ultimately, to the cataracts frequently found in the eyes of older people. If this protein could be made to turn over—that is, to replace the changed older molecules more rapidly—opacity and cataracts might be prevented. In a similar way, if other proteins in the body turn over more slowly in the aged, then damaged older proteins could accumulate and cause age changes. These are interesting ideas for which some evidence exists in old humans and several other animals. However, the evidence is far from compelling.

As if proteins were not complicated enough, the amino acids that compose them can be either right-handed or left-handed. Like our two hands they may look alike but really are not alike; right hands can shake with right hands and left hands with left, but for left and right to clasp each other, one must be turned upside down. In all other respects the shape of our two hands is identical. In the same way, chemists designate amino acid molecules as either right-handed or left-handed. Right-handed molecules are identified with the letter *D* (an abbreviation for dextro-, or right), left-handed molecules with the letter *L* (for levo-, or left).

What is astonishing is that almost all amino acids produced by any animal, including humans, are the L, or left-handed, form. Even cells in culture will not metabolize right-handed amino acids. For reasons that are unknown we have a left-handed biology! After proteins are made, however, some of the amino acids in them may slowly and spontaneously convert to the right-handed mirror images of themselves. These right-handed amino acids usually change the behavior of the protein that contains them. Right-handed amino acids in the lens proteins of the eye may contribute to the opacity, described above, that leads to cataracts.

An amino acid called aspartic acid is found in tooth enamel and in the dentine that lies beneath this hard outer shell. Naturally incorporated aspartic acid is left-handed, or L-aspartic acid. Over time some of it spontaneously converts to the right-handed form, or D-aspartic acid. There is good evidence that the rate of change over time is fairly constant—about 0.1 percent per year—so the switch from left-handed to right-handed aspartic acid might be a good measure of biological age. Patricia Masters of the Scripps Institution of Oceanography in La Jolla, California, studied the tooth of an Alaskan Eskimo woman whose frozen body was preserved in the permafrost of St. Lawrence Island for sixteen hundred years. The woman was found to be about fifty-three years old by determining the amount of right-handed aspartic acid in the enamel of one of her teeth. From general body appearance she was thought to be between fifty and sixty years of age. A man, ninety-three years old according to his birth certificate, was found to be about ninety-six years of age when the aspartic acid changes in one of his teeth were measured. These results do not yet provide absolute proof that a biological marker has been found to determine human biological age, but they do hold promise.

The error hypothesis of aging that was refined and popularized by Orgel received added support from a discovery made several years ago by Ronald Hart and Richard Setlow who worked, respectively, at Ohio State University and the Brookhaven National Laboratory. It was already known that cells have mechanisms for repairing certain kinds of errors that occur in DNA, that most essential of molecules of which our chromosomes are composed. Genes, then, are also made of DNA; this fundamental molecule therefore provides the blueprint for all of life's processes. It also has the unique property of being able to reproduce an exact copy of itself. The preservation of the fidelity of DNA is so important that cells have developed ways to repair it if it is damaged. Damage to DNA may occur from the effects of normal background radiation, ultraviolet radiation, cancer-causing chemicals, and even some normal metabolic processes. Cross-linking and free radicals also produce DNA damage. We know of at least six different kinds of DNA repair systems. It has been estimated that if DNA repair processes did not exist, enough damage to cells would accumulate in one year to render cells nonfunctional.

Working with sophisticated molecular biology techniques, Hart and Setlow found that the ability of a cell to efficiently repair its damaged DNA was better in cells taken from animals with greater longevity. This observation was immediately interpreted as supporting the error hypothesis of aging. If less efficient repair processes go hand in hand with shorter life span and more efficient processes with longer life span, then perhaps there is a vital link between repair and aging. Animals with longer life spans may have evolved more efficient methods for correcting errors in their vital DNA molecules.

In spite of the attractiveness of these ideas, not all scientists who have attempted to repeat the experiments have succeeded in confirming the original finding. All that we can say with certainty is that DNA repair does occur in cells, but we are not sure whether it is truly more efficient in longer-lived species. This area of cytogerontology is ripe for further exploration.

One intriguing finding about DNA repair and the aging process applies not to body (somatic) cells but to sperm or egg (germ) cells. Errors in the germ cells are more serious for a species than errors in somatic cells because germ cell errors can be passed on to the animal's offspring. It has been found that the cells that produce mature sperm and egg cells have an extraordinary capacity to correct errors. Any accumulation of errors in the line of cells that eventually forms the sperm and eggs is either repaired or selected against by a process that spontaneously aborts the embryo. Thus, the errors are corrected or eliminated, and each new generation is, in a real sense, rejuvenated. Maybe that is the reason why babies are born young!

In 1972 Medvedev proposed an error hypothesis more specific than the general theory he offered in 1961. The basic issue is the extent to which redundancy can protect vital information or processes from degradation. Medvedev speculated that if genes exist in multiple, identical copies, this would act as a reserve system for vital information. That is, if an important gene incurred an error, its backup gene would take over the crucial job and save the cell from death or failure. Thus, having multiple genes, all carrying the same message and therefore capable of doing the same job, acts as a reserve of vital information, protecting the cell from random errors that might occur in any one essential information-containing gene. Ultimately, Medvedev theorized, all of the repeated genes would incur errors and the aging process would begin. However, this idea may be better suited to explaining the differences in species longevity than to explaining age changes, because the greater the frequency of redundant genes, the longer will be the species' maximum life span.

In the previous chapter we saw how redundancy in rocket design might parallel both age changes and longevity determination in humans. The analogy with Medvedev's proposal is that when rocket engineers want greater certainty of a mission's success, they include several copies of the software used by the rocket's on-board computers. In that way if one copy of the vital program becomes muddled, a second copy can replace it.

It is now commonly accepted that repeated gene sequences do exist, but direct evidence of their effect on aging has not been forthcoming. However, few direct tests of the hypothesis have been made.

Error theories have much to recommend them and the expectation is that they will continue to be modified as new data accumulate. In the future there is a good chance that some version of an error theory will turn out to explain an important proportion of age changes. One of the main virtues of the error approach is its universality and the fact that errors do occur in some of the molecules that compose all cells. Furthermore, one could easily account for the rate of error accumulation and thereby explain why the rate of aging differs in different species.

THE ORDER TO DISORDER THEORY

One fundamental change that could lead to aging has been studied mostly by physicists. It involves orderliness.

From the moment of conception, most of the energy and activity of an organism is directed toward reaching sexual maturation and adulthood. We have seen how evolution has selected those features that best ensure that a developing animal will reach sexual maturity. The developing animal directs most of its energies to fulfilling a genetically determined plan for the orderly production and arrangement of an enormous number and variety of molecules. These, in turn, are housed in the billions of cells of various kinds that, when appropriately arranged, comprise the tissues and organs of the developing animal. After sexual maturation, deterioration in peak efficiency occurs because, as Harold Morowitz of George Mason University puts it, "Perfect order requires infinite work." No system can supply infinite work indefinitely, least of all a biological system. In addition, deterioration builds on itself. As the molecular order that was present in the mature organism deteriorates because the work to keep it perfect fails, the efficiency of the affected biological system diminishes.

Disorder increases. This is the realm of thermodynamics, the branch of physics that deals with heat, energy, and entropy. Physicists say that *in a closed system,* matter tends to a state of equilibrium, which means increasing disorder. The measure of this state is called entropy and is described in the second law of thermodynamics.

Some biogerontologists believe that the efficiency of systems that utilize energy and drive biological development begins to diminish after sexual maturation, displaying increasing entropy. They believe that increasing molecular disorder results from mistakes in molecules, which also form the basis of the error theories just described. Advocates of this idea claim that the disorder that begins in particular molecules produces errors in other molecules that, in turn, cause the cascade of changes in cells, tissues, and organs that we call aging.

However, increasing molecular disorder, if it does play a role in aging, does not occur in all cells at the same time. Nor does it progress at the same rate in all of the cells in which it occurs. Of equal importance is the fact that we and other animals are *open systems* through which matter and energy flow. Thousands of environmental factors constantly affect us, including the food that we ingest and the air that we breathe. Nevertheless, increasing molecular disorder is an important contributor to age changes. Variations in rates of increasing disorder in the molecules that compose our tissues may be the reason why some of our tissues and organs age faster than others and why the rate of aging varies from individual to individual.

Return for a moment to the clock shop, where each organ or tissue is represented by a different clock ticking at a different rate. The point at which a clock starts to slow and then stop is a function of how well it was constructed, how carefully it was maintained, and how many ticks were possible when the spring was first wound. Our rates of aging depend on how well we developed, how we have cared for ourselves, how efficient our repair systems are, and our genetic heritage.

We can't really blame nature for the aging process. As pointed out earlier, she only designed us to reach sexual maturity! It is we who have tampered with her plan by permitting ourselves to live far beyond sexual maturation and to open this Pandora's box of functional losses that we call aging. After maturity our destiny is to incur the same kind of disorder in our former orderly molecules as does any machine or complex system in time. Even the universe itself is believed to be rushing toward an ultimate state of increasing disorder, or entropy. We know of no good reason why living things should be an exception.

SO WHY DO WE AGE?

Now that we know all of the major theories that might explain why we age, what is the truth? The truth is that we still do not know. Some biogerontologists take the easy way out and suggest that each theory has something to recommend it. They conclude that aging has many causes, which might include aspects of all the theories described. Others adhere to one of the theories with great passion and discount the merits of any other theory.

Gerontology as a science has been, until recently, derided by most mainstream biologists, in large part because of the proliferation of untested theories. However, biogerontology is no different in this regard than other well-established disciplines such as theoretical physics.

Theories involving electromagnetic and weak nuclear forces were recently unified, and now theoreticians are seeking to meld this into the theory of strong nuclear forces to form a Grand Unified Theory of the universe. (As the physicist Stephen W. Hawking observes, "This title is rather an exaggeration: the resultant theories are not all that grand, nor are they fully unified, as they do not include gravity.") Gerontology is now at a stage where several of the theories are being collapsed into each other, and, although much important information is not yet included in the merger, we are making good progress toward the biogerontological counterpart of the physicists' Grand Unified Theory.

Perhaps the most reasonable position to take at this time is to say that, because gerontology is such a young science, we simply do not have the basic knowledge needed to offer a good explanation for why aging occurs. However, we might take some comfort in the fact that, for the first time in the history of biology, enough dedicated scientists are working in the field of aging to offer hope that the speculation might soon end.

A PERSONAL VIEW

I used to be indecisive, but now I'm not so sure.
—Boscoe Pertwee

Given the aforementioned caveats, I offer some personal beliefs about the cause of age changes. Although I present the ideas that follow as my own, they of course depend on the views and thoughts of many of my predecessors and contemporaries. I will also reconsider the determination of longevity because of its intimate relationship to the aging process. I will make few attempts to assign priority to the ideas that follow only because in most cases priority is unknown or in some dispute.

The premise upon which the following ideas rest is that the survival of a species depends upon a sufficient number of its members reaching sexual maturation and producing enough progeny that reach independence to guarantee the continuation of the species. Natural selection, guided by beneficial mutations, has molded the biology and the survival strategies of all living things to achieve this fundamental goal. As previously indicated, the best strategy to guarantee that an animal or human will survive long enough to mature sexually is to provide it with more than the minimum required capacity in its vital organs. In this way, if damage or pathology occurs in an essential system before sexual maturation, there is a greater likelihood that the animal will still survive to reproduce and pass on to its progeny its superior physiological capacity. This general strategy, essential for the survival of all species, has evolved in different ways for various life forms. Energy and purpose are concentrated to achieve reproductive success which assures the immortality of the genes. The continuation of the germ line is the driving force of natural selection. Longevity of individual animals is of secondary importance.

Animals are selected through evolution for having physiological reserves greater than the minimum necessary to reach sexual maturation and rear progeny to independence, but once this critical goal has been attained, they have sufficient excess reserve capacity to "coast" for a period of time, the remainder of which we call their life span. This time period, then, is *indirectly* determined genetically. During the coasting period the animal functions on its excess capacity. This physiological reserve of energy and functional capacity does not renew at the same rate that it incurs losses, so molecular disorder—entropy—increases. Random changes or errors appear in previously well-ordered molecules, resulting in the normal physiological losses that we call age changes. These changes increase the vulnerability of the animal or human to predation, accidents, or disease.

What happens after reproductive success and raising progeny to independence is not important for the survival of a species. What happens next, of course, is aging and, ultimately, death. Wild animals, because they rarely live long enough do not experience aging. The entire scenario is analogous to the ticking on of a cheap watch after the guarantee period has ended. The watch's guarantee period corresponds to the time spent by animals to reach sexual maturation and to finish rearing progeny. After the warranty period ends, the watch does not simply "die" because it would be prohibitively expensive to put a mechanism in a cheap watch that would cause it to self-destruct on the day after the guarantee expires. Likewise, it would cost too much in energy to make a system in an animal that would cause it to die precisely on the day that its progeny become independent. What happens after the guarantee period expires in watches and after the reproductive period in animals is aging, which inexorably leads to failure in watches and death in animals.

The ideas of Williams offer an alternative to the idea that increasing entropy occurs after sexual maturation. In his way of thinking, survival to sexual maturation is accomplished by postponing until after reproductive maturity the effects of genes that perform well in youth but become mischief-makers later. When these once good, now harmful genes eventually do switch on, they provide the blueprint for age changes.

This personal view of life span determination and why we age is necessarily provisional given the lack of basic information in this field; my views will no doubt change as new information becomes available. But if the general thrust of these ideas is correct, then it would be useful to think about aging in a different way than most people do. Experiments are designed to answer questions. Scientists have long known that important results are not so much predicated on what information is obtained experimentally as on whether the right question was asked when the experiment was designed. But it is often difficult to know what is the right question to ask. If the wrong question was asked, then the experimental results will answer a useless question.

Until now we have almost always thought about aging by asking, "Why do we age?" And biogerontologists have designed their experiments to attempt to answer this question. The results have not been impressive. With the exception of the discovery that age changes occur within individual cells, we do not know much more today about the fundamental cause of aging than we did a century ago. Most of what we have learned is descriptive: we know much more about *what* happens than we did before but very little about *why* it happens. Biogerontologists have described changes that occur as we age from the molecular level up to the level of the whole animal. However, these descriptive observations add little to our understanding of the basic process.

It is for this reason that George Sacher proposed that we have been asking the wrong question. Instead of asking "Why do we age?" we should ask "Why do we live as long as we do?" By asking that question we might reorder our thinking and be able to design experiments to obtain more fundamental information. I think this is a useful new approach and I hope that more biogerontologists will come to appreciate the subtle but important reason for asking this better question.

Implicit in the question "Why do we live as long as we do?" is the idea that our longevity has increased and may be capable of increasing further. That appears to be true, since the human life span is known to have increased since prehistoric times. If our life span has increased, then it is likely that the start of the aging process has changed within the new time frame. Based on this reasoning, we may conclude that the aging process is malleable, that we can understand how it occurs, and that perhaps we can tamper with it. The goal of experiments designed to answer this new question would be to obtain information on how the body has changed over the millennia such that longevity increased and the aging process slowed. In the next section, we will consider man's attempts to thwart aging and death and will evaluate the extent to which we have been successful in manipulating the aging process.

PART FIVE

Slowing Aging and Increasing Life Span

CHAPTER 16

Early Attempts to Control Aging

However old we are, our probability of death within
the next hour is never equal to one; there is therefore
no final barrier that we will encounter.

—A. Jacquard

O NLY in recent times have people become interested in what
scientists have learned about aging and how this knowledge can be applied to controlling or even reversing the aging process. In former
times, questions about aging, mortality, and immortality were largely
the province of philosophy and religion.

SHOULD WE TRY TO CHEAT DEATH?

In many religions, philosophies, and fields of science, old age and
death have been accepted as inevitable consequences of life. Indeed,
it has been argued by some that both benefit the human species and
consequently should not be tampered with.

Several ancient myths exemplify early human thought on the inevitable consequences of old age and the impossibility that humans can

change it. A Babylonian epic, carved into twelve clay tablets around 650 B.C., describes Gilgamesh's obsession with immortality. Gilgamesh, a ruler in southern Mesopotamia who lived around the year 3000 B.C., consults with a sage who tells him that to be victorious over death he must first conquer sleep by staying awake for seven days and nights. Gilgamesh tries and fails. Even Gilgamesh, who is part god, cannot defeat sleep, to say nothing of defeating aging and death.

The Greek legend of Tithonus, which dates from about the same time as the Gilgamesh epic, is told by Aphrodite, the goddess of love. Tithonus, a Trojan, loves Eos, the goddess of dawn. Eos asks Zeus to make Tithonus immortal, but unfortunately she neglects to ask also that Tithonus retain his youth. The lovers are happy for a while, but then Eos's terrible mistake slowly becomes apparent. Tithonus grows older and older and more and more frail until he is unable to move. He is shut into a room where he lies forever aging.

The concept of death as a benefit was methodically developed by the Greek philosopher Epicurus in the fourth century B.C. The idea found its way into Lucretius's poetic work *On the Nature of Things*, in which we read that it is necessary for each generation to grow old and die to make room for the next. This thought anticipated Thomas Malthus's hypothesis in the nineteenth century that populations tend to increase geometrically (1, 2, 4, 8, 16, 32, etc.), and the supply of food arithmetically (1, 2, 3, 4, 5, 6, etc.). Thus, overpopulation is inevitable and greater longevity undesirable. Lucretius noted that death is the fate of all men, even the greatest ones. He argued that it is presumptuous for those of us who have not achieved greatness to expect to accomplish what the greatest have been unable to do. Moreover, Lucretius employed the Epicurean concept of pleasure by stating that there is a finite number of pleasures and once they have been experienced there is no point in living longer. A modern interpretation of the Epicurean lament is the bumper sticker that reads, "So many women (or, if you prefer, men), so little time."

The Roman senator Marcus Tullius Cicero wrote, in the first century B.C., a defense of old age and death in his classic book *De Senectute*. It was printed in English in 1481 by William Caxton and in 1744, Benjamin Franklin reissued it in large type for the benefit of older readers.

SHOULD WE TRY TO CONTROL AGING?

Control of the aging process has probably been a goal ever since the first human realized that growing old reduced his or her prowess and heralded approaching death. Perhaps the oldest written record on aging appears in 1600 B.C. in an Egyptian papyrus called the "Book for Transforming an Old Man into a Youth of Twenty." It tells how to prepare an ointment for this purpose which, it says, has been "found effective myriad times."

Man's ability to exercise major control over nature was generally not recognized in the ancient Western world, so the possibility of prolonging life was seldom seriously considered. Since life, as a whole, was rarely a happy experience then, prolonging it was not a popular goal. Aristotle (384–322 B.C.) wrote at length on aging and death, accepting them as part of the natural and beneficial order of things. Thus, he extolled the brilliance of Nature, who arranged to make one's teeth fall out in old age precisely when death approached and they were no longer needed.

In the Far East, however, a different attitude prevailed. The belief that immortality and its corollary, eternal youth, could be attained had its origins in sixth century Taoist writings in China. Taoists believed that the universe and the human body are composed of two opposite principles in harmony with each other, the yin and the yang. Illness and aging were thought to result from an imbalance between these two fundamental forces. Taoist ideas about prolonging life permeate Chinese science and medicine to this day. In early Western civilization there was no comparable tradition of attempting to increase human longevity. That is not to say that there were no efforts to increase human longevity in early Western civilization, but they lacked the popularity that such efforts achieved in China.

In the eighteenth century, Benjamin Franklin, a man renowned for his common sense, encouraged the idea of increasing human longevity, which he believed to be possible with the advance of science. His view carried enormous weight with the public, coming as it did from a man who was associated with some of the time's most sensational scientific achievements—the invention of the lightning rod, the discovery of electricity and the principles of the steam engine. Speculation about flight, like talk of increasing human longevity, had long been a matter for ridicule, but the successful balloon ascent by the Montgolfier brothers silenced the naysayers. Franklin's belief that it was possible to extend human longevity influenced many previous doubters of his day.

Like Franklin, Marie-Jean-Antoine-Nicolas de Caritat Condorcet, a renowned French scientist and secretary of the French Academy of Sciences in the eighteenth century, reasoned that advancements in science would someday lead to greater longevity. He wrote:

> The day will come when death will be due only to extraordinary accidents or to the decay of the vital forces, and that ultimately, the average span between birth and decay will have no assignable value. Certainly man will not become immortal, but will not the interval between the first breath that he draws and the time when in the natural course of events, without disease or accident, he expires, increase indefinitely?

Here Condorcet is not just wondering about postponing age changes, but also about extending the human life span. He based his belief that the human life span would be increased on the belief that the environment would be improved, that acquired characteristics are inherited, and that profound advancements would be made in the medical sciences.

A contemporary of Condorcet, the Anglican clergyman Thomas Robert Malthus, who achieved immediate fame when he published *An Essay on the Principle of Population as it Affects the Future Improvement of Society*, attacked all three of Condorcet's basic assumptions. Malthus (a) denied that environmental improvements would significantly increase longevity, (b) was skeptical that the inheritance of acquired characteristics could proceed without limit, and (c) doubted that there existed a single example of an increase in life span through human intervention. To this day, Malthus is correct in respect to this third point, and the theory regarding the inheritance of acquired characteristics (Lamarckism) is unacceptable to modern geneticists. Most gerontologists do not believe that improvements in the environment play any role at all in influencing what appears to be the fixed human life span of about 115 years. Environmental changes may, however, influence life expectation, that is, how close we come to fulfilling the promise of our full life span.

Gerald Gruman is given credit for coining, in 1956, the term "prolongevity," which expresses the notion that extending human longevity is both possible and desirable. Gruman sees the Enlightenment as the dividing line between nonscientific notions about extending human longevity and progress in biology toward "a scientific foundation for prolongevitism" made possible by the scientific revolutions of the sixteenth and seventeenth centuries.

REJUVENATING SUBSTANCES

One of the most persistent themes in myths or legends about the reversal of the aging process or the defeat of death is the existence of a substance, usually water, with rejuvenating properties. Many describe a fountain with the power of restoring youth to those who drink from or bathe in it. The classic example of acting on these legends is that of Juan Ponce de León, who sailed for the new world in search of a fountain of youth. He did not find the fountain but accidentally discovered Florida in 1513.

The earliest reference to rejuvenation by a fountain of youth can be found in Hindu writings dating from about 700 B.C. References to rejuvenation by fountains also occur in the Old and New Testaments as well as in the Koran and Greek and Roman writings. The modern infatuation with mineral and thermal springs as cures for illnesses and sources of rejuvenation is doubtless derived from this tradition.

Many substances other than water have also been alleged to have rejuvenating properties. It was reasoned that if ordinary food and drink sustain life, then there must be a more perfect food or drink that will extend life. Examples are ambrosia and nectar of the Greek and Roman gods, the Hindus' soma, and *octli* of ancient Peru and Mexico. In the garden of Eden, the fruit from the tree of life conferred immortality. In addition to food and drink, precious stones, fire, charms, and magic ceremonies have all been considered means for increasing longevity.

ALCHEMY

In Western civilization the first major attempt to extend human longevity was alchemy in the Middle Ages. Like the first thoughts about increasing human longevity, alchemy had its roots in China. A Chinese alchemist in the first century B.C. advised the Han emperor to transmute mercury into gold and make tableware from it. By eating and drinking from these utensils, he would achieve immortality. In modern Japan, bathhouses can be found with solid gold tubs, in which a bather pays a handsome fee to sit, in the hope that an illness might be cured or longevity increased. Perhaps we should not be too quick to ridicule this practice. Today, Japan enjoys the greatest average life expectation of any country on earth! The ancient Taoists reasoned that if one substance could be changed into another, then human mortality also could be changed to immortality. The alchemists' goal was to find the elixir of life, or, as it was also called, the "philosophers' stone." By this time the Taoists in China had dominated Eastern attempts to increase longevity for centuries, while efforts in the West were just beginning.

Some of the Chinese alchemical thought was probably transmitted to the West by way of Arabic science. In the thirteenth century, alchemy in the West suddenly became a powerful enterprise that ultimately contributed to experimental science and to much of modern chemistry and medicine. It was the precursor of the belief that humans could significantly control nature through experimental science. Prior to this revolution in thought, it was generally assumed that the fate of humans was predetermined and immutable. Alchemists set for themselves two goals: to prepare a medicine that could cure all diseases and extend human life, and to transmute ordinary metals into silver or gold.

These goals were based on the belief that over long periods of time both immortality and the transformation of common metals into gold had actually occurred naturally. Alchemists reasoned that minerals evolved in the earth's crust in such a way that the base or lower minerals, like those containing iron or lead, were ultimately transformed by natural processes to nobler minerals containing silver or gold. It was known that in living things great changes occurred, such as the metamorphoses of caterpillars to butterflies and tadpoles to frogs. The belief in spontaneous generation was prevalent: living things such as worms and maggots were thought to arise from decaying matter, with mice formed *de novo* in dark places containing straw or abandoned cloth. Many animals were thought to live for centuries and some for millennia. If primitive animals could appear so suddenly, change so radically, and in some cases outlive humans, it was reasoned that humans also must have the potential for greater longevity and even immortality.

The greatest thirteenth-century advocate and popularizer of alchemy as a means for prolonging life was the Oxford scholar Roger

Bacon. His arguments in support of alchemy's potential embraced all of the earlier major themes for believing that longer life and immortality were attainable. Because he believed that people lived much longer in the past and in distant lands, he was convinced that the brevity of life was accidental and could be extended. He believed that longevity was reduced by the prevalence of immorality and sin and that the process was reversible. He argued that neglect of good health practices associated with diet, exercise, breathing, elimination, sexual activity, rest, and control of the emotions shortened life and that many animals learned how to avoid aging. Finally, he maintained that there were many examples of humans who had extended their lives considerably by finding or making secret potions, drinks, or foods. In these beliefs, Bacon stood against the prevailing medical dogma, which maintained that the length of human life was fixed and immutable.

The elixir of life, the curative, transformative philosophers' stone, was sought by all of the alchemists, but its discovery eluded everyone. Alchemy eventually evolved to become the basis for medical chemistry. Medical chemists were not interested in the transmutation of metals but sought to explain the workings of the human body in chemical terms. Most importantly, they believed that no single elixir or philosophers' stone could resolve all ills but that specific chemical cures must be found for each disease. Thus, a most extraordinary leap of thought had brought medical practice to a new level of sophistication.

CAVORTING

In Bacon's time it was recognized that many diseases were contagious and it was generally believed that good health was similarly contagious. Youths were thought to have the greatest store of the vital principle of good health. These beliefs formed the basis for Bacon's recommendation that one way to transmit the "vital principle" to old men and thus reverse the aging process was to have them lie with a young virgin in order to receive her "breath." This was certainly not a new idea. The practice, variously known as "shunamatism" or "gerocomy," was first described in the Old Testament (1 Kings 1:1–4), when the servants of King David, who "was old and stricken in years," said, " 'Let there be sought for my lord the king a young virgin; and let her stand before the king, and be a companion unto him . . . that the lord the king may get heat.'. . . So they sought for a fair damsel throughout all the borders of Israel . . . and brought her to the king. And the damsel was very fair; and she became a companion unto the king, and ministered to him; but the king knew her not." Nevertheless, as happens with modern yogurt eaters and recipients of cell therapy, "the days of David drew nigh that he should die."

Well into the eighteenth century there were those who covertly recommended the practice of rejuvenating old men by having them lie with young virgins. Marcilio Ficino's recipe for increasing a man's longevity in 1498 (quoted by Alex Comfort) dictated that "he should find a young, healthy, gay and beautiful girl, attach his mouth to her breast, and drink her milk while the moon is waxing and thereafter take *pulv foeniculi* with sugar."

Shunamatism was advocated by the great Dutch physician Boerhaave (1668–1738), who "recommended an old Burgomaster of Amsterdam to lie between two young girls, assuring him that he would thus recover strength and spirits."

Although there is no evidence that shunamatism works in humans, there are several reliable reports that regular mating increases the longevity of male rats. Researchers are as silent about the effect of mating on the longevity of the females as historians are on the effect of young virgin males on the longevity of co-habitating old females.

SCROTUM HOKUM AND OTHER NONSENSE

Erroneous beliefs about aging have been part of our culture for millennia. Although we have come to ridicule some of them—for example, ancient searches for the fountain of youth—many people still embrace equivalent panaceas in the belief that they can reverse or stop the aging process.

The suggestion that aging is caused by changes in the endocrine or hormone-secreting glands is certainly not new. In 1889, when he was seventy-two, the eminent French physiologist Charles-Edouard Brown-Séquard reported that he had rejuvenated his health by inoculating extracts of crushed domestic animal testicles into his arms and legs. Over the next several years, he and thousands of other physicians inoculated many older people. The press publicized the experiments sensationally and the medical journals were largely hostile. Brown-Séquard maintained that the extracts increased vigor, or, as he said, the "nervous force," so that the recipient could better vanquish diseases. The cult of injection spread throughout the world. Brown-Séquard distributed his extract to physicians without charge and forbid it to be sold. He personally paid for the costs of distribution. However, entrepreneurs were soon manufacturing the extract according to Brown-Séquard's directions, which were published in the open scientific literature. His lawsuits against them failed when he was advised that published scientific results were in the public domain and that his recipe no longer belonged exclusively to him. Although the extract prepared by Brown-Séquard has been proven to be ineffective, he is given credit for drawing attention to the use of tissue and glandular extracts as the sources of important therapeutic agents. He is considered to be the "father" of endocrinology.

In the 1910s and 1920s, the Russian Serge Veronoff grafted monkey testicles to gullible men, in the belief that transplants from nonhuman primates were more likely to be successful because monkeys are closer to man on the evolutionary scale than are domestic animals. Like Brown-Séquard's, Veronoff's early claims were soon disproven and the method was abandoned.

No one is known to have suggested the inoculation of monkey ovarian tissue into old women. In view of the dangers inherent in this procedure one might consider this to be a fortunate oversight and a rare example of women benefiting from unequal treatment.

In the early 1920s, John R. "Doc" Brinkley became a millionaire by transplanting the glands from goats and other animals into thousands of old people. Brinkley was a fundamentalist preacher who, without medical qualifications, opened a clinic in Kansas. There, with his wife, he ran a surgical assembly line in which grafts from goat testicles were inoculated into his ingenuous recipients. Goats were chosen as testicle donors because of Brinkley's belief that they were sexual athletes. Brinkley established convalescent centers, a radio station to advertise his services, and a line of pharmaceutical products. His wealth led him to run for governor of the state of Kansas, a race he lost.

In the 1920s and 1930s, prison doctors at California's San Quentin penitentiary implanted the testicles of executed felons into thirty prisoners in an effort to increase virility and stem the aging process. In view of the laws of immunology, which were discovered later, these transplants must have been uniformly rejected by the recipients.

Although a variation of this kind of rejuvenation therapy still persists in some countries in the form of cell therapy (see below), there is simply no evidence to support its validity. Modern biogerontological endocrinologists are more interested in the role of hormones as possible causes of age changes than as means of rejuvenation.

CELL THERAPY

The legacy of testicular transplants survives to this day in the form of "cell therapy," in which dried cells from the tissues of fetal or newborn sheep, pigs, or rabbits are inoculated into gullible humans in the unproven belief that the aging process will be slowed. The best-known practitioner of this trade was the Swiss surgeon Paul Niehans, who died at the age of eighty-nine in 1971. Like testicular transplants, animal cells are usually rejected by the recipients, who should count themselves lucky if they survive the potentially severe immunological reaction. Despite the risks and lack of evidence that it is beneficial, cell therapy remains a lucrative business in many countries, including Switzerland, Germany, Holland, and the Bahamas. It is not practiced legally in the United States.

A similar alleged remedy for aging was the practice of inoculating specific body fluids as a means of rejuvenation. In the 1940s Alexander Bogomoletz, president of the Ukranian Academy of Sciences and director of the Kiev Institute of Experimental Biology and Pathology, promoted the inoculation of a certain "cytotoxic" serum as a remedy for aging. A cytotoxic serum is literally an antiserum against cells. To prepare it, cells from one animal species are inoculated into another. The inoculated animal produces antibodies to the foreign cells, and those antibodies can be collected from its blood. Although antisera produced by inoculating animals with viruses or bacteria are extremely helpful in preventing or ameliorating some human diseases, there is no evidence that antibodies produced by inoculating whole animal cells are beneficial. In fact, there is the real threat that antibodies produced in an animal against, for example, human lung cells will attack those cells in a human recipient, causing a severe reaction and perhaps death.

YOGURT

When a Nobel Prize winner advocates a method for slowing the aging process, the world takes notice. This occurred during the first decade of this century when Élie Metchnikoff, a renowned microbiologist working at the prestigious Pasteur Institute in Paris, made a startling announcement. He claimed that humans are slowly poisoned by toxins produced by the bacteria that are normally found in their intestines. This, he claimed, was the main cause of aging. The remedy, Metchnikoff maintained, was to eat fermented milk, sour milk, or yogurt, because the lactic acid bacilli used to produce them are beneficial and would replace the harmful microorganisms. He bolstered his arguments by declaring that many of the allegedly longevous people of southeastern Europe and southern Russia ingested large amounts of yogurt. Thus was born the belief that yogurt and other forms of fermented milk could slow the aging process and even extend life.

Even if the gut flora is changed by ingesting yogurt—and there is considerable doubt that it is—there is no evidence that such a change will influence longevity. Even rodents with sterile guts raised under germ-free conditions for generations do not reveal any dramatic change in longevity.

The craze for sour milk products as a means of modifying the aging process lasted some twenty years. It created a new dairy industry and made the owners rich, yet no evidence has ever been obtained to prove Metchnikoff's claims. Modern yogurt eaters, largely unfamiliar with the food's history, ingest it because of its reputation as a high-protein, low-fat, low-calorie food. This reputation is not entirely warranted, either.

STERILIZATION

In 1920 a book appeared with the title *Rejuvenation through the Experimental Revitalization of the Aging Puberty Gland*. The author was Eugen Steinach, professor of physiology at the University of Vienna. He achieved instant fame, and his experiences parallel those of Brown-Séquard and Veronoff in several respects. Steinach argued that by tying shut the duct that carries sperm from the testicles (called vasoligation and distinct from vasectomy, in which the duct is removed), the hormone-producing part of the testicles would be stimulated and rejuvenation achieved. The operation results in sterility, but Steinach argued that it restored the health of several patients. In time, the results of vasoligation convinced objective observers that the procedure was worthless as a means of ameliorating poor health or reversing the aging process. Today, the operation survives as a means of sterilizing a male and limiting the progress of cancer of the prostate.

PROCAINE

The late Ana Aslan, a Romanian physician working at the Bucharest Institute of Geriatrics, promoted a compound called Gerovital for thirty years as a means of slowing the aging process. She achieved considerable popularity in Romania by promoting this substance, which is indistinguishable from the anesthetic called procaine hydrochloride, also known by the trade name Novocain. Procaine is used in the United States mainly as a dental anesthetic to reduce the pain of drilling or tooth extractions.

In 1951 Aslan found that procaine was unstable, so she added two chemicals called benzoic acid and potassium metabisulfate. The product was renamed Gerovital H3 (GH3). She claimed to have seen remarkable improvement in the health of older people to whom the material was administered. Most of the evidence was anecdotal, inadequately controlled, or based on subjective evaluation. Nevertheless, gullible believers from Western countries made sales skyrocket. With the proceeds she built a large research institute and earned substantial amounts of hard foreign currency for a grateful pre-*glasnost* Romania. She was a national hero when she died a few years ago.

Compelling evidence supporting the claims made for Gerovital H3 is unavailable. Studies done in the United States and the United Kingdom on Gerovital H3 produced no evidence for its efficacy. Gerovital H3 is not approved to ameliorate the aging process by the Food and Drug Administration in the United States, although it can be obtained in Nevada because of claims that it does not enter interstate commerce and therefore does not come under the jurisdiction of the FDA.

In the next chapter we will examine more reliable information based on modern scientific evidence about factors that affect aging, and we will see which ones hold the most promise for the future.

CHAPTER 17

How Exercise, Nutrition, and Weight Affect Longevity

Avoid fried meats, which angry up the blood. If your stomach disputes you, lie down and pacify it with cool thoughts. Keep the juices flowing by jangling around gently as you move. Go very light on the vices, such as carrying on in society; the social ramble ain't restful. Avoid running at all times.

—Satchel Paige

THE most direct way to increase our life expectation would be to delay or eliminate the causes of death—an observation that will surprise no one. Because the two leading causes of death in developed countries—vascular diseases and cancer—account for the majority of deaths, their delay or elimination would have the most profound impact on life expectation. In 1900 the leading causes of death were infectious diseases; their virtual elimination in developed countries has since resulted in a twenty-five-year gain in life expectation.

Short of eliminating all causes of death, we might hope to reduce their severity or incidence or to postpone their occurrence. Attempts to do so commonly focus on changes in lifestyle, particularly in exercise and diet. This chapter examines what we know about the effects of exercise and diet on aging and life span.

THE EFFECT OF EXERCISE ON AGING AND LIFE SPAN

Most people seem to exercise less as they grow older. Humans lose muscle fibers at an accelerated rate after about the age of sixty, becoming weaker, and aerobic capacity declines about one percent per year from the age of twenty to the age of sixty. Willingness to exercise is also generally reduced, perhaps due to cultural influences. Until relatively recently, in most cultures an older person was expected to "act his age." Now everyone is encouraged to exercise, and some formerly sedentary people, both young and old, are becoming exercise enthusiasts.

A common reason given for exercising is that it will increase longevity. This is true, but in a very limited sense. Exercise does not slow or otherwise alter normal aging processes or increase human life span. Exercise may increase longevity only to the extent that it modifies disease processes, notably that of cardiovascular disease. If it is true that exercise influences death rates, it is because it contributes to disease modification. There is simply no evidence that exercise, or lack of exercise, is capable of perturbing the fundamental aging processes.

There is considerable evidence that exercise can postpone or reduce the occurrence of heart attacks, angina, non-insulin-dependent diabetes, osteoporosis, and hypertension. There is also some evidence that exercise may elevate the level of high density lipoproteins (HDL) in the blood plasma (the so-called good cholesterol) and reduce the level of low density lipoproteins (LDL, or "bad cholesterol"). The higher the ratio of HDL to LDL, the lower the risk of cardiovascular disease. If exercise helps you to delay or avoid cardiovascular disease, the leading cause of death, it follows that your life expectation will increase. Exercise may also produce a general sense of well-being, reducing anxiety, depression, tension, and the effects of stress. However, this has not been shown to affect the fundamental aging process or to increase life span.

One of the earliest events that colored our beliefs about exercise was the collapse of the Greek runner Pheidippides, who died of exertion after running from the battlefield at Marathon to Athens to report the Greek victory over the Persians. Until the nineteenth century there was still a widespread belief that vigorous exercise was harmful to the body and reduced longevity. A sedentary centenarian professor once remarked, upon hearing of the death of a ninety-seven-year-old colleague, that in his youth the dead man was addicted to mountain climbing, which surely must have caused his early demise.

Studying exercise in experimental animals has not definitively established its relation to longevity. Forced exercise in laboratory rats has increased life expectation when started early in life; when started in later life, the results have been inconclusive. In experiments with fruit flies, high activity groups have shown a significant *reduction* in life expectation and life span when compared with more sedentary groups.

Simple observations lead to the general conclusion that exercise, per se, has little, if any, influence on life expectation. If it did, we would find lumberjacks, stevedores, and baseball players outliving taxicab drivers, sedentary businessmen, and general loafers. This does not seem to be the case. However, a classic study of London bus workers revealed that the sedentary drivers lived shorter lives than did the more active ticket takers. But was it lack of exercise that killed them, or the stress of coping with London traffic, or perhaps their greater exposure to vehicle exhaust? As is often the case, it is difficult to identify *the* cause from among many possible causes.

College athletes have become favorite subjects in studies on the effects of exercise on aging, health, and longevity, in part because many are willing to maintain contact with researchers for many years, as are their nonathletic classmates, who usually form the control groups. (Because of the belief that vigorous exercise could reduce longevity, early studies focused on college oarsmen, who were thought to engage in a particularly strenuous form of exercise.) Nevertheless, the perfect study of the effect of exercise on longevity has yet to be done. It would have to be longitudinal with decades of follow-up, for all the reasons given in chapter 9, so the cost would be enormous. But a bigger problem is the impossibility of assembling two study groups distinguished *only* by the fact that members of one exercise. The eating habits, health status, and genetic heritage of the athletes and the control group will never be identical. And even if the groups of students were perfectly matched, both might be distinguished from the general population by differences in health, motor skills, strength and stamina, personal habits, or lifestyle decisions, which may in themselves influence longevity and aging. Also, there is no way to ensure that the athletes remain active and the controls less so. The majority of athletes stop exercising when they stop competing. Athletic ability in youth seems to have little to do with whether physical activity is maintained in middle or old age. All of these considerations have, appropriately, been called *confounding variables*. For what they may be worth, here are the results of some less-than-perfect studies.

THE LONGEVITY OF COLLEGE ATHLETES

A report in 1932 found that, in a group of almost forty thousand men who graduated from college between 1870 and 1905, life expectation at age twenty-two was 45.6 years for athletes and 47.7 years for nonathlete "honor" students; for an average group of different men holding life insurance policies, it was 44.2 years. However, it was found subsequently that athletes graduating late in the period studied, between 1900 and 1905, had a lower mortality rate than all graduates. The researchers felt that this occurred because this group, unlike their predecessors, underwent a vigorous medical examination before they were permitted to engage in sports. Whether or not that explanation is valid, the discrepancy again demonstrates the likelihood of finding important variations that were not anticipated, hence not controlled for, which as a result cannot be explained with certainty. Applying studies as old as these today is also complicated by the fact that life expectation was much lower in 1932 and the causes of death were different—again, confounding variables.

In the early 1950s the *Alumni Cantabrigiensis* was published. This biographical list contains entries for all known students, graduates, and office holders at Cambridge University for several centuries up to 1900. A study was conducted on the longevity of 772 sportsmen who competed in athletic contests against Oxford University between 1860 and 1900. One control group consisted of 374 men who graduated with special academic honors and a second, of 336 random graduates. It is possible that the control groups included some athletes or that the random and athletic groups contained some intellectuals. Notwithstanding these complications, it was found that the intellectuals lived, on average, two years longer than the random group and almost one and a half years longer than the sportsmen. These small differences may well be attributed to chance, but it is clear that the athletes did not enjoy any marked increase in life expectation.

In a study undertaken at Michigan State University in 1951, 629 varsity letter winners were compared with 583 controls. Birth dates ranged from 1855 to 1919. The longevity of the athletes was found to be about the same as the controls. A Harvard study of men attending the university between 1880 and 1916 showed that the 275 letter winners in minor sports outlived the 177 letter winners in major sports and the 1,638 nonathletes. The letter winners had the shortest life expectation, although rates of death attributable to infections, cancer, and heart disease were no different among the three groups. A second Harvard study of 6,303 men confirmed that major lettermen lived one to three years less than the other groups. Little difference was found between the longevity of the minor lettermen and that of the nonathletes. In contrast, a study in which 172 Harvard and Yale graduates, each of whom rowed at least once between 1882 and 1902 in the four-mile varsity race, were compared with classmates picked at random found that the athletes lived six years longer than did the nonathletes. However, the control group was found to have a much higher than expected frequency of death caused by tuberculosis, which might explain this unique result. In five other studies, no difference was found between athletes and the general population with respect to deaths caused by infections, cancer, suicide or cardiovascular disease.

In 1986, a study of almost seventeen thousand Harvard alumni, aged thirty-five to seventy-four, by R. S. Paffenbarger, Jr., and his colleagues at Stanford University, concluded that death rates declined as energy expenditures devoted to physical activity increased up to 3500 kilocalories per week; above that level, death rates increased slightly. The expenditure of calories was calculated thus: walking seven city blocks, 56 kilocalories; climbing seventy stairs, 28; light sports, 5 per minute; vigorous sports, 10 per minute. The death rates were 25 to 33 percent lower among alumni who expended at least 2000 kilocalories per week in exercise than those among less active men. It was calculated that, by the age of eighty, those who exercised gained one to two additional years compared to those who were sedentary.

However, one commentator reasoned that, although eighty-year-old exercising alumni gain up to 2.15 additional years (depending on the form of exercise), the total time required to expend 2000 kilocalories per week in the sixty years between graduation and age eighty would range from 1.18 to 2.37 years. The years they gained were thus spent jogging!

Several more serious criticisms that are too technical to be considered here have been leveled against this study. The Harvard group studied, of course, is not representative of the general population. The results are also at variance with the other studies of university men described above, including several others at Harvard.

THE LONGEVITY OF BASEBALL PLAYERS

The Metropolitan Life Insurance Company examined the records of more than one thousand major league baseball players who played between 1876 and 1973, most for less than five years. As a group, these players had a death rate 25 percent lower than that of men in the general population. Their greater longevity may be attributed to the general good health needed to reach the professional ranks, to the "healthy worker effect" (epidemiologists recognize that employees with continuous access to quality medical care are maintained in better health and have lower mortality rates than the general population), or to genetic factors.

Baseball players are a highly selected group and factors other than athletic activity may affect these results. After retirement, the mortality of baseball players was found to increase rapidly, but it still remained lower than matched controls in the general population.

In virtually all of the above studies on athletes, the subjects exercised for only a brief period in their lives. This is a serious flaw because it does not answer the central question: Does regularly performed exercise throughout life have beneficial effects on health or longevity? Far too little pertinent information has been gathered to answer this question with any confidence.

THE LONGEVITY OF OLD ATHLETES

Several studies have shown that the best-trained older people who exercise achieve levels for many exercises that approach those found for most sedentary younger people. Some physically trained seventy- or eighty-year-olds can outperform a sedentary thirty-year-old, although genetic factors cannot be ruled out. Nevertheless, by age sixty-five most men have lost 25 to 30 percent of their muscle mass and a similar proportion of their strength.

We would like to have a well-controlled study that compares the longevity of athletes who have remained physically active all of their lives with comparably aged subjects who were sedentary. Regrettably, no studies have addressed this essential question, so we really do not know what effect, if any, habitual physical activity throughout life has on life expectation or on the aging process. If there is an effect, positive or negative, it must be small since we have difficulty observing it. Genetic factors, general health, socioeconomic conditions, and level of education are probably more important determinants, overriding any effect that exercise might have on aging and longevity. To the extent that exercise slows the progress of a life-threatening disease it could be said to indirectly increase life expectation. There is good evidence, for example, that exercise may slow the progress of cardiovascular disease. But as our discussion of the effects of banning motor vehicles demonstrated, not everything that increases life expectation has any affect at all on the aging process. If you exercise because it makes you feel good or because you believe that it might prevent, slow, or reverse the effects of a disease then, by all means, continue. However, if you exercise to slow the fundamental aging processes, we have no data that suggest you will succeed.

IS THERE AN ANTIAGING DIET?

A recurring theme in human attempts to slow aging or increase longevity is the belief that ingesting some special food or drink might do the trick. The candidates have included certain waters, ambrosia, nectar, yogurt, and even liquids containing dissolved pearls and gold.

As discussed in chapter 12, the sixteenth-century Venetian Luigi Cornaro, after a life of gluttony and sin, adopted a spartan diet and lifestyle, and achieved considerable fame by writing about his conversion and his belief that it allowed him to become a nonagenarian. Cornaro's convictions anticipated a remarkable discovery made more than four hundred years after his death.

The science of biogerontology has long been cursed with vociferous fringe groups that, without valid evidence, claim to have found ways to slow or stop the aging process. These people, almost always motivated by greed, prey on the gullibility of the uninformed with arguments that are to biogerontology what astrology is to astronomy. It is no wonder, then, that gerontologists responded with considerable skepticism to a claim made about sixty years ago that a way had been found to not only double but triple an animal's life span. Skepticism was increased by the additional claim that the method would also retard or eliminate the occurrence of cancer and other diseases of old age—and all of this could be accomplished by maintaining a slim and youthful appearance! These claims certainly sound impossible, but they have turned out to be true.

Building on work reported some twenty years earlier, Clive M. McCay and his colleagues at Cornell University astounded biogerontologists when in 1934 they reported that laboratory rats fed a diet containing normal amounts of vitamins, proteins, and minerals but extremely low in calories grew more slowly and lived much longer than rats fed a regular diet. In some cases they lived twice as long. It is important to understand that this calorie-restricted diet produced *under*nutrition in the animals, not *mal*nutrition. Malnutrition results from a diet that lacks components necessary to maintain life and good health. McCay provided all of the necessary nutrients but restricted the number of calories severely. The McCay diet is called "undernutrition without malnutrition" by some gerontologists and "caloric restriction" by others.

McCay reasoned that reduced caloric intake slowed an animal's development and, therefore, its longevity increased: if a lifetime of biological milestones were marked on a rubber band, then caloric restriction would simply stretch the band. Longevity, McCay thought, increased because the time between key developmental events was lengthened. Furthermore, in those rats whose growth was retarded by caloric restriction, the frequency of cancers was reduced and, like the aging process, postponed. In fact, all nonmicrobial disease processes were postponed in the underfed rats. Later, it was found that as the proportion of carbohydrates replaced with proteins increased, so did the longevity.

McCay's interpretation may, however, be seriously flawed. The reason is this: Laboratory rats are usually given all they want to eat and drink, and they normally live about two years. This we then assume is a rat's normal life span. But a wild, or feral, rat does not live that way. Its lifestyle is usually one of alternating periods of feast and famine. So wild rats may have their growth retarded normally by periodic, sometimes long-lasting, famines. McCay, by underfeeding his usually well-fed laboratory rats, may simply have reproduced what normally happens to a wild rat.

McCay may really have discovered the reverse of what he thought: that animals that eat all they want grow and age faster and live shorter lives than do their underfed cousins. We might conclude, therefore, that, under natural or wild conditions, animals whose nutritional needs are satisfied only intermittently represent the normal state of affairs. So, although the wild animal's potential for longevity may never be realized, it probably has the potential to outlive its caged counterparts who live a life of plenty.

McCay's experiments clearly show that the caloric content of food somehow influences longevity. He may have been looking through the telescope from the wrong end, but there is nothing wrong with the telescope.

One experiment that might help us to understand this problem would be to capture a number of wild rats or mice, mark them, turn them loose, and then recapture them periodically. Over many months the experimenter would be able to determine how long the wild animals lived as the older ones eventually failed to appear in the traps. The ages of these wild rats or mice then could be compared to a group of wild cousins who dine, for example, in a granary where unlimited amounts of food are available. The question to be answered is simply this: Which group lives longer? The experiment would have to include controls on the animals' predators and, perhaps, on differences in their physical activity. My expectation is that the underfed animals would live longer. But the experiment has not yet been done.

Undernutrition without malnutrition remained a laboratory curiosity until recent years, when its importance was recognized by mainstream scientists. McCay's experiment has now been performed on many other animals, including fish, mice, silkworms, spiders, fruit flies, rotifers, and daphnia (the last two are microscopic pond animals). The results with all these species have been the same: caloric restriction produced animals with greater longevity. But rodents, insects, and pond animals are not like humans, nor are they particularly long-lived. We would certainly like to know if this effect would occur in humans or at least some animal closer to man on the evolutionary scale than rodents. A few years ago a dietary restriction experiment was begun using monkeys. Although the study is only four years old, the first, tentative results show that physical and sexual development is delayed in the calorie-restricted animals and that these leaner monkeys appear to be in good health. It is too soon to know whether their longevity has been increased, but it appears that dietary restriction is the best way to study the possibility of decelerating the aging process and increasing longevity. Conversely, unrestricted feeding is the best way to study the acceleration of the aging process and the reduction of longevity.

Underfeeding may not be an unmixed blessing. Some of the older reports claim that underfed animals are generally smaller, have altered breeding cycles, and may exhibit aberrant behavior. However, in more recent research the health of calorie-restricted rodents and their ability to run through a maze do not seem to be impaired, although caloric restriction clearly delays sexual maturation.

These differences again emphasize the importance of distinguishing the chronological age of an animal from its biological age, as discussed in chapter 1. Nowhere is the importance of this distinction more vividly apparent than in caloric restriction studies. Here, animals on a restricted diet may be identical in chronological age to animals fed all they want but are only *half* as old biologically.

Despite the possible drawbacks of caloric restriction, the benefits of increased longevity and disease postponement are obvious. These results should be especially meaningful for those of us in developed countries who have learned to manipulate our environment and can, essentially, eat as much as we like. Like McCay's control animals, we may be dying sooner as a result. (It is important to appreciate that many underprivileged people have a short life expectation because of malnutrition, not undernutrition. Malnutrition may occur even when a sufficient amount of food is available if that food lacks essential nutrients.)

Scientists have discovered no more effective way to slow the rate of aging or increase longevity in warm-blooded animals than undernutrition without malnutrition. Nor do we know of a more effective means of postponing or eliminating so many kinds of cancers and other diseases.

Early experiments suggested that the sooner caloric restriction is imposed after weaning, the greater its effect. It was therefore believed that the fundamental aging process, and perhaps the factors involved in life span determination, might be manipulable only in youth. Today, there is persuasive evidence that undernutrition begun in young adults or even middle-aged animals will extend longevity. This implies that whatever factors influence longevity are active virtually throughout life.

HOW DOES CALORIC RESTRICTION WORK?

Despite extensive research the mechanism by which caloric restriction works is not clearly understood. As discussed, it was initially believed that it simply slowed developmental processes; it might, for example, take twice as long for a calorie-restricted rat to reach sexual maturity as it would for an animal that fed at will. But since caloric restriction has been found to extend longevity almost as much when begun in adulthood as when begun in youth, the old belief is no longer tenable. The true explanation has been the subject of intensive research during the past decade.

One approach that has yielded important results has attempted to answer this question: Is the increase in longevity attributable to caloric restriction caused by reducing the intake of energy or by reducing some specific component of the diet? Edward Masoro, Byung P. Yu, and their colleagues at the University of Texas have shown clearly that the antiaging action of dietary restriction is due to the reduced intake of energy rather than the reduced consumption of some particular food component or contaminant. These researchers believe that blood glucose levels are the key to understanding the mechanism. Their reasoning goes like this: Glucose, metabolized from carbohydrates in food, is the primary source of fuel for all animal cells. Masoro has found that although calorie-restricted and calorie-unrestricted animals burn the same amount of glucose per gram of tissue, the restricted animals have a much lower concentration of glucose in their bloodstreams. He believes that this lower amount of glucose in the bloodstream is beneficial because some of the products of glucose metabolism interact with important enzymes, proteins, and even the DNA of genes to impair or deactivate them.

As we discussed in chapter 15, when oxygen is used in metabolic processes, highly reactive free radicals are produced. The free radicals have enormous affinity for many different kinds of molecules and will combine with their closest susceptible neighbor. Thus, if a cell's free radical defense mechanisms are breached and unrepaired damage to important molecules accumulates, chemical mischief can occur that might be the basis for age changes. Glucose metabolism could contribute to the production of mischief-making free radicals.

All fuels are reactive and can cause damage, which is why they are fuels. Gasoline, when burned, produces products that may damage the engine—to say nothing of us and the environment—so we must design engines to blunt the damage. Engine repairs, necessitated by the trauma of internal combustion, must be made from time to time, yet despite these measures a gasoline engine eventually ages and dies. Similarly, the metabolism of glucose produces cellular damage and requires efficient repair processes. As with the gasoline engine, the repair processes are not perfect, and the cell must also eventually age and die.

In chapter 15 we discussed Max Rubner's "rate of living" theory. Rubner postulated that most animals use the same amount of energy per unit of body weight over the course of their life span. Thus, animals that use fuel quickly will have shorter life spans than animals that burn fuel slowly. Rubner reasoned that cells must incur damage as a function of the speed and magnitude of their metabolism: life cannot be sustained without damaging cells, however slow the metabolic rate might be. We have since come to believe that the rate of fuel use is only one of several factors that determines the rate and magnitude of cell damage. Genetic and environmental factors are probably involved as well.

Other than the formation of free radicals, glucose fuel might produce chemical mischief in another way. This possibility was suggested by Anthony Cerami and his colleagues when they were at Rockefeller University in New York City. It has been known for decades that molecules essential to life, such as proteins and the DNA of which our genes are composed, will react chemically with glucose. The process is apparent in food that has been stored for a long period or cooked. The glucose-protein or glucose-DNA reaction, called glycosylation, is revealed by the golden brown color of cooked food and the change in texture and taste of stored food. Any changes in such fundamental molecules as proteins and DNA can produce problems for a living cell. If one imagines this reaction occurring over time in the cells of living animals, one has the basis for an hypothesis that age changes in cells are caused by the cumulative effect of the glycosylation of proteins and DNA molecules. The ultimate products of the glucose-protein and glucose-DNA reactions have been called Advanced Glycosylation Endproducts (AGE).

Regardless of the chemical details, one view of how dietary restriction increases longevity and delays disease processes holds that in the cells of calorie-restricted animals reactive free radicals and Advanced Glycosylation Endproducts are formed at a reduced rate. With fewer free radicals and AGE present, the defenses against these chemicals and the repair of what damage they may cause are more rapid. One of the hallmarks of dietary restriction is a delay in reproductive maturity when undernutrition is begun in early life and a reduction in offspring produced when it is begun after sexual maturation. It makes good sense not to have babies when food is scarce—a fact that is known to animals but that seems to have been lost on the human populations of many less-developed countries. Thus, some biogerontologists believe that the diversion of energy from reproduction in times of food scarcity is an evolved strategy for survival. If true, this may explain why caloric restriction is beneficial to a species—but it still does not tell us how it works.

CAN HUMANS INCREASE THEIR LONGEVITY BY CALORIC RESTRICTION?

The waist is a terrible thing to mind.
—Ziggy, (The Palace Cafe, New Orleans)

It is tempting to conclude from our present knowledge that humans might increase their longevity by simply adopting a diet that includes all the necessary nutrients but is very low in calories. Most biogerontologists believe that is correct. Yet despite the fact that the discovery is more than fifty years old, few people have been sufficiently motivated to opt for a diet based on undernutrition.

In view of the overwhelming evidence that it will postpone disease and prolong life, why has there not been a mass movement to adopt the caloric restriction regimen? Aside from the fact that dietary restriction has not been proven conclusively to work in humans, I think the answer is that, for most people, the quality of their lives is more important than the quantity. I believe that a change in lifestyle, especially reducing daily caloric intake to levels of borderline hunger or near starvation, is too high a price for most people to pay for postponing disease and achieving greater longevity. Furthermore, we do not know what the long-term effects of caloric restriction might be on cognition. Although a few rodent studies imply that behavioral effects are minimal, rodents do not have human brains and many gerontologists worry that caloric restriction might impair some mental processes that are not possible to measure in rats or mice.

One individual who has opted in adulthood to live with a calorie-restricted diet is a respected biogerontologist, Roy Walford of the University of California, Los Angeles. Walford began his reduced calorie diet in mid-life after studies done by him and others indicated that longevity can be extended in mice even when the regimen is begun in mid-life. Walford disagrees with the idea that caloric restriction in laboratory animals simply mimics what occurs in wild animals. Control animals, he points out, have included not only those that may eat all they want, but also animals that are restricted by degrees; that is, some whose caloric intake is reduced by 10 percent, some by a greater fraction, from what animals eat when allowed to eat all that they want. Walford finds that the greater the caloric restriction, the longer-lived the animal—up to a point. That point is at about a 40 percent reduction in calories consumed, beyond which point real starvation results. Walford claims that even wild mice are not as calorie restricted as 40 percent-restricted laboratory mice because wild mice are not as small or as light.

I agree with Walford that wild mice surely vary in their caloric intake. My point is that most wild mice would not have the opportunity to eat all that they want whenever they want and, hence, whatever the level of caloric restriction, they would be expected to live longer in the wild (were predators and accidents somehow controlled) than laboratory mice that eat all that they want. My major criticism of the claim that undernutrition increases longevity still holds. I prefer to say that overnutrition increases disease incidence and reduces longevity. Although the difference may be subtle, it is important, because overnutrition is the more unusual situation in feral animals. Similarly, overfed humans are, on an evolutionary scale, a relatively recent development. The present human life span, which developed over several million years, probably did so under conditions of under-, rather than over-, nutrition.

Another point Walford makes concerns the correlation of the brain weight to body weight ratio with longevity. Walford maintains that the longevity of the animals that feed freely shows the correlation best. Therefore, he argues, caloric restriction is a true longevity extender because calorie-restricted animals live beyond what the brain weight to body weight ratio predicts. He maintains that the true state of affairs in the wild lies somewhere between feeding freely and living always on the verge of starvation. If extreme caloric restriction were the rule, then animals' development would be so delayed and litter size so small that normal predation would soon overcome the species. I agree with this but would emphasize that it only applies to cases of *extreme* restriction. Finally, Walford argues that for caloric restriction to work best all of the necessary vitamins, minerals, and trace elements must be provided. This, he argues, can be done easily in the laboratory, but would be unlikely to happen in the wild.

Walford also cites reports that Okinawans, who consume 17 to 40 percent fewer calories than the average for the rest of Japan, have, proportionately, more centenarians than do Japanese on the main islands and only 60 percent the incidence of heart disease, stroke, and cancer. A thirty-year-old report from Spain describes an experiment in which one group of clinically normal people in an old-age home were given calorie-restricted diets while a control group ate as usual. After three years, the calorie-restricted group had only half as many admissions to the infirmary for sickness and half as many deaths as the group that was fed normally.

Walford began his undernutrition diet in 1987. He does not regard his efforts as an experiment because, as a scientist, he understands that one subject does not make a valid experiment. His action will yield useful information only if a significant number of people can be persuaded to adopt his diet—or if he lives to some extraordinary age. He might reach age one hundred or so for the same unknown reasons that others have without restricting their intake of calories. However, if Walford lives to what we consider the limit of the human life span, about 115 years, the result could not be ignored, even with just one experimental subject. Walford deserves enormous credit for doing what few humans have attempted, and those of us who know of his efforts to increase our knowledge of human aging wish him well. We hope he outlives all of us.

In light of the results that undernutrition without malnutrition has yielded so far, we might amend a popular adage to read, "You are what you *don't* eat." However, a phenomenon seen in bees demonstrates an even more extreme effect of nutrition on longevity. When larval bees are fed royal jelly for about three days, they become worker bees. If a larval bee is fed royal jelly throughout its life, a queen is produced. Worker bees and the queen bee develop from fertilized eggs and are female. Unfertilized eggs produce male drones, which fertilize the queen. The female worker reaches half the weight of the queen bee, lives about one month, and lays no eggs. The queen lives five or six years and produces up to three thousand eggs a day, every day for her entire life span! No one knows why the constant feeding of royal jelly increases a bee's life span sixty or seventy times, but it is probably the most profound nutritional effect on longevity within a species known to biologists.

IDEAL WEIGHT AND LONGEVITY

Although the effect of caloric restriction on longevity of animals is well accepted, a recent observation in humans has muddied the waters. The challenge comes from results of the Baltimore Longitudinal Study of Aging (BLSA), the study of human aging described in chapter 9.

From the turn of the century to the 1960s so-called ideal height and weight tables for humans were prepared mostly by life insurance companies, based on actuarial experience with their policyholders. The insurance companies wanted to know how height and weight correlated with longevity. However, life insurance policyholders are not a valid sample of the general population. They represent a healthier, wealthier elite, more conscious of health problems and better able to afford health care and life insurance premiums than non-policyholders as a group. Also, the heights and weights used to construct the tables, especially in the last century, were often based on applicants' statements, not actual measurements. But even accurate height and weight measurements tell us little about actual body fat; determinations of build or frame were not taken into consideration until recently.

Despite these faults, the tables—especially those prepared by the Metropolitan Life Insurance Company in 1959 and updated with information from the Society of Actuaries in 1960—are widely used by physicians, public health officials, nutritionists, and the general public. In recent years these tables have broken down the numbers according to three body frames (small, medium, and large) and cover one broad age group (twenty-five to fifty-nine years), but they still do not give ideal numbers for each specific age.

Academic reports on death rates as a function of weight, height, *and specific age* began to appear about ten years ago. Forty different populations have been studied. The reports convincingly contradict earlier "ideal" height-weight tables. One study, by Reuben Andres and his colleagues at the BLSA, found that, contrary to popular belief, the lowest death rates among middle-aged people occur not in the leanest segment of the population but among those with weights ranging from the midpoint to at least 20 percent *over* the midpoint on the 1959 tables! The insurance industry reexamined its data and essentially confirmed the new finding; as a result, the 1959 height-weight tables were revised in 1983.

BLSA researchers found that being mildly to moderately "overweight" has been overemphasized as a risk factor for early death. They also found that individuals who are either extremely thin or extremely overweight live shorter lives. This surprising finding, that a little "extra" weight provides greater longevity, held for both sexes, so in recommending weights to promote longevity there is no reason to have separate male and female height-weight tables.

Metropolitan Life's 1983 height-weight table, for men and women aged twenty-five to fifty-nine, thus gives higher weights for heights than did the 1959 table. However, for reasons that remain unclear, these tables are still at variance with the BLSA data. Some people have suggested that applicants or examining physicians still understate weights to ensure that a new policy will be issued. No such cheating occurs in the BLSA study. A comparison of the recommendations for maximum longevity given in the 1983 insurance company tables and those based on BLSA data is given in table 17–1. Assuming the BLSA table is the more accurate of the two, the insurance company weight ranges are too high for those under age forty, and too low for those over forty. The Baltimore study has insufficient data to make weight recommendations for those aged seventy and over. Again, severe obesity is clearly a threat to life. In addition, people who have other significant risk factors, such as a family history of some disease, are cautioned that the values may not be applicable to them.

How can we resolve the BLSA finding—being thin does not favor longevity—with the apparently contradictory fact that caloric restriction increases longevity in animals? Roy Walford suggests that "heavier" people may live longer because the present American diet is so poor that people must eat more food, and hence more calories, simply to obtain all of the nutrients needed to live long.

The old height-weight tables may merely have reflected our cultural bias that "thin" is healthy and beautiful. When longevity, not beauty, determines the goal we find that we should weigh more than the pre-1959 tables said we should, especially in our middle years. To call this being *overweight* is unjustifiably pejorative; the greater weight should be called the *ideal* weight because we will live longer!

In the seventeenth century, Peter Paul Rubens painted subjects

**TABLE 17-1. Recommended weight ranges for height:
Insurance company versus Gerontology Research Center actuarial tables**

Height (ft and in)	Metropolitan Life 1983 weights (ages 25–59)		Baltimore Longitudinal Study of Aging weights for men and women (by age range)				
	Men	Women	20–29	30–39	40–49	50–59	60–69
4 10		100–131	84–111	92–119	99–127	107–135	115–142
4 11		101–134	87–115	95–123	103–131	111–139	119–147
5 0		103–137	90–119	98–127	106–135	114–143	123–152
5 1	123–145	105–140	93–123	101–131	110–140	118–148	127–157
5 2	125–148	108–144	96–127	105–136	113–144	122–153	131–163
5 3	127–151	111–148	99–131	108–140	117–149	126–158	135–168
5 4	129–155	114–152	102–135	112–145	121–154	130–163	140–173
5 5	131–159	117–156	106–140	115–149	125–159	134–168	144–179
5 6	133–163	120–160	109–144	119–154	129–164	138–174	148–184
5 7	135–167	123–164	112–148	122–159	133–169	143–179	153–190
5 8	137–171	126–167	116–153	126–163	137–174	147–184	158–196
5 9	139–175	129–170	119–157	130–168	141–179	151–190	162–201
5 10	141–179	132–173	122–162	134–173	145–184	156–195	167–207
5 11	144–183	135–176	126–167	137–178	149–190	160–201	172–213
6 0	147–187		129–171	141–183	153–195	165–207	177–219
6 1	150–192		133–176	145–188	157–200	169–213	182–225
6 2	153–197		137–181	149–194	162–206	174–219	187–232
6 3	157–202		141–186	153–199	166–212	179–225	192–238
6 4			144–191	157–205	171–218	184–231	197–244

NOTE: Values in this table are for height without shoes and weight without clothes.

SOURCE: Reproduced with permission from R. Andres, D. Elahi, J. D. Tobin, D. C. Muller and L. Brant, "Impact of Age on Weight Goals," *Annals of Internal Medicine,* vol. 103 (1985) Page 1030.

rather more ample than our current standards favor and clearly depicted them as beautiful. If our present vision of beauty regards people at their ideal weight for maximum longevity as less than beautiful, then perhaps we should revise our standard of beauty.

Although we have no good evidence to explain *why* being slightly "overweight" in middle age (heavier than was once thought ideal) should favor greater longevity, that it does appears to be beyond dispute. Life expectancy seems to be greatest at weights that exceed the old insurance company figures by 10 to 30 percent during middle age.

The resolution of the apparent discrepancy between the increase in longevity found in calorie-restricted animals and the BLSA finding that human longevity is increased at middle age when modest weight increases occur is probably due to several factors. Walford's speculation that, because of our poor diets, we must eat more calories to obtain the required nutrients, may be important. However, we must recall that the BLSA participants are a select group of educated and comparatively wealthy individuals. Their average longevity at all weights might be greater than that found in the general population because all are more likely to take better care of their health. The discrepancy may also be attributed to the possibility that caloric restriction in rats and other lower animals may, for some unknown reason, not have the same effect in primates. Thus, the study undertaken recently by the National Institute on Aging, and discussed earlier, in which monkeys have been put on a calorie-restricted diet, assumes great importance.

Other than eradicating diseases and manipulating diet and exercise, efforts to increase longevity have included changing the environment itself. Some of the more interesting approaches are discussed in the next chapter.

CHAPTER 18

How Temperature, Light, Transfusions, and Suspended Animation Affect Longevity

A man with a watch knows what time it is; a man with two watches isn't so sure.

—Anonymous

BIOGERONTOLOGISTS have attempted to manipulate many biological and environmental factors in an effort to perturb the processes of aging and life span determination. Some of the more important experiments and studies have already been discussed. What follow are the results of less well-known studies that investigate the effects of other factors on longevity.

TEMPERATURE AND AGING

It has been known for centuries that many biological reactions slow down at colder temperatures, so researchers have tried to determine whether reduced temperature slows the rate of aging. In many cases it does.

In 1917, Jacques Loeb and John H. Northrop, working at the Rockefeller Institute, discovered that the life span of fruit flies increased when they were kept at a cold temperature. The same effect has been found in various kinds of worms, water fleas, insects, rotifers, cuttlefish, sea hares, sea squirts, and fish. Longevity is generally two to three times greater for cold-blooded animals placed at temperatures several degrees lower than those in their normal habitat, even compared to animals kept at a temperature only ten degrees higher. Of course there are limits to the high and low temperatures that these animals can endure.

In some fish of the northern hemisphere, those that live in the southern part of their range, where the water is warmer, grow faster, mature earlier, and have a shorter life span than those in the northern, colder region. The stickleback, which lives about a year and a half in the south of France, doesn't even reach maturity for several years in the northern latitudes. Raymond Pearl used these findings arguing that as temperatures increase, so does the "rate of living": metabolism is higher, eggs develop faster, growth is more rapid, and most biological reactions are accelerated. Two cold-blooded animals of the same species raised at different temperatures will be the same age chronologically, but the animal raised at the colder temperature will be biologically younger.

Nevertheless, the simple observation that cold-blooded animals age more slowly in colder environments has become clouded by more recent experiments. It turns out that when fruit flies and members of some other cold-blooded species are kept at cold temperatures for only *part* of their lives, they do not live longer. Perhaps the cold increases longevity only when endured during a certain phase of life. Experiments testing this hypothesis have produced conflicting results. Today, we really do not know how cold influences the aging process. It is not as simple as Pearl thought, and temperature may have little, or nothing, to do with the rate of living.

We do know that several cold-blooded animals at higher latitudes can actually survive for some time in a frozen state. A reptile and four frog species have been reported able to do this trick, and recently hatchlings of the Canadian painted turtle have been shown to survive subfreezing winter temperatures with more than half of their total body water as ice. When warmed they had strong heartbeats, good blood flow, and normal breathing and movements. Animals that survive freezing do so, in part, by producing an antifreeze (technically, a cryoprotective or cryogenic agent). Frequently it is glycerol, but it may also be glucose. Ice crystals forming *within* a cell can pierce the cell's vital structures like microscopic spears and cause its death. But if ice formation is confined to the spaces *between* cells, then little damage is done and the animal will survive. The antifreezes seem to work by preventing the formation of intracellular ice crystals.

Temperature changes may not mean much to warm-blooded animals like ourselves, who maintain a constant internal temperature regardless of the surrounding temperature. Living in the cold should not be expected to perturb our aging processes, and in fact we have no evidence that Eskimos live longer than the inhabitants of equatorial countries. There are, however, examples of mammals that have survived freezing. In 1956, two articles reported that 30 percent of a group of golden hamsters survived without injury after being frozen for about an hour at a temperature of 23 degrees Fahrenheit. Almost half of their body water had turned to ice. It is not clear how the hamsters accomplished this feat. The arctic ground squirrel has been found to hibernate for eight months each year, with a body temperature a few degrees below freezing.

It is possible that a delay in aging and an increase in longevity may occur in animals that survive freezing in the normal course of their lives, though this has not been studied. As we discussed in chapter 8, normal human fetal cells will undergo about fifty doublings in culture. Cells frozen after any given number of doublings appear to remember that number indefinitely and resume doubling after thawing until the cumulative number is about fifty. Cells from human adults behave similarly, although the number of doublings that they undergo is reduced in proportion to the age of the donor. We know that this phenomenon occurs in normal animal cells as well. If surviving freezing delays aging and increases longevity in intact animals, it may do so in a similar way.

SUSPENDED ANIMATION

Zeus placed a beautiful boy in eternal sleep in the belief that his youth would thereby be preserved forever. In the more modern story of Sleeping Beauty, a princess and her court are put to sleep for a century and do not appear to have aged when awakened by the handsome prince. The idea of suspended animation also appears in Washington Irving's short story "Rip Van Winkle." However, the idea of increasing human longevity by extending sleep has been limited to the imagination of fiction writers, because neither the aging process nor longevity itself is known to be affected by sleep. But dormancy, in various guises, and hibernation do appear to influence longevity in other animals.

In lower animals, dormancy, often provoked by unfavorable environmental conditions, can take several forms. Insects may stop their growth at some stage (diapause), rotifers dry out (desiccation), or other small animals envelope themselves in a tough membrane (encystment). Rotifers, with life expectations of eight days to five months depending on the species, have been revived from the desiccated state after twenty-seven years. Encysted rotifers have survived for fifty-nine years. Some desiccated worm eggs have been revived after twenty years of dormancy. A water animal scientifically called the tardigrade but commonly known as the "water bear" can dessicate and revive many times, remaining dried out for as long as seven years. Wasps can live for several years arrested in the pupal stage. These states of suspended animation can be caused by many conditions, including extreme temperatures or changes in humidity, day length, or the availability of food.

There is a general belief that animals do not age, or that the aging process is slowed during these periods of dormancy. Once revived, the animals seem to resume their developmental programs from the point at which they became dormant. However, it is doubtful that the aging process is completely arrested because biochemical reactions stop completely only at temperatures approaching absolute zero, a temperature far more extreme than any of the conditions that produce a state of suspended animation. Chemical reactions might be slowed in dormant animals, but it is doubtful that they stop completely.

In the case of hibernating higher animals, like the bear, it is difficult to determine whether aging continues during the dormant state, but there is good reason to believe that the process is slowed. When animals are refrigerated and thereby tricked into hibernating longer than they ordinarily would, they do tend to live longer. Conversely, animals that normally hibernate but are prevented from doing so have shorter life spans.

CRYONICS

Benjamin Franklin wrote, "I wish it were possible from this instance, to invent a method of embalming drowned persons, in such a manner that they may be recalled to life at any period, however distant; for having a very ardent desire to see and observe the state of America a hundred years hence, I should prefer to any ordinary death, being immersed in a cask of Madeira wine, with a few friends, till that time, to be then recalled to life by the solar warmth of my dear country." In a modern variation on Franklin's wish members of the Cryonics Society advocate freezing humans in liquid nitrogen when they die (or immediately before legal death, the subject of a recent lawsuit filed by a terminally ill believer), to be stored until a cure for what killed them can be found. Then, they propose, each individual will be thawed, treated, and sent on his or her way. Their motto: "Freeze—Wait—Reanimate." (Those who cannot afford freezer space for their entire body may opt to preserve only the head. It will, presumably, be attached to a healthy body when resurrection occurs.)

There are several flaws in this procedure. As discussed earlier, animal tissue cannot be viably preserved in a frozen state unless a cryoprotective agent penetrates all of the cells. Whole, live animals that tolerate freezing are able to distribute this antifreeze through a functioning circulatory system. Without a functioning circulatory system the cryoprotective agent cannot penetrate into all cells. In the laboratory, this limits the amount of tissue that can be frozen and thawed with most cells surviving to scraps no bigger than a matchstick head. Furthermore, the thousands of different types of cells in the body probably require different rates of freezing and thawing to maintain their viability. Thus, freezing and thawing a whole body or head at a single rate (as is done) would probably not permit the survival of most cell types. Finally, when even tiny portions of animal brains are frozen and then thawed using the methods of the cryonicists, considerable cell destruction can be seen.

Modern cryonicists might be compared with the ancient Egyptians, who believed that mummification and a well-furnished tomb would allow the deceased to carry on in the afterlife. Modern-day cryonicists are no doubt as devout in their belief in resurrection as were the practitioners of mummification, and most biologists would give their present cryogenic practice about the same chance of resurrecting life as that of mummification.

Some biogerontologists have suggested that, although freezing is an impractical method for increasing human longevity, we might accomplish the feat by fiddling with the thermostat in our brain to lower our internal body temperature. The thermostat is thought to be located in the region of the brain called the hypothalamus. Surgical and chemical means have succeeded in "turning down" the thermostat in monkeys and rats, and the experiments suggest an increase in the longevity of the animals. However, much more work needs to be done to obtain unequivocal results. Even if proved successful, it is doubtful that many rational people would risk the possible side effects of such tricky brain surgery in order to increase their longevity.

AGING IN THE DARK

Fruit flies reared in total darkness live longer than those reared in continuous light. If raised in alternating light and darkness, they live longest when the dark and light periods add up to twenty-four hours, as opposed to an artificially shorter or longer "day." It is thought that internal clocks, affected by light and dark, influence longevity. Octopuses, cuttlefish, and squid, unlike fruit flies, live longer if raised in constant light. The explanation is intriguing. These animals usually reproduce only once and then die. Light stimulates the eye, which sends a chemical message through the optic nerve to the optic gland in the brain, where, in these animals it inhibits the secretion of a hormone that causes maturation of the eggs and sperm. Thus longer periods of light, like the long days of summer, inhibit spawning and extend the animal's life. Long nights have the opposite effect.

It appears that light influences longevity only in a few primitive animals. Several researchers have attempted to determine whether the longevity of higher vertebrates can be perturbed by artificially changing the light and dark periods each day. The results of these experiments have been equivocal, with the difficulties of interpretation further compounded by the role of undernutrition, which sometimes occurs in these experiments. We have no reason to believe that we can increase our longevity by light manipulation and no evidence that the annual differences in light and dark that do exist at different latitudes have any effect on human longevity.

CAN TRANSFUSIONS AFFECT LONGEVITY?

An old idea has it that there is something in the blood of old animals that can accelerate aging in young animals. Or, the reverse, that something in the blood of young animals might rejuvenate the old ones. The results of actual blood transfusions have not convincingly supported this idea, but some evidence has come from what are called parabiosis experiments. Parabiosis is a technique in which two inbred animals are surgically joined like Siamese twins, so that they share a common circulatory system, though their hearts continue to beat independently. The joining is done in such a way that the paired animals can move around. One experiment was done with over five hundred rat pairs by Frederic C. Ludwig of the University of California, Irvine. When a young and an old animal are paired, the older member is found to live significantly longer than a normal, unpaired control. When one animal dies, the other may continue to live but, unless surgically separated, it does so at the cost of dragging around the dead twin, which may contribute to its early demise. There does not seem to be a clear effect on the longevity of the younger member of the pair.

The experiments have not demonstrated whether any rejuvenating factor actually exists in the blood of the young animals or, if there is, what it might be. Perhaps, instead, the old animal produces an aging factor, which is inactivated by the young animal. Maybe the young animal's more vigorous immune system protects the older animal or the hormones produced by the younger neuroendocrine system delay the aging process in the older partner. Parabiosis experiments are difficult to do, and merely attaching two animals surgically does not necessarily result in a shared blood system. This technique is not currently popular in aging research, and little follow-up to Ludwig's experiments has been done.

Manipulating environmental factors can perturb the aging process in some animals, but we have no convincing evidence that this can be done in humans. Biogerontologists have long been interested in the possibility that environmental factors that perturb the aging process in animals might do so by affecting an imaginary internal clock. The search to locate this clock and discover how it works has led to some remarkable findings.

CHAPTER 19

The Clocks That Time Us

3,155,414,400	Seconds
52,590,240	Minutes
876,504	Hours
36,521	Days
5,218	Weeks
1,200	Months
400	Seasons
100	Years
1	Life

THE old saw, "If Mother Nature doesn't get you, Father Time will," has received its best support from efforts to find the biological clock in each of us.

Given an awareness of jet lag and the difficulty of adapting to night shifts, it is surprising that biologists have accepted the notion of biological rhythms in plants and animals only within the last twenty-five years. Only within the last ten years have some physicians and clinicians become believers. Biogerontologists are only now recognizing that biological rhythms might also be important in understanding the aging process. Biological rhythms are now accepted as important in the development and behavior of animals. The medical implications of these rhythms for humans are only now being appreciated. Rhythms, and the clocks that time them, are now thought to be good candidates for roles in the aging process. Even our perception of time seems to change as we age.

OUR PERCEPTION OF THE PASSAGE OF TIME

Guy Pentreath put it well when he inscribed the following verse on a clock in Chester cathedral:

> For when I was a babe and wept and slept, Time crept, When I was a boy and laughed and talked, Time walked; Then when the years saw me a man, Time ran, But as I older grew, Time flew.

Time seems, to most of us, to pass more rapidly as we grow older. The reason why is not known with certainty, but we can hardly be surprised: at the age of ten, one year is 10 percent of one's completed life and one or two percent of what remains; at sixty, the percentages are more or less reversed. If we think of time as a line on which we move from past to future, then as we age, each movement diminishes future time more conspicuously but adds less noticeably to what is past. But even as time seems to accelerate, we may find fewer novel events to commit to memory and feel that mental stimulation is reduced. For a child, everything is new; for an older person there are few surprises.

A statement attributed to Albert Einstein may have some merit in explaining why most people perceive time to fly faster as they get older: "When you sit with a nice girl for two hours, you think it is only a minute. But, when you sit on a hot stove for a minute, you think it is two hours. That's relativity." Put less graphically, in pleasant times we feel less time urgency and in unpleasant times we feel more. It might be that with aging, pleasant events appear to pass even more quickly than they did in youth, while unpleasant things are perceived to last longer. There comes a time, usually in the fifties, when most people change their perspective of time. Until then we measure time from birth to the present but look to the future. Middle age is a mélange of past, present, and future. And in old age we look more to the past but measure time remaining until anticipated death.

CIRCADIAN RHYTHM

Several biological rhythms are well documented; the availability of food and the activity of predators, for example, change with the seasons. One of the most common and familiar rhythms, the twenty-four-hour cycle, is technically called a circadian rhythm (*circa* in Latin means "about," *dies* means "day"; the word was coined in 1959 by Franz Halberg). Our body's metabolism obeys circadian rhythmicity, and circadian clocks may affect distant body parts by controlling the release of hormones. Circadian rhythms appear to be governed by the daily changes in light and temperature caused by the spinning of our globe on its axis, but biological rhythms do not just passively respond to cues from the sun. When animals—humans included—are isolated from the environmental cues, in caves or special laboratory rooms where such things as light, food, temperature, and sound are kept constant, they come to depend on an internal biological clock that is itself independent of the sun. This "free-running" clock has a period of close to, but not exactly, twenty-four hours. Because the period changes under certain conditions it is said to fluctuate or oscillate.

The first demonstration of the free-running period, or internal clock, was made in plants in 1729 by the astronomer Jean Jacques d'Ortous de Mairan. He found that a plant that opens its leaves during the day and folds them at night continues to do so when it is hidden from the sun. It took almost 250 years for the importance of this observation to be appreciated.

In 1910 the Swiss physician August Forel noticed that each morning worker bees arrived from more than a hundred yards away to join his family for breakfast on the terrace of their summer home, seeking to dine on the marmalade. They soon began to arrive even before the table was set, in anticipation of breakfast, and eventually drove the family indoors. The persistent bees arrived on the terrace at breakfast time anyway, and Forel concluded that they were able to remember time.

In 1929 Karl von Frisch and his student Beling marked bees with a dye dot and gave them sugar water each day at the same time. One day the sugar water was not presented. The bees arrived anyway. When the experiment was conducted in a salt mine far below the surface of the earth and away from any environmental cues, the results were the same. The oscillations of the bees' biological clock were determined by showing that the bees could be trained to arrive only when the sweet water was presented at close to twenty-four-hour intervals. When it was presented at nineteen- or forty-eight-hour intervals, the bees could not be trained to recognize the pattern.

The definitive experiment was done in 1955 when a French experimenter trained forty bees to drink sugar water between 8:15 and 10:15 each night in a closed room. Then he flew with the bees to New York City where he set up the same experiment. The next day the bees flew to the feeding table between 8:15 P.M. and 10:15 P.M.—French time. This proved that no environmental cue stimulated the bees to feed at a particular time. It seemed that they carried their own watches. As Parisian bees, they did not reset their watches to coincide with those worn by New York bees.

An internal clock apparently helps bees conserve energy by avoiding futile visits to flowers, which produce nectar and pollen according to their own circadian rhythms. This was first discovered in 1751 by Carolus Linnaeus, the Swedish biologist best known for inventing the system by which all living things are scientifically named. Linnaeus devised a clock that took advantage of the different times various plants opened and closed their flowers. He grew these plants in his garden and by looking at the flowers he could determine the time of day with good accuracy.

In the 1950s, Colin Pittendrigh at the University of Pennsylvania found that the circadian clock, unlike other metabolic processes, is not influenced by temperature. It is of no importance to the bee whether the sun is shining or not, or whether there are other temporal cues. The bee will visit the flowers of its choice at the time of greatest nectar production according to its internal clock.

Although biological rhythms are not as precise as mechanical or electronic watches, evolution has selected for tight enough constraints on their oscillations that they can be used as clocks. Engineers spend a lot of time pursuing the same result. Oscillations, or variations in timing can interfere with the functioning of complex machines, so they must be minimized. The timing gear in your car's engine must run at a precise period or the spark plugs will not fire at the right time and motor efficiency will drop. If the oscillations are too great, the motor may not run. Jet lag occurs in a similar way. When you arrive at a distant location after passing through several time zones, efforts to synchronize with the new time often generate unusual oscillations in the timing of simple events like wakefulness, sleep, and hunger. Soon the oscillations are dampened and your rhythms become synchronous with those of the people in the new time zone.

There are also noncircadian biological rhythms, some with periods of less than a second, and others with periods of more than a year. In humans, the electrical activity of the brain has a period of one-tenth of a second, the heart beats about once per second, and we breathe about once every six seconds. The cycle of sleeping and waking repeats once a day. So does the slight rise in body temperature in the afternoon and its fall early in the morning. Low-frequency (long-period) cycles include the 28-day human menstrual cycle and the annual, seasonal cycle for some hibernating animals.

WHERE IS THE CLOCK?

If an internal clock exists in animals, as appears to be the case, where is it located and how does it work? In recent years it has become apparent that there are actually several clocks, discrete but synchronized, and finding them has been the subject of much research. The finite ability of normal cells to divide could be one kind of clock. Curt Richter found the location of what might be the master clock in 1972, at the base of the brain in the anterior part of the hypothalamus. The exact location is called the suprachiasmatic nuclei or SCN. The SCN is really a pair of small clusters totaling about two thousand nerve cells situated just above the point where the optic nerves converge as they come from the retinas of the eyes on their way to the visual cortices of the brain. When Richter removed the SCN in animals, their circadian rhythms were disrupted. A later experiment confirmed the location: the researcher again removed this tiny group of neurons from the brain of a hamster, but this time replaced them with SCN from a hamster with an abnormal circadian rhythm. The graft recipient was subsequently found to have the circadian rhythm of the abnormal donor.

AGING CLOCKS

> Time is nature's way of keeping everything from
> happening at once.
> —J. C. (graffiti in the men's room,
> Strictly Tabu Club, Dallas, Texas)

How internal clocks actually work remains a mystery. Biogerontologists have only recently begun to study them but can make at least one important generalization: as a human ages, there is a loss of coordination among his or her internal clocks. Sleep patterns change, and periods of wakefulness increase, as discussed in chapter 11. More subtle changes occur in our capacity to regulate temperature. Desynchronization of our internal clocks may, in fact, play a key role in the origin or control of the aging process. It appears certain that more than one clock influences aging because age changes in our various organs and tissues seem to occur at different rates.

A SURE WAY TO SLOW AGING

> "Time flies like an arrow,
> fruit flies like a banana."
> —Anonymous

There is one certain, simple way to slow the aging process and significantly increase your longevity. The method, based on Einstein's special theory of relativity, requires only a wall clock and means of traveling at the speed of light. Start by facing the clock. You can tell the time because your brain reacts to the light reflected to your eyes from the face of the clock. However, it takes time for the light to get from the clock to your eyes—not much time, but in a story about time any interval is important. So if you start walking away from the clock, it will take just a little bit longer for each ray of light to catch up and let you know that another minute has passed. Now, suppose that at the instant you receive the news that it is midnight you begin moving away from the clock at the speed of light, the same speed as the light rays that brought the news from the face of the clock. Instead of letting the light—and time—pass, you begin traveling with the particular ray carrying the stroke of midnight in a particular direction. When the hands of the clock reach 12:01, the light rays that register and distribute that fact will never catch up with you. Time is frozen at 12:00 midnight.

To reverse the aging process, you simply have to move faster than the speed of light. Theoretically that is not possible, but in the movie *Superman* our hero circled the earth at a speed faster than light, forcing time backward and allowing him to save Lois Lane, who had earlier suffocated in a landslide. Superman did not, however, invent this way of reversing time. The method had been described in an earlier limerick, as follows:

> There was a young lady named Bright,
> Who traveled much faster than light.
>   She started one day
>   In a relative way,
> And returned on the previous night.

Actually, you don't have to travel at the speed of light, which is about 186,000 miles per second, to make time pass more slowly. Proof was obtained in 1971 by scientists who strapped supersensitive cesium-beam atomic clocks into specially reserved seats aboard four jet airplanes. Each jet then circled the world, two traveling west, and the other two east. Compared to a sister clock that stayed on the ground, the clocks that flew east lost a small amount of time and those that traveled west gained time. The loss or gain was measured in billionths of a second, but it was nonetheless detectable.

If you were to travel in an eastward direction relative to the earth, you too would lose time or age more slowly, but the amount would be infinitesimal. Magellan's decision to sail west may have shortened his life significantly, but few physicists attribute the loss to relativistic effects. To make a noticeable difference, you would have to travel much faster than is now possible. Nevertheless, airline crews who always circle the globe in an eastward direction will age more slowly than their westbound counterparts! Theory says that the greater the speed, the greater the effect. Travelers on a spaceship going about 87 percent of the speed of light will, after four years flying, discover that eight years have passed on earth.

Of course, we do not know what effect travel at or near the speed of light might have on the behavior of the molecules that compose us. In theory, an object moving at the speed of light would have zero thickness and infinite mass. Perhaps the effect would be so undesirable that we would abandon any dreams of slowing our aging process by accelerating to the speed of light.

The phenomenon of aging slowing down as bodies approach the speed of light is only paradoxical if you believe there is such a thing as absolute time. Einstein showed us that there is no absolute time. Time is dependent upon where we are and how we are moving. Physics suggests something else about aging: the universe itself is believed to have a finite life span, and it is generally agreed that most subatomic particles decay. If both the largest and smallest things in the universe are transitory, then the same must be true of everything in between. Thus, there is no such thing as immortality on a cosmological time scale. Fifteen billion years, the age of the universe, may, compared to our much shorter life span, seem to go on forever, but in fact forever doesn't exist.

AN EASY WAY TO INCREASE YOUR LONGEVITY

If increasing your longevity by traveling at the speed of light does not appeal to you, perhaps the following suggestion will. You need only accept this premise: When you are asleep you are not a productive, conscious, functioning person—you are not living life in any way comparable to the way you live it when you are awake. The time, then, is essentially wasted (although not in the biological sense). If this premise is granted, then extending longevity becomes a question of increasing one's waking hours, a relatively easy task.

If, for example, you set your alarm clock for thirty minutes less sleep each night from age twenty-five to age sixty, you would gain about 266 days in additional waking hours, or "life." This gain in "longevity" is equivalent to completely eliminating your risk of dying in an automobile accident! If you maintained this practice until age eighty-five, your increase in "longevity" would be about 1.25 years, equivalent to finding a cure for stroke as a cause of death!

PART SIX

The Future of Human Aging and Longevity

Life Extension and Antiaging Therapies

[Aging] is what happens to you while you're busy making other plans.
                    —with apologies to John Lennon

AMONG the many controversial ideas in the field of aging, at least one fact stands out as incontrovertible. No one has ever shown unequivocally that, in humans, any medical intervention, lifestyle change, nutritional factor, or other substance will slow, stop, or reverse the fundamental aging process or the determinants of life span. It is easy to understand why this statement is true. Proving it wrong would require a double-blind, placebo-controlled study of the proposed intervention in a sufficiently large number of humans over a long enough period of time to demonstrate an effect with statistical accuracy. ("Placebo-controlled" means that one group of test subjects gets the real substance or procedure and the control group gets a "phony." "Double-blind" means that neither the person administering the test substance or procedure nor the person to whom it is administered knows which one has been used.)

Even so, there are frequent claims that an antiaging substance has been found. Hundreds of different cosmetics have claimed to restore skin or hair to some subjectively more youthful appearance or texture. Such changes do not affect the fundamental aging process; they simply cover up or disguise some of its inexorable effects.

ANTIAGING THERAPIES AND PROFITS

The Consumer's Union of the United States estimates that Americans spent three to four billion dollars on cosmetic surgery in 1990—mostly in pursuit of a more youthful appearance—and another billion dollars for moisturizers. Add to these sums the unknown billions spent on vitamins, nutrients, medications, and antiaging programs and it is easy to see why this area is such a magnet for the unscrupulous. The monkey gland injections of several decades ago have given way to the life-extension movement, whose proponents distribute a formidable array of chemicals through mail-order houses, health-food stores, and youth doctors. Because they are sold as dietary supplements, with no therapeutic claims on the label, they escape supervision by the Food and Drug Administration. The alleged therapeutic benefits are instead described in separate pamphlets or books that, because they are not part of the packaging, sidestep the law.

Double-blind, placebo-controlled studies on the efficacy of antiaging nostrums have not been conducted because the cost is prohibitive; such studies, regularly performed for drugs and biologicals developed by pharmaceutical companies, can last several years, cost tens or hundreds of millions of dollars, and require advance approval by the FDA. A proper study of the effect of any alleged antiaging substance or program would require a testing period long enough to demonstrate an effect on the aging process, probably at least a decade or two. Many of the alleged antiaging compounds are common substances that cannot be patented or easily monopolized. The selling price of such nostrums is thus too low to cover the cost of a proper study.

Testing the efficacy of an antiaging compound or intervention is made even more difficult because we have no objective way of knowing whether it is affecting the basic causes or processes of aging. We simply do not know what the fundamental causes of aging are or what exactly determines longevity.

HOW DO WE TEST WHAT CANNOT BE MEASURED?

Alex Comfort, the English biogerontologist, believes that a large battery of tests might be used to assess objectively the effects of an antiaging intervention over a period of time that might be less than a decade. No single test reliably measures biological age changes, but Comfort and others argue that a large number of tests, taken together, could provide an objective measure of the rate of aging. Such a battery of tests was used in the 1960s to determine the rate of aging in survivors of the atomic bombing of Hiroshima.

The kinds of tests suggested for inclusion include anthropometric measurements, such as seated stature and trunk height; clinical measurements of skin elasticity, systolic blood pressure, pulmonary function, hand grip strength, light extinction, visual acuity, and auditory function; chemical measurements of blood serum cholesterol and albumin levels; and psychometric testing of such things as vocabulary, reaction time, digit-symbol, similarity, and tapping tests. Cells grown from skin biopsies also might be used to determine the rate of loss of doubling potential or the rate of cell migration from the biopsy.

No one has yet conducted such an evaluation of a possible antiaging substance or procedure with positive results. As suggested earlier, the financial and temporal cost of doing a proper study would be prohibitive.

WHAT WOULD HAPPEN IF WE LEARNED HOW TO MANIPULATE LONGEVITY?

I have already discussed what might happen were all causes of death now written on death certificates to be resolved. The survival curve would probably become much more rectangular, with deaths from "natural causes"—the normal loss of function in some vital organ—compressed into a few years close to the maximum life span. Of course, we haven't reached this point yet, but it is clear that we are moving in that direction as biomedical scientists progress in their efforts to control the leading causes of death. Amelioration of diseases, which may increase life expectation, is the task of the biomedical scientist, but efforts to understand the aging process and the determination of life span are the province of the biogerontologist. What, then, might be the pattern of human life if biogerontologists were successful, or partly successful, in tampering with the fundamental clocks that govern aging and longevity?

Alex Comfort suggests that biogerontologists may find it easier to alter the rate of aging than to thoroughly understand, and potentially perturb, the aging process. What outcome an alteration in the rate of aging would produce would depend on how much the rate was changed and when in life the changes began. It might be undesirable to alter the rate of aging before, say, age twenty, when developmental changes are still occurring. A lengthened infancy, childhood, or adolescence would probably not appeal to many people. Alteration of the rate of aging might not be possible before about the age of thirty, when the exponential part of the Gompertz curve begins (see chapter 6) and age changes first become manifest. Thus, altering the rate of aging in adulthood seems to be the most plausible consideration.

At the other extreme, few people would opt to slow their rate of aging when they are already old and infirmities are most likely to occur. The scenario likely to have the greatest appeal is one in which a slowing of the aging process is effected at a time, closer to, or in, middle age. Alex Comfort puts this succinctly when he suggests that we might choose as a goal to spend seventy or more years becoming a forty- or fifty-year-old. This might occur if caloric restriction worked as a means of slowing the rate of aging in humans.

Active life expectancy, as previously discussed, is also a critical concern. Most people would not wish for an increase in longevity that added only years of ill health, misery, or unhappiness. Of course the severity of illness that people would consider acceptable would vary, but if we succeed in slowing the rate of aging we may not be able, especially at first, to switch back to the normal rate if the slow rate becomes undesirable. A determination of when, in life, one is happiest poses the following dilemma: you must pass through the whole of life to provide an answer. The possibility of returning to an earlier and happier age once a determination is made leads to the realm of science fiction, where a time machine may be available to return one to an earlier age. There are many variations on this theme, some of which I will discuss in a moment.

AT WHAT AGE ARE WE MOST PRODUCTIVE?

Given the ability to slow the aging process, when might the best time be to begin? Most people would opt for slowing their aging process when life satisfaction is greatest. Determining when that is would involve a highly subjective, intensely personal decision. One way in which this question can be approached with some objectivity is to consider when in life work productivity is greatest or best. Of course, accomplishments in our work and overall happiness do not necessarily coincide but at least productivity can be measured objectively; the results provide some enlightening insights. Perhaps the most extensive study ever done on when in our lives accomplishments are greatest, was made in the early 1950s by Harvey C. Lehman. His monumental investigation entitled "Age and Achievement," evaluated productivity across a vast array of endeavors.

Lehman found that most creative achievements occur in the thirties, and the highest levels of leadership are reached in the fifties and sixties. He found a narrow range of ages for peak accomplishment but creativity and leadership can be observed at almost any age. Lehman measured creativity and leadership not only among his contemporaries but also for humans born at earlier times. Lehman's data and his conclusions have been criticized because he did not consider the number of people who were alive in each age group that he studied. The number of people in many of the groups that he studied grew rapidly, thus the age distributions were skewed to the young. Lehman also did not adjust his data for life expectation at the time he collected his data. Despite these reservations, his findings merit consideration.

Creativity seems to peak in the thirties and then it falls off rapidly. For a variety of reasons, including the prerequisite of years of experience, high levels of leadership are usually reached in mid-life or later. Athletes, depending on which parts of their neuromusculature provide the basis for excellence in their particular sport, may reach world-class levels in their early teens (gymnasts), late teens or twenties (sprinters), or early thirties (marathon runners).

What is clear from Lehman's data is the fact that superior human accomplishments span almost the entire lifetime, from the early teens for gymnasts to the eighties and nineties for popes and justices of the United States Supreme Court. Yet, with respect to creative endeavors, whether people live past the age of eighty-five or die at age forty, most do their best work in their thirties.

Aging and Longevity in the Twenty-first Century

Never make forecasts, especially about the future.
—Samuel Goldwyn

TODAY people in developed countries can, for the first time in history, expect to live long enough to become old. The enormous medical, social, and economic progress made in these countries in the twentieth century has added about twenty-five years to life expectation at birth. This dramatic rate of change will not continue into the next century—annual gains have declined and in some years not appeared—but the cumulative increase in life expectation has already had profound social effects. Matilda White Riley, a renowned sociologist on the staff of the National Institute on Aging in Bethesda, Maryland, has described the degree to which gains in life expectation have outrun the ability of society to adjust to the change.

Our society is still centered around youth. Until recently many businesses and institutions mandated retirement at age sixty-five, although many people that age are fully capable of continuing to work productively. Riley believes that while the twentieth century has been the era of increasing longevity, the twenty-first century will bring greater social opportunities "for older people to age in new and better ways." She argues that a decline of most physical and mental attributes is not inevitable with age, as formerly believed. I agree up to a point. We know, for example, that most people over age sixty-five have not suffered significant decrements in their previous physical or mental condition. However, with advancing years the number of older people who do experience decrements surely increases. The different rates at which age changes occur in each individual mean that some fortunate people will be found at almost any age in whom no losses are obvious.

Sixty-five may have been a reasonable standard of "being old" when it was first established as a retirement age in Germany in 1870, when life expectation at birth was less than forty-nine years. In the 1990s, however, it is unrealistic because life expectation at birth in Germany and many other developed countries is over seventy-five years.

THE EFFECT OF GENETICS ON FUTURE LONGEVITY

Today, two-thirds of all deaths occur in persons over the age of sixty-five. Almost one-third of these occur in persons over the age of eighty. Only 15 percent of those who die after age sixty-five and 5 percent of those over eighty are ever autopsied, so except for legally suspect deaths what is certified as the cause of death is often an educated guess or a physician's unsubstantiated notion of what the cause of death should be. Without an autopsy we rarely know for certain the cause of death in the old-old.

In one study, 30 percent of people over the age of eighty on whom autopsies were performed were found to have died of no known cause. The researcher concluded that the cause of death was probably the normal loss in physiological function attributable to aging, often called "natural causes," but that category does not appear on the death certificates used by the National Center for Health Statistics. In a recent Connecticut study of 280 people, whose deaths occurred from birth to age ninety-five, the cause of death stated on the death certificate varied in a major way from what was found at autopsy in 29 percent of the cases. In an additional 26 percent the certificate and the autopsy results agreed on the major disease category but the autopsy attributed death to a different specific disease. Nevertheless, we continue to base important research decisions, theoretical considerations, program development, and health policies on misleading or outright spurious information about the causes of death in the fastest growing segment of our population. About 10 percent of all medical costs are incurred during the last year of life; this alone should argue for a better understanding of the causes of death in the elderly.

There is ample evidence that our longevity is influenced strongly by our genetic heritage. As discussed earlier, a study by Raymond and Ruth Pearl more than fifty years ago found that 87 percent of people over age seventy had at least one parent or grandparent who lived to seventy or older. Forty-eight percent of ninety-year-olds and 53 percent of centenarians had two such parents. These percentages are significantly higher than those found for people who die at younger ages. Also, it seems that the age of the mother at death is a bit more likely than that of the father to predict a child's age of death. This correlation may not be entirely due to genetics; the lifestyle, nutritional habits, health care, and even the working careers of children may be similar to those of their parents, and these environmental similarities may in part explain intergenerational similarities in longevity. If you favor the genetic argument, the message is clear: choose your parents and grandparents wisely. Or, if you find the environment and lifestyle argument more persuasive: live like the long-lived.

To the extent that genetic heritage influences longevity, we would expect that identical twins living in similar conditions would die at closer to the same age than would fraternal twins. As noted earlier, they do. The difference between the ages at death of fraternal twins is almost twice as great as it is for identical twins. Longevity is not, however, determined by some genetic program that plays out from birth to old age. The genetic program directs development toward reproductive success and determines longevity only indirectly after sexual maturation. Longevity, then, is a measure of how far we are able to "coast" on the excess physiological capacity or redundancy remaining after reproductive maturity. The age changes that occur during the "coasting" period are random events, attributable to the increasing likelihood of molecular disorder.

Other observations also suggest that genes play an important role in indirectly determining longevity. The most notable is the obvious difference in longevity among animal species. An adult mayfly lives for a few hours, while a housefly is old in fifty days, a mouse in three years, and a human in eighty years. More subtle evidence for the role of genes in determining longevity is based on a phenomenon called heterosis or hybrid vigor. When a male member of one inbred strain of animals is mated with a female of a second inbred strain of the same species, their offspring live longer than either parent, are often larger, and reproduce for a longer time. (An inbred strain is produced by making more than twenty consecutive brother-sister matings, usually in experimental laboratory rodents. The resulting animals are almost identical in genetic composition, much like identical twins.) The effect has been found to occur in the fruit fly. Hybrid vigor is also displayed when a male horse is bred to a jackass. The mule offspring lives longer than either parent.

THE EFFECT OF NURTURE ON FUTURE LONGEVITY

Although our genetic heritage plays an essential role in determining potential longevity, the choices that we make about how to live clearly affect the outcome. Even the best of genes cannot compensate for carelessness in crossing busy intersections, or decisions to expose our lungs to tobacco smoke or our bodies to HIV or other microorganisms.

Several studies have documented what may be self-evident, that lifestyle influences life expectation (but not the basic aging process, nor the life span). It is not possible to quantify the effect of hypothetical longevity-assurance genes, but it is possible to measure the influence of certain lifestyles on longevity. A given lifestyle may increase life expectation simply by reducing the chances of contracting a particular life-threatening disease. This is quite different from slowing the rate of aging or affecting the mechanism that indirectly determines longevity. The life expectation of tobacco smokers, for example, is so persuasively less than that of nonsmokers that most life insurance companies charge nonsmokers a lower premium for the same amount of coverage. The use of tobacco can and does increase the likelihood of developing fatal lung cancer, thus lowering life expectation. However, lifestyle influences life expectation by altering the probability of certain diseases or accidents. There is no evidence that tobacco use or any other lifestyle trait alters the fundamental rate of aging or the mechanism that determines longevity.

Most of the reliable lifestyle studies have been made on nonsmoking members of health-conscious religious groups. Not all participants had practiced "healthy" lifestyles all of their lives. Some even smoked a little at one time in their lives; most drank little, if any alcohol. Only the Seventh Day Adventists studied restricted their intake of protein and fat. The Mormons studied had few restrictions on their intake of meat and sugar, as did the group of Catholic nuns. Not much in the tenets of these religious groups addresses exercise or physical fitness. These, and similar populations that have been studied, show large reductions in the risk of dying at various ages compared to averages for the general population.

Highly-educated members of the group of 306 Catholic nuns studied had a median survival of 89.4 years. In a group of 4,342 Seventh Day Adventist physicians, mortality for each age group was, on average, 44 percent lower than that for the white male population in the United States. A group of people in Dallas, Texas, selected on the basis of physical fitness and lower risk factors for disease, was also found to have significantly greater life expectation.

The findings from a few of these studies are summarized in table 21-1, with life expectation figures for the United States general population included for comparison. Note that each group has a significantly greater than average expectation of life at each age. But no one has specifically identified anything these groups have in common that explains their outliving the general population by so many years.

TWENTY-FIRST-CENTURY DEMOGRAPHICS

In 1991, the world's population of people over the age of sixty numbered almost half a billion. Almost half of these people lived in one of four countries: the People's Republic of China, India, the former Soviet Union, and the United States. More than 20 percent of all people over the age of sixty live in China. Fifty-seven percent of all people over the age of sixty live in the developing countries; this proportion is expected to reach 69 percent in the year 2020.

The segment of the world's population age eighty and over now numbers fifty million people, or 10 percent of all people over the age of sixty. These oldest old are the fastest growing fraction of the population in many countries, and 54 percent reside in the developed countries. However, after the year 2000, the majority of the oldest old will be found to reside in the developing countries.

Today, the world's "oldest" countries, those with the largest percent of their population aged sixty-five and over, are all developed countries: 17.9 percent of the Swedish population is sixty-five and older, compared with 12.6 percent of the United States population (figure 21-1). Sweden also has the highest proportion of people eighty years

TABLE 21-1. Life expectation of selected groups compared with U.S. general population

		Males				Females		
Group	Number in group	Life expectation			Number in group	Life expectation		
		Birth	65	85		Birth	65	85
Mormon high priests (1980–88)	5,231	86.5	25.5	12.7	-ª	86.5	24.9	11.0
Alameda County, California, with Mormon lifestyle (1974–88)	1,036	92.4	30.4	16.4	1,254	87.5	25.7	11.6
Insured Mormons (1980–88)	-	85.7	24.8	12.2	-	88.1	26.3	12.0
Dallas, Texas, Selected Population (1989)	10,224	88.4	27.0	13.8	3,120	98.1	35.0	19.0
Seventh Day Adventists (1960)	9,484	80.5	20.8	9.0	-	-	-	-
United States General Population (1989)	-	71.8	15.2	7.1	-	78.6	18.7	9.0

ªNot available.

Modified with permission of the Population Council. From Kenneth G. Manton, Eric Stallard, and H. Dennis Tolley, "Limits to Life Expectancy: Evidence, Prospects, and Implications," *Population and Development Review* 17 no. 4 (December 1991):, and *Vital Statistics of the United States,* 1989, National Center for Health Statistics, Vol. II, sec. 620, Life Tables, Washington, D.C. 1992.

old or older (3.5 percent). Japan, with the greatest life expectation at birth in 1991 (82.1 years for women, 76.1 for men), will "age" rapidly: 10 percent of its current population is over sixty-five; in 2005 the figure will reach about 17 percent. In 2025 half of the population of Italy will be older than fifty years. During the next sixty years, men and women aged sixty-five and over will comprise the fastest-growing segment of the United States population; the number of those aged eighty-five and over will increase at a rate four times greater than the rate for the entire group aged sixty-five and over.

If we assume that no extreme changes in fertility, mortality, or net

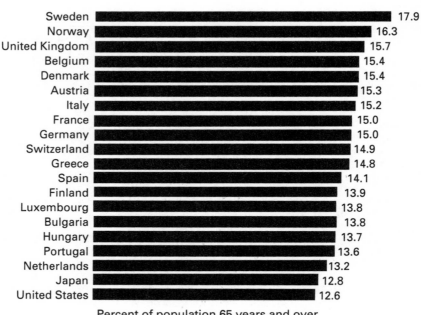

FIGURE 21-1. World's oldest countries, 1992

Country	Percent
Sweden	17.9
Norway	16.3
United Kingdom	15.7
Belgium	15.4
Denmark	15.4
Austria	15.3
Italy	15.2
France	15.0
Germany	15.0
Switzerland	14.9
Greece	14.8
Spain	14.1
Finland	13.9
Luxembourg	13.8
Bulgaria	13.8
Hungary	13.7
Portugal	13.6
Netherlands	13.2
Japan	12.8
United States	12.6

Percent of population 65 years and over

SOURCE: U.S. Bureau of the Census, Center for International Research, International Data Base on Aging and "An Aging World II," *International Population Reports*, P95/92–3, U.S. Government Printing Office, Washington, D.C., 1992.

immigration and emigration occur in the United States, then in the next sixty years our total population will grow relatively slowly, but the age structure will undergo the profound changes depicted in figure 21-2. This change will be unlike anything experienced before in this country. The number of people under thirty-five will almost stop increasing after 2010, and the number under sixty-five after 2030. However, there will be a sharp increase in the number of persons sixty-five and over beginning in 2010. The rapid increase in the number of older people after 2010 depends mostly on a single past event—the baby boom of 1946 to 1964. Today this generation comprises one-third of our population.

FIGURE 21-2. Age structure of U.S. population, 1980–2050.

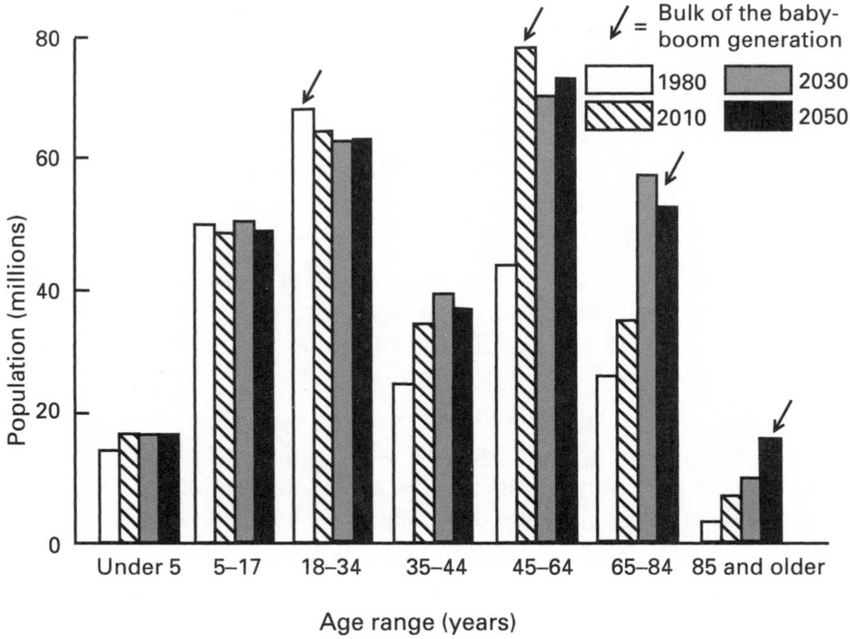

SOURCE: U.S. Bureau of the Census, Statistical Brief, SB1–86; December, 1986.

OUR FUTURE SELVES

The baby boom generation will advance the median age in the United States from about thirty-one today to over thirty-eight in 2010 and almost forty-two in 2050. The generation will be most economically productive from 1985 to 2020. In 2010 the oldest baby boomers will be almost sixty-five years old and the youngest about forty-five. As the group begins to reach age sixty-five starting in 2011, the number of older people will rise dramatically. By 2030 the baby boom cohort will be the "young-old," sixty-five to eighty-four years of age.

In 1992, there were approximately thirty million people aged sixty-five and over in the United States. This number will increase about 17 percent to about 35 million by the year 2000. By 2050 this group may number about 67 million, or about 125 percent more than today. Persons eighty-five years of age or older could by then constitute almost 5 percent of the total population, compared to 1 percent today. They will represent 25 percent of those over age sixty-five at that time. In 2030 the last phase of the baby boom explosion will begin. By that year those eighty-five years of age and over will be the only older age group still growing, having increased from about 2.7 million now to 5 million in 2000 (an 85 percent increase), 8.6 million in 2030 (a 220 percent increase) and 16 million in 2050 (a 500 percent increase). Those over eighty-five will increase from 9 percent of the population sixty-five years of age or older now to almost 17 percent by 2010 and 25 percent by 2050. There will be an increasing disparity between the numbers of eighty-five-year-old females and males between 1970 and 2050.

All of these statistics are included in table 21-2 and some of these data are abstracted to produce figures 21–3 and 21–4.

Actuaries at the Social Security Administration have calculated life expectation for males and females at birth and at age sixty-five for several years in the twenty-first century, assuming a medium rate of mortality (table 6-3). If mortality rates fall from what they are today, then the life expectation figures in the table will increase; if the mortality rate increases, the values will fall.

The distribution of the entire United States population by age and sex is depicted in figure 21-5 for the years 1950, 1987, and as projected for the year 2050.

Today, among the aged, women outnumber men three-to-two. The imbalance increases to more than two-to-one for persons eighty-five and over. There may be as many as 12.5 million more women than men sixty-five and older in 2050. Older women are more likely to be widowed, living alone, poor, and suffering from chronic physical ailments. More persons will be caring for very old parents after they themselves reach retirement in the next century. If generations are assumed to be separated by twenty-five years, persons aged eighty-five to one hundred could have children who are sixty to seventy-five years of age. When the baby boom cohort reaches eighty-five and over in 2050, some of these eighty-five-year-olds could have a living parent. In the next century many middle-aged children (thirty-five years old) might have both parents (sixty years old) and grandparents (eighty-five years old) to care for. There will be more and more four-generation families. These events portend enormous social and economic changes in our society. Increasing life expectation for all age groups is a phenomenon that has never before occurred in human history.

TABLE 21-2. Population age 65 and older, United States, 1970–2050

Year	Male (age)				Female (age)			
	65 and older	65–74	75–84	85 and older	65 and older	65–74	75–84	85 and older
Numbers (thousands)[a]								
1970	8,413	5,461	2,456	496	11,693	7,032	3,727	934
1980	10,363	6,787	2,886	691	15,345	8,861	4,901	1,583
1990	12,652	7,861	3,827	964	19,147	10,193	6,456	2,496
2000	13,734	7,764	4,577	1,393	21,302	9,930	7,630	3,743
2025	24,210	15,089	7,053	2,069	34,426	17,999	10,819	5,609
2050	27,044	13,914	8,504	4,627	40,016	16,108	12,472	11,436
Age distribution[b]								
1970	100.0%	64.9%	29.2%	5.9%	100.0%	60.1%	31.9%	8.0%
1980	100.0	65.5	27.8	6.7	100.0	57.8	31.9	10.3
1990	100.0	62.1	30.3	7.6	100.0	53.3	33.7	13.0
2000	100.0	56.5	33.3	10.2	100.0	46.6	35.8	17.6
2025	100.0	62.3	29.1	8.6	100.0	52.3	31.4	16.3
2050	100.0	51.5	31.4	17.1	100.0	40.2	31.2	28.6
Percent change								
1970–1980	23.2%	24.3%	17.5%	39.3%	31.2%	26.0%	31.5%	69.5%
1982–1990	17.4	12.2	25.4	33.3	19.3	11.6	24.3	44.9
1990–2000	8.6	−1.2	19.6	44.5	11.3	−2.6	18.2	50.0
2000–2025	76.3	94.3	54.1	48.5	61.6	81.3	41.8	49.9
2025–2050	11.7	−7.8	20.6	123.6	16.2	−10.5	15.3	103.9
1982–2000	27.4	10.9	50.0	92.7	32.8	8.8	47.0	117.4
1982–2050	150.9	98.7	178.6	540.0	149.4	76.4	140.2	564.1

[a]Figures have been independently rounded, hence, totals may not equal the sum of the parts.
[b]Percent of population aged 65 and over.

SOURCE: U.S. Bureau of the Census and *Statistical Bulletin*, Metropolitan Life Insurance Co., April–June 1984. Permission granted courtesy of *Statistical Bulletin*.

The imminent increase in the number of older people will have a substantial impact on institutions providing health care, financial services, housing, and social security. The elderly have more health problems than do younger people. Those problems tend to be more complex and chronic, requiring longer periods of hospitalization, more extensive nursing care, and greater utilization of home health care and extended-care facilities. Clearly, the economic and social impact of extending longevity will be enormous.

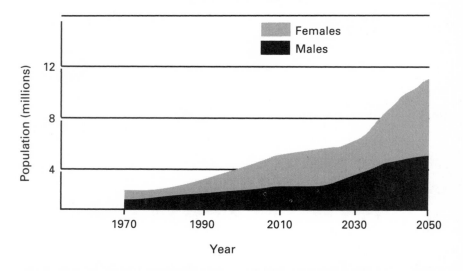

FIGURE 21-3. Population age 85 and older by sex, United States, 1970–2050

SOURCE: U.S. Bureau of the Census and *Statistical Bulletin*, Metropolitan Life Insurance Co., April–June 1984. Permission granted courtesy of *Statistical Bulletin*.

FIGURE 21-4. Population age 65 and older, United States,1970–2050.

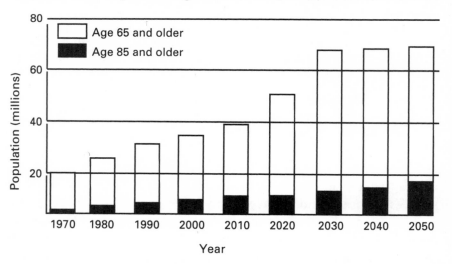

SOURCE: U.S. Bureau of the Census and *Statistical Bulletin*, Metropolitan Life Insurance Co., April–June 1984. Permission granted courtesy of *Statistical Bulletin*.

FIGURE 21–5. Percent Distribution of U.S. Population by Age and Sex 1950, 1987 and Projections for 2050

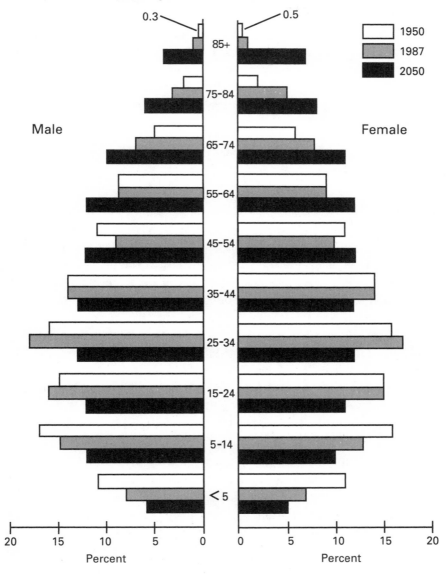

SOURCE: U.S. Brureau of the Census, Current Population Reports. *Statistical Bulletin*, Metropolitan Life Insurance Co., July–September, 1989. Permission granted courtesy of *Statistical Bulletin*.

Before we despair over this, however, let's remember that the fact that so many people in developed countries are reaching old age proves that the medical, public health, economic, social, and educational advances of the last hundred years have been successful. It seems to me that every old person should be a cause for the celebration of our success and not for lamentation. Why have we striven to increase biomedical research, health care delivery, and social services during this century if not to allow more of us to become old? Every success in biomedical research has the potential to increase human life expectation. If that goal is undesirable, then why conduct biomedical research at all?

LIVING THE RECTANGULAR LIFE

In chapter 6, I described how the achievements of biomedical scientists have resulted in fewer people dying at younger ages and more people dying at older ages. As discussed, this has resulted in the further rectangularization of the survival curves. If the human life span is fixed, then the progressive postponement of death by biomedical advances will reduce both the span of years in which death is most likely to occur and the duration of chronic illnesses that precede death. Of course the human life span and those of other animals are not precisely fixed. If it is possible to live 115 years, then it is possible to live 115 years and one day more.

In chapter 7, I showed how resolution of the leading causes of death would add more than a decade to our life expectation, but even eliminating all of them would not make us immortal. When all of the goals of biomedical research have been achieved, the limit in extending life expectation will be reached: we will die, not from heart disease, stroke, or cancer—the causes now written on death certificates—but from the effects of the normal decrements of old age. We will then have to coin succinct terms to say that death was caused by a normal loss in physiological function, ultimately resulting in the failure of the kidney, heart, liver, nervous system, or some other vital organ. Our fate will be to die only from "natural causes."

Resolution of the two leading causes of death, cardiovascular diseases and cancer, would increase our life expectation by about seventeen years. To extend our longevity by significantly more than that, we would have to perturb the processes that determine longevity or produce age changes. However, any benefits of increasing human life expectation—whether by eliminating disease, manipulating longevity-assurance genes or slowing the rate of aging—might be tempered by the economic impact that the achievement could have.

For example, if we were able to eliminate cardiovascular diseases and cancer, people would live longer and thus be exposed to an increased incidence in the remaining causes of death. Economists at the Office of Management and Budget calculate the increase in social security, medicare, medicaid, retirement benefits, and other costs would be profound. If cardiovascular disease were eliminated, the additional annual federal cost would be over sixty-seven billion 1983 dollars. If cancer were eliminated as a cause of death, more than eighteen billion 1983 dollars would have to be spent annually on those whose lives would be extended. Even if these figures are off by a factor of two, resolving the two leading causes of death in the United States would cost us from about ten (cardiovascular disease) to over fifty (cancer) times the present annual cost of our efforts to cure the diseases! Cynics might carry this reasoning to its logical conclusion and argue that if everyone would die suddenly in middle age, we could eliminate our national debt and balance the budget in a few years.

CAN WE EXTEND OUR LIFE SPAN?

Few researchers now study the normal losses in physiological function that occur as we age and how those losses might be slowed or reversed, but these normal losses may eventually become the leading causes of death. If at some future time all deaths in old age result from natural causes, most will occur within a diminishing span of ages. If you live a healthy life until, say, the age of 110 but succumb to ultimately lethal age changes by age 112, you will have approached the maximum human life span. Assuming many others do the same, average life expectation will almost catch up with maximum life span.

I do not believe that we will soon have the ability to manipulate what appears to be the fixed human life span of 115 years. Even if we concede that, on an evolutionary time scale, the human life span will increase naturally, the increase will be imperceptible even over several millennia. If the past is any guide, it might be ten thousand years or more before the maximum human life span reaches even 120 years. I am quite pessimistic that, in the next century, we will learn enough about human evolution to be able to accelerate the processes that drive our increasing life span.

Successful tampering with the processes of biological fitness and adaptation is probably beyond our ability to master, although some of our present actions are certainly having a negative influence on the fitness and adaptation of humans. For example, biomedical sciences and our culture have conspired to preserve and increase the presence of many unfavorable traits in the human gene pool that, without our intervention, would remain at a low level, or disappear entirely. These traits include many genetically determined pathologies that are treatable to the extent that their victims are able to survive long enough to pass on those traits to their progeny. In this way the undesirable traits survive and spread in the human gene pool. The usual processes of fitness and selection, which would have eliminated the biologically unfit before they had a chance to reproduce, are frequently thwarted by human intervention, allowing many of the biologically unfit to survive and reproduce. Our culture demands that we do everything we can to permit all people who suffer from illness to survive as long as possible. Although our intentions obviously are benign, the effect of our actions is to undermine the fundamental process of evolution in which only the fittest survive.

RESEARCH ON LONGEVITY AND AGING TODAY

A complete understanding of aging and longevity is surely one of the most difficult problems in all of biology. If you think understanding cancer is difficult, try aging. Scientific efforts to understand the aging and longevity processes have never been greater than they are today, but the resources invested in understanding the biology of aging and longevity equal only a fraction of what is spent on efforts to understand and control the two leading killers, cardiovascular disease and cancer.

The budget requested by the Congressional Conference Committee for the National Institutes of Health (NIH) in 1993 is about 10.4 billion dollars. The only institute at the NIH where funds are spent specifically in an effort to understand the aging process is the National Institute on Aging (NIA). The 1993 budget request for the NIA was about 401 million dollars, much of which will be used to fund research unrelated to understanding the normal aging process. About half of the

NIA budget is now spent on investigating Alzheimer's disease and other diseases most common in the aged. Another substantial part of the budget is spent to study other matters of great concern to the aged, such as brain disorders other than Alzheimer's disease, incontinence, falls, and psychological, psychiatric, and social problems. I do not challenge the merit of undertaking research to ameliorate these conditions, but it is essential to understand that resolution of these problems will not increase our understanding of the aging process. In the 1992 appropriations for the NIH, the National Cancer Institute and the National Heart, Lung and Blood Institute together received more than sixty-two times the fifty-one million dollars spent on basic research in biogerontology by the National Institute on Aging.

A recent example illustrates why I believe that resolving geriatric medical problems without understanding the basic biology of aging will not advance our understanding of the aging process. During the surge of poliomyelitis research in the 1950s and 1960s a substantial amount was spent on fundamental research on the biology of the virus. Without that basic research, instead of a vaccine we would probably have state-of-the-art, computer-driven iron lungs in which to house tens of thousands of polio victims. Basic knowledge about the virus brought about the development of a vaccine and the virtual elimination of the disease. In the same way, no amount of money spent on the care of the elderly, or the resolution of Alzheimer's disease or any other age-associated disease, will ever lead to an understanding and slowing of the aging process. Again, I do not advocate the cessation of attempts to control the diseases that afflict the elderly, but it should be appreciated that these efforts are mere palliatives and will not increase our knowledge of the basic processes of aging and longevity.

Although difficult to assess with absolute precision, my belief is that less than fifty million dollars of the 401 million-dollar NIA budget in 1993 will be spent on research on the basic aging process, about one-half percent of the NIH budget and less than the price of television advertising during the 1993 Super Bowl. Some scientists have suggested that basic knowledge about the normal aging process may come unexpectedly from some other place, like fundamental cell biology research sponsored by the National Cancer Institute. Nevertheless, triple the amount spent for basic research in aging and longevity would still be about one and one-half percent of the entire NIH effort. The biomedical research establishment in the United States and elsewhere clearly places a higher priority on finding cures for cardiovascular disease and cancer. As a result, that research is much more likely to affect human longevity than is fundamental biogerontological research, but without in any way affecting the normal physiological decline that is characteristic of old age. If our goal is in fact to maximize opportunities to increase human longevity, then our current priorities are seriously out of balance. If this imbalance continues, there is little likelihood that the research accomplishments of a handful of underfunded biogerontologists will ever result in an increase in the human life span.

Another measure of our cultural priorities is the attention that longevity is given in the education of young people. About 84 percent of secondary school biology text books do not mention aging. Those that do devote only one to three pages to the subject. Of introductory college biology texts, 51 percent do not mention the biology of aging and none devotes more than four pages to the subject. The emphasis in all of these books is on early growth and development, with what happens biologically after maturity substantially ignored. Thus, our students receive an indirect message that what is important in biology is what happens before adulthood—that is, the developmental processes that student readers are experiencing or have experienced personally. It seems reasonable to expect that students should also be exposed to at least a modicum of knowledge about the biological changes that most of them will live to experience.

Many scientists and policymakers do not recognize the fact that death occurs in older people because of their greater vulnerability to diseases and that this is a consequence of the normal aging process. The greater incidence of cardiovascular disease, stroke, cancer, and Alzheimer's disease in old cells, as compared to the dramatically less susceptible young cells, is not fully appreciated by most biomedical scientists. I believe that if it were more widely appreciated that older cells are more susceptible to disease, research on why this is so could provide new insights into our understanding of the normal aging process and the changes that make late-occurring diseases more likely in old tissue.

WHAT SHOULD OUR GOALS BE?

Our increasing ability to control many aspects of our biological destiny has persuaded many people that a technique for slowing the aging process or extending the human life span cannot be more than a few years away. The optimists see the conquering of the major killers—viral and bacterial scourges like poliomyelitis, measles, rubella, tuberculosis, scarlet fever, and diphtheria—during the first half of this century as evidence for their position. Resolution of these diseases depended upon the implementation of better hygienic conditions, the discovery of effective vaccines, and the development of antibiotics. The transplantation of hearts and other organs, enormous advances in diagnostic techniques, and the promise of anticancer therapy are examples of more recent successes by the biomedical research community. All of these accomplishments are thought to herald a second revolution in which recombinant DNA technology and the production of monoclonal antibodies will eliminate the remaining chronic diseases. Because of these monumental achievements, gerontological optimists reason that reversing the aging process, or increasing longevity, are attainable goals.

I am not one of the optimists, and I do not believe that we have a sufficient understanding of either the aging process or the determinants of life span to expect to significantly manipulate either during our lifetime. A more important issue, however, is whether it would be desirable to manipulate either process. The capacity to halt or slow the aging process, or to extend longevity, would have consequences unlike most other biomedical breakthroughs. Virtually all other biomedical goals have an indisputably positive value. It is not at all clear whether or not the ability to tamper with the processes that age us or determine our life span would be an unmixed blessing. As pointed out earlier, resolution of all disease and other causes of death would result in a life expectation of about one hundred years. I am apprehensive about extending average life expectation beyond age one hundred once the leading killers are resolved because the result would be disease-free but nonetheless functionally weaker, still inexorably aging people. We would suffer the fate of Tithonus as memorialized by Alfred, Lord Tennyson: "And after many a summer dies the swan. Me only cruel immortality consumes." Old people will simply become older, condemned to the vicissitudes of a continuing aging process. And that outcome, I believe, is undesirable for most people. (Roy Walford disagrees with my expectation and suggests that calorie-restricted mice not only live longer but that infirmity occupies a smaller proportion of their total life span.) However, I maintain that to extrapolate to humans what is found in mice is a dangerous game.

It might also be argued that aging and natural death are the only humane ways of ridding us of the tyrants, serial killers, and other undesirables who would otherwise continue to threaten or harm us. Biology works this way now. Few of us would welcome increased longevity for those who bring misery to others.

Gerald Gruman, a historian of aging, has called those who advocate that we should not tamper with the human condition "apologists" and numbers among them Lucretius, Aristotle, and Cicero. I am not advocating apologism, but I am advocating that the ethical dilemmas created by achieving some scientific goals, like slowing the aging process, should be settled by citizens *before* the consequences of our actions come crashing down on the heads of future generations. Surgical and drug-induced abortion, the transplantation of human fetal tissue, and the right to die come immediately to mind as examples of biological advances made before the ethical consequences were resolved. The penalty for dealing with ethical issues raised by biomedical discoveries *post facto* is a climate of extreme emotionalism and the drawing of rigid battle lines in the face of the immediacy of the problem.

It is not yet possible for us to perturb the aging phenomenon in humans or to increase our life span. In my view, those who believe that it is possible or about to happen have an obligation to initiate a public dialogue on the question *now*. Little has been said about the social, psychological, and economic effects of slowing the aging process or extending our longevity. Less still has been said about its impact on institutions such as social security, life insurance, retirement, and health care.

The present debates over the use of elaborate life-support systems ("when to pull the plug") and abortion rights are trivial in comparison with the ethical dilemmas that would arise if we had the ability to slow the aging process or increase longevity. As I've said, I think it's unlikely that the fundamental processes of aging and life span determination will be understood in the near future. Furthermore, I suggest we view this as a blessing in disguise, because it gives us an opportunity now to address the consequences of tampering with the processes of longevity and aging before citizens are confronted with a fait accompli.

NO MORE AGING: BLESSING OR NIGHTMARE?

It is important to contemplate and publicly discuss now the impact that manipulation of the aging process would have on virtually every aspect of our lives, before such manipulation becomes possible. If we reach the point of understanding the aging process well enough to slow or stop it, we probably will have the means to perturb it at any time during or after development. As already discussed, there could be many complications. Regardless of the age at which you chose to arrest the clock, there always would be the possibility that life satisfaction might have been greater at a later time. The particular age you chose probably would depend in part on the ages chosen by important people in your life, especially your family and friends. This freedom of choice could create any number of social, biological, economic, and political problems and a bizarre asynchrony of ages. An example: You stop the aging process at age forty-five, but your older brother or sister chose thirty-five and your parents chose twenty-five. Your children may choose other ages or choose not to arrest their aging process at all. How will you relate to parents who are younger than you, children who are older than you, or siblings aging at a different rate? There are other, equally grotesque scenarios. Would manipulation of the aging process even interfere with the evolution of our species? In short, the problems created by having the power to arrest or even slow the aging process could be enormous and damaging to both the individual and society in general.

One must also assume that any method for reversing or slowing the aging process will cost something. How will we select the recipients? If the cost is high, will only the rich benefit or will society extend access to everyone by using public funds? What about convicted felons, tyrants, and other unsavory characters? Will the technique be made available in third world countries where starvation and disease are rampant? Surely, no one will want to starve or suffer for longer periods of time.

Old age is not necessarily synonymous with pain and unhappiness. Many older people find they have never been happier than in their later years. Why, then, if you are still young and have not yet had the opportunity to experience a happy old age, risk not experiencing what might be the best years of your life?

A few of my gerontological colleagues claim they can envision a scenario in which the ability to tamper with the clocks that govern the aging process and life span would benefit most individuals or society in general, but I can see no more advantage either to stopping or slowing the aging process than to stopping or slowing developmental processes at some arbitrary young age. The power to control either developmental or aging processes becomes even more undesirable when one realizes that it might be available only to the few who could afford it.

Why then, have I spent my lifetime learning more about aging and longevity if it is not my goal to manipulate the processes? First, as a scientist, I am curious about how the world works. But learning how something works does not necessarily mean that one must then tamper with the mechanism. As a boy I wanted to know how my wristwatch worked, but, after I learned, I had no desire to tamper with the watch. Scientists fundamentally love to solve puzzles. Biologists who work in the field of biological development are interested in how a fertilized egg grows and multiplies to become an adult form. I doubt that any developmental biologist has as his or her ultimate objective stopping or slowing the human developmental process. Similarly, many biogerontologists are interested in their subject simply because they want to know why and how the process occurs. Manipulating the process is not a goal of most biogerontologists. If it is a goal of some biogerontologists then they have an obligation to deal with the consequences before they begin to tinker.

Matilda White Riley views aging in the twenty-first century with much optimism. She believes that society will recognize that most older people are still productive and that the restrictions on self-expression that now characterize society's attitude toward the elderly will change. Choices will increase; lifelong learning will replace education only for the young; ageism will end; new methods for ensuring financial security will be established; retirement as we know it will disappear; and life will consist of periods of work, leisure, and learning regardless of age. Society will, in short, be forced to create new roles for this, the most rapidly expanding portion of our population.

IMMORTALITY

Few would question the goal of resolving all of the causes of death that now appear on death certificates. One of these causes, however, is accidents, which, because they are statistically unavoidable, will never be completely eliminated. Even if we eliminate all the diseases that now cause death, death will be common, attributable to accidents or to natural causes. Would this be paradise? Certainly we would live longer; just as certainly we would become weaker and weaker as the normal, inexorable aging process made our vital organs increasingly less efficient. In *Gulliver's Travels*, Jonathan Swift imagined just such a society, a group of people called the Struldbrugs who grew older and older and more and more frail but never died, even when the functional capacity of their aging organs eventually dropped below the point necessary to sustain a minimum quality of life. The Struldbrugs longed for the blessing of death, but it never came. They suffered immortality as a curse as the aging process continued interminably.

The desire for immortality is, like the desire to control the aging process, usually expressed glibly, with little thought to the consequences. However, the undesirable scenarios that could occur were the aging process controlled pale in comparison to what might happen if immortality were possible. Suppose that immortality could be achieved by the simple expedient of taking a daily pill. Who would get the pill if the cost were low, medium, or high? Who would have access to it if it was in short supply? Would its existence be kept a secret by its discoverers or some government to benefit friends and outlive enemies? What would happen if control of the pill fell into the hands of the unscrupulous? If the pill were universally available, our already serious problems with overpopulation would become mind-boggling. The unpleasant scenarios that one can imagine are virtually without limit. It is more difficult to imagine a scenario that would benefit anyone. In my view, those who believe that controlling the aging process or bestowing immortality is desirable should reconsider.

A cynical view has it that there is little need to be concerned about the consequences of manipulating the processes of aging and longevity because there is little chance that a few underfunded biogerontologists will be able to achieve that goal. More to the point, however, is the fact that few serious scientists are directing their research to extending human longevity or achieving immortality.

THE POPULATION BOMB

In my view, the most serious objection to the argument that longevity should be extended is that doing so would exacerbate a problem that underlies virtually all of the other problems faced by the world today. These subordinate problems range from the indiscriminate destruction of the planet to mass starvation, wars, economic inequities, and health failures. The underlying problem is overpopulation.

Conservative estimates indicate that the current population of the planet will double by the year 2050. Eleven thousand people are born every hour, more than a quarter million each day. In the United States, we add four times the population of Washington, D.C., annually— another New Jersey every three years or another California every twelve. World population increases by the number of people in San Francisco every two days, and it will gain the equivalent of the population of China from 1990 to 2000. It took three million years for the number of humans to reach one billion, in 1800. It took only one hundred thirty years, until 1930, to add a second billion, and thirty more, until 1960, to reach three billion. The fourth billion was added by 1975, in the space of only fifteen years, and in 1987, twelve years later, we reached the present five billion. Over one billion of these people suffer from malnutrition and fourteen million children under the age of five die each year. At the present rate of population growth, in about five hundred years there will be about one person for every square meter of land! The magnitude of the overpopulation problem is illustrated in figure 21-6.

FIGURE 21-6. World Population Growth through History

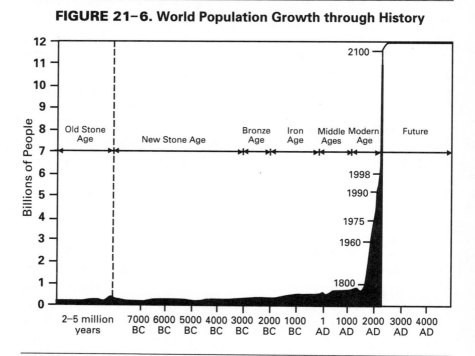

SOURCE: "Population: A Lively Introduction," Joseph A. McFall, Jr., *Population Bulletin*, Volume 46, Number 2, October, 1991, pages 1–43, Population Reference Bureau, Washington, D.C.

Unless human overpopulation is controlled soon, the planet will suffer irreversible degradation and humanity will experience a continued increase in poverty, starvation, and virtually all of the other ills that presently concern us. Nothing is more urgent today than solving the problem of human overpopulation. Even if manipulating our biological clocks to increase individual longevity is desirable, that goal should be subordinated to defusing this even more fundamental problem.

HOW TO INCREASE LIFE EXPECTATION

Because immortality and the complete elimination of aging are probably both undesirable, some believe that just slowing the aging process might be the best compromise. This view has many advocates, and the objective may well be useful. We still do not know how to slow the aging process in humans, but we do know how to increase our life expectation by eliminating or reducing causes of death. This approach has, in fact, been remarkably successful throughout most of this century. Nevertheless, the "success" has come at a great cost. Increased life expectation and birth rates have resulted in an explosive increase in the world's population, bringing us dangerously close to destroying what is left of the pristine surface of the planet. Unless the number of humans populating this planet is soon reduced, there will be little purpose in considering the question of slowing the aging process or increasing the human life span. The planet will not be a place on which it is worth spending more time.

After years of thinking about these kinds of issues, I've decided that there is only one objective that is both practical and desirable and that is to strive for maximimum human life expectation by eliminating the present leading causes of death. I see no value to society or to the individual in seeking to slow or stop the aging process or to achieve immortality.

The scenario that provokes the least concern is the one in which all humans reach the maximum life span, still in possession of full mental and physical abilities, with death occurring quickly as we approach, say, our 115th birthday. This is the goal that we are tacitly pursuing at this time. Virtually all biomedical research has the implicit goal of eliminating disease in all of its forms. It is logical to ask what will happen if we are successful. The answer seems to be that if we are successful, our life expectation will be increased but we will eventually die from the basic aging processes that lead to failure in some vital system.

Oliver Wendell Holmes put this idea nicely:

> Have you heard of the wonderful one-hoss shay,
> that was built in such a logical way
> It ran a hundred years to a day,
> And then, of a sudden, it—ah but stay,
> I'll tell you what happened without delay,
> Scaring the parson into fits,
> Frightening people out of their wits—
> Have you ever heard of that, I say?
>
> At half past nine by the meet'n'-house clock,—
> Just the hour of the Earthquake shock!
> What do you think the parson found,
> When he got up and stared around?
> The poor old chaise in a heap or mound
> As if it had been to the mill and ground!
>
> You see, of course, if you're not a dunce,
> How it went to pieces all at once,—
> All at once, and nothing first,—
> Just as bubbles do when they burst.
>
> —From "The Deacon's Masterpiece; or,
> The Wonderful 'One-Hoss Shay' " (1857–58)

Further Reading

Introduction

Cowdry, E. V., ed. *Problems of Aging.* Baltimore: Williams and Wilkins, 1939.

Freeman, Joseph T. "The History of Geriatrics." *Annals of Medical History* 10 (1938):324–55.

Nascher, Ignaz L. *Geriatrics: The Diseases of Old Age and Their Treatment.* New York: Arno Press, 1979.

———. "A History of Geriatrics." *Medical Reviews of New York* 32 (1926): 281–84.

Shock, Nathan W. *The International Association of Gerontology.* New York: Springer Publishing Co., 1988.

PART 1: What is Aging?

Chapter 1

Kohn, Robert R. *Principles of Mammalian Aging.* 2nd ed. Englewood Cliffs, N. J.: Prentice Hall, 1978.

Strehler, Bernard L. *Time, Cells and Aging.* 2nd ed. New York: Academic Press, 1977.

Chapter 2

Clapp, Roger B., M. Kathleen Klimkiewicz, and John H. Kennard. "Longevity Records of North American Birds, Gaviidae through Alcidae." *Journal of Field Ornithology* 53 (1982):81–124.

Comfort, Alex. *The Biology of Senescence.* 3rd ed. New York: Elsevier North Holland, 1979.

Diamond, Jared M. "Big-bang Reproduction and Ageing in Male Marsupial Mice." *Nature* 298 (1982):115–16.

Heller, J. "Longevity in Molluscs." *Malacologia* 32, no. 2 (1990):259–95.

Hughes, T. P., and J.B.C. Jackson. "Do Corals Lie about Their Age? Some Demographic Consequences of Partial Mortality, Fission, and Fusion." *Science* 209 (1980):713–14.

Jones, Marvin L. "Longevity of Captive Animals." *Zoological Garten N. F. Jena* 52 (1982):113–28.

Klimkiewicz, M. Kathleen, and Anthony G. Futcher. "Longevity Records of North American Birds, Coerebinae through Estrildidae." *Journal of Field Ornithology* 58 (1987):318–33.

———. "Longevity Records of North American Birds, Supplement 1." *Journal of Field Ornithology* 60 (1982):469–94.

Pamilo, P. "Life Span of Queens in the Ant *Formica exsecta.*" *Insect Society* 38 (1991):111–19.

Robertson, O. H., and B. C. Wexler. "Histological Changes in the Pituitary Gland of the Pacific Salmon (Genus *Oncorhynchus*) Accompanying Sexual Maturation and Spawning." *Journal of Morphology* 110 (1962):171.

Chapter 3

Ferguson, C. W. "Bristlecone Pine: Science and Esthetics." *Science* 159 (1968):839–46.

Janzen, Daniel H. "Why Bamboos Wait So Long to Flower." *Annual Review of Ecological Systems* 7 (1976):347–91.

Mohlenbrock, Robert H. "Ancient Bristlecone Pine Forest, California." *Natural History* 94 (1985):38–41.

Nooden, L. D., and A. C. Leopold, eds. *Senescence and Aging in Plants.* San Diego: Academic Press, 1988.

Osborne, Daphne. "Seeds of the Past." *New Scientist* 63 (1974):252–54.

Ross, E. E., and D. A. Davidson. "Record Longevities of Vegetable Seeds in Storage." *HortScience* 27 (May 1992):393–96.

Thimann, Kenneth V., ed. *Senescence in Plants.* Boca Raton, Fla.: CRC Press, 1980.

Toole, Vivian K. "Ancient Seeds: Seed Longevity." *Journal of Seed Technology* 10 (1986):1–23.

Chapter 4

Bell, Graham. *Sex and Death in Protozoa.* New York: Cambridge University Press, 1988.

Blumenthal, Herman T. "Aging: Biologic or Pathologic?" *Hospital Practice,* 1978, 127–37.

Evans, J. G. "Ageing and Disease." In *Research and the Ageing Population,* 38–57. Ciba Foundation Symposium 134. Chichester: Wiley, 1988.

Murphy, Timothy F. "A Cure for Aging?" *Journal of Medicine and Philosophy* 11 (1986):237–55.

PART 2: Aging by the Numbers

Chapter 5

Aging America, Trends and Projections, U.S. Dept. of Health and Human Services Publication No. (FCoA) 91-28001, 1991.

Brock, D. B., J. M. Guralnick, and J. A. Brody. "Demography and Epidemiology of Aging in the United States." In *The Handbook of the Biology of Aging,* 3rd ed., eds. Edward L. Schneider and John W. Rowe, 3–23. San Diego: Academic Press, 1990.

Commonwealth Fund Commission on Elderly People Living Alone. "Aging Alone: Profiles and Projections." Baltimore: Judith B. Casper, 1988.

Kinsella, Kevin. "Aging in the Third World." U.S. Department of Commerce, Bureau of the Census. International Population Reports. Series P-95, no. 79. September 1988. Washington, D.C.: U.S. Government Printing Office.

"A Profile of Older Americans." Washington, D.C.: American Association of Retired Persons, 1992.

Siegel, Jacob S., and Maria Davidson. "Demographic and Socioeconomic Aspects of Aging in the United States." Current Population Reports, Special Studies. Series P-23, no. 138. August 1984. Washington, D.C.: U.S. Government Printing Office.

Taeuber, Cynthia M. "America in Transition: An Aging Society." Current Population Reports, Special Studies. Series P-23, no. 128. December 1983. Washington, D.C.: U.S. Government Printing Office.

Torrey, Barbara B., Kevin Kinsella, and Cynthia M. Taeuber. "An Aging World." U.S. Department of Commerce, Bureau of the Census. International Population Reports. Series P-95, no. 78, September 1987. Washington, D.C.: U.S. Government Printing Office.

U.S. Senate Special Committee on Aging. "Aging America: Trends and Projections." Washington, D.C., 1984.

Chapter 6

Boxenbaum, Harold. "Gompertz Mortality Analysis: Aging, Longevity Hormesis and Toxicity." *Archives of Gerontology and Geriatrics* 13 (1991):125–38.

Brody, Jacob A. "Prospects for an Aging Population." *Nature* 315 (1985):463–66.

Dublin, Louis I., Alfred J. Lotka, and Mortimer Spiegelman. *Length of Life.* New York: Ronald Press, 1949.

Gompertz, Benjamin. "On the Nature of Function Expressive of the Law of Human Mortality and on a New Mode of Determining Life Contingencies." *Philosophical Transactions of the Royal Society* (London), series A, 115 (1825):513–85.

Metropolitan Life Insurance Company. "Longevity Gains Continue." *Statistical Bulletin* 71 (1991):19–26.

———. "Major Improvements in Life Expectancy: 1989." *Statistical Bulletin* 71 (1991):11–17.

National Center for Health Statistics. *Vital Statistics of the United States.* Vol. 2, sect. 6, 1989. Life Tables. Washington, D.C.: Public Health Service, 1992.

Pearl, Raymond, and Ruth DeWitt Pearl. *The Ancestry of the Long-lived.* Baltimore: Johns Hopkins University Press, 1934.

Sacher, George A. "Life Table Modification and Life Prolongation." In *Handbook of the Biology of Aging*, ed. C. E. Finch and L. Hayflick, 582. 1st ed. New York: Van Nostrand Reinhold, 1977.

Chapter 7

Cassel, Cristine K., and Berniece L. Neugarten. "A Forecast of Women's Health and Longevity." *Western Journal of Medicine* 149 (1988):712–17.

Fries, James F. "The Compression of Morbidity: Near or Far?" *Milbank Quarterly* 67 (1989):208–32.

Goldstein, Samuel. "Human Genetic Disorders That Feature Premature Onset and Accelerated Progression of Biological Aging." In *The Genetics of Aging*, ed. E. L. Schneider, 171–224. New York: Plenum Press, 1978.

———. "Lifespan of Cultured Cells in Progeria." *Lancet* 1 (1969):424.

Hazzard, William R. "Biological Basis of the Sex Differential in Longevity." *Journal of the American Geriatrics Society* 34 (1986):455–71.

Holden, Constance. "Why Do Women Live Longer Than Men?" *Science* 238 (1987):158–60.

Martin, George M. "Genetic Syndromes in Man with Potential Relevance to the Pathobiology of Aging." In *Genetic Effects on Aging*, ed. D. Bergsma and D. Harrison. Birth Defects, Original Article Series, no. 14. New York: Alan Liss, 1978.

Metropolitan Life Insurance Company. "Longevity of Presidents, Vice Presidents, and Unsuccessful Candidates for the Presidency." *Statistical Bulletin* 61, no. 3. (July–September 1980).

———. "Longevity of Symphony Conductors." *Statistical Bulletin* 61, no. 4. (October–December 1980).

Myers, George C., and Kenneth G. Manton. "Compression of Mortality: Myth or Reality?" *Gerontologist* 24, no. 4 (1984):346–59.

Salk, D., Y. Fujiwara, and G. M. Martin, eds. *Werner's Syndrome and Human Aging*. New York: Plenum Press, 1985.

Smith, David W. E. "Is Greater Female Longevity a General Finding among Animals?" *Biological Reviews* 64 (1989):1–12.

Smith, David W. E., and Huber R. Warner. "Does Genotypic Sex Have a Direct Effect on Longevity?" *Experimental Gerontology* 24 (1988):277–88.

Verbrugge, L. M. "Gender, Aging and Health." In *Aging and Health: Perspectives on Gender, Race, Ethnicity and Class*, ed. K. S. Markides. Newbury Park, Calif.: Sage Publications, 1989.

PART 3: How Do We Age?

Chapter 8

Carrel, Alexis, and Albert H. Ebeling. "Age and Multiplication of Fibroblasts." *Journal of Experimental Medicine* 34 (1921):599.

Cristofalo, Vincent J. "The Destiny of Cells: Mechanisms and Implications of Senescence." *Gerontologist* 25 (1985):577–83.

Cristofalo, V. J., and B. M. Stanulis-Praeger. "Cellular Senescence In Vitro." In *Advances in Tissue Culture*, ed. Karl Maramorosch, 2:1–68. New York: Academic Press, 1982.

Goldstein, Samuel. "The Biology of Aging." *New England Journal of Medicine* 285 (1971):1120–29.

Hayflick, Leonard. "Cell Aging." In *Annual Review of Gerontology and Geriatrics*, ed. Carl Eisdorfer, 1:26–67. New York: Springer Publishing Co., 1980.

———. "The Cell Biology of Human Aging." *Scientific American* 242 (January 1980):58–66.

———. "The Cellular Basis for Biological Aging." In *Handbook of the Biology of Aging*, ed. Caleb E. Finch and Leonard Hayflick, 159–85. 1st ed. New York: Van Nostrand Reinhold, 1977.

———. "The Coming of Age of WI-38." In *Advances in Cell Culture*, ed. Karl Maramorosch, 3:303–16. New York: Academic Press, 1984.

————. "The Limited in Vitro Lifetime of Human Diploid Cell Strains." *Experimental Cell Research* 37 (1965):614–36.

Hayflick, Leonard, and Paul S. Moorhead. "The Serial Cultivation of Human Diploid Cell Strains." *Experimental Cell Research* 25 (1961):585–621.

Kirkwood, Thomas B. L. "Towards a Unified Theory of Cellular Ageing." *Monographs in Developmental Biology* 17 (1984):9–20.

Kirkwood, T.B.L., and T. Cremer. "Cytogerontology since 1881: A Reappraisal of August Weismann and a Review of Modern Progress." *Human Genetics* 60 (1982):101–21.

Martin, George M. "Cellular Aging-Clonal Senescence." *Journal of Pathology* 89 (1977):484–511.

Norwood, Thomas H., and James R. Smith. "The Cultured Fibroblast-like Cell as a Model for the Study of Aging." In *Handbook of the Biology of Aging*, ed. Caleb E. Finch and Edward L. Schneider, 291–321. 2nd ed. New York: Van Nostrand Reinhold, 1985.

Röhme, D. "Evidence for a Relationship between Longevity of Mammalian Species and Life Spans of Normal Fibroblasts In Vitro and Erythrocytes In Vivo." *Proceedings of the National Academy of Sciences* (U.S.) 78 (1981):5009–13.

Stanulis-Praeger, B. M. "Cellular Senescence Revisited: A Review." *Mechanisms of Aging and Development* 38 (1987):1–48.

Weismann, August. "The Duration of Life." In *Collected Essays upon Heredity and Kindred Biological Problems*, ed. E. B. Poulton. Oxford: Clarendon Press, 1889.

Witkowski, J. A. "Alexis Carrel and the Mysticism of Tissue Culture." *Medical History* 23 (1979):279–96.

————. "Dr. Carrel's Immortal Cells. *Medical History* 24 (1980):129–42.

————. "The Myth of Cell Immortality." *Trends in Biochemical Sciences* 10 (1985):258–60.

Chapter 9

Older and Wiser: The Baltimore Longitudinal Study of Aging. NIH publication no. 89-2797. Washington, D.C.: U.S. Government Printing Office, September 1989.

Shock, Nathan W., Richard C. Greulich, Reubin Andres, David Arenberg, Paul T. Costa, Jr., Edward G. Lakatta, and Jordan D. Tobin. *Normal Human Aging: The Baltimore Longitudinal Study of Aging.* NIH publication no. 84-2450. Washington, D.C.: U.S. Government Printing Office, November 1984.

Chapter 10

Busse, E. W., Maddox, G. L., eds. *The Duke Longitudinal Studies of Normal Aging 1955–1980: An Overview of History, Design, and Findings.* Springer Publishing Co. New York, 1985.

Hazzard, William R., Reubin Andres, Edward L. Bierman, and John P. Blass. *Principles of Geriatric Medicine and Gerontology.* 2nd ed. New York: McGraw-Hill, 1990.

Katzman, R., and J. E. Jackson. "Alzheimer Disease: Basic and Clinical Advances." *Journal of the American Geriatrics Society* 39 (1991):516–25.

Meites, Joseph "Effects of Aging on the Hypothalamic-Pituitary Axis." *Review of Biological Research in Aging* 4 (1990):253–61.

Terry, R. D., R. DeTeresa, and L. A. Hansen. "Neocortical Cell Counts in Normal Human Adult Aging." *Annals of Neurology* 21 (1987):530–39.

Chapter 11

Brant, L. J., and J. L. Fozard. "Age Changes in Pure-Tone Hearing Thresholds in a Longitudinal Study of Normal Human Aging." *Journal of the Acoustical Society of America* 88, no. 2 (1990):813–20.

Dement, William C. *Some Must Watch While Some Must Sleep.* New York: W. W. Norton and Co., 1978.

Kallman, D. A., C. C. Plato, and J. D. Tobin. "The Role of Muscle Loss in the Age-related Decline of Grip Strength: Cross-sectional and Longitudinal Perspectives." *Journal of Gerontology* 45, no. 3 (1990):M82–88.

Kallman, H., and M. S. Vernon. "The Aging Eye." *Postgraduate Medicine* 81, no. 2 (1987):112–30.

Kligman, Albert M., Gary L. Grove, and Arthur Balin. "Aging of Human Skin." In *Handbook of the Biology of Aging,* ed. Caleb E. Finch and Edward L. Schneider, 820–41. 2nd ed. New York: Van Nostrand Reinhold, 1985.

Kraus Whitbourne, S. *The Aging Body.* New York: Springer-Verlag, 1985.

Lakatta, Edward. "Heart and Circulation." In *Handbook of the Biology of Aging,* ed. Edward L. Schneider and John W. Rowe, 181–218. 3rd ed. San Diego: Academic Press, 1990.

Miller, I. J., Jr. "Variation in Human Taste Bud Density as a Function of Age." *Annals of the New York Academy of Sciences* 561 (1989):307–19.

Orentreich, N., and N. P. Durr, "Nail Changes with Aging." In *Aging and the Skin,* ed. Arthur K. Balin and Albert M. Kligman, 285–306. New York: Raven Press, 1989.

Orentreich, N., and V. J. Selmanowitz. "Levels of Biological Functions with Aging." *Transactions of the New York Academy of Sciences,* series 2, vol. 31, no. 8 (1969):992–1011.

PART 4: Why Do We Age?

Chapter 12

Allard, M. *A la recherche du secret des centenaires.* Paris: Le cherche midi editeur, 1991.

Beregi, Edit, ed. *Centenarians in Hungary.* Basel: Karger, 1990.

Cornaro, Luigi. *The Art of Living Long.* Milwaukee: William F. Butler, 1918.

Freeman, Joseph T. *Aging, Its History and Literature.* New York: Human Sciences Press, 1979.

———. "The Old, Old, Very Old Charlie Smith." *Gerontologist* 22, no. 6 (1982):532–36.

Gruman, Gerald J. "A History of Ideas about the Prolongation of Life." *Transactions of the American Philosophical Society* (Philadelphia), 56, pt. 9 (1966) 1–102. Reprinted by Arno Press (*New York Times*), N.Y., 1977.

Gruman, Gerald J., ed. *Roots of Modern Gerontology and Geriatrics.* New York: Arno Press, 1979.

Mazess, Richard B., and Sylvia H. Forman. "Longevity and Age Exaggeration in Vilcabamba, Ecuador." *Journal of Gerontology* 34, no. 1 (1979):94–98.

Medvedev, Zhores A. "Age Structure of Soviet Populations in the Caucasus: Facts and Myths." In *The Biology of Human Ageing*, eds. A. H. Bittles and K. J. Collins. Cambridge: Cambridge University Press, 1986.

———. "Caucasus and Altay Longevity: A Biological or Social Problem?" *Gerontologist* 13, October 1974, 381–87.

Ropp, Robert S. de. *Man against Aging.* New York: Arno Press, 1979.

Spencer G., A. A. Goldstein, and C. M. Taeuber. *America's Centenarians.* U.S. Department of Commerce, Bureau of the Census. Washington, D.C.: U.S. Government Printing Office, 1987.

Suzman, Richard M., David P. Willis, and Kenneth G. Manton, eds. *The Oldest Old.* New York: Oxford University Press, 1992.

Thoms, William J. *Human Longevity, Its Facts and Its Fictions.* London: John Murray, Albemarle St.; New York: Scribner, Welford and Armstrong, 1873.

Chapter 13

Charlesworth, B. *Evolution in Age-structured Populations.* Cambridge: Cambridge University Press, 1980.

Cutler Richard G. "Evolution of Human Longevity: A Critical Overview." *Mechanisms of Ageing and Development* 9 (1979):337.

———. "Evolution of Longevity in Primates." *Journal of Human Evolution* 5 (1976):169.

———. "On the Nature of Aging and Life Maintenance Processes." In *Interdisciplinary Topics in Gerontology*, vol. 9, ed. Richard G. Cutler, 81. Basel: Karger, 1976.

————. "Evolutionary Biology of Aging and Longevity in Mammalian Species." In *Aging and Cell Function*, ed. J. E. Johnson, Jr., 1–148. New York: Plenum Press, 1984.

————. "Evolutionary Biology of Senescence." In *The Biology of Aging*, ed. John A. Behnke, Caleb E. Finch, and Gairdner B. Moment, 311. New York: Plenum Press, 1978.

————. "Evolutionary Perspective of Human Longevity." In *Principles of Geriatric Medicine*, ed. Reubin Andres, Edwin L. Bierman, and William R. Hazzard, 22–29. New York: McGraw-Hill, 1985.

Hofman, Michel A. "Energy Metabolism, Brain Size and Longevity in Mammals." *Quarterly Review of Biology* 58 (December 1983):495–512.

Holliday, Robin. "Toward a Biological Understanding of the Ageing Process." *Perspectives in Biology and Medicine* 32 (1988):109–20.

Kirkwood, Thomas B. L. "Comparative Evolutionary Aspects of Longevity." In *Handbook of the Biology of Aging*, ed. Caleb E. Finch and Edward L. Schneider, 27–45. 2nd ed. New York: Van Nostrand Reinhold, 1985.

————. "Evolution of Ageing." *Nature* 270 (1977):301.

Kirkwood, Thomas B. L., and Michael R. Rose. "Evolution of Senescence: Late Survival Sacrificed for Reproduction." *Philosophical Transactions of the Royal Society of London B* 332 (1991):15–24.

Medvedev, Zhores A. "Repetition of Molecular-Genetic Information as a Possible Factor in Evolutionary Changes of Lifespan." *Experimental Gerontology* 7 (1972):227–38.

Rose, Michael. *The Evolutionary Biology of Aging*. New York: Oxford University Press, 1991.

Sacher, George A. "Longevity, Aging and Death: An Evolutionary Perspective." *Gerontologist* 18, no. 2 (1978):112–20.

————. "Relation of Lifespan to Brain Weight and Body Weight in Mammals." In *The Lifespan of Animals*, ed. G.E.W. Wolstenholme and M. O'Conner, 115–33. Ciba Foundation Colloquia on Ageing, vol. 5. London: Churchill; Boston: Little, Brown and Co., 1959.

Woodhead, A. D., and K. H. Thompson, eds. *Evolution of Longevity in Animals: A Comparative Approach*. New York: Plenum, 1987.

Chapter 14

Adelman, Richard C., and George S. Roth, eds. *Testing the Theories of Aging*. Boca Raton, Fla.: CRC Press, 1982.

Brody, Harold "Neuronal Loss." In *Biological Mechanisms in Aging*, ed. R. T. Schimke, 563–66. NIH publication no. 81-2194. Washington, D.C.: U.S. Government Printing Office, 1980.

Burnet, F. M. *Intrinsic Mutagenesis: A Genetic Approach to Aging*. New York: John Wiley and Son, 1974.

Denckla, W. D. "A Time to Die." *Life Sciences* 16 (1975):31.

Everitt, Arthur V. "The Hypothalamic-Pituitary Control of Ageing and Age-related Pathology." *Experimental Gerontology* 8 (1973):265–77.

Everitt, A. V., and J. A. Burgess, eds. *Hypothalamus, Pituitary and Aging.* Springfield, Ill.: Charles C. Thomas, 1976.

Hayflick, Leonard. "Theories of Biological Aging." *Experimental Gerontology* 20 (1985):145–59.

Medvedev, Zhores A. "An Attempt at a Rational Classification of Theories of Aging." *Biological Reviews* 65 (1990):375–98.

Rockstein, Morris, ed. *Theoretical Aspects of Aging.* New York: Academic Press, 1974.

Roth, George S. "Age-related Changes in Hormone Action: The Role of Receptors." In *Biological Mechanisms in Aging*, ed. Robert T. Schimke, 678–85. NIH publication no. 81-2194. Washington, D.C.: U.S. Government Printing Office, 1980.

―――. "Changes in Hormone Binding and Responsiveness in Target Cells and Tissues during Aging." In *Explorations in Aging*, ed. Vincent J. Cristofalo, Jay Roberts, and Richard C. Adelman, 195. New York: Plenum Press, 1975.

Sacher, George A. "Evolutionary Theory in Gerontology." *Perspectives in Biology and Medicine* 25 (1982):339.

―――. "Theory in Gerontology" (in two parts). In *Annual Review of Gerontology and Geriatrics*, vols. 1 and 3, ed. Carl Eisdorfer. New York: Springer Publishing Co., 1980, 1983.

Schneider, Edward L., ed. *The Genetics of Aging.* New York: Plenum Press, 1978.

Strehler, Bernard, L. "Genetic Instability as the Primary Cause of Human Aging." *Experimental Gerontology* 21 (1986):283.

Szilard, Leo. "On the Nature of the Aging Process." *Proceedings of the National Academy of Sciences* (U.S.) 45 (1959):30–45.

Warner, Hubert R., Robert N. Butler, Richard L. Sprott, and Edward L. Schneider, eds. *Modern Biological Theories of Aging.* New York: Raven Press, 1987.

Williams G. C. "Pleiotropy, Natural Selection, and the Evolution of Senescence." *Evolution* 11 (1957):398–411.

Chapter 15

Armstrong, D., R. S. Sohal, R. G. Cutler, and T. F. Slater. *Free Radicals in Molecular Biology, Aging and Disease.* New York: Raven Press, 1984.

Bjorksten, Johan. "Crosslinkage and the Aging Process." In *Theoretical Aspects of Aging*, eds. M. Rockstein, M. L. Sussman, and J. Chesky, 43. New York: Academic Press, 1974.

Burnet, F. Macfarlane. *Intrinsic Mutagenesis: A Genetic Approach to Aging.* New York: John Wiley and Sons, 1974.

Curtis, Howard J. *Biological Mechanisms of Aging.* Springfield, Ill.: Charles C. Thomas, 1966.

Harman, Denham. "The Aging Process." *Proceedings of the National Academy of Sciences* (U.S.) 78, no. 11 (1981):7124.

Hausman, P. B., and M. E. Weksler. "Changes in the Immune Response with Age." In *Handbook of the Biology of Aging*, eds. Caleb E. Finch and Edward L. Schneider, 414–32. 2nd ed. New York: Van Nostrand Reinhold, 1985.

Hofman, M. A. "Energy Metabolism, Brain Size and Longevity in Mammals." *Quarterly Review of Biology* 58 (1983):495–512.

Kay, Marguerite M. B. "The Thymus: Clock for Immunological Aging?" *Journal of Investigative Dermatology* 73, no. 1 (1979):29.

Lints, Fred A. "The Rate of Living Theory Revisited." *Gerontology* 35 (1990):36–57.

Mahlhorn, R. J., and G. Cole. "The Free Radical Theory of Aging: A Critical Review." *Advances in Free Radical Biology and Medicine* 1 (1985): 165–223.

Makinodan, Takashi. "Immunity and Aging." In *Handbook of the Biology of Aging*, ed. Caleb E. Finch and Leonard Hayflick, 379. 1st ed. New York: Van Nostrand Reinhold, 1977.

Makinodan, Takashi, R. Good, and Marguerite M. B. Kay. "Cellular Basis of Immunosenescence." In *Immunology and Aging*, eds. T. Makinodan and E. Yunis. New York: Plenum Press, 1977.

Makinodan, Takashi, and Marguerite M. B. Kay. "Age Influence on the Immune System." In *Advances in Immunology*, eds. H. G. Kunkle and F. J. Dixon, 678. New York: Academic Press, 1980.

Medvedev, Zhores A. "The Role of Infidelity of Transfer of Information for the Accumulation of Age Changes in Differentiated Cells." *Mechanisms of Aging and Development* 14 (1980):1–14.

Miller, Richard A. "Aging and the Immune Response." In *Handbook of the Biology of Aging*, eds. Edward L. Schneider and John W. Rowe, 157–80. 3rd ed. San Diego: Academic Press, 1990.

Miquel, J., A. C. Economos, J. Fleming, and J. E. Johnson. "Mitochondrial Role in Cell Aging." *Experimental Gerontology* 15 (1980):575.

Nagy, I. Zs., ed. "Lipofuscin-1987 State of the Art." *Excerpta Medica*, International Congress Series 782, 1988.

Orgel, Leslie E. "Ageing of Clones of Mammalian Cells." *Nature* 243 (1973):441.

Pearl, Raymond. *The Rate of Living.* New York: Alfred A. Knopf, 1928.

Prigogine, I. *Introduction to Thermodynamics of Irreversible Processes.* 2nd ed. New York: John Wiley and Sons/Interscience Publishers 1961.

Pryor, William A. *Free Radicals in Biology*. 6 vols. New York: Academic Press, 1986.

Richardson, Arlen. "A Comprehensive Review of the Scientific Literature on the Effect of Aging on Protein Synthesis." In *Biological Mechanisms of Aging*, ed. Robert T. Schimke, 339 NIH publication no. 81–2194. Washington, D.C.: U.S. Government Printing Office, 1980.

Sohal, R. S. *Age Pigments*. New York: Elsevier North Holland, 1981.

Sohal, R. S., and R. G. Allen. "Relationship between Metabolic Rate, Free Radicals, Differentiation and Aging: A United Theory." In *Molecular Biology of Aging*, ed. A. D. Woodhead, A. D. Blackett, and A. Hollaender, 75–104. New York: Plenum Press, 1985.

———. "Relationship between Oxygen Metabolism, Aging and Development." *Advances in Free Radical Biology and Medicine* 2 (1986):117–60.

Verzar, Fritz. "Ageing of Collagen Fibres." In *Experimental Research on Aging. Experientia*, supplement 4:35. Basel: Birkauser Verlag, 1956.

Verzar, F., and K. Huber. "Thermic Contraction of Single Tendon Fibers from Animals of Different Ages after Treatment with Formaldehyde, Urethane, Glycerol, Acetic Acid and Other Substances." *Gerontologia* 2 (1958): 81–103.

Walford, Roy L. *The Immunologic Theory of Aging*. Copenhagen: Munksgaard; Baltimore: Williams and Wilkins Co., 1969.

———. "Studies in Immunogerontology." *Journal of the American Geriatric Society* 30 (1982):617–25.

Walford, Roy L., et al. "The Immunopathology of Aging." In *Annual Review of Gerontology and Geriatrics*, vol. 2, ed. Carl Eisdorfer. New York: Springer Publishing Co., 1981.

Weksler, Marc E. "The Immune System and the Aging Process." *Proceedings of the Society for Experimental Biology and Medicine* 165 (1980):200.

PART 5: Slowing Aging and Increasing Life Span

Chapter 16

Bogomolets, Alexander A. *The Prolongation of Life*. New York: Essential Books/Duell, Sloan and Pearce, 1946.

Child, Charles M. *Senescence and Rejuvenescence*. Chicago: University of Chicago Press, 1915.

Gruman, Gerald J. "A History of Ideas about the Prolongation of Life." *Transactions of the American Philosophical Society* (Philadelphia), 56, pt. 9 (1966):1–102. Reprinted by Arno Press (*New York Times*), N.Y., 1977.

Gruman, Gerald J., ed. *Roots of Modern Gerontology and Geriatrics*. New York: Arno Press, 1979.

Hamilton, David. *The Monkey Gland Affair.* London: Chatto and Windus, 1986.

Metchnikoff, Élie. *The Prolongation of Life.* New York: G. P. Putnam's Sons; London; Knickerbocker Press, 1910.

Minot, Charles S. *The Problem of Age, Growth and Death.* New York: G. P. Putnam's Sons; London: Knickerbocker Press, 1908.

Olmstead, J.M.D. *Charles Édouard Brown-Séquard.* Baltimore: Johns Hopkins University Press, 1946.

Chapter 17

Andres, R., D. Elahi, J. D. Tobin, D. C. Muller, and L. Brant. "Impact of Age on Weight Goals." *Annals of Internal Medicine* 103 (December 1985):1030.

Holehan, A. M., and B. J. Merry. "The Experimental Manipulation of Ageing by Diet." *Biological Review* 61 (1986):329–68.

Holliday, Robin. "Food, Reproduction and Longevity: Is the Extended Lifespan of Calorie-restricted Animals an Evolutionary Adaptation?" *BioEssays* 10, no. 4, (1989):125–27.

Holloszy, J. O. "Exercise and Longevity: Studies on Rats" (minireview). *Journal of Gerontology* 43, no. 6 (1988):B149–51.

Masoro, Edward J. "Food Restriction and the Aging Process." *Journal of the American Geriatrics Society* 32 no. 4 (1984):296–300.

———. "Food Restriction in Rodents: An Evaluation of Its Role in the Study of Aging" (minireview). *Journal of Gerontology* 43, no. 3 (1988):B59–64.

———. "Metabolism." In *Handbook of the Biology of Aging,* eds. Caleb E. Finch and Edward L. Schneider, 540–66. 2nd ed. New York: Van Nostrand Reinhold, 1985.

Masoro, E. J., I. Shimokawa, and B. P. Yu. "Retardation of the Aging Processes in Rats by Food Restriction." *Annals of the New York Academy of Sciences* 621 (July 1991):337–52.

McCay, C. M., L. A. Maynard, G. Sperling, and L. L. Barnes. "Retarded Growth, Life Span, Ultimate Body Size and Age Changes in the Albino Rat after Feeding Diets Restricted in Calories." *Journal of Nutrition* 18 (1939):1.

Monnier, V. M., D. R. Sell, S. Miyata, and R. J. Nagara. "The Maillard Reaction as a Basis for a Theory of Aging." In *Proceedings of the Fourth International Symposium on the Maillard Reaction,* ed. P. A. Finot, 393–414. Basel: Birkhausert-Verlag, 1990.

Paffenbarger, R. S., Jr., R. T. Hyde, A. L. Wing, and C. Hsieh. "Physical Activity, All-Cause Mortality, and Longevity of College Alumni." *New England Journal of Medicine* 314 (1986):605–13.

Polednak, Anthony P., ed. *The Longevity of Athletes.* Springfield, Ill.: Charles C. Thomas, 1979.

Ross, M. H. "Nutritional Regulation of Longevity." In *The Biology of Aging*, ed. J. A. Behnke, C. E. Finch, and G. B. Moment, 173–89. New York: Plenum Press, 1978.

Walford, Roy L., S. B. Harris, and R. Weindruch. "Dietary Restriction and Aging: Historical Phases, Mechanisms and Current Directions." *Journal of Nutrition* 117, no. 10 (1987):1650–54.

Weindruch, Richard, and Roy L. Walford. *The Retardation of Aging and Disease by Dietary Restriction.* Springfield, Ill.: Charles C. Thomas, 1988.

Chapter 18

Barnes, B. M. "Freeze Avoidance in a Mammal: Body Temperatures below 0 C. in an Arctic Hibernator." *Science* 244 (1989):1593–95.

Diamond, Jared M. "Resurrection of Frozen Animals." *Nature* 339 (1989): 509–10.

Chapter 19

Boxenbaum, Harold. "Time Concepts in Physics, Biology, and Pharmacokinetics." *Journal of Pharmaceutical Sciences* 75, no. 11 (1986):1053–62.

Brock, Mary Anne. "Chronobiology and Aging." *Journal of the American Geriatrics Society* 39 (1991):74–91.

Hafele, C. J., and R. E. Keating. "Around-the-World Atomic Clocks: Predicted Relativistic Time Gains." *Science* 177 (1972):166–67.

Schroots, J.J.F., and J. E. Birren. "The Nature of Time: Implications for Research on Aging." *Comparative Gerontology* 2 (1988):1–29.

PART 6: The Future of Human Aging and Longevity

Chapter 20

"Anti-Aging Cures and Quackery." In *Quackery: A $10 Billion Scandal*, 73–95. House Select Committee on Aging, Subcommittee on Health and Long-term Care. Washington, D.C.: U.S. Government Printing Office, 1984. Publication no. 98–463.

Hochschild, Richard. "Can an Index of Aging Be Constructed for Evaluating Treatments to Retard Aging Rates? A 2,462 Person Study." *Journal of Gerontology* 45 (1990):B187–214.

Kinsella, Kevin. "Aging in the Third World." U.S. Department of Commerce, Bureau of the Census. International Population Reports. Series P-95, no. 79. September 1988. Washington, D.C.: U.S. Government Printing Office.

Lehman, Harvey C. *Age and Achievement*. Princeton: Princeton University Press for the American Philosophical Society, 1953; Ann Arbor: University Microfilms.

Levin, Sharon G., and Paula E. Stephan. "Age and Research Productivity of Academic Scientists." *Research in Higher Education* 30 (1989):531–49.

Chapter 21

"An Aging World II," U.S. Bureau of the Census, International Population Reports, P25, 92-3, U.S. Government Printing Office, Washington, D.C., 1992.

Branch, Laurence G., Jack M. Guralnik, Daniel J. Foley, Frank J. Kohout, Terrie T. Wetle, Adrian Ostfeld, and Sidney Katz. "Active Life Expectancy for Ten Thousand Caucasian Men and Women in Three Communities." *Journal of Gerontology* 46 (1991):M145–50.

"Can You Live Longer?" *Consumer Reports*, January 1992, 7–15.

Grigsby, Jill S. "Paths for Future Population Aging." *Gerontologist* 31 (1991):195–203.

Keyfitz, Nathan. "What Difference Would It Make If Cancer Were Eradicated? An Examination of the Taeuber Paradox." *Demography* 14, no. 4 1977:411–18.

Kohn, Robert R. "Cause of Death in Very Old People." *Journal of the American Medical Association* 247, no. 20 (1982):2793–97.

Krupka, L. R., and A. M. Vener. "Treatment of Aging in Secondary School Biology Textbooks: A Neglected Phenomenon." *American Biology Teacher* 44 (1982):264–69.

Kurtzman, J., and P. Gordon. *No More Dying: The Conquest of Aging*. Los Angeles: J. P. Tarcher, 1976.

Manton, Kenneth G., Eric Stallard, and H. Dennis Tolley. "Limits to Human Life Expectancy: Evidence, Prospects, and Implications." *Population and Development Review* 17 (December 1991):603–36.

Neugarten, Berniece L., and Robert J. Havinghurst, eds. *Extending the Human Life Span: Social Policy and Social Ethics*. Washington, D.C.: U.S. Government Printing Office, 1977.

Riley, Matilda White. "Aging in the Twenty-first Century." Boettner Lecture. Boettner Research Institute, American College, Bryn Mawr, Pennsylvania, 1990.

Schneider, E. L., and J. D. Reed, Jr. "Life Extension." *New England Journal of Medicine*, 2 May 1985, 1159–68.

Taeuber, Cynthia M. "If Nobody Died of Cancer?" *Kennedy Institute Quarterly Report* 2, no. 2 (summer 1976):6–9.

———. "Sixty-five Plus in America." U.S. Department of Commerce, Bureau of the Census. Current Population Reports, Special Studies, P23–178 and

P23–178RV Washington, D.C.: U.S. Government Printing Office, 1992 and 1993.

Torrey, Barbara B., Kevin Kinsella, and Cynthia M. Taeuber. "An Aging World." U.S. Department of Commerce, Bureau of the Census. International Population Reports. Series P-95, no. 78. September 1987. Washington, D.C.: U.S. Government Printing Office.

"What Limits Lifespan?" In Population and the New Biology, ed. B. Benjamin, P. R. Cox, and J. Peel, 31–56. New York: Academic Press, 1974.

General Texts and Reviews

Adelman, Richard C., ed. Modifications of Proteins during Aging. New York: Alan Liss, 1985.

Arking, Robert, Biology of Aging: Observations and Principles. Englewood Cliffs, N.J., Prentice Hall, 1991.

Beauvoir, Simone de. The Coming of Age. New York: G. P. Putnam's Sons, 1972.

Bergsma, D., and D. E. Harrison, eds. Genetic Effects on Aging. New York: Alan Liss, 1978.

Collatz, K.-G., and R. S. Sohal, eds. Insect Aging: Strategies and Mechanisms. Heidelberg: Springer-Verlag, 1986.

Comfort, Alex. The Biology of Senescence. 3rd ed. New York: Elsevier North Holland, 1979.

Cristofalo, Vincent J., Jay Roberts, and Richard C. Adelman, eds. Explorations in Aging. New York: Plenum Press, 1975.

Finch, Caleb E. Longevity, Senescence and the Genome. Chicago: University of Chicago Press, 1990.

Finch, Caleb E., and Leonard Hayflick, eds. Handbook of the Biology of Aging. 1st ed. New York: Van Nostrand Reinhold, 1977.

Finch, Caleb E., and Thomas E. Johnson, eds. Molecular Biology of Aging. Vol. 123. UCLA Symposium on Molecular and Cellular Biology. New York: Wiley-Liss, 1990.

Finch, Caleb E., and Edward L. Schneider, eds. Handbook of the Biology of Aging. 2nd ed. New York: Van Nostrand Reinhold, 1985.

Fries, James F., and Lawrence M. Crapo. Vitality and Aging. San Francisco: Freeman, 1981.

Lamb, Marion J. Biology of Aging. Halstead Press, New York: John Wiley and Sons, 1977.

Lints, Fred A. Genetics and Ageing. Basel: Karger, 1978.

———. "Insects." In Handbook of the Biology of Aging, eds. Caleb E. Finch and Edward L. Schneider, 146–72. 2nd ed. New York: Van Nostrand Reinhold, 1985.

McGrady, Patrick M., Jr. *The Youth Doctors.* New York: Coward-McCann, 1968.

Medawar, Peter B. *Aging: An Unsolved Problem of Biology.* London: H. K. Lewis, 1952.

Reff, M. E., and E. L. Schneider, eds. "Biological Markers of Aging." Bethesda, Md.: National Institutes of Health, 1982. Publication no. 82-2221.

Rose, Michael. *The Evolutionary Biology of Aging.* New York: Oxford University Press, 1991.

Rosenfeld, Albert. *Prolongevity II.* New York: Alfred A. Knopf, 1985.

Rothstein, Morton. *Biochemical Approaches to Aging.* New York: Academic Press, 1982.

———. *Biochemistry of Aging.* New York: Academic Press, 1982.

Schimke, Robert T., ed. "Biological Mechanisms in Aging." Bethesda, Md.: National Institutes of Health, 1980. Publication no. 81-2194.

Smith-Sonneborn, Joan. "Aging in Unicellular Organisms." In *Handbook of the Biology of Aging*, eds. Caleb E. Finch and Edward L. Schneider, 79–104. 2nd ed. New York: Van Nostrand Reinhold, 1985.

Walford, Roy L. *Maximum Life Span.* New York: W. W. Norton and Co., 1983.

Woodhead, A. D., and A. D. Blackett, eds. *Molecular Biology of Aging.* Vol. 35. Basic Life Sciences. New York: Plenum Press, 1984.

Index

ABOUT THE AUTHOR

LEONARD HAYFLICK, PH.D., is Professor of Anatomy at the University of California, San Francisco, Medical School, and was Professor of Medical Microbiology at Stanford University School of Medicine. He is a past president of the Gerontological Society of America and was a founding member of the council of the National Institute of Aging. The recipient of several research prizes and awards, including the 1991 Sandoz Prize for Gerontological Research, he has studied the aging process for more than thirty years.